Japanese Philosophers on Society and Culture

Japanese Philosophers on Society and Culture

Nishida Kitarō, Watsuji Tetsurō, and Kuki Shūzō

Graham Mayeda

LEXINGTON BOOKS
Lanham • Boulder • New York • London

Published by Lexington Books
An imprint of The Rowman & Littlefield Publishing Group, Inc.
4501 Forbes Boulevard, Suite 200, Lanham, Maryland 20706
www.rowman.com

6 Tinworth Street, London SE11 5AL, United Kingdom

Copyright © 2020 The Rowman & Littlefield Publishing Group, Inc.

All rights reserved. No part of this book may be reproduced in any form or by any electronic or mechanical means, including information storage and retrieval systems, without written permission from the publisher, except by a reviewer who may quote passages in a review.

British Library Cataloguing in Publication Information Available

Library of Congress Cataloging-in-Publication Data

Names: Mayeda, Graham, author.
Title: Japanese philosophers on society and culture : Nishida Kitarō, Watsuji Tetsurō, and Kuki Shūzō / Graham Mayeda.
Description: Lanham : Lexington Books, 2020. | Includes bibliographical references and index. | Summary: "What is culture? What can we learn from art, architecture, and fashion about how people relate? Can cultures embody ethical and moral ideals? These are just some of the questions addressed in this book on the cultural philosophy of three preeminent Japanese philosophers of the early twentieth century, Nishida Kitarō, Watsuji Tetsurō and Kuki Shūzō" — Provided by publisher.
Identifiers: LCCN 2020039552 (print) | LCCN 2020039553 (ebook) |
ISBN 9781498572088 (cloth) | ISBN 9781498572101 (pbk)
ISBN 9781498572095 (epub)
Subjects: LCSH: Philosophy, Japanese—20th century. | Japan—Civilization—20th century.
Classification: LCC B5241 .M39 2020 (print) | LCC B5241 (ebook) | DDC 306.01—dc23
LC record available at https://lccn.loc.gov/2020039552
LC ebook record available at https://lccn.loc.gov/2020039553

This book is dedicated to my parents, Lloyd and Phyllis Mayeda. Thank you for inspiring me to ask important questions, to think critically, and to live ethically.

Contents

1	Japanese Cultural and Social Philosophy in Context	1
2	Watsuji Tetsurō's Early Views on Culture: A Study of *Pilgrimages to the Ancient Temples in Nara* (*Koji Junrei*)	31
3	The Development of Watsuji's Theory of Culture and Climate: An Interpretation of *Fūdo*	61
4	Watsuji's Three Climatic and Cultural Zones: Anti-essentialist and Deterministic Readings	85
5	Kuki's Hermeneutic Approach to the Floating World: *Iki* as the Living Form of Japanese Idealism	125
6	Kuki and Heidegger: The Method for Interpreting Culture	145
7	Kuki Shūzō's Concepts of Culture and Society: The Intuition at the Heart of Ethics	165
8	Nishida: Who I Am and Who You Are	197
9	Nishida's Views on Morality and Culture: The Moral Individual and the Moral Culture	225
10	Conclusion: Japanese Cultural and Social Philosophy in the Twentieth Century	257

Works Cited	271
Index	285
About the Author	289

Chapter 1

Japanese Cultural and Social Philosophy in Context

Who am I? Part of the answer to this question usually involves a second question, Who are we? I live in a network of social relationships, and most of these relationships have a cultural aspect: the things I do and say, the way that I view the world, all take their meaning at least in part from my relationships. The question of who I am can be interpreted as a question about an individual, but it can also be framed as a question about the society and culture in which I live, the themes of this book. We will explore these themes as they were addressed in the social and cultural philosophy of three twentieth-century Japanese philosophers, Nishida Kitarō (1870–1945, 西田幾多郎), Watsuji Tetsurō (1889–1960, 和辻哲郎), and Kuki Shūzō (1888–1941, 九鬼周造).[1] By "social philosophy," I mean their views about the nature of the social relation: the relationship between myself and other people. By "cultural philosophy," I mean the things that people do and make: the cultural activities in which they engage, the language they use to express themselves, and the cultural objects they produce.[2] These activities and objects can be considered cultural in the sense that their significance—that is, why we do them, the meaning of doing them—is at least in part determined by the culture to which we belong. Culture thus indicates a way of life of a people, the activities and things they produce, and the symbolic meaning of the things they do and make (Mitchell 2000, 13–14). Each of the philosophers whom we will study in this book emphasizes a slightly different aspect of culture, and part of our study will involve clarifying these differences.

NEW TEXTS AND NOVEL PERSPECTIVES: THE FOCUS OF THIS BOOK

I have tried in this book to focus on aspects of the writings of Nishida, Watsuji, and Kuki that have generally received less attention in English-language scholarship. In the case of Watsuji, one chapter explores one of his earliest works, a sort of travel diary he made while visiting temples in the ancient Japanese capital city of Nara, called *Pilgrimages to the Ancient Temples in Nara* (*Koji Junrei*, 『古寺巡礼』) which has as yet been of little interest to philosophers. In the next two chapters, I concentrate on his famous work *Climate and Culture* (*Fūdo*, 風土; Watsuji 1961; *NKZ* 8:1–256), in which he explores the relationship between climate and culture. However, here too, I have tried to focus on parts of the work that have been neglected, such as the final chapter on the history of the study of climate, which deals with the work of European philosophers such as Immanuel Kant (1724–1804), Johann Gottlieb Fichte (1762–1814), Johann Gottfried Herder (1744–1803), and G. W. F. Hegel (1770–1831). This part of *Climate and Culture* has not been translated into English, which explains its neglect in the English-speaking world.

In the case of Kuki, I have chosen well-known works such as *The Structure of Iki* (*Iki no kōzō* 『「いき」の構造』, Kuki 2004; *KSZ* 1:1–86) and *The Problem of Contingency* (*Gūzensei no mondai*, 『偶然性の問題』, *KSZ* 2:1–264), but I have focused on aspects that have not yet been fully studied by European or North American philosophers such as his hermeneutic method and the influence of the intuitionism of French philosophers François Pierre Gontier Maine de Biran (1766–1824) and Henri-Louis Bergson (1859–1941). Many scholars have noted Kuki's use of a hermeneutic method, which he announces at the beginning of *The Structure of Iki*, but few have really described the method he actually uses in this text or compared it to Martin Heidegger's hermeneutic method from which Kuki apparently derives it. In regard to intuitionism, here I am referring to his discussion both in *The Structure of Iki* and more fully at the end of *The Problem of Contingency* about the way that humans experience their essential nature and that of reality itself, which Kuki believes involves intuition. While the influence of French philosophy on Kuki is well known, it has not been explored in as much depth as it might, no doubt because of the relative obscurity of Maine de Biran in the English-speaking world (and even in the Francophone world). However, a recent English translation of Maine de Biran's *The Relationship between the Physical and the Moral in Man* by Darian Meacham and Joseph Spadola (Maine de Biran 2016; originally published as *Sur les rapports du physique et du moral de l'homme* in 1811) makes consideration of this aspect of Kuki's work timely. Also, French influence on Japanese philosophy is pervasive: for instance, Nishida wrote an early essay called "Bergson's Philosophical

Method" (*NKZ* 1:255), and he mentions Bergson throughout his works, such as in his lectures titled "The Historical Body" (Nishida 1998b, 50).[3] Thus, further study of the links between Japanese and French philosophy contributes to our understanding of the former.

I have been less original in my exploration of Nishida's philosophy: what the two chapters on his philosophy contribute to the literature is a concerted study of what he says about who "I" am and who "You" are and how it is that "We" live together as the expression of what Nishida calls the "historical body" and later the "historical world," the concrete world that is always in motion around us and of which we are simply the expression. I have tried to draw together the whole body of his work in order to articulate Nishida's concept of the relationship between the individual and society and the importance he places on each culture developing its ability to express the morality that his view of the nature of human existence entails. Nishida chose different idioms throughout his life for expressing his basic thought: he began with the phenomenological psychology of William James, then switched to the dialectical model articulated as the logic of place (*basho*, 場所), before finally exploring the same topics from the point of view of what he called the "historical world" (*rekishiteki sekai*, 歴史的世界), which is a world of "action-intuition," a world of constant dynamic activity of which our thoughts are just a part. But despite the diversity of ways in which he expressed it, as Nishida himself noted, his philosophy focused on a handful of issues which he explored through these various idioms (Nishida 1998b, 37; see also Fujita 2016). Because of my interest in the social and cultural implications of Nishida's work, I begin by exploring his notion of self and other and the relationship in which the two always already exist before they become separated in conscious thought. I then explain how this dynamic relationship between self and other is expressed through the cultural activities and cultural production of the "historical body"—the unfolding of the actual cultural and social world as a process of dynamic activity. Finally, I try to explain in as specific a way that I can how Nishida thought we should live our lives as individuals, as cultural groups, and as a world society sharing ever-shrinking space on this small planet.

Some might find the order of the chapters somewhat odd: Would it not be better to begin with Nishida, the "father" of twentieth-century Japanese philosophy, before moving on to Watsuji and Kuki, whom he influenced? I have decided to put my study of Nishida's work last for three reasons. First, I believe the reader will be better able to appreciate Nishida's somewhat abstract presentation of the nature of society and culture after having read the more concrete works of Watsuji and Kuki. Second, Watsuji's and Kuki's works deal very explicitly with Japanese cultural practices such as art, architecture, clothing, language, greetings, and so on—topics of intrinsic interest to Japanophiles who make up the majority of students of Japanese philosophy outside Japan. Hopefully, once readers have been regaled with the specific cultural examples discussed by Watsuji and Kuki, they will then be willing to embark on the more daunting task of studying Nishida's elaboration of his ideas in philosophical and religious terms. Third, my own reading of the work of these three philosophers has proven to me that it becomes much easier to understand Nishida once one has read Kuki and Watsuji. Their philosophical methods were very much influenced by Nishida, but they are expressed using European phenomenology and hermeneutics, methods that are quite well known to students of European and North American philosophy; reading how they believed these methods built on what they learned from Nishida is very helpful for interpreting Nishida's abstract theoretical approaches.

For instance, I found that I could more easily understand the role of intuition in Nishida's philosophy after understanding how Kuki adapted Heideggerian hermeneutics by incorporating the intuitive method of Maine de Biran and Bergson. This was particularly the case because Kuki's writing is very clear, while Nishida's way of expressing himself can be highly technical and abstract. Also, after reading Watsuji's description of the dialectic of space and time that underlies his study of culture as the spatial and temporal (historical) manifestation of climate, I found it easier to understand Nishida's dialectic interpretation of the relationship between the self and other in his middle work and his articulation of the relationship between individual and society in the unfolding of the concrete world as a historical body in the last phase of his philosophy. Again, the resonance becomes more apparent if one first reads Watsuji's engaging and dynamic expression of this dialectic before reading the more academic texts of Nishida.

Also, the final place is one of honor, and Nishida deserves to be accorded it. In reading Nishida, Kuki, and Watsuji together, one comes to appreciate Nishida's genius. In contrast with his two students, he experimented with many more philosophical methods than they did. Also, one begins to appreciate the profundity of his philosophy, which aimed at expressing a very simple but therefore radical truth about human existence. When one compares his work to that of Kuki and Watsuji, one is inevitably left with a feeling that the latters' views were somewhat superficial despite their evident genius and originality. Only Nishida really delves deeply into the fundamental question of the nature of reality, of the self, and of the others with whom we live.

WATSUJI, KUKI, AND NISHIDA ON CULTURE AND SOCIETY

We begin our exploration of the philosophical study of culture and society in the philosophy of these three philosophers with Watsuji, whose thought is perhaps the most straightforward of the three. Watsuji was particularly interested in the social relationship: the relation between the individual and society that he called "betweenness" (*aidagara*, 間柄). In *Ethics* (*Rinrigaku*, 『倫理学』 [3 volumes: 1937, 1942, and 1949]),[4] he articulated this relationship as the basic structure of human existence, which is both spatial and temporal. The term "betweenness" with which Watsuji described this basic structure clearly conveys its spatial dimension: we are not just points or pure egos; we exist in a web of social relations: we are truly what exists "between" each of us. Moreover, whatever physical place we find ourselves in, or whenever we move from place to place, the meaning of these places and the significance of these movements is social in nature: home, office, honeymoon, vacation—the meanings we associate with each place are determined by society. Temporally, humans exist between the individual and the group: at times, they identify more as individuals and so reject the group; at others, they identify with the group and so deny their individuality. The dynamic movement back and forth between these poles unfolds in time. Watsuji considered this movement to be dialectical in structure, and he called its basic precondition "emptiness" (*kū*, 空), a concept commonly used in Japanese philosophy and East Asian philosophy in general.

In the works we will study, Watsuji referred to many elements of Japanese culture, including art, architecture, and language. *Pilgrimages to the Ancient Temples in Nara* (Watsuji 2012; *WTZ* 2:1–192; hereafter *Pilgrimages*), written early in his career in 1919, describes and interprets the art and architecture of Nara, the ancient capital of Japan. It is not generally studied as a philosophical text, but since its publication 100 years ago, it has remained a much-loved guide to these ancient treasures. In the book, Watsuji's descriptions of the cultural artifacts and the history of Buddhist art in Japan provide an opportunity to characterize his early views on the nature of culture and the importance of social interaction in experiencing it. The work also displays his openness to cultural change and his acknowledgment that Japanese culture is the result of an amalgam of influences ranging from ancient Greece to South, Central, and East Asia.

In his mature philosophy, exemplified in *Climate and Culture* (Watsuji 1961), Watsuji addresses the topic of Japanese culture in an explicitly philosophical study. The book was based on lectures he gave in 1928–1929, and it was published as a complete book in 1935. Unlike *Pilgrimages*, which was written for the general public, *Climate and Culture* was truly philosophical, and in order to study the relationship between climate and culture, Watsuji developed a new philosophical method—a spatial phenomenology—inspired by Martin Heidegger's phenomenology as described in his first major work, *Being and Time* (Heidegger 1996). However, Watsuji corrected what he considered to be a weakness in Heidegger's method. As he explains in his introduction to the first edition of *Climate and Culture*, while he was impressed by the German philosopher's "attempt to treat the structure of man's existence in terms of time," he "found it hard to see why, when time had . . . been made to play a part in the structure of subjective existence, at the same juncture space also was not postulated as part of the basic structure of existence"[5] (Watsuji 1961, v; *WTZ* 8:1). As we will see, this insight led to a spatialized notion of culture: cultural objects and activities are themselves ways of experiencing the contextual and climatic nature of human existence, that is, its spatial nature. When we greet another with "Cold enough for you?" or when we don toques, scarves, and mittens, we are directly expressing the climatic nature of our existence. Indeed, the donning of warm clothes is in fact one way that we experience the cold of winter.

As *Climate and Culture* has been extensively studied both in Japan and outside it, I have decided to emphasize the lesser-known final section of the book, currently not translated into English, which discusses the similarities and differences between Watsuji's understanding of the relationship between climate and culture and that of European, especially German, philosophers such as Kant, Herder, Fichte, and Hegel. The comparison allows us to see how Watsuji rejected the tendency toward geographic determinism in the philosophy of these Europeans and instead drew out the aspects of their thought that would justify his phenomenological analysis. Thus we can see the chapter as a description of a dialogue between Watsuji and his European predecessors as he sought to develop and deploy his phenomenological method. At the same time, he was not entirely successful in eschewing cultural determinism for a phenomenological, experiential approach to the relationship between climate and culture; cultural essentialism also crept in (Berque 2011, 22–25; see also fn. 2 on p. 322). These two problematic aspects of his study are in large part due to the influence of the Europeans on him: located at the center of the "modern" world, they were content to generalize about the nature of culture, thus leading to cultural essentialism, and they did not interrogate in a rigorous, critical way the causal role of geography in cultural development.

As we can see, Watsuji's study of climate and culture displays an inherent tension which I have tried to emphasize in my study. On the one hand, he clearly viewed culture as malleable and porous; on the other, there are also elements of essentialism and determinism that emerge in his later work. In *Pilgrimages*, we get a clear sense that Watsuji is *creating* Japanese culture, molding and solidifying its historical development through apparent description of it. The history he created in that period of his thought emphasized that Japanese culture was simply the mixing of many influences both from within and outside Japan. However, by the time of *Climate and Culture*, published fifteen years later, while resisting cultural determinism in some aspects of his study, Watsuji also reified culture to the extent that he considered it an expression of a special attunement of the Japanese to nature and thus an expression of the Japanese spirit.⁶ This reification, which led to a problematic cultural essentialism, became even more apparent in his three-volume *Ethics* published during the late 1930s and 1940s. A detailed study of the sources of essentialism and geographic determinism in *Climate and Culture* thus provides a useful window on Watsuji's later philosophy, since it contains the seeds of those views. The trajectory I describe makes it possible to understand how the later philosophy, subject to much criticism for promoting Japanese nationalism, emerged.

Kuki Shūzō's philosophy provides an interesting counterpoint to that of Watsuji because he was inspired by the same phenomenological methodology (that of Martin Heidegger), but he interpreted and modified it in a different way. Moreover, he had a radically different notion of Japanese culture: while Watsuji used examples with which Japanophiles would be familiar such as Buddhist art and architecture, Kuki was inspired by a rather unusual set of cultural practices, namely those of the *geisha* from a rather obscure period in Japanese history at the end of the Tokugawa era called *Kasei* (化政 [1804–1830]).⁷ His choice seems to have been animated by the ethics that he saw exemplified in the relationship between *geisha* and their lovers at that time, which was characterized by a detached disinterest, a realistic resignation to the impossibility of permanent personal attachment, and a plucky resolve to live according to ideals despite the impossibility of achieving them.

Like Watsuji, whose concept of the social relation was influenced by Japan's Confucian and Buddhist heritage, Kuki also sought to articulate traditional East Asian philosophy in a modern idiom. However, he interpreted the tradition as radically as he interpreted modern European philosophy. For instance, one would not typically associate the "floating world" of the *geisha* with Buddhism, especially the stereotype of Zen austerity held by most people, nor would one link it with the rigid Confucian hierarchy and sense of duty of the samurai, expressed in their moral code, *Bushidō* (武士道). And yet Kuki did both, developing a complex and highly modern ethics based on the ideals that he saw embodied by the *geisha*. Moreover, as I already mentioned, Kuki was very innovative in his adaptation of Heideggerian hermeneutics. Our examination of *The Structure of Iki* will focus on this methodology, which we will examine to understand both the way it adopts and the way it departs from Heidegger's method. Indeed, as we will see, Kuki introduces a kind of intuitionism into the method that allows him to incorporate a metaphysical, transcendent dimension into Heidegger's otherwise secular framework.

To make Kuki's intuitionism more apparent and to draw out the ethical implications of it more clearly, in the third chapter on Kuki's philosophy, we examine closely the end of Kuki's book *The Problem of Contingency* (*Gūzensei no mondai* 『偶然性の問題』; *KSZ* 2), in which he writes about the mystical and metaphysical implications of his study of the relationship between necessity and contingency. This will give us an opportunity to identify the influence of French philosophy, especially that of the "spiritualist" school that had its origins in the work of Maine de Biran and culminated in the vitalist philosophy of Henri Bergson. I think that this emphasis on the French connection is warranted because it provides us with insights not only into the role of intuition in Kuki's hermeneutic phenomenology but also about the mystical element that Kuki shares with both Frenchmen: for all three philosophers, the individual is able through encounters with others to access the mystical source of reality from which the ethical obligations that underlie social structures and cultural practices are derived.

As I mentioned earlier, Nishida's philosophy had a profound influence on both Watsuji and Kuki; however, it is not always apparent in their writing. In order to draw out the influence, in the first chapter on Nishida's philosophy, I focus on his understanding of the dialectical concept of the social, that is, his description of the relationship between self and other. This dialectical approach was one of the sources of Watsuji's dialectical interpretation of human existence as a constant movement between the poles of individual and group which was fully achieved in his three-volume *Ethics*. In the last chapter on Nishida's thought, I try to develop the ethical implications that Nishida recognized in his description of the relationship between the individual and the other. Here, too, the influence on Watsuji and Kuki is clear, for like Nishida, both of them were interested in the ethical nature of human existence, although they developed quite different ethics due to the different ways in which Nishida inspired them.

As well, the spatial and temporal dimensions of human existence that both Watsuji and Kuki emphasized in their philosophy have their origins in Nishida. Indeed, in the middle period of his thought, he identified these two aspects clearly in his notion of *basho* (place, 場所), the place where all creative activity that is the basic form of reality occurs. The spatial aspect is the fact that *basho* is the place where this dynamic activity takes place (Tremblay 2007, citing *NKZ* 4:208–209), and the temporal aspect is the dynamic activity itself (Tremblay 2007, 68): both are the self-determination of *basho*. Watsuji's view, elaborated in *Ethics*, that emptiness is the transcendental precondition of the dialectic of self and other (McCarthy 2017; McCarthy cites Watsuji 1996, 117; see also 223–224, 233) was no doubt inspired by Nishida's philosophy in this regard. But I think that Kuki's interest in articulating the mystical and metaphysical nature of reality was also inspired by this aspect of Nishida's thought (*KSZ* 1: [89]).[8]

In the final chapter of the book we will also explore the connection between Nishida's social and religious philosophy and discuss the implications of his social philosophy for world politics, a topic addressed in his last work, *The Logic of Place and the Religious Worldview* (『場所的論理と宗教的世界観』, NKZ 11:371). His emphasis on the cosmopolitan implications of his philosophy is both an inspiring note on which to end the book and draws out more clearly the cosmopolitan goals of Watsuji and Kuki's philosophies of culture and society. For while all three philosophers were guilty of Japanese chauvinism, they were all animated by the hope that a better understanding of the individual, the group, and the relationship between the two would inspire the Japanese to look outward and see the whole world as the expression of the creative reality of which we are all a part.

THE PHILOSOPHY OF CULTURE IN EUROPE IN THE NINETEENTH AND EARLY TWENTIETH CENTURIES

Before answering the question of why we should study Japanese cultural and social philosophy, we should ask ourselves what "culture" meant in the period in which Nishida, Watsuji, and Kuki lived and wrote. At the beginning of this introduction, I defined what I meant by culture very broadly. But what was the definition that the subjects of our study used? Until shortly after the Second World War, culture was relatively easy to define. T. S. Eliot's definition in his *Notes towards the Definition of Culture*, published in 1948, is emblematic:

> [By culture] I mean first of all what the anthropologists mean: the way of life of a particular people living together in one place. That culture is made visible in their arts, in their social system, in their habits and customs; in their religion. But these things added together do not constitute the culture. . . . A culture is more than the assemblage of its arts, customs, and religious beliefs. These things all act upon each other, and fully to understand one you have to understand all. (1948, 124)

We can see in this definition several features of "culture" that are largely shared by the three Japanese philosophers whom we will study in this book:

1.) Culture is related to a defined and homogeneous group of people.
2.) Those people live close to each other, "in one place."[9]
3.) Culture involves activities such as "habits and customs," religious and social practices.

4.) Culture also involves objects—Eliot cites the arts, but culture is often thought to include food, clothing, architecture, and so on.
5.) Culture is a shared way of living in the world and interpreting it.

Today, culture is primarily studied scientifically by anthropologists, sociologists, and human geographers, or else in a critical way by critical theorists, critical geographers, and others; unlike in the nineteenth and early twentieth centuries, it is a topic seldom addressed by philosophers.[10] Why this is the case no doubt has many causes. Perhaps it can be explained by the increasing recognition throughout the world of the importance of diversity, which led to skepticism about "culture" as a monolithic category and the acceptance of subcultures and alternative cultures, which makes "culture" a problematic category. Also, the promotion of multiculturalism in many countries has made clear that people can have multiple cultural competencies, especially if they belong to families with mixed cultural, linguistic, or religious backgrounds. There are many cultures, but "culture" as a general concept has become somewhat meaningless, or at least less important.

Moreover, beginning after the First but increasingly after the Second World War, intellectuals have been influenced by critical approaches such as Marxism, the Frankfurt School, Freudianism, and those found in the works of Michel Foucault, Gilles Deleuze, Felix Guattari, and Judith Butler, to name only a few. The approach to the study of society and culture that these schools, theories, and individuals promote have made it impossible to naively accept cultural products and practices as simple facts; rather, they must be seen as the result of particular social, political, or economic conditions, and they should only be studied from a specific standpoint rather than from an unproblematic objective one.

Take for example the cultural practice of educating the young as embodied in a school system composed of preschool, primary, secondary, and postsecondary institutions. Education can be analyzed as the product of particular economic effects, political choices, or social and cultural practices specific to a particular group. For instance, as sociologists Pierre Bourdieu and Jean-Claude Passeron have shown, success in French schools depends on the "cultural capital" that students have acquired in their home from their family and friends: the more a student shares the musical and artistic tastes of her future schoolmates, the more her extracurricular life is similar to that of others, the easier it will be for her to succeed in the system (Bourdieu and Passeron 1964). In light of the obviously contingent nature of social and cultural practices, that is, their dependence on systems of norms and values that are not obvious by superficial observation of them, the less it is possible to take "society" or "culture" to be a homogeneous phenomenon (Robbins 2005, 23).

If we were to adopt a Foucauldian perspective, we might analyze education as a system of knowledge that sets certain behaviors as normal and gives those who determine the standard of normalcy power over others who are subject to normalization. Foucault explains that normalizing judgment creates

> a whole range of degrees of normality indicating membership of a homogeneous social body but also playing a part in classification, hierarchization, and the distribution of rank. In this sense, the power of normalization imposes homogeneity, but it individualizes by making it possible to measure gaps, to determine levels, to fix specialities, and to render the differences useful by fitting them one to another. (1979, 184)

Institutions of all kinds, educational, carceral, governmental, social, and cultural, can be critically analyzed by uncovering the power structure that they represent and the technologies they use to acquire knowledge, and thereby power, over those subject to them.[11]

Nishida, Watsuji, and Kuki lived in an era in which such cultural critique was emerging but did not yet dominate, at least not in Japan. There were of course hints of it in the work of each: critical elements that questioned the possibility of a common Japanese culture and society. But they still operated within the paradigm of society and culture that they had inherited from Japanese philosophy and religion and that they found in the European philosophy they studied so assiduously in order to derive from it ways to modernize Japan. Thus their concepts of society and culture were influenced by Confucianism and Buddhism and the social system that, while it was crumbling around them in the early twentieth century, still informed the intellectual world in the Meiji (1868–1912), Taishō (1912–1926), and early Shōwa (1926–1989) periods.

The European philosophers they read were likewise enamored with the topics of society and culture: as the influence of the individualist tendencies of early modern European philosophy (Descartes, Leibiniz, Spinoza, Locke, etc.) waned, Europeans became interested in who they felt they were as a group. Thus Kant, Herder, Fichte, Hegel, and many other German idealist philosophers explored what social and cultural practices and their historical development over time reveal about the nature of human existence, human experience, and human knowledge. They attempted to identify the social and cultural preconditions of human rationality, justice, and morality. For instance, Sonia Sikka explains how Herder's philosophy of culture must be read in light of his view that philosophy should aim at understanding and promoting the basic humanity common to all people. She writes,

> Herder actually argues emphatically in favor of the existence of common properties among *all* human beings, regardless of the nation to which they belong

(*Ideas for a Philosophy of the History of Mankind*, 377; Herder 1985, vol. 6). All possess reason, language and the drive towards *Humanität* (humanity). In this context, *Humanität* signifies benevolence and respect, consideration for the humanity of others, as opposed to the *in*humanity of oppressors and assassins (ibid., 372). Herder maintains that all human beings possess the same basic aptitudes and predispositions (*Anlagen*) (ibid., 379), but, in line with the principle of unity in multiplicity that is so pervasive in his thought, these broad common capacities and tendencies are, he thinks, realized in diverse forms, at varying levels of advancement, across different societies. (Sikka 2011, 21) [Emphasis in original]

Though cultures vary from each other and change over time, the study of culture by Enlightenment and post-Enlightenment thinkers often focused on the common humanity that is shared despite these differences.

While Nishida, Watsuji, and Kuki clearly read these philosophers and their views on culture, society, and history, they were also aware of more modern European philosophy, which Watsuji and Kuki studied firsthand during their trips to Europe, and which they brought back with them to Japan. Here, five strands of influence are notable, including that of Herder, Kant, and the German idealists:

1.) German thought, as exemplified in the work of Herder; Kant's reaction to Herder; and the post-Kantian idealism of Fichte, Schelling, and Hegel;
2.) scientific approaches to culture and society as exemplified by the views of French philosophers Auguste Comte (1798–1857) and Hippolyte Taine (1828–1893);
3.) the transcendental approach of the Neo-Kantians (both the Marburg and Baden varieties): Wilhelm Windelband (1848–1915), Heinrich Rickert (1863–1936), Paul Natorp (1854–1924), Hermann Cohen (1842–1918), and Ernst Cassirer (1874–1945);
4.) intuitionism and *Lebensphilosophie* (life philosophy or vitalism) as typified in the work of Henri Bergson (1859–1941); and
5.) phenomenology as found in the work of the early phenomenologists and in their successors Edmund Husserl (1859–1938) and Martin Heidegger (1889–1976).

Though it will be impossible to go into detail about all of these developments in the philosophy of culture, a brief word should perhaps be said about this landscape in which the works of Nishida, Watsuji, and Kuki are situated. We will leave out phenomenology from our overview as it will be a major subject of our study of the views of Watsuji and Kuki on culture and society.

Cultural Diversity and Cultural Essentialism
in Herder, Kant, Fichte, and Hegel

I will not go into much detail in regard to the views of Herder, Kant, Fichte, and Hegel on the nature of culture and society and the influence of the natural environment on them: these are the subject of a detailed study in Chapter 3, the second chapter on Watsuji, who dealt extensively with their views in the final part of *Climate and Culture*. However, the general trajectory of the debate in German philosophy is helpful as it figures importantly in the background of the thought of all three philosophers. We will use Watsuji's interpretation of this trajectory in order to provide a Japanese perspective that will be useful in our study.

According to Watsuji, there are similarities between the cultural philosophy of Herder and Kant, but they differed in that Herder took a spatial approach and Kant a temporal one. Herder, Watsuji explains, was interested in cultural differences that could be found throughout the world in any given period,[12] whereas Kant was interested in changes in culture as it evolved over time and developed toward the achievement of a truly moral society (Dupré 1998). Watsuji also noted the universalist tendencies of both Herder and Kant: despite acknowledging the diversity of cultures, Herder believed that each was a unique expression of the divine;[13] Kant rejected Herder's view, instead arguing that what was universal in each culture was not its present state of development but the social and political goals toward which it strove, and which must embody the ethical and moral obligations of all humanity (Allison 2009, 42).[14] As Ernst Cassirer explained, from Kant's point of view, "As ethical subjects, we act not from freedom but towards freedom" (2015, 230). Watsuji interpreted Herder and Kant as agreeing that culture disclosed something universal about human existence while emphasizing different aspects of it: Herder prioritized the spatial dimension of human existence, and so he emphasized the diversity of cultures spread out across the physical space of the Earth (*WTZ* 8:220); Kant prioritized the temporal dimension of human existence, and so he emphasized the historical development of each culture as it strives to achieve a rational political and social structure (*WTZ* 8:222).

Watsuji was also inspired by the view of both Fichte and Hegel that a given nation expresses the spirit of the people who comprise it.[15] Fichte outlined these ideas in his famous and controversial *Addresses to the German Nation* (Fichte 2008), and Hegel expressed his version in many works, the most well-known being his comments in the *Encyclopedia of the Philosophical Sciences in Outline* (Hegel 1990). What impressed Watsuji in Fichte's thought was his view that culture takes the form of a "metaphysical spiritual nature" (*WTZ* 8:225), although Fichte did not relate this directly to climate. Hegel, however, did so, writing that "ethical spirit . . . exhibits its totality in the form of geographical and climatic determinacy" (1990, §442). Watsuji adopts the terminology of "spirit" in some of his work, but he rejects Hegel's metaphysics, no doubt for the same reason that Cassirer did so. The latter wrote in 1939, "Hegel's philosophy seeks to be a philosophy of freedom. And yet the idea of freedom of metaphysical Idealism as it undergirds the Hegelian system only guarantees freedom for the infinite, the absolute subject, but not for the finite subject. The latter remains from start to finish stoutly bound, for it is nothing but a mere transient point within world events, a means of which the World Spirit makes use" (Cassirer 2011, 146). Watsuji's view, developed in his later philosophy, was that while each individual manifests the absolute within her, the constant dynamic movement of the absolute is not working toward any particular telos: its movement is simply the activity of reality itself (McCarthy 2016).

The Scientific Approach to the Study of Culture: Auguste Comte and Hippolyte Taine

French philosophers had a significant impact on Japanese philosophy during the careers of Nishida, Watsuji, and Kuki. Auguste Comte's positivist empiricism sets the stage for our study in two ways. Comte was one of the first preeminent French philosophers to suggest a systematic scientific approach to the study of human society. In this regard, he, along with Étienne Bonnot de Condillac (1714–1780), was of interest to Kuki as a counterpoint to Maine de Biran's intuitionism, which influenced Kuki's interpretation of phenomenology and hermeneutics. However, Comte was also of importance because of his views about human history and the evolution of human societies, which was also positivistic: Comte believed that it must be possible to explain history as the expression of a series of sociohistorical laws. Indeed, in his *Courses on Positive Philosophy* (*Cours de philosophie positive*, 1830–1842), he contrasts the traditional unscientific approach to the study of human history with his suggested scientific approach. First, he describes the unscientific approach of two schools which he labels "Theological" and "Metaphysical":

> In politics it is obvious that, in spite of the undeniable tendency today to a sounder philosophy, the prevailing disposition of statesmen and even of publicists, both in the theological and in the metaphysical school, is to conceive social phenomena as arbitrarily modifiable to an indefinite extent, and to suppose that the human species is without any innate inclination, and is always ready to undergo passively the influence of the legislator whether temporal or spiritual, provided he be invested with sufficient authority. . . . The metaphysical school

has recourse to the device of Providence in a much vaguer and less specific way, without ceasing to base itself on the same hypothesis, and habitually introducing its unintelligible entities into these vacuous political explanations, especially the great entity of nature, which today embraces all the rest, and which is nothing but an abstract derivative of the theological principle. Disdaining even any subordination of effect to cause, it attempts to elude the philosophical difficulty by attributing to chance the production of observed events, and sometimes, when the inanity of this procedure becomes too glaring, by exaggerating to the point of absurdity the influence of individual genius on the course of human affairs. Whatever the mode adopted, the result in both schools is always to represent the political action of man as essentially indefinite and arbitrary, exactly as in the past biological, chemical, physical and even astronomical phenomena were believed to be, during the more or less prolonged theologico-metaphysical infancy of these sciences. (Comte 1974, 143–144)

Having described the views that he rejects, he then prescribes a corrective in the form of a scientific study of human society, which would allow for social phenomena to be understood in terms of "natural laws" that would in turn enable one to rationally predict the future direction society would take (Comte 1974, 147). According to Comte, sociology as a rigorous science is to have both a static and dynamic aspect. He describes the static aspect of sociology as analogous to the study of anatomy, which locates the various elements relative to each other:

The social anatomy which constitutes static sociology must have as its permanent object the positive study, at once experimental and rational, of the various parts of the social system in their action and reaction upon one another, abstracting for the time being as much as possible the movement which is always modifying them. Sociological predictions, founded on the exact knowledge of these interrelations, are thus destined to derive the various static indications on each mode of social existence in conformity with further observation, in a manner analogous with what takes place habitually in individual anatomy. (Comte 1974, 149)

Comte's scientific and sociological approach to culture was the foil of the concept adopted by the Neo-Kantians of the Baden School, Wilhelm Windelband and Heinrich Rickert, as we shall see shortly.

Interestingly, Comte's scientific conception accepted the mutual influence of cultures, limited only by the distance (and hence the possibility of exchange) between them. In this regard, Comte's view is similar to that of Watsuji, who also accepted the importance of cultural interaction. For instance, in his early work *Pilgrimages*, Watsuji noted the flow of cultural influence as Greek aesthetics bled into Indian art, which in turn traveled through Western China to Eastern China, Korea, and so to Japan (see also Watsuji 1998, 250–260). Comte writes about this interaction as follows:

> Looking farther afield, we see the continuous interrelation of the systems of sciences and of arts, if we allow for the solidarity becoming less intense as it becomes more indirect. It is the same with the totality of social phenomena, not within one nation, but among the various contemporary nations, whose influence on one another cannot be denied, especially in modern times, though here the consensus will as a rule be less pronounced, and decrease gradually with the diminishing affinity of the cases and number of their contacts, to the point of disappearing altogether, as for instance between Western Europe and Eastern Asia, whose societies have appeared up till now to be practically independent of one another. (Comte 1974, 150–151)

Here we also note the importance Comte, like the Japanese philosophers we shall study, placed on the continuity between politics, society, and culture. He emphasized, "A political regime is never to be considered except in its continuous relation, sometimes general, sometimes special, to the corresponding state of civilisation, apart from which it cannot be properly judged, and by the gradual pressure of which it is produced and modified" (Comte 1974, 155). By examining Comte, one begins to understand why the political and social upheaval that Japan was experiencing during the time that Nishida, Watsuji, and Kuki lived caused them to reflect on Japanese culture and the nature of social relations. Having read Comte, it became obvious to them and their contemporaries that the political changes brought about by the Meiji Restoration and increasing democratic reforms during the Taishō period (1912–1926) must inevitably influence Japanese social structures and culture. How this would occur and what would remain of traditional Japanese culture was an open question. In this regard, the scientific approach of Comte also had something to contribute: it allowed one to study the process of cultural development over time (Comte 1974, 162) by examining the cause-and-effect relations between earlier states of society and present ones (Comte 1974, 163). Comte believed these to be "subject to a definite order" which could in turn be described by natural laws (Comte 1974, 164). Japanese philosophers, witnesses to significant social changes, must have been intrigued by the possibility of studying them in a systematic way.

While Hippolyte Taine (1828–1893) will not figure prominently in our exploration of Nishida, Watsuji, and Kuki, it would be impossible to imagine that his philosophy, extremely well known in the nineteenth century, would not have influenced them. Taine continued the development of the French scientific approach to the study of culture and society established by Comte.[16]

In his view, history advanced by the acts of "great men," whose influences were attributable to their souls,[17] and which could therefore be studied via psychology, a field of science that revealed the laws of human action. He explains in his *History of English Literature* that all the external habits of a person reveal an inner life which is the "genuine man," and which is the proper subject matter for the historian:

> All these externals are but avenues converging to a centre; you enter them simply in order to reach that centre; and that centre is the genuine man, I mean that mass of faculties and feelings which are produced by the inner man. We have reached a new world, which is infinite, because every action which we see involves an infinite association of reasonings, emotions, sensations new and old, which have served to bring it to light, and which, like great rocks deep-seated in the ground, find in it their end and their level. This underworld is a new subject-matter, proper to the historian. If his critical education suffice, he can lay bare, under every detail of architecture, every stroke in a picture, every phrase in a writing, the special sensation whence detail, stroke, or phrase had issue; he is present at the drama which was enacted in the soul of artist or writer; the choice of a word, the brevity or length of a sentence, the nature of a metaphor, the accent of a verse, the development of an argument—everything is a symbol to him; while his eyes read the text, his soul and mind pursue the continuous development and the everchanging succession of the emotions and conceptions out of which the text has sprung: in short, he unveils a psychology. (Taine 1871, 4–5)

Taine goes on to develop this scientific approach by noting the different psychologies of people from different cultures with the aim of identifying "the moral constitution of a people or an age" that is as "distinct as the physical structure of a family of plants or an order of animals" (Taine 1871, 5). A scientific study can reveal the "system in human sentiments and ideas" which "has for its motive power certain general traits, certain marks of the intellect and the heart common to men of one race, age, or country" (Taine 1871, 7). Thus according to Taine, to understand the history of human societies, the scholar must study the effects of three elements: "the *race*, the *surroundings*, and the *epoch*" (Taine 1871, 10) [emphasis in original]. As the neo-Kantian cultural philosopher Ernst Cassirer explains, Taine believed that all of human history could be explained based on these three elements:

> Once we have established these three elements [race, surroundings and epoch] and taken them firmly in hand, the problem is solved: By combining these three basic elements in the right way, we can magically conjure the whole breadth of historical appearances and the phenomena of culture in all of their gleaming colours. . . . [Taine] never tired in casting light on the character and basic

outlook of a particular epoch by means of the combination of innumerable details. (Author's translation) (Cassirer 2011, 142–143)

Taine's scientific mindset built out of the myriad of empirical details of history a complete understanding of the development of human culture over time (Cassirer 2011, 145). One sees in Taine's approach the embryonic form of Watsuji's interest in studying the relationship between climate and culture, though the method that he would use would be completely different. One can also see in Taine an exemplar of the French positivist school which Bergson, and so too his student Kuki, rejected.[18]

Bergson's Intuitionism

Henri Bergson is not normally considered a philosopher of culture; but his work on morality and religion such as *The Two Sources of Morality and Religion* (1932) can provide us insight into his views on the subject of society and social organization. His intuitionist philosophical method had a tremendous influence on both Nishida and Kuki. They were also drawn to the distinction he makes between the sad world of everyday life in which people act based on habitat and social pressure (Bergson 1932, 5–19, 20–21) and the world of the true individual whose connection with life and God gives rise, through an intuition of the moral life, to a vital, living sense of morality. Bergson describes morality as contact with life itself in the following way:

> The other attitude is that of the open spirit. To what is such a spirit open? If we said that it encompasses the whole of humanity, we would not be far off the mark. Indeed, we might not have gone far enough, since he embraces animals, plants, and the whole of nature. And yet what falls within his circle of concern would not suffice for defining his outlook, because strictly speaking, he could do without anyone [to whom to direct it]. The form that this outlook takes does not depend on its content. It is filled with beings; but we could also empty it. And yet the spirit of charity would continue to persist in a person who possesses it, even were there nothing living left on Earth. (132, 21)

Culture need not be a set of empty and lifeless obligations: it is capable of expressing something fundamental about the living world. However, to do so, individuals must gain intuitive access to what the life living as our world expresses. If we fail, we collapse into the directionless, uninspired life of the everyday individual. But humans are capable of loving truly, of being selflessly charitable, and of living authentically, and they can do so when they connect in a direct way with the continuous and dynamic flow of life prior to its stultification by the imposition of habit, concepts, and theoretical abstraction. We will delve in greater detail into Bergson's theory of culture and his method of intuition in Chapter 7, and so we will defer a more thorough interpretation until then.

The Transcendental Approach of the Neo-Kantians

The Neo-Kantians had a significant impact on Japanese philosophy, especially that of Kuki, who studied with Paul Natorp and Heinrich Rickert. Like Watsuji and Kuki, the Neo-Kantians were particularly interested in both social and cultural philosophy.[19] Indeed, in many ways their approach to the topic can be seen as the foil to the views of Watsuji and Kuki. The Neo-Kantians shared a scientific approach with Comte, but they disagreed with the French philosopher about the nature of the object of study. As we have seen, Comte believed that all scientific study must take phenomena—things that actually happen—as its starting point. One then determines what laws can account for these phenomena. As an example, Comte proposed to study literature by examining the writings of a particular author to reveal her soul—that is, her inner psychology—which could then be analyzed to discover the psychological rules that it follows.

In contrast, Wilhelm Windelband (1848–1915) and Heinrich Rickert (1863–1936), the preeminent philosophers of the Baden branch of Neo-Kantianism, believed that the subject of the social sciences had to be fundamentally different from that of the natural sciences. In his well-known lecture in 1894 upon assuming the position of Rector of Kaiser-Wilhelm University in Strasburg, Windelband drew a distinction between natural sciences, which he labeled "nomothetic" (i.e., "law-like") because they sought the natural law ("laws of occurrence," Windelband 1998, 12) that explained particular natural phenomena (Windelband 1998, 13), and the social sciences, which were "idiographic" because they aimed at "reproducing or rendering intelligible a creation of human life in its factuality" (Windelband 1998, 12), for instance, by describing the form (*Gestalt*) of a particular historical event (Windelband 1998, 13). While the natural sciences studied laws, the social sciences studied "events" (ibid.). Windelband went on to explain that while both natural and social sciences examined empirical phenomena, which he called "facts of perception," and did so critically in order to form general concepts (Windelband 1998, 14), the two differed in regard to using facts (Windelband 1998, 15): natural scientists tended to seek general rules, while social scientists portrayed the character of a historical episode. He wrote,

> The difference between the study of nature and history begins where the concern is with the knowledge-appropriate utilization of the facts. Thus we see: the one

seeks laws, the other forms. In the one, thought pushes from the identification of the particular to the grasping of general relationships, in the other one remains with the painstaking characterization of the particular. For the student of nature, the single, given object of his observation never has scientific merit in itself; it serves him only insofar as he considers himself justified in regarding it as a type, as a special case of a categorical concept and to further develop the latter from it. In this he reflects only on those features which lend insight into a lawful generalization. For the historian, the task consists of bringing to life in an imagined present some or other artifact of the past in its entirely individual character. With respect to that which once really existed, the historian has a task to fulfill similar to that of the artist with respect to that which is in his creative ideas. . . .
From this it follows that the tendency toward abstraction dominates in the thinking of natural science, while that toward concreteness [*Anschaulichkeit*] dominates in history. (Windelband 1998, 15–16)

We need not go into the details of Windelband's philosophy except to note its influence on Kuki's theory of contingency (see Mayeda 2008) and to emphasize that Nishida, Watsuji, and Kuki all rejected the scientific approach of the Neo-Kantians to the study of culture.

Rickert believed that a proper social scientific approach to the study of history must focus on values, not facts or events: the individuals and events of history take on more or less importance when seen through the lens of a system of values. Cassirer explains Rickert's value-oriented history of philosophy as follows: "To understand a fact historically and to organize it historically, one must relate it to general values. The fullness of individual facts cannot be ignored, and yet cannot be grasped as such. Only by relating facts to general values is it possible for historical knowledge to proceed along particular lines and to divide it internally" (author's translation) (Cassirer 2011, 40). Whether history is studied as a series of events (Windelband) or by relating events to values (Rickert), the general impulse of the Neo-Kantians was transcendental: it was to discover behind the happenings of the world the conditions of their possibility and to build a science of culture and society on an understanding of them (Cassirer 2011, 40; 2015, 223). The problem for the Neo-Kantians was in the end a metaphysical one: Are the forces that connect historical events really similar to the material forces that link physical events? In other words, is there a proper analogy between the study of natural phenomena and the study of society and culture? The suspicion that the similarity was solely metaphorical created a metaphysical crisis that led among other things to the development of phenomenology, first in order to securely ground the natural sciences in experience (Husserl), and then later to radically question the metaphysical presuppositions of the whole history of European philosophy until that time (Heidegger).

As we will see in this book, Nishida, Watsuji, and Kuki were all to lesser or greater degrees influenced by and reacting to the failures of Neo-Kantianism that were becoming more apparent as the twentieth century wore on. What they preserved from the long history of cultural philosophy that we have traced is first the interest in culture as a legitimate subject of philosophical inquiry, and second, the Enlightenment impulse to discover in culture something essential about both individual and social existence.

JAPANESE CULTURE AND JAPANESE NATIONALISM

Each of the three Japanese philosophers whose theories of culture we will study in this book has been subject to criticism for the political views that their theories support. Beginning in the 1930s, Nishida Kitarō's views were subject to serious criticism by his students such as Tanabe Hajime (1934) and Marxists such as Tosaka Jun (*TJZ*, 3:172–173). John Maraldo is of the view that whereas Nishida was not initially concerned with politics or political philosophy, he was inevitably, though reluctantly, drawn into the politics of the time (2017, 164; see also Yusa). His writing just prior to and during the war was not meant to justify Japanese aggression, but it was interpreted in that way by the government (Maraldo 2017, 167–168), and government adoption of it reinforced postwar critique of his philosophy (ibid.). As Arisaka Yoko points out in her detailed study of Nishida's "The Principle of the New World Order," published in 1943, Nishida presented the uncontroversial claim that there are a variety of cultures in the world and that each has the duty to develop itself to its utmost potential. But this was accompanied by the more problematic claim that Japan was the most highly developed culture in Asia and therefore the natural political leader of the new "coprosperity sphere" which the Japanese government was considering creating both to dominate the region and to act as a balance against European hegemony. Arisaka writes,

> At the abstract and universal level, Nishida's ontological theory of globalized cultures is not in itself politically problematic; it simply describes a dialectical process through which nations become what they are. What made it problematic was Japan's purported position in this dialectic at the time of Japanese colonialist expansion in Asia: it so happens that, according to Nishida, it was Japan that most fully expressed this universally applicable, globally significant, world-making dialectic, and, as such, it was the "historical mission of Japan" to bring this insight to the greater world ravaged by Euro-American imperialism and materialism (which Nishida criticized to be operating under the principle

of the egoistic expansionism of the nineteenth century that merely dominates and subjugates others for one's own purposes). The creation of the Greater East-Asian Co-Prosperity Sphere was said to be a step toward consolidating the world-historical expressions of the peoples of East Asia (against Euro-American domination), and Japan was to self-appoint itself as the leader of this mission.

As we will see, Nishida adopted an internationalist approach: societies should be free to discover within themselves a "world-historical" element—an element that reflects the basic truth of what it means to live in a world of constant creation, production, and change. Once they have done this and put this "world-historical" perspective into action, they will inevitably reject nationalism and imperialism (Parkes 1997, 311). But as Arisaka points out, there is an inherent danger in a philosophy of culture that posits a universal goal for cultural development: such a view can very easily slip into both cultural essentialism (the tendency to reduce particular cultures to a few key features) and cultural comparison (the tendency to compare different cultures with one another and create a hierachy) (see also Maraldo 2017, 171). A universalist theory of culture provides a ready yardstick for measuring "progress" along the path toward the goal of greater cultural development, and it also encourages stereotyping cultures in order to more readily determine where they fall along the ruler. Thus while one can see in Nishida's adoption of an internationalist and "world-historical" approach many points of resistance to Japanese ultranationalism (Yusa 1994; Parkes 1997), as Yusa notes, "any attempt to address the immediate political issues of Japan philosophically was bound to invite misunderstanding" (131). Indeed, the political context leading up to and during the Second World War has heavily influenced how several interpreters have read Nishida's texts (see Narita and Harootunian 1993; Faure 1993).

But while Nishida's philosophy of culture invites necessary criticism and caution, I think it does provide some insight into problems that still exist today. As we will see in this book, his ultimate view was quite close to that of Immanuel Kant: cultures should work toward achieving truly ethical societies that embody moral ideals. Moreover, the ideal that Nishida thought we should achieve was one in which we abandon selfish goals and pursue lives that reflect the absolute in us. For Nishida, this meant simply accepting that as human beings, we are the expression of the dynamic unfolding of reality, and therefore we must act on this recognition not only by respecting this common humanity, but also by recognizing the deeper unity between ourselves and others. It is hard to see how this exhortation to respect others as one wishes oneself to be respected is problematic. Of course, the fact that Nishida himself saw the ethics he proposed as compatible with Japanese domination in Asia should be a caution against wholesale acceptance of his view.

As we will see in this book, Watsuji's theory of culture went through a number of changes as it evolved during his career. He started out viewing culture as malleable, subject to change due to interaction with other cultures and changing social, economic, and political factors. But with the publication of *Climate and Culture*, we see a view of culture emerge that could easily slip into essentialism and geographic determinism (Berque 2011, 22). This tendency results from the fact that once one sees culture as climatic, it can easily become tied to a specific place; and the more that a culture is tied to a specific place, the more it becomes associated with specific ethnic groups that live there. Thus Sakai Naoki writes, "As his work Fūdo or *Climate and Culture* amply indicates, the totality to which a person belongs is circumscribed in terms not only of historical, political, and sociological factors but also of climatic, geographic, and ethnographic specificities" (1997, 90).

Another problem with Watsuji's philosophy is that he believed that his climatic theory of culture could provide insight into the basic structure of human existence, which as we have seen is both temporal and spatial. The goal of understanding human existence is thus tied to the goal of understanding the link between climate and culture. But again, this can easily slip into the specific project of understanding myself as an individual in relation to the specific culture to which I belong. Now if understanding who we really are means understanding the nature of the culture to which we belong, and if this culture is identified with an ethnic group inhabiting a particular place as Watsuji believed, then understanding oneself requires understanding the uniqueness of one's culture. Once one goes down this path, a philosophy of culture in general is quickly transformed into the philosophy of a particular culture. Sakai points out this very transformation from a general climatic theory of culture to a theory of the particularity of each culture. He also picks up on the fact that in the philosophy of Watsuji (as is also the case with Kuki), the investigation of Japanese particularity inevitably sets up an opposition between East and West (Sakai 1997, 90–91). For to understand who I am as a Japanese person requires me to understand what the characteristics are of the Japanese, and in turn, how I am different from non-Japanese. Indeed, this dualism is one way of reading *Climate and Culture*, as we will see in the chapters devoted to that text.

When we shift from an assessment of the possibilities latent in Watsuji's philosophy of culture and society to his actual political views, one must acknowledge an inherent ambiguity. Steve Bein captures this ambiguity when he writes, "Watsuji's reputation would see significant damage during the Second World War, some of it arguably deserved, much of it not" (2011, 6). Not only does Arisaka note Watsuji's direct involvement in supporting and justifying Japanese aggression and nationalism (2014, 18–19), she also explains how his theory of culture as embodying the unique features of a specific ethnic group fed into Japanese nationalism prior to and during the Second World War: "Watsuji's writings made it clear that the Japanese culture possessed unique characteristics (such as the notion of nothingness and deep aesthetic sensibilities) which were superior to the vulgar and materialistic Euro-American cultures. His cultural nationalism supported the common nationalistic sentiments of the time" (Arisaka 2014, 19; see also Bellah 1965; for a contrary view, see LaFleur 1990). I have a tendency to read Watsuji's views of culture in the context of the late Meiji and Taishō periods when the Japanese intellectual world was in crisis as it sought to modernize (which at that time meant Westernize) while still maintaining a tie to tradition (see also Lucken 2015): such a crisis inevitably invites those living through it to reflect on Japanese tradition, to romanticize the past and to devalue foreign elements. Whatever the case might be with Watsuji's political views, we will use an exploration of his cultural and social philosophy to reflect on how to avoid a cultural theory from slipping into a justification for cultural essentialism and nationalism.[20] What is interesting about his theory is his view that to correct Heideggerian phenomenology, it is necessary to place more emphasis on the spatial (and hence climatic and social) elements of human existence. The question is whether it is possible to use culture as the subject of phenomenological analysis with the aim of drawing out the spatiality and sociality of human existence without sliding into cultural essentialism or geographic determinism.

Kuki's philosophy displays a modern and cosmopolitan approach that in many instances contrasts with the attempts of Nishida and Kuki to set up traditional Japanese philosophical views as a counterweight to the increasing influence of European currents of thought in Japan. This is most clear in the works we will study in this book, which question the traditional interpretations of Japanese cultural ideals, ethics, and religion as much as they constitute a critique of European views.

Some have given Kuki's project a different interpretation. For instance, Leslie Pincus, while acknowledging that Kuki was reacting against certain strains of modernization and Europeanization that he witnessed in Japan during the Taishō and early Shōwa periods, nonetheless served the interests of Japanese nationalism by finding in its past (in the *geisha* culture of the Tokuagawa era) a "rarefied space of 'Japanese culture'" that could then be "imprinted [with] the stamp of a unitary 'Japanese character,' subject to the mandates of a repressive and imperialist state" (1996, 246–247). She thus gives a warning to the scholars of today not to separate texts such as *The Structure of Iki* from "the history in which those texts are implicated" (ibid.). This is an important point: we should hesitate to read *The Structure of Iki* purely as a postmodern text that plays with notions of Japanese identity in a critical way; rather, one must have an eye toward the social and political context in which Kuki was writing as well as the other texts that he produced, some of which are more clearly connected with Japanese nationalism and the creation of Japanese culture as "unique" and, in its uniqueness, somehow superior to others.

For instance, while acknowledging that Kuki wrote chauvinistic essays such as "The Japanese Character," Sakabe Megumi contrasts these with *The Structure of Iki*, "The History of Early Modern Western Philosophy," and his "Lecture on Contemporary French Philosophy," which he believes avoid simplistic nationalism (Sakabe 1990, 103). However, even Sakabe recognizes some nationalist tendencies in *The Structure of Iki*, particularly near the beginning when Kuki describes *iki* as embodying the "ethnic particularity" of the Japanese. In contrast, Tanaka Kyūbun argues that these passages are not meant to be nationalistic but cosmopolitan. In his view, Kuki's theory of culture is animated by a recognition of the interchange between cultures (Tanaka 1992, 90–93). Of course, defining cultural difference often involves defining particularities of each culture. As with the texts of Nishida and Watsuji, it would be dangerous to definitively label Kuki's philosophy of culture in a particular way: he wrote texts that sought to elevate Japanese culture and preserve its traditions, but as Sakabe points out, he also wrote texts that resisted this trend and identified unique Japanese culture with very nontraditional values.

WHY STUDY JAPANESE CULTURAL AND SOCIAL PHILOSOPHY?

In her study of Herder's cultural philosophy, Sikka answers the question "Why should we study Herder?" After all, he, like Nishida, Watsuji, and Kuki, has been accused of cultural essentialism and cultural chauvinism, attitudes that are generally considered incompatible with our modern liberal democratic views, which value differences and assert the importance of maintaining them. Sikka makes two useful points in defending the study of Herder that can be applied to our study of Nishida, Watsuji, and Kuki. First, while we might be skeptical about the permanence of cultural identity, cultures do seem to exist as a matter of fact: people share, either consciously or subconsciously, ways of speaking, acting, dressing, and so on (Sikka 2011, 8). Given this fact, it can be useful to consider theories about what this shared life means. Second, she points out that cultural membership implies a kind of relationship to others that is different from that of voluntary groups or associations: for instance, it is generally easier to leave a voluntary association than it is to leave a culture, and cultural membership has a much different impact on our lives as individuals than does our joining and leaving other kinds of groups (Sikka 2011, 8–9). In other words, a study of culture can be the basis of a social theory: a theory about the nature of social relations.

The Japanese philosophers whom we will study have made significant contributions to our understanding of what culture is and what its existence implies about the nature of intersubjective relationships. Watsuji's theory of the dialectic of self and other, which has its origins in his study of climate and culture and would be fully developed in his three-volume *Ethics* (*Rinrigaku*), accurately captures the tug of war that we all feel between asserting our individualism and wanting to belong to a group, be it family, friends, colleagues, coreligionists, or a political party. But even the early works of Watsuji, on which we will focus in this book, lead us to question what culture is and what kinds of interpersonal relationships give rise to it. For instance, *Pilgrimages* does not just document Buddhist art, an important part of the Japanese cultural tradition; instead, Watsuji is engaged in creating its modern meaning by imagining the lives, attitudes, and sensibilities of the artists and patrons who made it possible for temples, statues, and paintings of profound beauty and power to be created. Imagined relations with past ancestors thus play an important role in Watsuji's creation of Japanese culture. And his interactions with friends, family members, and the strangers he encounters during his tour of the temples of Nara and the surrounding area heavily influence his experience of Japanese culture, lending to this experience the tinge of the emotional and intellectual exchanges he has with them. Similarly, *Climate and Culture* inspires us to reflect on culture not just as a response to geography and the physical environment, but as a way of experiencing it: according to Watsuji, the greeting "Cold enough for you?" and variations of it found in the cold regions of our planet *is* climate more so than air of a particular temperature or humidity. The French philosopher Augustin Berque has made this aspect of Watsuji's philosophy, the idea that human existence is situated in a *milieu* (Berque's translation of *fūdo*, "climate"), the starting point for very inspiring reflections on the relationship between humans and their natural and social environment.

Kuki's analysis of the relationship between a *geisha* and her lover portrays a conundrum of the modern world: How to be in a romantic or sexual relationship and yet maintain one's freedom and individuality? Indeed, Kuki's analysis leads us to fundamental questions such as "What is freedom?" and "What is idealism?" Kuki answers the first question by saying that to be free, we must maintain distance from others and that others must respect this distance. He answers the second question by saying that to live according to ideals requires acceptance that they are unrealizable. The study of the specific relationships that he describes to answer these questions and the examples that he gives drawn from Japanese culture both provide concrete examples to illustrate his notions of freedom and idealism while at the same time causing us to reflect critically on our stereotypes of *Bushidō* (*the way of the samurai*) and Buddhism, the strands within Japanese culture that he sees as providing the models for them. For instance, one tends to think of samurai as blindly giving up their lives for the sake of the group; they are by no means free. And one common stereotype of Buddhism is that it involves recognizing a simplistic oneness with others. Comparing these stereotypes with Kuki's insistence that these Japanese traditions promote and protect very modern ideals such as freedom and individuality causes us to take a healthy second look at them.

Finally, all three philosophers lead us to reflect on a universal problem: How do we negotiate the constant change that societies and cultures undergo? Nishida, Watsuji, and Kuki lived in a period of rapid modernization in Japan, a modernization that involved exploration, adaptation, and adoption of political, economic, social, and cultural institutions from foreign, mostly European, countries. Their theories of culture and society reflect the challenges they faced in their times, such as how to balance the preservation of traditional values with the need to adapt them to meet changing times. Their experience is also useful for considering the push and pull that goes on within multicultural societies as we struggle to decide how to live together when we have different concepts of marriage, romantic and sexual relationships, family, privacy, ethics, and law, to cite just a few dimensions of them. Nishida, Watsuji, and Kuki give us three different answers about how culture changes, how it incorporates new elements, and how it reconciles the new with the old.

NOTES

1. I will be using the traditional Japanese name order of "family name" followed by "given name" when writing about Japanese philosophers.

2. As an example, Watsuji includes within his definition of Japanese culture clothing, food, and shelter, the fine arts and religion (Watsuji 1998, 256–259).

3. Fujita Masakatsu discusses this in his article in the *Oxford Handbook of Japanese Philosophy* (Davis 2017).

4. For an excellent overview of the content of the three volumes, see Sevilla (2014).

5. 「人の存在の構造を時間性として把捉する試みは、自分にとって非常に興味深いものであった。しかし時間性がかく主体的存在構造として活かされたときに、なぜ同時に空間性が、同じく根源的な存在構造として、活かされて来ないのか、それが自分には問題であった。」(*Fūdo*, WTZ 8:1).

6. In his essay "The Japanese Spirit" (*Nihon seishin*, 1935), Watsuji explains that spirit is grasped concretely in the way that a people experience climate and culture. He wrote, "Fundamentally, spirit is . . . matter as living active subject. What is called the physical body as active subject from the standpoint of an individual

person corresponds to climate and nature as active subject for the race as active subject. Spirit expresses itself in matter precisely in this latter sense. If it is correct to call spirit this kind of natural-climatic subject that continuously actualizes itself in objective forms—in other words, which itself is certainly not an object and yet causes us to grasp it only through what is objective—then it is hardly inappropriate to call a race of people an active subject in the sense of a living whole" (Dilworth et al. 1998, 231–261, 244).「根源的には精神はまた生ける主体的なる物質ででもあるのである。個人の立場において主体的なる肉体と呼ばるるものが、主体的民族にとっては主体的なる風土自然に相当する。だからこそ精神は物質的なるものにおいて己れを現わし得るのである。もしこのような、己れを絶えず客体的な姿に実現して行くものを、——すなわちそれ自体は決して対象たることなくしてしかもただ対象的なるものを通じてのみ己れを我々に把捉せしめるものを、精神と呼ぶのが正しいならば、生ける全体性としての主体的民族をこの名によって呼ぶことは決して不当ではない。」(WTZ 4:299).

7. *Kasei* is a combination of two era names: *bunka* (文化時代, 1804–1818) and *bunsei* (文政時代, 1818–1830).

8. In his essay, "Bergson in Japan," he writes, "Mr. Bergson has 'reanimated the absolute' [in Japanese philosophy]. And the philosophy of Nishida, perhaps the most profound thinker in Japan today, is presented as an effort to synthesize transcendental philosophy with that of Bergson" (author's translation).

9. Watsuji's concept of culture was slightly different in that he acknowledged that a culture could be exported throughout the world. Examples in his works usually focus on religions: in *Pilgrimages*, he demonstrates the migration of Buddhism and of Buddhist art from South and Central Asia to China, Korea, and Japan. In *Climate and Culture*, he discusses the migration of the culture of the desert through the transportation of messianic religions (Judaism, Christianity, and Islam) from the Middle East to Europe.

10. A renewed interest in culture in philosophy circles has been inspired by the work of Daniel C. Dennett (see, for instance, *From Bacteria to Bach and Back: The Evolution of Minds* [New York: W.W. Norton & Company, 2017]). It complements ongoing work in the area, for instance, in the the work of those studying Ernst Cassirer (see Edward Skidelsky, *Ernst Cassirer: The Last Philosopher of Culture* [Princeton, NJ: Princeton University Press, 2008]).

11. For an example of a study applying Foucault's work to educational institutions, see Ball (2010).

12. See Sikka (2011, 250–251) to confirm Watsuji's assessment on this point.

13. This follows from his view that all things are the expression of God. Sikka writes, "The ultimate ground and explanation of reality, which Herder defines as force or power, *Kraft*, is not merely, for him, an indication of God, but *is* God" (2011, 224) [emphasis in original].

14. Kant's teleological interpretation of history and nature was overshadowed for many years by the idealists, who were more interested in Kant's epistemology and his transcendental idealism—the view that all knowledge is constituted by the faculties of the experiencing subject. It only became a subject of study for the Neo-Kantians,

who were very influential in Europe and in Japan during the time of Nishida, Watsuji, and Kuki. For the Neo-Kantians, the teleological interpretation of nature and history could in some sense be said to have supplanted interest in the *Critique of Pure Reason*. According to John Michael Krois, this is particularly clear in the case of Ernst Cassirer, for whom "the historical writings, Kant's ethical works, and the *Critique of Judgment* together form a general teleological system of philosophy" (Krois 1987, 21).

15. See the extract from "The Japanese Spirit" quoted in note 6. He also wrote in *Fūdo* that the "problem of climate exists, within . . . metaphysical spiritual nature" (*WTZ* 8:225; author's translation). 「我々の風土の問題はまさに形而上的な精神的自然の内に、…「神的なるものの特殊法則」として、存するのである」. The term "the special law of the divine" is a quote from Fichte, whose theory Watsuji was commenting on in this passage.

16. For a helpful introduction to the philosophy of history of Taine and to the influence of Hegel on him, see Dumas (1972).

17. "When you consider with your eyes the visible man, what do you look for?" he wrote. "The man invisible. The words which enter your ears, the gestures, the motions of his head, the clothes he wears, visible acts and deeds of every kind, are expressions merely; somewhat is revealed beneath them, and that is a soul. An inner man is concealed beneath the outer man; the second does but reveal the first" (Taine 1871, 4).

18. On Bergson as an exemplar of the "spiritualist" school that rejected Taine's positivism, see Gunn (1922, 73).

19. The term *Kulturwissenschaft* was often used by Neo-Kantians to indicate what we would today call the "social sciences."

20. Sakabe Megumi undertakes such an analysis in Sakabe (1988).

Chapter 2

Watsuji Tetsurō's Early Views on Culture

A Study of Pilgrimages to the Ancient Temples in Nara (Koji Junrei)

THE THREE FACETS OF CULTURE: CONSTRUCTED, DYNAMIC, AND PHILOSOPHICAL

Culture is not just old temples and Buddhist art. It is not just about how we use language or social conventions. According to Watsuji Tetsurō, the artifacts and practices that make up our everyday notion of culture are clues that point to something fundamental about how we relate to our natural and physical environment and to other people: a study of culture reveals something about the social nature of human existence and the phenomenological structures that make it possible. One of the principal tasks of Watsuji's mature philosophy is to identify these structures by analyzing the cultural clues. In this chapter, we will study *Pilgrimages to the Ancient Temples in Nara* (hereafter *Pilgrimages*; *Koji Junrei*, 『古寺巡礼』, Watsuji 2014) in order to better understand Watsuji's views about what culture is and what it reveals about human existence, especially its social aspects.

Pilgrimages is an early text: Watsuji wrote it in 1919 at the beginning of his professional career. It is generally considered a work about art history, and even today, it is used as a guide for Japanese tourists visiting Nara and its many temples. As a result, philosophers have on the whole ignored it.[1] However, the book foreshadows the trajectory that Watsuji's social and cultural philosophy would eventually take.

Pilgrimages was written for the educated public, not philosophers, and therefore the philosophical ideas that exist in embryo form in the text are expressed simply and directly; Watsuji leaves out many of the technical details of his later social philosophy. This makes reading *Pilgrimages* enjoyable, and it can serve as an accessible introduction to Watsuji's thought.

The picture of culture that emerges from a study of Watsuji's book is the following:

1.) *Culture is constructed*: people, including cultural experts (historians of art and music, sociologists of popular culture, and so on), identify what counts as "culture" and interpret the meaning of cultural objects and practices; there is no objective criterion for determining if something is "cultural";
2.) *Culture is eclectic and dynamic*: it is composed of many elements from diverse sources that have accumulated over time, and it is subject to evolution and change;
3.) *Culture has philosophical significance*: cultural objects and practices can be analyzed philosophically in order to discover something about us—the people who participate in a cultural activity and who use cultural objects.

We will discuss each of these aspects in turn as they emerge in *Pilgrimages*. Our goal will be to reveal the embryo of Watsuji's later philosophy of the social that can be found in the text. The three aspects of culture identified above demonstrate that Watsuji already had a concept of human existence as social existence, which he would later describe as "betweenness" (*aidagara*) to indicate that we exist between the individual and the group.

Pilgrimages demonstrates that Japanese culture is something constructed and that relationships are important for this process of construction, in particular the imagined relationship between the past and present and the concrete interactions between the interpreter and the objects and the interpreter and those around him. Indeed, the very form of the book, which is written as a travel journal and privileges the author's impressions, feelings, and reflections, indicates that Watsuji is constructing the history of Japanese Buddhist art and its significance. In the journal, he records his interactions with his friends and family and with the people he meets during his pilgrimage to Nara. He also describes what he imagines the artists and artisans were like who created and imported cultural objects and artistic and architectural styles to Japan hundreds of years ago. It is impossible to know for certain how the medieval Japanese interpreted the Buddhist art that Watsuji encounters during his trip; it is likewise impossible to be certain about how they used the temples and buildings that remain from the period. But this does not stop Watsuji in *Pilgrimages* from imagining how the people of a thousand years ago lived, felt, and thought. He thus constructs culture, rather than simply identifying it as if it were an object of scientific study.

Watsuji characterizes Japanese culture as eclectic and dynamic: Buddhist art and architecture in Japan are largely the result of the importation and modification of artistic styles from East Asia, styles that had themselves developed in Europe and Central and South Asia before landing on Japan's shores. Indeed, Watsuji mentions at various points in *Pilgrimages* the superiority of immigrant artists over native Japanese ones. The fluidity of Japanese culture that Watsuji acknowledges in this early work is also present in his later works, although it tends to be ignored. A study of *Pilgrimages* will help the student of Watsuji to identify both similar notions of cultural fluidity and eclecticism in subsequent works while also allowing her to identify the rigidity and chauvinism that later emerges to undermine Watsuji's early views.

Watsuji's study of Buddhist art and architecture hints at its philosophical significance, which he will develop in his later work by explicitly adding a theoretical dimension to his study of culture and identifying the structures of human existence that make our experience of culture possible. In the philosophy of his middle and later period, Watsuji introduced the technical term *aidagara* (間柄)[2] to identify this structure (McCarthy 2010, 28). *Aidagara* is a basic mode of human existence that indicates that humans always exist in a web of relationships. Betweenness is not our capacity to relate to others or a faculty for doing so since this would presuppose the existence of an individual who possesses this capacity or faculty; rather, betweenness is the fundamental form of human existence of which both being an individual and being part of a group are manifestations. In his later thought, Watsuji describes the structures of our experience (namely space and time) that make this betweenness possible, and he explains how our experience of ourselves as individuals is derived from existence as betweenness (Watsuji 1996, 68–74).

Although in *Pilgrimages* Watsuji does not provide a philosophical analysis of the culture he describes, here and there in the text one can glimpse his philosophy of culture: cultural objects (paintings, statues, buildings) and our experiences of them express Japanese ways of feeling and thinking about things—they are basic stances that the Japanese take toward reality. For example, through the study of cultural objects and spaces, we discover how Japanese people relate to nature and to other people because they are expressed in their preferences for particular forms of artistic expression. In the next chapter, we will look at what culture as a stance of this kind tells us about basic aspects of human existence.

We turn now to showing how these three features of culture—the fact that it is constructed and contingent, that it is eclectic and dynamic, and that it can be studied philosophically to learn something fundamental about human existence—are implicit in Watsuji's description of his trip through the ancient temples in Nara. At the end of the chapter, we will see how *Pilgrimages* uses a phenomenological method that focuses on the interpreter's experience of culture, which in turn justifies Watsuji's emerging idea that culture is a manifestation of the way that we relate to our environment and to others from which he later derives the fundamental temporal and spatial structures of human existence as betweenness.

However, before examining these aspects of *Pilgrimages*, a bit of background about the text will be helpful.

BACKGROUND: *PILGRIMAGES TO THE ANCIENT TEMPLES IN NARA*—PUBLICATION, THEMES, AND STRUCTURE

Watsuji Tetsurō's *Climate and Culture* (*Fūdo: ningengakuteki kōsatsu*, 風土―人間学的考察, Watsuji 1961; *WTZ* 8) is his best-known book outside of Japan. This is no doubt because a partial English translation was published in 1961 as part of the UNESCO World Culture Series, and so the text was available long before many of Watsuji's other works that did not appear in English until the 1990s and the early part of this century. However, in Japan, *Pilgrimages* is at least as well-known if not more so than *Climate and Culture*. The book consists of an account of his visit to various old temples in and around Nara, the ancient capital of Japan from 710 to 794 CE. It was first published serially beginning in August 1918 and then as a complete book in 1919. The text takes the form of a self-conscious travel diary—I say "self-conscious" because it does not consist of extracts of Watsuji's actual diaries. Rather, as he writes in the introduction to the text, it is a "record of his impressions" (*inshōki*, 印象記; *Pilgrimages* 5) made during a trip with a few friends to Nara in May 1918. Nara Hiroshi sees similarities between *Pilgrimages* and Goethe's *Italian Journey* (Nara 2012, xx–xxii).[3] The comparison conveys what the reader can expect from the form of the book, including the spiritual transformation that Watsuji undergoes during the pilgrimage. However, in terms of style, Watsuji's work lacks the poignancy of Goethe's. Perhaps a more accurate way of characterizing it would be as Watsuji himself does—it is a contribution to research on Japanese culture with the secondary purpose of acquainting non-Japanese with it.[4]

Societies undergoing modernization (in the sense of Europanization or Americanization) are often particularly interested in culture, not necessarily to answer the more general question "What is culture?" but rather to ask "What is *my* culture?" and "How is *my* culture different from that of others?" Modernization often requires people to abandon old ways of doing things to which they have become attached, and this is accompanied by a sense of loss which new ways of thinking, dressing, eating, working, and living cannot replace.[5] Watsuji Tetsurō likely wrote *Pilgrimages* while involved in this kind of reflection. Influenced by Japanese modernists such as the author Natsume Sōseki (夏目漱石, 1867–1916),[6] he sought to identify and uncover the meaning of Japanese culture at a time when this culture was undergoing rapid change.

I believe that it makes sense to read *Pilgrimages* as an account of the *experience* of culture rather than as simply an objective account of a *concept* of culture because of how Watsuji describes the work in his preface to the new edition, published in 1946. There, he writes that "the account of my first impressions was organically connected to the rest of the book, making it difficult to make patchwork repairs."[7] It is clear from this comment that the text was not conceived as a scholarly work on Japanese Buddhist art history approached from the detached perspective of a scholar; rather, the articulation of Japanese culture was intimately linked to Watsuji's description of what he was experiencing while visiting the temples of Nara. This intimate connection between Watsuji's academic reflections and his account of the emotions he felt while visiting the temples made later modification of the text by the mature philosopher difficult. In this regard, the text has links to *Climate and Culture*, which shares with *Pilgrimages* the fact that its observations about the relationship between climate and culture are embedded in a personal account, in the case of *Climate and Culture*, of his experience of the boat trip from Japan to Europe.

THE THREE FACETS OF CULTURE AS CONSTRUCT

In the following subsections, I examine how Watsuji conceives of culture as something constructed—something created by the interpreter in interaction with the past and with people and objects in the present. Doing so will involve examination of a few passages from *Pilgrimages* that sustain this view. As I mentioned at the beginning of this chapter, although *Pilgrimages* contains no philosophical analysis, we can still extract from it some of Watsuji's embryonic views about culture and the nature of social existence and the spatial and temporal structures that he will later identify as fundamental to it.

Watsuji's view that culture is constructed is evident from the form of the text, which contains the following:

1.) Descriptions of Watsuji's interactions with other—culture is something that is experienced and interpreted together with others;
2.) Descriptions of the personal feelings that are evoked in Watsuji by visiting the sites of Nara—part of the meaning of cultural artifacts and practices is the emotions that they evoke;
3.) Watsuji's imagination of the past (intertemporal interaction) as a means of describing present Japanese culture—we should not adopt a scientific

or anthropological approach to culture; imagination can play a role in creating cultural meaning.

By studying each of the forms that the text takes, we will gain a first glimpse of the idea of culture that is implicit in *Pilgrimages*. At the end of this chapter, we will then reflect on how this idea of culture presages future developments in Watsuji's theory of culture and the emergence of a social philosophy in his later works.

Watsuji's Interactions with People: The Role of Relatives, Friends, and Others Encountered during the Trip to Nara

In Watsuji's later philosophy, a basic feature of human existence is that it is a constant movement between two poles: the individual and the group. He calls this movement "betweenness" (*aidagara*). While this term is not used in *Pilgrimages*, the text demonstrates that Watsuji already held this view at this early stage in his career. One piece of evidence for this is that Watsuji's recounting of his trip to visit the temples of Nara involves many descriptions of interactions with others: his relatives, friends, acquaintances, and staff at the various temples who provide access to the art he and his party views. These interactions are not just incidental; they play an important part in his experience of the art: some of the interactions arouse thoughts and feelings that color his experience of it, while others point to the generalizability of the experience Watsuji identifies. The experience of Japanese culture that Watsuji describes in *Pilgrimages* is thus both an individual activity—something that Watsuji reflects on and records in his book—and a group activity—something that is done together with others.

Interactions with Others in the Construction of Culture: Watsuji's Visit to His Parents' Home—Watsuji's State of Mind on Setting Out on His Trip to Nara

Culture is determined by the relationship in which we stand to others. At the beginning of *Pilgrimages*, Watsuji describes his emotional state before setting out on his trip by recounting an interaction with his father at his family homestead. Watsuji's pilgrimage, and so the whole of his experience of Buddhist art and architecture, is colored by his rejection of the links to his family and his spiritual transformation during the trip. Before setting off for Nara, Watsuji is beset by feelings of guilt and oppressed by familial and social obligation; during the trip, he gradually develops a feeling of transcendent equanimity and an ability to accept his present circumstances rather than striving to fulfill the ideals that family and society have imposed on him.

The send-off for the trip is set at the house of Watsuji's parents. Anticipating that the pilgrimage will transform him, he feels wistful (*aishū no kokoro*, 哀愁のこころ) (Watsuji 2012, 10) for the family relationships he is about to leave behind, a feeling that contrasts with the liberation he feels at the end of the book upon seeing the dilapidated state of Hōrinji Temple (法輪寺) set against the transcendent natural and pastoral beauty of the surrounding landscape and the piercing eyes of the Buddha rupa enshrined at the temple (Watsuji 2012, 185). Watsuji's wistfulness is triggered by a conversation with his father, whose worldview is Confucian:

> Last night my father asked me, "What you're doing now—how much does it contribute to rescuing the decadent spirit?" . . . I could not help but lower my head in shame at the thought that prompted my father to ask me this question. My father is a man with a very strong passion for staying on the path. Not even for a moment has he forgotten the maxim that "medicine is an art of benevolent compassion," and in order to pursue that he has forsaken his own interest or pleasure and never looked back.[8] (Watsuji 2012, 10)

The description of his father's outlook on life as a medical doctor and the shame that his father's unwavering adherence to it prompts in Watsuji evoke the relationship between father and son, one of the Five Confucian Ethical Relationships that serve as models for a virtuous life.[9] While at home, Watsuji felt keenly his father's reproach for wasting his time touring Buddhist temples; but by the end of his journey, his spiritual awakening allows him to recognize the vanity of rigidly pursuing social and family ideals. Here is his description of his feelings upon seeing the Hōrinji Temple:

> After we finished with Chūgūji, we then walked to nearby Hōrinji. The pastoral beauty of a quiet farming village, the pond with brasenias flowering, the gently rolling hills in the distance—all was just perfect. The ancient tower of Hōrinji and the image of the Buddha with large eyes were also exquisitely pleasurable to see. I also enjoyed looking at the time-worn temple complex of Hōrinji itself, dilapidated and crumbling in places. I noticed that the bell tower had been appropriated to store a pile of rice straw bales. I also noticed that in the shade of a tree behind the main hall of worship, they'd put out a weaving machine on a straw mat.[10] (Watsuji 2012, 185)

His description of the dilapidated temple represents the pointlessness of ideals—they belong to the fruitless strivings of those who live in the world of samsara. In contrast, Watsuji's exultation in the beautiful natural surroundings and in seeing the Buddha's eyes demonstrates that he has realized the benefit of abandoning Confucian virtue: a glimpse of transcendence seems to justify Watsuji in setting out on a journey that his father initially criticized as frivolous.[11]

This episode taken from the beginning of *Pilgrimages* illustrates that culture for Watsuji is something constructed: the meaning that Watsuji ascribes to the Buddhist art and architecture that he encounters in Nara is informed by his mixed feelings as he leaves behind the Confucian orthodoxy of his parents and sets out on a path of spiritual transformation. The book contains many more stories about his interactions with his friends, and the academic analysis of history and artistic style that Watsuji formulates is often embedded in an account of some of these interactions such as his debate with his friend Z about dating the eleven-headed statue of the Bodhisattva Kannon (Sk. Avalokiteshvara) at Hokkeji Temple (法華寺), and his description of the exchange of letters with Kinoshita Mokutarō (木下杢太郎)[12] about the Shō Kannon (聖観音) in the Tōindō Hall (東院堂) of Yakushiji (薬師寺). These discussions are not dry and academic but heated and full of excitement[13] (Watsuji 2012, 79–84). In his description of them, Watsuji point out the emotional context in which culture is both experienced and interpreted: the experience of viewing the statue of the Eleven-Headed Kannon provokes an emotional response that Watsuji feels compelled to share and discuss with others.

The interactions Watsuji describes illustrate his philosophical view that culture discloses something important about the nature of human experience. The turmoil of Watsuji's family life, described as he sets out on his journey, is replaced in the end by a transcendent equanimity. His experience of Japanese culture and his interpretation of it for others occur against a backdrop of emotion evoked by human social interaction. One can see in the features of *Pilgrimages* a demonstration of the importance of human interaction and the emotions it gives rise to both for characterizing features of Japanese culture and for inciting the unique experiences that constitute it.

Interactions with the Past in Creating Japanese Culture

For Watsuji, culture has both a spatial and a temporal dimension. One aspect of the temporal dimension of culture is that it is *intertemporal*, that is, it involves people today "interacting" with those in the past. For instance, contemporary culture is influenced and sometimes even defined by how we think about the past and what we believe past cultural practices to be. We constantly engage in "remembering" or imagining the past, be it through historical fiction or television shows and films, period recreations of historical battles, or modern fictional universes modeled on images from the past.

Today's culture is defined through interaction with past culture both in fact and fiction.

Because time travel is impossible, we must resort to imagining the intertemporal space in which culture is created: *Pilgrimages* demonstrates how important imagination is for engaging with history. It also demonstrates that this imaginative engagement is intersubjective—it is created in the present through interactions with Watsuji's contemporaries, and it involves interaction with the past as these contemporaries imagine the life and reactions of historical figures. We have already mentioned one example of this which arose in the context of Watsuji's debate with his friend Z about the date of the Eleven-Headed Kannon at Hokkeji. This debate is followed by Watsuji imagining how the legends surrounding the creation of the statute came about. Let us look into this intertemporal reverie in more detail.

Apparently, there is a legend that an Indian sculptor was sent to Japan to carve the Eleven-Headed Kannon as a likeness of the Japanese empress Kōmyō (光明皇后, 701–760 CE; Watsuji 2012, 80–84). The sculptor is said to have been sent by King Kensei,[14] an Indian ruler, who had a vision of the empress in a dream. While Watsuji explains that "there is little doubt that this story does not tell the truth," he nonetheless engages in a fantasy to explain why this legend may have come about (Watsuji 2012, 81). He writes,

> Empress Kōmyō must have given passionate attention to the building of the West Golden Hall [of Kōfukuji temple (興福寺)] because of her devotion to her mother Tachibana no Michiyo [in commemoration of whom it was being built]. Hence, as the legend has it, it is not impossible to imagine that Empress Kōmyō stepped into the workshop of the sculptors. And it is equally possible to entertain a hypothesis that the sculptor received creative inspiration from her majesty's personal appearance. Empress Kōmyō, who was then about thirty-two or -three years of age, could have been perfect for a model of the *kannon* statue. If we were to think in this way, then the Kōfukuji legend would seem to be rewarded with a breath of life, though tenuously. At least it was possible.[15]
> (Watsuji 2012, 82)

Watsuji carries on his reverie, providing explanations of how the Eleven-Headed Kannon, which he dates to the Jōgan period (859–876 CE) slightly over 100 years after the Tenpyō period (729–749 CE) when Empress Kōmyō reigned (*b.* 701–*d.* 760 CE; Watsuji 2012, 80), could nonetheless have been influenced by a much earlier statue carved in her likeness (ibid., 83–84). It is interesting to see how the history of this Kannon statue, one of the national treasurers of Japan and an important part of its cultural history, is constructed by Watsuji as he interacts with his contemporaries and imagines the past when it was created. Again, this illustrates that culture is not something objective: its meaning is constructed by cultural interpreters interacting with each other and also standing before the cultural objects they interpret.

We get a sense in these and other passages that Watsuji is consciously making a theoretical point about the role of imagination and bodily experience in experiencing and constructing culture: both space (bodily experience) and time (imagination of the past) are essential to constructing culture because they are basic structures of human existence. An example of this is in the juxtaposition of past and present in Watsuji's discussion of the vapor bath in the Hokkeji compound. Watsuji imagines the situation described in the legend that Empress Kōmyō, a "representative of the aesthetic sense of the Tenpyō period," sucked the puss out of the blisters of a leper and was rewarded by a vision of an asura (a divine being in Buddhist mythology) that praised her for her mercy and virtue (Watsuji 2012, 74). The concrete image of the empress sucking out the puss from a wound brings the image of the empress, distant from us in time, closer to us as we imagine the bodily sensations involved in doing this.

In discussing the baths, Watsuji does not just recount the legend but also uses the experiences of contemporary Japanese who enjoy steam baths to explain how the old baths of Hokkeji could inspire ethical values. He writes,

> I hear people say that the steam bath in Osaka today can give sensual pleasure, not unlike smoking opium, and if one frequents steam baths, one would not be able to go without it for any length of time. So, if a steam bath is capable of creating a physiological sensation of this sort, we must assume that the bather after emerging from the bath would be in a special state of mind. At this point, if Empress Kōmyō, intent on performing a penance of mercy, were to make a visit to the bathhouse with her ladies-in-waiting at a time like this and treated the sick as prescribed, it would not be unthinkable at all that a type of intoxication inherent in steam bathing and the joy of arising from performing a merciful act would combine, resulting in a fusion of religious ecstasy and sensual intoxication. The Tenpyō period was a time when people felt an affinity for this sort of phenomena, so my conjecture is not entirely absurd. If we were to allow ourselves this sort of fantasy, this legend of "administering bathing" could have arisen from the people themselves.[16] (Watsuji 2012, 75)

The legend of the virtuous Empress Kōmyō is made vivid and plausible by pointing to the fact that both present and past bathers could be prone to mystical experiences as a result of bathing. This example illustrates how culture is constructed across time (intertemporally), but it also emphasizes that this is possible because experience is also spatial—we can imagine the past because our bodily experiences today (that of the bathers in modern Osaka) are shared by those who lived during the Nara period. Indeed, Watsuji affirms that bodily experience creates a link between present and past and facilitates the interpretation (or construction) of the culture of the bath. He writes,

> The still existing steam bath, though minor in importance, is nonetheless fascinating to me, perhaps because bathing is much closer to the flesh or perhaps because the flesh is far more effective in making immediate ties between the present and the past. I would get a more concrete sense of steam bathing if I were to experience a steam bath firsthand and judge for myself how it would warm my body, how the skin would feel, how languid I would feel afterward, and what the pleasant sensation would be after sweating out every drop of moisture. It may not be tactful or even wise to imagine the past from these very physical sensations; however, it is the easiest way.[17] (Watsuji 2012, 76)

To understand what steam bathing is, one must experience it bodily. To understand the culture of the steam bath that has existed since the Nara period, one combines this bodily experience with imagination of how the baths were enjoyed in the past. We find here Watsuji's reflection on the role of body, experience, space, and time in the creation of an image of the past that is essential to the definition of Japanese culture.

Throughout *Pilgrimages*, Watsuji is constantly seeking ways to relate his portrayals of Japanese culture during the Nara period to the present. He uses three techniques to achieve this. The first is by referring to bodily experience, which is shared between past and present because we, like our ancestors, share the same body. This technique is used in the description of the steam baths at Hokkeji. Watsuji seeks to anchor intertemporal imagination in a plausible account of bodily feelings because he presumes that such feelings are shared between present and past human beings. The second technique, used in the case of Watsuji's discussion of the women of the Tempyō period (Chapter 13 of *Pilgrimages*), is to emphasize the unity of the spiritual and the bodily, the sacred and the secular. Finally, Watsuji builds a link between past and present by showing how Japanese culture then as now is syncretic and open to foreign influence, a theme to which we turn in the next section.

Constructing Japanese Culture—Culture as the Emotional Response to the Environment

A final example of Watsuji's use of his imaginative powers as he constructs Japanese culture does not involve Buddhist art but rather an experience more familiar to modern Japanese people: the experience of nature. His description of the countryside around Nara foreshadows the views that he develops in *Climate and Culture* in which he interprets culture as emerging from the interaction between people and the landscape—it is the subjective response of human beings to their location in a social and natural environment (Watsuji 1961, v; *WTZ* 8:1).

At one point in *Pilgrimages*, Watsuji describes a landscape he sees during a train trip. The rolling hills inspire Watsuji to reflect on the ties between natural landscape and the Yamato people—the ethnic group that has taken on mythic importance in Japanese cultural self-understanding. Traveling through the Taima hills to the Taimadera Temple (當麻寺), Watsuji writes of the connection between nature and the Yamato people thus:

> The scenery around here was quite different from that of [the city of] Nara in that it was much more tranquil, and I thought I could sense the feeling of our ancestors who loved this area. Once upon a time, many temples and pagodas towered high between those hills beyond Kaguyama, where the new cultures of the Suiko and Hakuhō periods (ca. 600-700 CE) spawned. If we go back even further in history, we can say that the human emotions of our ancestors during the times of legends, be it love or hate, is etched deeply into these mountains and rivers. The fact that this was the original place for the *Yamato people* is apparently closely connected to the peculiar characteristics of the Yamato clan. We could see the gloomy-looking Tō no Mine Mountains on the right, then the train changed direction toward the foothills of Miwayama Mountain [三輪山]. This mountain plays an important role in ancient legends, and it is very fitting for the land of Yamato—it is gently sloping with long foothills and shows off superbly its soft roundness that is not unlike *kofun*, ancient burial mounds. The worshipping of mountains, because deities were thought to reside there, was common throughout ancient Japan, but it occurred to me that it was not perhaps rare for a people to admire a mountain like this with its gentle round curves. I have a hard time imagining how people in those days could feel any *supernatural power* from a mountain in this shape. Instead, doesn't this reflect people's vague admiration for a perfect object or an object in flawless harmony? If I am right, this mount too is not unlike a book in ancient legends.[18] (Watsuji 2012, 154) [emphasis in original]

The interdependence of humans and the natural environment was an important part of the ancient culture of Japan that Watsuji depicts; but Watsuji's example illustrates that it is also important to modern Japanese. For while art ages the moment it is made, landscapes remain largely unchanged in a thousand years. And so when contemporary Japanese behold the rolling hills of Tō no Mine, a link is built across time to the feelings of their ancestors from the Nara period. Yamato culture, Watsuji seems to be saying, is built through such intertemporal links made concrete by the experience of the landscape today.

In this section, we have demonstrated that *Pilgrimages* discloses a theory of culture as something constructed. Watsuji's relationships with his friends and family are the context in which he interprets the cultural meaning of Buddhist art and architecture. He uses his imagination freely to construct the modern image of Japanese culture. Culture has a history, but we do not have to approach this history in a purely academic way; our imagination of the past can also play an important role. This is most effective when the imagination invokes bodily sensations shared across time: the baths, the lives of women past and present, the inspiration of artists, modern and ancient syncretism, and the feeling evoked by a landscape. The spatial and temporal elements that Watsuji later uses to characterize the protean dialectical movement of human existence (*ningen sonzai*, 人間存在) as betweenness (*aidagara*, 間柄) take embryonic form in *Pilgrimages*, and they will be developed further in his later works.

Culture Is Eclectic and Dynamic: The Role of Cross-Cultural Exchange in Watsuji's Conception of Japanese Culture

As we have seen, what constitutes Japanese culture is not determined objectively by reference to specific criteria; it is about a specific experience when confronted with Buddhist art and architecture. Indeed, the emotions Watsuji experiences both while together with others and alone during his pilgrimage are essential elements of Japanese culture: culture evokes feelings and emotions. We have also seen that the meaning of culture is constructed intertemporally: understanding what makes art and architecture great involves imagining the lives of people during the Nara period and the emotions that they attempted to express in their creations and relating them to the feelings and experiences of Watsuji's contemporaries.

Another important aspect of Japanese culture according to Watsuji is that it is eclectic and dynamic: it is influenced by the culture of other places, and it changes over time as these influences are felt. Watsuji highlights this dynamism in part because it is an important feature of how modern Japanese understand their society, culture, and politics. For instance, one of the principle story lines that modern Japanese use to explain their history during the Tokugawa period (1603–1867) is the tug of war between the policies of openness (*kaikoku*, 開国) and closure (*sakoku*, 鎖国) to foreign influence.[19] Receptivity to and resistance against foreign influence are an essential part of Japanese cultural self-understanding.

The importance of foreign influence on Japanese Buddhist art during the Nara period is obvious from the very beginning of *Pilgrimages*, which begins not with a discussion of Japanese art but of Indian art—the Ajanta wall paintings, photos of which Watsuji examined before leaving on his trip to Nara. The viewing of the photos sets the exploration of Japanese culture that is to follow in the context of the history of the Buddhism as it radiates from its Indian origins. In Watsuji's opinion, the colors and forms used in the paintings demonstrate the influence of the climate of South Asia on Indian culture. He describes the palette used in them as "a reflection of the land and people of a tropical region" (Watsuji 2012, 3), and he explains that the faces of those depicted are moody because "the Indians then were not as cheerful as the Greeks at that time" (Watsuji 2012, 4). Here, we see a foreshadowing of Watsuji's view, expressed most clearly in *Climate and Culture*, that culture is really a mood or emotional attitude that influences our experience of the natural and social world and is expressed through cultural practices.

The reader might wonder why Watsuji begins the book with a description of Indian rather than Japanese art. In addition to setting the scene for his identification of the syncretism in Japanese Buddhist art, Watsuji's imagination of the Buddhist monks who created the paintings foreshadows the spiritual transformation that he will undergo during his pilgrimage. As we have already seen, Watsuji sets out on his journey in a wistful state of mind brought about by the guilt caused by his father's implicit criticism of his upcoming trip. Watsuji's description of the monks who painted the Ajanta wall paintings is free of such guilt. He speculates that the sensual images of the wall paintings could only have been created by monks who did not feel overly restricted by the monastic precepts. Free from moral restriction, the monks must have "believed in . . . a tolerant Buddha, who forgave everything and lead [*sic*] everyone to Buddhahood; he wasn't a strict leader who commanded believers to follow precepts and devote themselves diligently to religious practice" (Watsuji 2012, 7). The sunny culture of India that emerges through the paintings expresses "ultimate religious joy" (Watsuji 2012, 7), a joy whose muted tones Watsuji will have absorbed by the end of his journey (Watsuji 2012, 185).

In addition to Indian influences, Watsuji also identifies Greek elements in the Buddhist art he surveys. Though we typically associate classical Greek art with the pinnacle of aesthetic beauty, Watsuji does not always hold up Greek art as the ideal. For instance, in Chapter 2 of *Pilgrimages*, Watsuji compares a statue of Buddha from Gandhara[20] that was heavily influenced by Greek art with a stucco head of Maitreya from Central Asia. The former, he notes, portrays the Buddha as an idealized human, while the latter depicts the Buddha Maitreya as a supernatural being in human form (Watsuji 2012, 15). Watsuji concludes the paragraph comparing the two by claiming that both Greek and Buddhist art were only "truly perfected" in China (Watsuji 2012, 15). The subsequent inflow of Buddhist art into Japan is thus explained by the superiority of Chinese, not Greek, art. For while the stucco head of Maitreya in the Suiko Tenpyō Room of the Nara National Museum "comes closest to sculpture of the West," the statue "achieved that which Gandhara art attempted but could not achieve" (Watsuji 2012, 15). Chinese Buddhist art captures the otherworldly in a way that eludes the naturalism of the Greeks.

Throughout *Pilgrimages*, Watsuji acknowledges the dependence of Japanese culture on its openness to outside influence and the importance of cultural blending to its creation.[21] For instance, he discusses the likelihood of Chinese influence on the statues of the Four Guardian Kings (四天王, *shitennō*) that used to stand in the Kaidanin temple (戒壇院) (Watsuji 2012, 29), on the Kudara Kannon[22] at Hōryūji Temple (法隆寺) (Watsuji 2012, 41–43), and on the works at Tōshōdaiji (唐招提寺), created by Chinese artists who accompanied the Chinese monk Ganjin[23] from China. He is impressed by the work of foreign artists from Gandhara located in Kōfukuji temple (興福寺) (Watsuji 2012, 45),[24] and he discusses at length the possible influences on Japanese masked dance (called *gigaku*) from Western China, India, and even Greece (Watsuji 2012, 50–68).[25]

Traces of the Greek approach to life resonate with aspects of Japanese culture. For instance, in his description of the wall paintings of the Golden Hall of Hōryūji, which may have been painted by either Japanese or Chinese artists (Watsuji 2012, 171), he notes the Greek tendency, shared by the Japanese, to express the beauty of life in a cheerful and pure way without descending into the "abnormal interest in the breasts and bellies" found in the Ajanta wall paintings from India (Watsuji 2012, 171). In concluding Chapter 23, Watsuji emphasizes the commonalities between Greece and Japan:

> The fact that the mood of an Indian wall paintings [*sic*] changed like this in Japan is related to the idea that, although Japan is far to the east of Greece, Japan is more similar to Greece, far more so than Greece is to Persia, India, China's west, or China proper. The vast continent is so different from the Mediterranean peninsula in terms of climate, land, people, and so on, but Japan and Greece are considerably similar. It is not entirely impossible that a person, whose sentiment was never understood by anyone while migrating through the continent, could come to Japan and find life truly agreeable for the first time. In comparison to the creativity in China and India, Japan's creativity was quite meager. But even while the Japanese effaced themselves and strove to copy masterworks of art, their own particular ethnic personality could not be suppressed. If, for the moment, we assume that the land of Japan is characterized as possessing a sweet, luscious, and lyrical mood filled with a sad melancholy, these things can also be thought of as an innate disposition of the Japanese people. The gentleness of the country's legends as recorded in the *Kojiki* and the mercy and the grief expressed in the *kannon* at Chūgūji are probably manifestations of this national character. There, one always finds quietness and tears. So those tears cast a shadow onto the soul to all sorts of earthly pleasures. Therefore, when sensual paintings from India are filtered through these tears, they change into works with transparent beauty. There we witness the aesthetic consciousness of the Greek, which has finally found its soul brother in the faraway land.[26] (Watsuji 2012, 172)

There is an equivocation in regard to whether the Japanese inherit the Greek sensibility transmitted to them via China, or whether Watsuji is simply indicating that the nature of the Japanese spirit is such that when foreign art comes to Japan, it is refracted through the Japanese spirit, and the Greek influences are what survive the refraction. I think it is probably the latter—Watsuji wants to express that Japanese creativity is independent of foreign creativity, but at the same time, because culture is both temporal and spatial, it is also linked to other times and places.

What is the role of this eclectic dynamism in the construction of Japanese culture? Why is it such an important feature? Two explanations are possible. Nara Hiroshi, the translator of *Pilgrimages* into English, suggests that Watsuji emphasizes the foreign influence on Japanese Buddhist art in order to elevate its status by associating it with the "great" artistic traditions. By identifying Greek influences on Japanese art, Watsuji may have hoped that the iconic status of the Greeks in European art history would rub off on Japan (Nara 2012, xix).

An alternate explanation is that the syncretic, multicultural origin of Japanese art is a manifestation of the intersubjectivity (betweenness, *aidgara*) that Watsuji later articulated as the fundamental aspect of human existence (*ningen sonzai*, 人間存在). On this view, culture emerges from the interactions between people, and so the phenomenon of Japanese Buddhist art can only be truly understood through such interactions, which as a matter of fact included interactions between Japan, China, Korea, India, and Greece.

Many examples support the latter theory over the former. In *Pilgrimages*, Watsuji never places Japanese art alongside Greek at the pinnacle of artistic accomplishment. Rather, where he finds Greek influences in Japanese art, it is only as a trace. For instance, he emphasizes that the influence of the Greeks on Chinese art was at best impressionistic: the Chinese only adopted those influences that were congenial to them. He wrote, "The Chinese absorbed only Grecian grandiosity and sensuous beauty. Then, the Chinese added a typical Han influence to this, that is, a measure of simplification. As a result, a classical art was born, which was fresh, clean, vigorous, and spirited" (Watsuji 2012, 128). Chinese art bears only traces of Greek influence, and it is these traces within a bold and vigorous Chinese style that were transmitted to Japan. Thus elements of Greek design are only found in subtle aspects of Japanese temple architecture such as the use of entasis (a slight convexity to pillars to give them a feeling of strength and perhaps additional height). Watsuji writes,

> Though we cannot say with any degree of certainty that the Chinese could not have invented this slight convex curvature of the pillars, we can say that this feature has not been seen in Han-style architecture. ... If a variety of buildings from the Han dynasty period to the Tang dynasty period remained in China, we would be able to trace unequivocally how art styles of the west of China influenced East Asian architecture due to the transmission of Buddhism. But

the architecture that can provide evidence for this line of thought remains only in Japan.[27] (Watsuji 2012, 163)

The influence of Greek architecture on Japan is limited to the slight bulging of the pillars of Hōryūji Temple, and the Chinese buildings that would allow this slight trace to be followed back to its Greek origin have disappeared.

The Greeks are not always held up as an ideal; Watsuji sometimes criticizes them. For instance, while he acknowledges that Greek art is able to capture "naturalistic and humanistic characteristics" (Watsuji 2012, 66), in other places, he points out the failure of the Greeks to express how transcendence is always situated in immanence. For instance, he finds that they have difficulty depicting "a transcendent being in human form," and he points out that while Greek sculpture may express beauty as "a pinnacle of human desire," Buddhist art "reflects our desire for reaching the 'Other Shore'" (Watsuji 2012, 114, 142).

Watsuji's understanding of the relationship between cultures in the creation of Japanese culture is really one of syncretic blending rather than wholesale adoption. The blending tends to be dependent on preexisting resonances between the cultures, rather than simply on the supplanting of domestic by foreign culture. The interplay of similarity and difference is essential to his account. For instance, Watsuji compares the vision of the Buddhist Pure Land with the Christian vision of Heaven, explaining that while the former may arouse curiosity, Dante or Rossetti's images of Heaven "jolt [us] violently with both sadness and joy" in a way that images of the Pure Land do not (Watsuji 2012, 140). However, despite that difference, both Eastern and Western depictions are able to arouse our imaginations and stimulate us "to love and daydream about the ancient times" (ibid.).

Watsuji's theory of syncretic blending resulting in Japanese eclecticism is demonstrated in his account of the influence of Chinese dress, language, and writing on the Japanese during the Nara and Heian periods (Watsuji 2012, 109–111). The influence, he writes, was not one of "indigenizing" Chinese culture to suit Japanese needs, but rather one of true syncretic creativity. For instance, the development of *kana* (the native Japanese syllabary) from simplified cursive forms of *kanji* (Chinese characters) was not simply "an indigenization of *kanji*." Instead, he argues that the Japanese were inspired by Chinese culture and created something new "*based on the foundation* of foreign culture" (Watsuji 2012, 110) [emphasis in original]. He specifies,

> It is not that a culture specific to Japan embraced foreign culture, but that peculiarities of the Japanese people developed in this particular way in a society where the air was thick with foreign culture. This point of view is different from the one that contends that foreign culture was simply inserted into existing

Japanese culture in that, I argue, that foreign culture provided the soil for the development of native Japanese culture. If one takes this point of view, we may say that Japanese creativity is not something that stands as the opposite of foreign culture but that it was actually born out of foreign culture.[28] (Watsuji 2012, 110)

This is a view of culture that I think would appeal to postmodernits because it both recognizes the independence of cultural traditions and accepts syncretic influence. The model is somewhat similar to Hans-Georg Gadamer's "fusion of horizons," whereby each individual has a horizon that influences his interpretation of the world around him, which is broadened and modified through interactions with others who have different horizons.[29] While the idea of "fusion" may seem to favor sameness (the creation of a single "fused" horizon) and the eradication of difference, Gadamer emphasized that complete fusion is impossible. As Dermot Moran explains, "The attempt to understand the other must begin with the recognition that we are separated by different horizons of understanding, and that mutual understanding comes through overlapping consensus, merging of horizons, rather than through the abandonment by one of the interlocutors of his or her initial horizon" (Moran 2000, 252). When Watsuji writes that foreign culture cannot be simply "imported" or "indigenized," he is articulating a similar idea: there may be creative resonances, perhaps even a consensus, but not the absorption of one culture into another.

Japanese culture is constructed syncretically through the interaction between Japan, China, India, and Greece. It has transformed through time thanks to the constant influx of foreign artists, scholars, religion, and art. And yet Japanese culture is not simply a jumble as a result: where homologies are found, especially at an experiential, attitudinal, or emotional level, blending and transformation can occur.

TOWARD A PHILOSOPHICAL ANALYSIS OF CULTURE: *PILGRIMAGES* AS A PRELUDE TO WATSUJI'S LATER WORKS

Watsuji's study of Japanese Buddhist art is not meant to be an explicitly philosophical study; but it foreshadows in many ways the philosophical analysis that he would develop later in his career. For instance, in *Pilgrimages*, Watsuji explicitly links culture to climate as he would do in *Climate and Culture* (*Fūdo*), published in 1935 and based on his impressions during a boat trip from Japan to Europe in 1926, where Watsuji engaged in a period of foreign study. The book has become well-known because of its phenomenological analysis of both climate and culture and the link that Watsuji makes between the two. While culture has always been understood as a temporal phenomenon since it evolves through time, in *Climate and Culture*, Watsuji emphasized its spatial dimension, which he characterized as "climatic." Culture plays a big role in the book because cultural practices are evidence of how we experience climate. As with his examination of climate, Watsuji's phenomenological study of Buddhist art in *Pilgrimages* reveals the same fundamental structures of human existence, namely, time and space. A beautiful example is to be found in *Pilgrimages* when Watsuji describes his reaction to the many-armed Senju Kannon statue in Toshodaiji temple. On one occasion, its seemingly innumerable arms are so attractive that they evoke a symphony of sound (Watsuji 2012, 100). Yet on another occasion when Watsuji observed the statue being repaired, its arms detached and lying on the floor, he came away with an eerie, "otherworldly, grisly feeling" (ibid., 101). Here, we see how our experience of art is created by the interaction of the viewer with the spatial context in which we view it and how both the context and our experience of art change over time. *Pilgrimages* provides excellent examples of how culture is both a way of experiencing one's physical surroundings and evidence of the temporal and spatial nature of human existence.

In *Pilgrimages*, Watsuji does not articulate the dialectical nature of space and time that he will emphasize later; but there are many places in the work where one can see that Watsuji is aware of the relationship between climate and culture. Indeed, *Pilgrimages* begins with just such an episode: the examination of the Ajanta wall paintings which we have already studied. In examining the images, Watsuji notes the influence of the climate in which their creators lived, for instance, in the interplay of light and dark, which he notes is very different from what one sees in Japanese art and reflects "the land and people of a tropical region." He is initially surprised by the strange feeling of coolness in certain figures and plants; but then he realizes that this is only natural for artists living in a hot country, for whom "snow-capped mountains [are] the ideal earthly paradise" (Watsuji 2012, 3). He contrasts the "healthy, fleshy Greek women" that reflect the cheerfulness of Greek culture with the "melancholic faces" of the characters in the Indian paintings, attributing this to the Indian preference for shadow to light, which reflects "a tendency to find more pleasure in the dark of the night and to fear broad daylight" (Watsuji 2012, 4)

Of course, as spatial and temporal beings, humans change when they move to a new climatic environment. For instance, Watsuji muses about how traveling to Japan from China might have transformed the personality of the Chinese artists of the Tang dynasty and affected their artistic sensibilities. In his view, the works of art that they created in Japan provide evidence of the change in landscape. He writes,

> I wonder if the people born during the Tang dynasty's melting pot culture or those who were nurtured by it did not feel a change in their emotional constitution when they traveled across the Yellow Sea and reached the Inland Sea of

our beautiful country. Would the difference between the dusty parched brown continent and Japan's green and luscious landscape not unlike the features of a sixteen-year-old maiden, be not enough to cause a change in one's emotional perspective? If we were to assume a change occurred, the image that the inner eye of the artist saw must also have changed to some degree. For instance, take the facial expression of the [Eleven-headed] *kannon* [of Shōrinji Temple]. It is no longer unfocused or vague, a feature typical of the continent; it is a bit more attentive and sharper. Can I not consider this as evidence of change? When we stand in front of this Eleven-headed Kannon, we obtain a direct, tangible feel that the imagery for it was conceived in this land of Yamato.[30] (Watsuji 2012, 36)

In *Pilgrimages*, Watsuji also makes the kind of links between cultural practices and climate that he would be famous for in *Climate and Culture*. For instance, his discussion of the difference between the Turkish steam bath and the Japanese steam bath at Hokkeji Temple "may have come about from the way steam bathing was utilized in the life of an ethnic group, for example, depending on whether it was continual or with interruptions" (Watsuji 2012, 76).

There are also other links between *Pilgrimages* and Watsuji's later works. For instance, in *Ethics* (*Rinrigaku*), roads play a prominent role since they are means of communication that exemplify for Watsuji the intersubjective and spatial nature of human existence (Watsuji 1996, 159–162). He explains that when roads and other modes of communication are blocked, we become separated from our community, and this can have such a significant effect on us that we can feel the separation as a psychic wound (ibid., 159). In *Pilgrimages*, roads also appear, for instance, in Watsuji's discussion of the road between Nara and the later Northern capitals of Nagaoka (784–794 CE) and Kyōto (from 794 CE). As in *Rinrigaku*, this road is a physical manifestation of both the political and spiritual activity of Japan during this period. He writes,

> There was a big ado about moving the capital, which caused all court nobles to move in droves to the north.[31] Then, in Ōmi, the bronze casting of a large Buddhas [*sic*] began. The old capital of Nara, with its roads covered with tall grass due to a lack of traffic and neglect, became dilapidated and desolate, making one feel the evanescence of the world. It was then that court nobles began to return to Nara. A hubbub soon followed this as people worked to make the mold for the large statue of Buddha [at Tōdaiji Temple]. Thousands of carpenters, metalworkers and laborers began working busily. One would have been able to see workers carrying lumber and hunks of copper to the Narazaka area day after day. The mound of dirt where workers stood was created, and, just beyond it, one would have been able to see ferocious flames for copper founding. This would have continued for several years. Then the day of the

Buddha's consecration ceremony would arrive. The night sky above the woods around Tōdaiji would light up with more than 15,000 lanterns. Several thousand monks' singing and chanting of praises to the Buddha would echo like waves of distant thunder. The east side of town would then become quiet, and then the activity would pick up again because the construction began for temples like Tōshōdaiji, Saidaiji, and Sairyūji on the west side of town. It was said that there were already as many as forty-eight temples by the time the capital moved to Nara and, by the time these temples on the westside of town began to be built, the number had doubled.[32] (Watsuji 2012, 78)

The Buddhist art of Nara was not just the product of sculptors, architects, and builders. Rather, its production was influenced by social and political change and by the movements of artisans and craftspeople, worshippers and townsfolk. Culture is not just composed of cultural objects or cultural practices; it also includes ways of doing things, and it is influenced by the reasons for doing them.[33]

Watsuji muses specifically about the relationship between cultural difference and climatic difference in his discussion of the beauty of Tōshōdaiji, which is located in a grove of pines. He reflects on the architecture of other countries and concludes that only Japanese architecture fits well with pines. He writes,

Strolling in the area in front of the Golden Hall, I passed a short period of blissful time. The tall pines trees that surround this hall caused in me a sense of intimacy that was hard to describe. A pine grove and this building, for some reason, certainly go together perfectly. It is hardly possible to find any work of Western architecture, regardless of what style it is built in, that goes well with pine trees. It is not possible to place the Parthenon in a pine forest. Likewise, no Gothic cathedral would look right surrounded by those gently curing pine boughs. We should associate these buildings only with the cities, open fields, and forests of the countries in which they are found. Therefore, temples and shrines in Japan, too, are endowed with those intrinsic connections with the Japanese climate and customs. If we agree that Gothic buildings have vestiges of northern European forests, can we not also assume that our temples and shrines have the fragrances of pine and Japanese cypress trees? I wonder if the roof of this hall hints at the bowing boughs of pine and cypress trees. Does the hall as a whole not suggest a feeling of vigorous pine trees or even perhaps old, craggy, and gnarled cypress trees? The fact that wooden structures in the East have these roots is enormously interesting to consider when we ponder about how we might reduce cultural differences down to climate differences.[34] (Watsuji 2012, 98–99)

Watsuji then goes on to describe the line of the eaves, which he says "is specific to Eastern architecture." He also notes that the colors of the temple have the dullness and indistinctness that communicate *sabi*, evoking "a sad, quiet sentiment" (Watsuji 2012, 99). The mention of *sabi*, which indicates an emotion that is often associated specifically with Japanese culture, makes it clear that Watsuji considers Japanese culture to be climatic—a response to the spatial dimension of human existence.

While some scholars consider *Climate and Culture* to be an example of geographic determinism, I do not believe that in these passages from *Pilgrimages* Watsuji means that climate is the sole cause of culture. Since his reflections on culture and climate here are situated in a book about Buddhist art, the individual effort of architects and artists must clearly play some role. Thus in *Pilgrimages* it is clearer than in *Climate and Culture* that culture has many causes, individual, social, and environmental.

Moreover, Watsuji makes it clear that he considers culture to be malleable. An example is his documentation of the cultural changes in the Nara period and the beginning of the Heian period that resulted from the influx of Chinese influence, which affected clothing style, architecture, poetry, and religion (Watsuji 2012, 109). Since climate did not change, these cultural changes must have had other causes, both temporal (historical influx of Chinese culture) and spatial (interaction with climate and place).

Within a given climatic zone, Watsuji notes how different spaces precipitate different emotional responses. While the mountains of Yamato (i.e., Nara) "evoke cheerfulness and tenderness," the "rugged mountains [of Taima], deep and dark with trees," create a "dark and dreary feeling," and to him, it was "as if they hid some sort of special life energy and held deep secrets" (Watsuji 2012, 148). Watsuji's observations on the landscape on his way to Taimadera also indicate that the natural environment can invoke different emotions at different times. Thus the ancient Yamato people, who practiced primarily animistic religions, valued the soft hills that evoked ancient burial mounds (Watsuji 2012, 154) while the mountains around Taimadera evoke a different feeling—a welling up of life that inspired its residents to build a Buddhist temple. We thus see that for Watsuji, climate is not monolithic; rather, it captures features of the spatial and temporal aspects of human existence that are inherently open to various responses to the natural environment.

In the construction of Japanese culture in *Pilgrimages*, Watsuji hints at some of the themes he would take up in his later work, including the relationship between climate and culture (or rather, climate *as* culture). As well, we have already pointed out some of the ways in which Japanese art and architecture illustrate the spatial dimensions of human existence that would emerge in Watsuji's phenomenological analysis of human existence in both *Climate and Culture* and his three-volume *Ethics*.

CONCLUSION: TRACES OF WATSUJI'S PHILOSOPHICAL ANALYSIS OF CULTURE

In *Pilgrimages*, Watsuji introduces both his philosophy of culture and a way of studying it: a phenomenological and hermeneutic method that involves first a description of the experience of Watsuji and his friends as they tour the ancient temples of Nara followed by an interpretation of this experience that aims at identifying a basic attitude toward reality. In his later work, Watsuji will add a transcendental element to his method by analyzing what this attitude discloses about the basic structures of human existence. Watsuji's view of culture differs in many respects from that of his European contemporaries that we sketched in Chapter 1. He does not adopt a scientific approach like Comte, nor does he seek to express culture in logical form as a system of values as did the Neo-Kantians. Indeed, the journal form that Watsuji adopts in *Pilgrimages* is emblematic of the distance between his approach to culture and that of his European contemporaries.

At this early stage in his career, what is culture according to Watsuji? In terms of the objects and practices that Watsuji studies, his choices are the most conventional among the three philosophers we will study. While Nishida Kitarō defined culture broadly to include all forms of human activity, including artistic, artisanal, and industrial production,[35] Watsuji limits his discussion primarily to the visual arts, music, language and modes of communication, dress, attitudes, customs and so on; in short, precisely the topics that we conventionally include under the heading "culture."

But while his definition of culture is narrower than that of Nishida, it is far broader than that of Kuki Shūzō, who, as we will see, wrote about a very specific manifestation of culture in the world of the *geisha* during the Kasei era (化政, 1804–1830) at the end of the Tokugawa period (1603–1868). Indeed, Kuki's choice is as unusual as Watsuji's is conventional, since few if any Japanese people prior to Kuki's work would have considered the period to be one worth studying, let alone as the origin of Japanese culture. In contrast, in *Pilgrimages*, Watsuji provides a survey of Buddhist art from an iconic era that spans roughly the Nara period (奈良, 710–794 CE) and a bit beyond into the early Heian (平安, 794–1185 CE) after the Japanese capital shifted from Nara to Kyōto. And while Kuki concentrated narrowly on aesthetics and the literary arts,[36] Watsuji included everyday cultural practices such as bathing, language, the form of writing, and so on.

Apart from cultural objects and practices, what is culture? In *Pilgrimages*, Watsuji's answer is that culture is not just objects but the experience of encountering them and engaging in cultural practices. In other words, culture is the manifestation of spatial and temporal relationships. We discover aspects of our culture by experiencing the spaces created by temples and depicted in paintings, mandalas, and statuary. This experience is not distanced and scientific, but immediate and human: it involves emotional responses and heated exchanges with fellow travelers, friends, and family. Indeed, because for Watsuji space is not just physical but also social, the places that Watsuji visits are also described as social spaces.

Experience is not just spatial but temporal. Thus it is no surprise that *Pilgrimages* features imaginative recreations of the lives, feelings, and attitudes of people in the past who were responsible for sponsoring and creating classical Japanese Buddhist art. Of course, Watsuji could not have naively believed that he was accurately portraying what people long dead thought or felt. Rather, his imagination of the past aims at constructing and articulating present Japanese culture, which naturally incorporates a particular relationship between the present and the past.

Culture thus points to the spatial and temporal dimensions of human existence as *betweenness*. As we have seen, this is disclosed by the social nature of culture, which is manifest in *Pilgrimages* in three ways. First, Watsuji demonstrates that Japanese Buddhist art is the result of ongoing interaction between artists, craftspeople, and artisans and their wealthy patrons: without these social relations, Buddhist art would not have evolved as it did. Second, in *Pilgrimages*, Watsuji demonstrates that culture is something that we experience together with others: cultural experience is social experience, and as a result, cultural experiences reveal something about the nature of human social interaction. Third, *Pilgrimages* illustrates the dialectical nature of human sociality that features prominently in his *Ethics*. In that book, he explains that humans exist in a constant back-and-forth between asserting their individuality, which entails rejection of the group, but then identifying with the group and deemphasizing their individuality. In the journal of Watsuji's visit to the ancient temples contained in *Pilgrimages*, Watsuji illustrates just such a dialectical movement between individuality and the group: through the diary entries, Watsuji documents the social nature of cultural experience—the discussions he has with friends and family about the art and architecture he encounters—and also his personal experience and analysis of it.

As we turn in the next chapter to a study of *Climate and Culture*, it will be helpful to compare the depiction of Japanese culture in that book with the one we have studied in *Pilgrimages*. Such a comparison should help us identify how problematic nationalist ideas found their way into Watsuji's thought (Nara 2012, xvii; LaFleur 1990; Bernier 2006, 91; see generally Heisig and Maraldo 1994). In *Pilgrimages*, Watsuji rejected an essentialist approach to culture, seeking instead to demonstrate the link between Japanese, Korean, Chinese, Indian, and Greek cultures (Nara 2012, xviii). Nevertheless, as we have seen, Watsuji's search for a link between the Japanese and the Greeks can be interpreted as an attempt to rank Japan among the great European cultures in order to rectify the inferior position which he, like many of his contemporaries, felt that Japan occupied at the end of the Meiji period (明治, 1868–1912 CE) and the beginning of Taishō (大正, 1912–1926 CE). On this view, Japanese chauvinism is a response to a Japanese inferiority complex. In studying *Climate and Culture*, we will be alert to subtle changes in Watsuji's analysis especially in so far as these open the door to such chauvinism.

Finally, Watsuji's interest in *Pilgrimages* with the context in which Buddhist art was imported, transformed, and created provides a partial explanation for his affinity with phenomenology, especially Heideggerian existential phenomenology, which he studied during his trip to Europe between 1927 and 1928. Watsuji's descriptions of bathing practices, the atmosphere of the workshops in which the art was created, and the roads and trains along which he and the ancient artists and architects traveled evoke Heidegger's description of the woodworker in his workshop in *Being and Time*. *Pilgrimages* thus provides an excellent preparation for understanding Watsuji's interest in but also critique of Heidegger's early philosophy.

NOTES

1. The exception outside Japan is of course the author of the English translation, Nara Hiroshi (Nara 2012).

2. This is the translation adopted by most translators and scholars of Watsuji who use the English language (see, for example, the use of "betweenness" in Watsuji 1996 and Carter 2013). Augustin Berque, a French philosopher, uses the French term *médiance*, which has the connotation of "mediation" rather than "betweenness."

3. Watsuji's text invites the comparison—he mentions *Italian Journey* in Chapter 6 (*Pilgrimages to the Ancient Temples*, 31). However, it is not clear whether Watsuji alludes to Goethe to create a parallel between his text and Goethe's or whether he alludes to Goethe in order to better evoke the feeling of personal inadequacy and fecklessness that he is describing. Watsuji writes,

> I mentioned to my friend T, when we were talking about something else, what sort of work would be worthy of devoting one's life to it. I became envious of T, who was calm and purposeful and paid attention only to deepening his knowledge of the field of his choice. . . . I felt like rootles water grass and I thought I must recalibrate my path. Think of Goethe, who was extremely endows with talent, I thought to myself. Even he regretted the fact that when he traveled to Italy he felt that he had not spent the necessary time to perfect his craft and that he hadn't taken the time to acquire the necessary skills for it.

4. See the excerpt from Watsuji's letter to his wife from August 1, 1920, excerpted in Nara (2012, xiv).

56   *Chapter 2*

5. For a good example of Watsuji's acceptance of Westernization and nostalgia for Japanese tradition, see his essay, "The Japanese Spirit" (*Nihon seishin*, 『日本精神』), where he writes,

> In Japan, liberation from a feudal legacy appeared at the same time as liberation from Japanese tradition—it appeared, that is, as Westernism. Moreover, Westernization—that is, adoption of the various particular customs of the West—was felt as a transformation into a universal humanity. However, that kind of Westernization itself was a conceptual and not an actual Westernization. The essence of day-to-day Japanese footwear is still the *geta* [wooden clogs]; the essence of foreign clothes worn by Japanese is holiday finery. In such cases the tools of life may take on various new forms, while the ways of existence for which the tools are used remain unchanged. (Dilworth 1998, 247; see also his comments on "layering" in Japanese culture at p. 256) 「... 日本においては、封建的遺風からの脱却は同時に日本的伝統からの脱却、すなわち欧化主義となって現われたのである。しかも「欧化」することが、すなわち西洋のそれぞれの国民的特殊風習を学び取ることが、普通人間化することででもあるように感ぜられたのである。しかしその欧化は観念的な欧化であって現実の欧化ではなかった。日本人の靴の本質は下駄であり、日本人の洋服の本質は外出着である。そこでは道具がそれぞれ新しい形を取っただけであって、道具の示す存在の仕方そのものは依然として変わらない。」(*WTZ* 4:303–304)

6. For Watsuji's discussion of the influence of his teacher Sōseki, see Watsuji (1963).

7. *Pilgrimages to the Ancient Temples* 1 (*WTZ* 2:3). Watsuji writes, 「幼稚であるにもせよ最初の印象記は有機的なつながりを持っている。部分的の補修はいかにも困難である。」

8. 「昨夜父は言った。お前の今やっていることは道のためにどれだけ役にたつのか、頽廃した世道人心を救うのにどれだけ貢献することができるのか。...しかし今は、父がこの問いを発する心持ちに対して、頭を下げないではいられなかった。父は道を守ることに強い情熱を持った人である。医は仁術なりという標語を片時も忘れず、その実行のために自己の福利と安逸とを捨てて顧みない人である。」(*WTZ* 2:18).

9. The others are: ruler-ruled, husband-wife, older sibling-younger sibling, and friend-friend. See Carter (2013, 138–140), Ching (1993, 57–59), and Tu (1985, 113–130).

10. 「中宮寺を出てから法輪寺へまわった。途中ののどかな農村の様子や、蓴菜の花の咲いた池や、小山の多いやさしい景色など、非常によかった。法輪寺の古塔、眼の大きい仏像なども美しかった。荒廃した境内の風情もおもしろかった。鐘楼には納屋がわりに藁が積んであり、本堂のうしろの木陰にはむしろを敷いて機が出してあった。」(*WTZ* 2:192).

11. Watsuji's later philosophy will suggest that human existence is always between these two ideals—the Confucian and the Buddhist. In his early work, however, Watsuji appears to present the transcendent experiences evoked while viewing Buddhist art as an important step in growing up and growing beyond family obligation. Of course, a deconstructive reading of the text might suggest that neither set of goals—Confucian or Buddhist—can be pursued in isolation. After all, there are many passages in

Pilgrimages in which Watsuji extolls the value of ideals, for instance, in his praise of the various artists who traveled to India and China to learn new techniques and styles for expressing Buddhist ideas through the visual arts: Confucian dedication creates images of Buddhist transcendence. Perhaps one might see the back-and-forth between transcendence and immanence as a depiction of the dialectical movement between individual and group that Watsuji later identifies as the movement of betweenness (*aidagara*).

12. Kinoshita Mokutarō was the pen name of Ōta Masao (太田正雄, 1885–1945), an art-historian who was well-known in the Japanese literary world of his time. He was also a dermatologist.

13. This may simply be a device to engage the reader, but it is worth nothing that a similar emotional tone is used in the discussion of the date of the Shō Kannon.

14. This is the Japanese name of the king; we do not know his Indian name.

15. 「光明后は亡き母に対する情熱のために西金堂の建立について特に熱心な注意を払われたに相違ない。だから伝説にあるように、みずから制作場に臨まれたというようなこともないとは限らない。そこでまたこの芸術家が光明后を見て創作欲を刺戟せられたという仮定も可能になる。当時三十二、三歳ぐらいであった光明后は、観音像のモデルとしてもふさわしい。——かく考えれば、興福寺の伝説は一縷の生命を得て来るであろう。」(*WTZ* 2:88).

16. 「人の話によると、現在大阪に残っている蒸し風呂はアヘン吸入と同じような官能的享楽を与えるもので、その常用者はそれを欠くことができなくなるそうである。もし蒸気浴がこのような生理的現象を造り出すならば、浴槽からでた出たときの浴者は、特別の感覚的状態に陥っているというわなくてはならない。ちょうどそこへ慈悲の行に熱心な皇后が女官たちをつれて入場し、浴者たちを型通りに処置されたとすると、そこに蒸気浴から来る一種の陶酔と慈悲の行が与える喜びとの結合、従って宗教的な法悦と官能的な陶酔との融合が成り立つということも、きわめてありそうなことである。天平時代はこの種の現象と親しみの多い時代であるから、必ずしもこれは荒唐な想像ではない。こういう想像を許せば「施浴」の伝説は民衆の側からも起こり得たことになるであろう。」(*WTZ* 2:81).

17. 「風呂の方が肉体に近く、肉体の方が昔と今とを結びつけるに生々しい効果をもっているというせいでもあろうか。自分でこの蒸し風呂を試みて、その温まり具合や、肌の心持ちや、体のグッタリとする様子や、またありたけの汗を絞り出したあとのいい気持ちなどを経験してみたら、一層その感じがあるだろうと思う。こういう官能的な現象で昔を想像するのはあまり気のきいたことではないが、しかし最も容易な道である。」(*WTZ* 2:82).

18. 「奈良とはまた異なった穏やかな景色で、そこにこの土地を熱愛した祖先の心も読まれると思う。香久山の向こうのあの丘の間に多くの堂塔の聳えていた時代もあった。そこで推古白鳳の新鮮な文化は醸し出された。さらにさかのぼれば、伝説の時代のわれわれの祖先の、さまざまな愛と憎みとが、この山と川とに刻み込まれている。この地が特にやまとであったということと、日本民族の著しい特質とは、密接な関係を持つらしい。

多武の峯の陰欝な姿を右にながめながら、やがて汽車は方向を変えて、三輪山の麓へ近づいて行く。古代神話に重大な役目をつとめているこの三輪山はまた特に大和の山らしい。なだらかで、長く尾をひいて、古代の墳墓に見られると同様なあの柔らかな円味を遺憾なく現わしている。山を神として拝むのは原始時代に通有のことであるが、しかしこういうなだらかな線や円味を持ったやさしい山を崇拝するのは、比較的にまれなことではないであろうか。あの山の姿から超自然的な威力を感ずるという気持ちは、どうも理解し難い。むしろそれは完全なるもの調和あるものへの漠然たる憧憬を投射しているのではなかろうか。もしそうであるとすれば、この山もまた神話の書である。」(*WTZ* 2:158-159).

19. On this dialectic, see, for instance, Maruyama 1974 at 351.

20. "Ghandara" is both the ancient name of a region in modern Pakistan and a term used to refer to art and architecture created in that region between the first and sixth centuries CE (Ray 2018, 1). For a critical perspective on the terminology and discourse of Ghandaran art, see Falser (2015).

21. Both of these tendencies can be seen in Okakura Tenshin's *The Ideals of the East*, where he writes,

> The temples of Nara are rich in representations of Tâng culture, and of that Indian art, then in its splendour, which so much influenced the creations of this classic period—natural heirlooms of a nation which has preserved the music, pronunciation, ceremony and costumes, not to speak of the religious rites and philosophy, of so remarkable an age, intact.
>
> . . .
>
> Thus Japan is a museum of Asiatic civilisation; and yet more than a museum, because the singular genius of the race leads it to dwell on all phases of the ideals of the past, in that spirit of living Advaitism which welcomes the new without losing the old. (2007, 12)

22. "Kudara" is the Japanese name for the Korean Baekje empire.

23. Ganjin, the Japanese form of the name of the Chinese monk Jianzhen (鑒真, 688–763 CE), was a Chinese monk who attempted to come to Japan many times, finally succeeding and founding Tōshōdaiji temple in 754 CE. He brought many Chinese artists with him, and they produced the various wooden figures in that temple (Watsuji 2012, 47). Watsuji also discusses the craze of the Japanese court for Chinese Tang culture, which impressed the Japanese, transforming their tendency to moroseness and depression with the "admiration for that wide world of Tang, which was so full of life" (ibid., 83).

24. Watsuji is of the opinion that the artist must have been trained in China before traveling to Gandhara (ibid.).

25. On *gigaku*, a form of masked dance imported into Japan from China, see Kleinschmidt (1966).

26. 「インドの壁画が日本に来てこのように気韻を変化させたということは、ギリシアから東の方にあって、ペルシアもインドも西域もシナも、日本ほどギリシアに似ていないという事実と関係するであろう。気候や風土や人情において、あの広漠たる大陸と地中海の半島

はまるで異なっているが、日本とギリシアとはかなり近接している。大陸を移遷する間にどこでも理解せられなかった心持ちが、日本に来たって初めて心からな同感を見いだしたというようなことも、ないとは限らない。シナやインドの独創力に比べて、日本のそれは貧弱であった。しかし己れを空しゅうして模倣につめている間にも、その独自な性格は現われぬわけに行かなかった。もし日本の土地が、甘味な、哀愁に充ちた抒情詩的気分を特徴とするならば、同時にまたそれを日本人の気稟の特質と見ることもできよう。『古事記』の伝える神話の優しさも、中宮寺観音に現われた慈愛や悲哀も、恐らくこの特質の表現であろう。そこには常にしめやかさがあり涙がある。その涙があらゆる歓楽にたましいの陰影を与えずにはいない。だからインドの肉感的な画も、この涙に濾過せられる時には、透明な美しさに変化する。そうしてそこにギリシア人美意識がはるかなる兄弟を見いだすのである。」(WTZ 2:177–178).

27.「シナ人がこういう桂のふくらみを案出し得なかったかどうかは断言のできることでないが、しかしこれが漢式の感じを現わしているのでないことは確かなように思う。...もしシナに漢代から唐代へかけてのさまざまの建築が残っていたならば、仏教渡来によって西方の様式がいかなる影響を与えたかを明白にたどることができたであろう。しかるにその証拠となる建築は、ただ日本に残存するのみなのである。」(WTZ 2:168)

28.「固有の日本文化が外来文化を包摂したのではなく、外来文化の雰囲気のなかで我が国人の性質がかく生育したのである。この見方は外来文化を生育の素地とする点において、外来文化を単に挿話的のものと見る見方と異なっている。この立場では、日本人の独創は外来文化に対立するものではなく、外来文化のなかから生まれたものなのである。」(WTZ 2:114).

29. *Stanford Encyclopedia of Philosophy*, s 3.2 "The Happening of Tradition" (online: https://plato.stanford.edu/entries/gadamer/). See also Johnson (2014), which discusses the similarities and differences between Gadamer and Nishida.

30.「．．．唐の融合文化のうちに生まれた人も、養われた人も、黄海を越えてわが風光明媚な内海にはいって来た時に、何らか心情の変移するのを感じないであろうか。漠々たる黄土の大陸と十六の少女のように可憐な大和の山水と、その相違は何らか気分の転換を惹起しないであろうか。そこに変化を認めるならば、作家の心眼に映ずる幻像にもそこばくの変化を認めずばなるまい。たとえば顔面の表情が、大陸らしいボーッとしたところを失って、こまやかに、幾分鋭くなっているごときは、その証拠と見るわけに行かないだろうか。われわれは聖林寺十一面観音の前に立つとき、この像がわれわれの国土にあって幻視せられたものであることを直接に感ずる。」(WTZ 2:44–45).

31. Hiroshi Nara notes that this must refer to the moving of the capital to Nagaoka in 784, and later to Kyōto in 794. However, I think this is incorrect: what Watsuji is referring to here is the brief move of the capital from Nara to Kuni-kyo (modern Kizugawa) from 740 to 744 CE. This makes sense because subsequent sentences in

this passage mention that work on the construction of the Daibutsu at Tōdaiji had begun. This was in 741 CE.

32. 「遷都騒ぎがあって大宮人がぞろぞろと北の方へ行ってしまう。近江では大銅像の鋳造などがはじめられている。古き都は「道の芝草長く生い」世の中の無常を思わせるほどに荒れて行く。そうかと思うとまた大宮人がぞろぞろ奈良へ帰ってくる。そうして大仏の原型などを造るので大騒ぎがはじまる。何千という大工や金工や人足がいそがしそうに働きはじめる。毎日毎日奈良坂の方に材木や銅塊などを運ぶ人の影が見える。足場には土がもられ、その上には鋳銅のすさまじい焔がひらめいている。それが幾年か続く。やがて供養の日になると一万五千の灯で東大寺一円の森の上が赤くなる。歌唄讃頌する数千の沙門の声が遠雷のように大きくうねって聞こえてくる。——東の方が少し静かになって来たかと思うと、今度はまた西の方唐招提寺や西大寺や西隆寺などの造営がはじまる。奈良遷都の際すでに四十八箇寺あったという奈良の寺々は、このころはもう倍にはなっていたであろう。...」(*WTZ* 2:83–84).

33. It would be interesting to compare Watsuji's notion of culture as a set of "ways of doing things" that are shaped by social and political events and the environment and that are transmitted through history and "memes," which are used by Richard Dawkins and Daniel C. Dennett to explain the emergence and persistence of certain cultural practices (Woodcock 2000; Dawkins 1976; Dennett 1995).

34. 「堂の正面をぶらぶらと歩きながら、わたくしは幸福な少時を過ごした。大きい松の林がこの堂を取り巻いていて、何とも言えず親しい情緒を起こさせる。松林とこの建築との間には確かにピッタリと合うものがあるようである。西洋建築には、たとえどの様式を持って来ても、かほどまで松の情趣に似つかわしいものがあるとは思えない。パルテノンを松林の間に置くことは不可能である。ゴシックの寺院があの優しい松の枝に似合わないことも同様であろう。これらの建築はただその国土の都市と原野と森林とに結びつけて考えるべきである。われわれの仏寺にも、わが国土の風物と離し難いものがある。もしゴシック建築に北国の森林のあとがあるとすれば、われわれの仏寺にも松や檜の森林のあとがあるとは言えないだろうか。あの屋根には松や檜の垂れ下がった枝の感じはないか。堂全体には枝の繁った松や檜の老樹を思わせるものはないか。東洋の木造建築がそういう根源を持っていることは、文化の相違を風土の相違にまで還元する上にも興味の多いことである。」(*WTZ* 2:102–103).

35. "The real world," Nishida writes, "is the world of production" (Nishida 1998b, 41).

36. For a study of Kuki's approach to poetry, see Marra (2004).

Chapter 3

The Development of Watsuji's Theory of Culture and Climate
An Interpretation of Fūdo

FROM *PILGRIMAGES TO THE ANCIENT TEMPLES IN NARA* TO *CLIMATE AND CULTURE*

Why do cultural practices differ in different places? What makes a culture unique? If it is unique, why is this so? These questions preoccupied Japanese philosophers such as Watsuji Tetsurō during the first half of the twentieth century. Finding that Japan lagged behind the modern European nations, the Japanese government sent scholars to England,[1] France, and Germany,[2] countries synonymous with "modern" prior to the Second World War. The feelings of dislocation, alienation, and loneliness that these scholars all felt to some degree while abroad inspired them to reflect on what made them feel different and how different they really were from others. In *Climate and Culture as a Study of Human Being* (*Fūdo: ningengakuteki kōsatsu*, 『風土——人間学的考察』), written after his return from Germany, Watsuji addressed the question of cultural difference head on. A study of this book provides us an opportunity to discover his answer to the question of cultural difference as well as to learn his views on the nature of culture and the features of human existence that make cultural experience possible.

To appreciate Watsuji's philosophical analysis of the phenomenon of climate and its relationship to culture, it is helpful to understand how he situated it in relation to classic European treatments of the same topic. This comparative analysis is often overlooked by contemporary Watsuji scholars in the English-speaking world because the second half of *Climate and Culture* has not been translated into English.[3] In that part of the book, Watsuji provides a detailed interpretation of Immanuel Kant's, Johann Gottfried Herder's, and G. W. H. Hegel's answers to the same questions that preoccupied him during this period. Examining how Watsuji positioned himself relative to this classic cannon can help us to understand what he adopted and what he adapted from them. As well, studying *Climate and Culture* from this perspective helps us to make sense of why climate and culture are important *philosophical* topics. For while they are primarily studied today by social scientists in departments of sociology, anthropology, and human geography, until the Second World War, culture and geography were legitimate subjects for philosophical study.

Watsuji's later philosophy has been justly criticized for its nationalist tendency (Inoue 1979; Bernier 2006; Pinkus 1996). However, as other scholars have noted, there are aspects of his work that resist nationalism and celebrate cultural difference (Bein 2011, 8–9; Yuasa, 313–315). If we wish to sustain interest in his work today, it is therefore necessary to focus on useful aspects of his study of culture. Winnowing the wheat from the chaff is a secondary goal of this chapter. In the last chapter, we examined Watsuji's early work, *Pilgrimages*, in which he articulated a view of Japanese culture that was fluid and malleable, open to influences from other cultures, and constructed by cultural interpreters. In *Climate and Culture*, he shifts away from this paradigm somewhat. However, not all the traces of the fluid and open concept of culture from his early work disappear. My hope in this study of *Climate and Culture* is to identify some of these strands that persist in that work that acknowledge the value of cross-cultural exchange and the possibility of learning from cultural difference. It is these features that make Watsuji's investigation of culture worth studying today in an era in which people from across the globe migrate to new places and encounter different ways of thinking and doing.

Of course, identifying the continuity between *Pilgrimages* and *Climate and Culture* also brings the differences into starker relief and allows us to identify why there is a shift between 1919 and 1935. I hope to demonstrate through my analysis that the shift is in part a consequence of the phenomenological methodology that Watsuji adopts in the later work. His transcendental approach to phenomenology, which focuses on identifying the conditions for the possibility of human experience, introduces a universal aspect into *Climate and Culture* that was absent in *Pilgrimages*. In consequence, in his work on climate, "culture" is not just "Japanese culture" but "culture in general." Generalizations about culture are inevitably inaccurate given the diversity of definitions of culture and the continual migration of people across the Earth's surface. And to the extent that culture is "simply . . . the system of humanly expressive practices by which values are renewed, created, and contested" (Inglis 1993, 38, quoted in Mitchell 2000, 71), at the heart of culture is contestation and change.

The problems of universalism inherent in Watsuji's application of the phenomenological method to a study of climate are not solely attributable to the method; they are also a result of the subject to which Watsuji applied it, namely his own experience of different climates. In *Pilgrimages*, we can to some degree forgive the fact that he took it upon himself to be the sole interpreter of Japanese culture, since he was after all an educated man from the very culture he interpreted, and he was an expert in the Buddhist art he was interpreting. But in *Climate and Culture*, Watsuji bases his characterizations of climate on his personal observations during his boat trip from Japan to Europe and his personal (unquestioned) stereotypes about the mindset, philosophy, aesthetic, and values of the people whom he observed during the trip. As Augustin Berque points out, Watsuji is guilty of "substituting the observations of a traveler for a study of the vision of the world held by the societies" he describes (Berque 2011, 22 [translated by author]).

Watsuji's tendency to propose that his own subjective perspective is in fact objective is reinforced by a similar tendency in the European philosophers he studies at the end of the book. While the phenomenological approach predominates in the first half of *Climate and Culture*, at the end, Watsuji surveys other philosophical studies of climate and geography in order to locate his own approach in relation to them. The studies of interest to him include those by philosophers of German romanticism such as Johann Gottfried von Herder and German idealists such as J. G. Fichte, Friedrich Schelling, and G. W. F. Hegel. There is also a brief consideration of Immanuel Kant's view since he was a contemporary of Herder and an important influence on the idealists. While these philosophers acknowledged that cultures differed widely across the globe and that they changed throughout history, they also believed that culture disclosed certain universal structures of human existence. Moreover, they proposed that cultural diversity is somehow derived from the different geographic features of the region of the Earth in which each culture developed: humans are affected by the physical landscape, the climate, and the natural environment in which they live, but they also have an effect on the environment by engaging in agriculture, foraging, construction of shelters, and so on.

It is the universal nature of the claims that both the older German philosophers and Watsuji wish to make about the relationship between climate and culture which arguably introduces some problematic political elements into Watsuji's study, and which gave rise to later criticism that Watsuji was a Japanese nationalist (Bernier 2006). Indeed, Watsuji adopts some of the language that the German philosophers he admired employed such as "spirit" or "national character," which were labels for the universal or generalizable aspects of particular cultures that they identified. To greater or lesser extent, these thinkers believed that because German culture and German philosophy, or in the case of Watsuji, Japanese culture and Japanese philosophy, were expressions of the interaction between these groups and their social and geographic environment, these cultural practices were somehow objective expressions of universal aspects of human experience and existence. Watsuji applauds Fichte's *Addresses to the German Nation* because Fichte acknowledges that the Germans are a "unified natural whole"—a nation (*WTZ* 8:225). Each of the German philosophers had a different view as to what unified them into a nation—Herder maintained it was God,[4] Kant's teleology led him to believe that the unity was was a rational necessity, a step toward achieving what he called "a hidden plan of nature to bring about . . . a . . . perfect state constitution" (2014, Eighth Proposition, 116). For Watsuji, what unifies the Japanese and constitutes their spirit (*seishin*, 精神) are their shared culture and the ethical life that it embodies. In his essay "The Japanese Spirit," he explains that the Japanese spirit is captured "in the full gamut of Japanese culture in which all the aspects of our life are realized" (1998, 244),[5] and this spirit is embodied climatically as "a living whole" (ibid.).[6] The embodiment of the Japanese spirit in cultural and ethical practices leads Watsuji to identify this spirit with "the Japanese race as a totality as an active subject" (ibid.).[7]

In this chapter, we will familiarize ourselves with Watsuji's general theory of climate and culture. We will first situate his view in the context of the European philosophers who influenced him: there is a long line of German romantic and idealist thinkers who were interested in culture as a subject of study and who early on recognized that geography and the environment—that is, spatial aspects of human existence—have a significant impact on cultural practices. We will then turn to Watsuji's phenomenological methodology with the goal of understanding how he proposes to approach the study of culture and its relationship to climate. Watsuji did not intend to simply write a new chapter in the book begun by his European predecessors; instead, he wished to find a philosophical method that would enable him to look below the surface of the relationship between climate and culture to explain why the two are so intimately linked and to tease out the nature of the linkage.

SITUATING *CLIMATE AND CULTURE* IN RELATION TO EUROPEAN PHILOSOPHY

To understand what Watsuji intended to do in *Climate and Culture*, it is helpful to examine how he relates his project to that of other (mostly European) philosophers who had written on similar subjects. In the last chapter of the book, Watsuji discusses the work of thinkers beginning with Hippocrates (460–370 BCE), Aristotle (384–322 BCE), Polybus (*ca.* 400 BCE), Strabo (64 or 63 BCE to 24 CE), and Jean Bodin (1530–1596) before moving on to modern German philosophy and German idealism. We will join him in his study of this history beginning with Johann Gottfried von Herder (1744–1803), and will follow him through his analysis of the views of Immanuel Kant (1724–1804), Johann Gottlieb Fichte (1762–1814), and G. W. F. Hegel

(1770–1831), all of whom appreciated the philosophical significance of climate and its effect on society and culture.

What was Watsuji looking for in his study of these philosophers? He recognized in their views about culture and climate an implicit acknowledgment of the importance of the spatial dimension of human existence, which he felt had been ignored at the expense of an emphasis on time in German phenomenology. The comments that Herder, Kant, Fichte, and Hegel make about human history demonstrate that the evolution of human societies is closely tied to spatial phenomena such as geography and climate. Moreover, Watsuji also investigated how these philosophers understood the relationship between the universal and the particular, which interested him because one of his goals was to understand what the development of particular cultures reveals about time and space as universal features of human experience.

After a thorough review of ancient, medieval, and early modern European views on the subject, Watsuji turns to Herder with a study of two of his works, *Another Philosophy of History* (*Auch eine Philosophie der Geschichte zur Bildung der Menschheit*; 1774) and *Ideas for a Philosophy of the History of Mankind* (*Ideen zur Geschichte der Menschheit*; 1784). According to Watsuji, Herder recognized that human history was not just a temporal matter but a spatial one: he proposed that a history of humankind required a study of the diversity of cultures that exist at particular times in history;[8] a proper study of history could not simply trace the history of a particular cultural group over time. Watsuji explains, "To consider the form of specific peoples solely as if they were a single unique process of development toward the final goal of humanity, that is, as to consider them simply as a succession ordered based on 'before and after,' is [precisely] what [Herder] vehemently rejected. [Rather,] they must be grasped as a simultaneous order" (*WTZ* 8:220).[9] In Herder, Watsuji finds someone who, like him, wished to understand the nature of human existence by beginning from its multiple forms at a particular time—that is, its spatial element, its extension throughout the world.

Herder explains that human culture is the result of an interaction between cultural groups and their geographic milieu. Watsuji describes this view:

> Having observed that humans on Earth come in many different forms, and yet that they also comprise a single human species, he is led to the conclusion that this single species acclimatizes (*fūdoka suru* 風土化する) to various *places* (*tokoro* ところ) on its surface. Now whether we are dealing with the Mongols on the steppes of Asia, the Arabs in the desert, or the Indigenous people of California on the other side of the world (the California that is in the process of becoming the centre of today's world), he demonstrates that the character of the people results from their physical environment [literally, "land"] and daily ways of doing

things; in other words, the *living form of everyday life* that he describes is climatic (*fūdoteki* 風土的).[10] (Emphasis in original) (*WTZ* 8:213) (author's translation)

Herder's understanding of the relationship between culture and geography is very different than that which Watsuji develops in *Climate and Culture* because Herder sees a direct causal link between the two, whereas Watsuji considers culture to be a phenomenon that provides evidence of certain features of human experience—it is human experience which is "climatic," not culture per se. Or rather, both culture and climate are phenomena pointing to aspects of human experience. But what draws Watsuji to Herder is the recognition that culture takes place in and responds to a spatial milieu in addition to developing purely historically (temporally).[11]

Watsuji next turns to Kant, whose views he adopts in part and criticizes in part. What he accepts is Kant's view that the study of human history discloses certain universal aspects of human existence. What he criticizes is the over-emphasis on temporality at the expense of space. Kant was critical of Herder's approach to culture, a criticism recorded in his essay, "Review of J.G. Herder's *Ideas for the Philosophy of the History of Humanity*" ("Rezensionen von Herders Ideen zur Philosophie der Geschichte der Menschheit," 1785).[12] According to Watsuji, the difference between the two philosophers stemmed from the fact that Kant emphasized temporality and Herder spatiality. As we have seen, Herder's theory of culture and climate acknowledged the simultaneous existence of a diversity of forms of human life spread throughout the world (i.e., space), and his goal was to demonstrate through a variation of Spinoza's argument that it was this diversity that expressed the universal (i.e., God).[13] In contrast, Kant, who rejected the Spinozistic argument, emphasized time rather than space. In consequence, God's imprint was not in every creature by reason of its mere existence; instead God was manifest in the goal toward which each thing was oriented and toward which it strove over time. For Kant, God is manifest in the unfolding of history rather than in any single moment of its existence (*WTZ* 8:222). Henry Allison provides a helpful summary of Kant's teleological view of human history in this regard:

> Kant's application of teleology to humankind and its history . . . featured the following four theses. (1) If nature is to be regarded as a teleological system, it must be thought of as having an ultimate end, which can only be humankind. (2) Humankind may be considered as such an end only if it is also related to a final, unconditioned end, which must be moral. (3) Nature, by itself, cannot produce such an end, since that can only result from freedom; but it nevertheless can be thought of as preparing the way for or facilitating the development of morality. (4) It does this through culture, mainly the culture of skill, which, since it requires the development of humankind's rational capacities, is a lengthy

historical process, culminating in republican institutions, which maximize freedom under law, and a confederation of states guaranteeing perpetual peace. (Allison 2009, 42)

One can see in this description that, according to Kant, as long as all human activity is directed toward moral ends, the unfolding of history will guarantee the achievement of God's will. Indeed, according to Watsuji, the emphasis on rationality was yet another reason that Kant's account of history prioritized time over space: the rational values the universal, not the simultaneous multiplicity of particular individuals (i.e., space) (ibid.).

Watsuji was critical of Kant's theory of history and culture, which he believed was inconsistent with other aspects of Kantian philosophy (*WTZ* 8:223). In his view, Kant failed to recognize that a teleological approach to history was not necessarily inconsistent with a diversity of ends. In Watsuji's view, different cultures pursue different ends; not every society pursues the end of "attaining a civil society which can administer justice universally" that Kant considered the rational end for all (Kant 2007, 45).[14] Moreover, a teleological interpretation of history does not require the presupposition of a universal end of all humankind. Indeed, empirical observation confirms the diversity of culture and hence the diversity of social aims: (*WTZ* 8:223). Watsuji writes, "Nature desired climatic differences, and in consequence it also desired the individual differences that flow from it. In other words, it desired that humankind be realized in a variety of different forms. In which case one must now acknowledge that the end of nature is in fact Herder's so-called 'simultaneous order.' One cannot separate climatic particularity from the various destinies of the many forms of humankind" (*WTZ* 8:223).

We learn something about Watsuji's approach to culture from this discussion of Kant: Watsuji admired Herder's interest in the diversity of human cultures and the way that he related this to the diversity of geography and climate. But he was also drawn to the universal tendencies he recognized in Herder and Kant, both of whom believed that humanity is the expression of something universal. For Watsuji, this universal aspect, which we will explore further in this chapter, is the phenomenological structures of spatial and temporal experience which culture and climate disclose;[15] in contrast, for Herder, the universal was the idea of God expressed through the diversity of nature and humans, and for Kant, the capacity for reason expressed through the ideal of humanity, which is ultimately a pursuit of the divine (Kant 2007, 64–65).[16] Watsuji called the universal aspects of human existence (time and space) revealed by culture its "metaphysical" sense, by which he meant that these aspects were properties of human nature that transcend individual humans and cultures. He announces this in his discussion of J. G. Fichte's concept of "nation" in the latter's *Addresses to the German Nation* (*Reden an die deutsche Nation*, 1808), which Watsuji praised as an example of the recognition of the metaphysical status of culture in German idealism.[17] Watsuji writes,

> The nation submits to *the special law* of the self-development of the divine (ein gewisses besonderes Gesetz der Entwicklung des Göttlichen).[18] Compliance with this special law, both in the eternal world and in the temporal, brings together a group of people in a single unified natural whole. Thus, this foundational law of development can be considered to provide through and through the national character of a people (Fichte, *Schriften*, VII, p. 381). Although we know that such a law exists, the individuals who are subject to it are *completely unable to grasp it conceptually*. A nation or a people can only *awaken* to its unity historically. Acting and suffering together, namely through common rulers, territory, wars, triumphs and defeats, this is what allows the group to realize that it is a people. But even in cases in which this does not occur as is the situation with the Germans, it is by means of the strength of a *metaphysical existence* that the concept of the unity of the people can be maintained. Indeed, this is the remarkable characteristic of the German people. It is in this way that the unique characteristic of a people comes to possess a transhistorical meaning. It is realized concretely through the process of historical development, but its own foundation is in its *metaphysical and spiritual nature*. For his part, Fichte does not grasp this in terms of climate, but our problem of climate exists precisely within this kind of metaphysical spiritual nature, and thus within what he himself called "the special law of the divine."[19] (*WTZ* 8:225) [emphasis in original]

Watsuji sees the culmination of the metaphysical concept of culture in the Hegelian notion of "spirit," a term which he adopts in other parts of *Climate and Culture* to refer to what culture discloses. Indeed, his use of this term, for instance, when he refers to the "spirit" of the Japanese or of the Chinese or the Indian, is no doubt meant to evoke this Hegelian concept.[20] This spirit expresses itself concretely in each culture, and insofar as it is concrete, it is what Watsuji calls "climatic"—culture expresses itself through specific responses to the geography and climate of its surroundings. And following Hegel, each of these concrete manifestations of spirit—each particular cultural spirit—is a necessary expression of spirit as it develops universally. Watsuji gives his gloss on Hegelian philosophy:

> The totality of a given people directly expresses nature; this is its *determination by geography or climate*. The spiritual life of peoples that are so determined exists at various specific stages of development, and it is only within those particular stages that they are able to grasp themselves. At a given stage, an ethical spirit develops either as an order of "simultaneity" or of "succession,"

and a people is precisely that which expresses itself as determined individually by it. In other words, it is "spirit as a particular people." The particular spirit of a people that is thus established is the development of its reality in accordance with a *particular principle*; this is its "history." However, precisely because it is a limited form of spirit, it tends to move toward the universal history of the world.[21] (*WTZ* 8:229) [emphasis in original]

Like Watsuji, Hegel describes three kinds of climatic regions. However, Watsuji is critical of Hegel's ignorance of the world outside of Europe, and so proposes to correct his approach in his own work.[22] He writes, "Unlike Hegel, we cannot countenance that [the developments of] world history treat Europeans as the 'chosen people.' Enslaving nations other than Europe is not the way to realize the freedom of all; world history must assign a place to each different nation in a way that recognizes its climatic [specificity]"[23] (*WTZ* 8:232–233). No doubt, Watsuji bristled at Hegel's chauvinistic view, common in Europe at the time, that while the history of the world may begin in the Orient, it is only in the West that it reaches its full glory (*WTZ* 8:232).

Thus Watsuji's theory of climate is to be understood roughly along Hegelian lines as a theory that describes universal aspects of human existence as expressed in individual concrete cultures.[24] Where he differs from Hegel is in his understanding of what these universal aspects are—they express spirit in a quasi-Hegelian sense, but Watsuji gives them a phenomenological twist, such that what is disclosed in individual cultures is certain universal aspects of human experiencing. He explains in *Ethics* that what distinguishes his philosophy from that of Hegel is that for him, space and time are forms "of the subjective structure of *ningen*" (Watsuji 1996, 230)—they are structures of human experience rather than forms of Hegelian spirit "as the ultimate totality" (Watsuji 1996, 229) in what Watsuji calls its "in-itself-form" as *Idee* (Watsuji 1996, 232). In other words, he rejects Hegel's view that time and space are the structures of concrete human experience understood as the manifestation of a universal "idea"; rather, Watsuji's view, time and space are simply the forms through which all knowledge and experience are constituted.[25]

While I have tried to demonstrate the difference between the "universality" of Watsuji's phenomenological approach in *Climate and Culture* and the universalism of Hegel's philosophy of history, there are many indications that Watsuji was very drawn to the Hegelian approach, but also indications that he misunderstood it. In his later three-volume *Ethics*, for instance, Watsuji admits the similarity between his characterization of the absolute and that of Hegel (Watsuji 1996, 119). However, he tries to distinguish his characterization from that of Hegel by explaining that in his philosophy, the absolute is "the principle of ethics alone," not "the principle of all philosophy" as is the case with Hegel (ibid.). Thus it is legitimate to interpret Watsuji's concept of dialectic in his book, *Ethics*, in Hegelian terms. But in my view, Watsuji's insistence that his dialectic is the basis of ethics as the study of human being but not also the dialectic of "all philosophy" creates a division between the philosophical and the concrete (the ideal and the real, to use Watsuji's terms from *Ethics* [Watsuji 1996, 229–232]) that Hegel's philosophy sought to avoid. Rüdiger Bubner explains this unity between the concrete and the theoretical very well:

> For Hegel, "spirit" is not itself some transcendent entity whose status could simply be challenged by invoking examples of historical relativity. It is conceived rather as living movement of self-actualisation on the model of the Aristotelian *Energeia*, which seeks expression in its own appropriate form. The life of spirit for Hegel thus consists precisely in the ongoing process of externalisation and re-appropriation. The various historical forms it assumes do not represent a loss of its essential substance, but rather demonstrate its intrinsic power to express its own character. For these forms are the forms of spirit itself as manifested through time. They are its forms, but spirit is not simply identical with them.
>
> ... The single enduring spirit, which the labour of the philosophical concept perpetually serves, expresses itself in historical terms, and does so necessarily. . . . For Hegel, there is no such thing as the existence of "time," and in addition the existence of "spirit," in such a way that the two could essentially come into conflict with one another. (Bubner 2003, 170) (author's translation)

Watsuji rejects Hegel's philosophy of spirit because he felt that the Hegelian concept of "spirit" separated the ideal from the real—idea and material. He explains, "The standpoint of Spirit [in my philosophy] cannot be idealism. And insofar as Spirit [in Hegelian philosophy] is, generally speaking, opposed to matter, the term *Spirit* is not appropriate here. This is why we must call [Spirit] *subjective ningen*" (Watsuji 1996, 232) [emphasis in original]. However, this interpretation of Hegel overlooks the unity of the ideal and the real in the latter's philosophy.

Our discussion of Watsuji's survey of the role of climate in the history of philosophy has helped us to get a general idea of what Watsuji wishes to achieve in *Climate and Culture*: a reassertion of the importance of space alongside time as a structure of human experience, and a justification of why it is through culture that one can study this universal aspect. Watsuji sees in the history of modern German philosophy (Herder, Kant) and German idealism (Fichte, Hegel) a recurrent recognition of the importance of space—of the particularity of human cultural existence developed through interaction between humans (intersubjectivity) and through interaction between humans and their environment (climate, milieu). Heideggerian phenomenology, on Watsuji's assessment, overlooks this spatial aspect of human existence, placing too much emphasis on temporality and, hence, individuality. A corrective is needed to phenomenology, and Watsuji finds this in the philosophers he, and we, have reviewed.

As we have seen, Watsuji was interested in the relationship between climate and culture because he wished to correct the overemphasis of European phenomenology on temporal aspects of human existence. By studying this relationship, he was able to draw out the fundamentally spatial aspects of this existence that were overlooked in Husserlian and Heideggerian phenomenology. In the next section, we turn to a study of the phenomenological method he proposes to use in *Climate and Culture*. The goal will be to see how he modifies this method to bring out the spatial aspects of human existence.

THE PURPOSE OF *CLIMATE AND CULTURE*: IDENTIFYING THE PHENOMENOLOGICAL STRUCTURES OF INTERSUBJECTIVITY

Having begun our interpretation of *Climate and Culture* with the last chapter of Watsuji's text, which dealt with the history of philosophical approaches to climate, we now return to the first chapter, in which Watsuji explains why he became interested in the study of climate and culture, and in which he sets out his philosophical approach to the topic. Watsuji has two primary goals in the text. The first is to conduct a phenomenological analysis of culture in order to discover what cultural practices (dress, food cultivation and preparation, language, greetings, customs, etc.) reveal about the structures of human experience. The second is to underline the importance of intersubjectivity as a feature of human existence and by doing so, to emphasize the spatial nature of human existence which is often overlooked in European accounts of human nature. This second goal is primarily carried out as a critique of Martin Heidegger's *Being and Time*, which appeared in 1927, the year before Watsuji's return to Japan and the beginning of his work on the essays that comprise *Climate and Culture*.

In addition to the intrinsic interest of the topic of climate and culture, study of *Climate and Culture* is interesting for two further reasons: it sheds light on Watsuji's later work, and it highlights unique features of Japanese phenomenology that differ from European strands. In regard to the first point, the theory of intersubjectivity that Watsuji develops in the book is the basis for his later important work on ethics in which intersubjectivity is a crucial foundational concept. In regard to the second, studying Watsuji's theory of intersubjectivity illustrates how Watsuji is both attracted to and inspired by European philosophy while at the same time being critical of its chauvinism. Watsuji makes it clear at the outset of *Climate and Culture* that he is inspired by Heideggerian phenomenology, but he also wants to correct certain aspects of it. He will do so by using Japanese cultural and philosophical perspectives as a counterpoint to European phenomenology.

The phenomenological approach that Watsuji adopts in *Climate and Culture* is based on Heidegger's *Being and Time*. Watsuji does not simply apply Heideggerian phenomenology unmodified; he corrects it based on his critique of it.[26] His primary criticism is that *Being and Time* prioritizes the temporal aspects of human existence and underestimates the importance of its spatial aspects. One of the purposes of *Climate and Culture* is thus to demonstrate the importance of the spatiality of human experience and human existence, which Watsuji identifies with the climatic nature of human experience. Watsuji believed that a study of culture reveals the spatial and temporal context in which humans exist "climatically."

Watsuji criticizes Heidegger's philosophy in *Being and Time*, particularly his exposition of the structures of human being (which Heidegger calls its "existential" structures, 1996, 10–11/12–13), for placing too much emphasis on the individual and too little on the role of others (intersubjectivity) in human existence. In sociological terms, Watsuji believed that Heidegger did not acknowledge the important role that community, society, and the group play in our lives. In phenomenological terms, Watsuji is critical of the fact that Heideggerian phenomenology gives priority to the temporality of human existence over its spatiality. How does the phenomenological analysis map on to the sociological critique? The spatial aspect of human experience is the condition for the possibility of social relations, while the temporal aspect according to Watsuji is primarily about how an individual experiences her own world: space is about intersubjectivity, while time is about the succession of thoughts and feelings in an individual's consciousness.

The individualist reading of Heidegger that Watsuji proposes has been criticized by many Heidegger scholars (see, for example, McMullin 2013, 3; Figal 2000, 71). When considering these criticisms, it is important to remember that Watsuji wrote the various chapters that comprise *Climate and Culture* between 1928 and 1935, not long after the publication of *Being and Time* in 1927. In contrast, modern scholars have had the benefit of interpreting Heidegger's groundbreaking book in the context of his later work. When one reads his later books and essays, it becomes clear that Heidegger's discussion of the environment, art, and creative activity is intersubjective and spatial, thus correcting the emphasis on temporality in *Being and Time*. There has also been significant recent work on Heidegger's ethics (McMullin 2013; Hatab 2000; Hodge 1995; Marx 1992), which naturally relies on what he writes about intersubjectivity, an element of the spatiality of human existence (Sikka 2006, 318).[27] However, in this chapter, my goal is not to provide an accurate interpretation of Heidegger but to understand Watsuji's phenomenology. To do so, we must provisionally accept his criticism of Heidegger and use it to understand Watsuji's goal in studying climate, which is to uncover the spatial structures of human experience and existence.

SPACE AND TIME: FUNDAMENTAL STRUCTURES OF HUMAN EXPERIENCE DISCLOSED THROUGH CULTURE AND CLIMATE

What structures of human existence are disclosed through the phenomenological study of culture? Watsuji identifies two: space and time. The temporal aspect is revealed by the fact that all cultures have a history: they emerge and evolve over time. The spatial aspect is revealed first by the diversity of cultures, which are spread across different geographic and climatic zones, but also by the fact that cultural practices are the result of interaction among humans (which take place in the "external" spatial world and not in a single individual's mind) and between humans and their environment. The intersubjective aspect of cultural creation is evidence, Watsuji argues, of the importance of a fundamental characteristic of human existence that he labels "betweeness" (*aidagara* 間柄; Watsuji 1961, 9:12; *WTZ* 8:15–17).[28]

How does Watsuji characterize these two aspects of human existence, the individual and the social? He writes, "By 'man' I mean not the individual (anthrōpos, homo, homme, etc.) but man both in this individual sense and at the same time man in society, the combination or the association of man. . . . For a true and full understanding, one must treat man both as individual and as whole"[29] (Watsuji 1961, 8–9; *WTZ* 8:14–15). The social aspect manifests itself in culture, which is the product of interactions between humans. Watsuji thus assigns a fundamental role to culture in understanding the nature of human experience. In consequence, in *Climate and Culture*, the exploration of the existential structures of human existence disclosed by human sociality becomes an investigation of the existential structures disclosed by culture.

Culture has a temporal aspect: all cultural practices have a history and evolve over time (Watsuji 1961, 9; *WTZ* 8:15). And culture also has a spatial aspect, which Watsuji labels "climatic" (Watsuji 1961, 10; *WTZ* 8:16), by which he means that culture is a response to the human and natural environment. We can see the dual nature of climate when Watsuji writes,

> Mankind is saddled not simply with a general past but with a specific climatic past. . . . Climate as this specific content does not exist alone and in isolation from history, entering and becoming a part of the content of history at a later juncture. From the very first, climate is historical climate. In the dual structure of man—the historical and the climatic—history is climatic history and climate is historical climate.[30] (Watsuji 1961, 10; *WTZ* 8:16)

As we can see from this formulation, time and space are closely intertwined. It is not that humans exist as bodies in geometric space and that this space is then situated in time. Rather, climate (space) is in its concrete form a historical (temporal) phenomenon because culture as a climatic phenomenon unfolds in time and because humans have a history of being influenced by climate and influencing their geographic environment over time. Canada can be said to have a "cold climate" not simply in virtue of the average temperature in any given year, but because climate has affected the development and evolution of Canadian culture and because the activity of Canadians and the Indigenous people in Canada have affected the geographic environment and climate in which they live.

The spatial and temporal aspects of climate have both an ontological and a phenomenological significance.[31] Ontologically, that is, viewed from the point of view of the human mode of existence, humans are both individuals and part of a social group. Culture, as we will see, is an expression of both of these aspects of human existence. This dual mode of existence also shapes how humans experience the world: it has phenomenological repercussions. Thus culture, which is an expression of the temporal and spatial nature of human existence, mediates human experience—our culture is the context in which we find meaning in the world around us. And if culture mediates human experience, then there must be something about the structure of this experience that is both temporal and spatial: climate and culture are structured by time and space. To identify these structures, Watsuji applies his version of Heideggerian phenomenological analysis to culture.

Why does Watsuji adopt Heideggerian phenomenology? How does it help to identify the features of human experience disclosed by culture? Culture can be understood as a context in which we find meanings for the interactions we have with objects and other humans. Heideggerian phenomenology provides a theory about how humans relate to (or in Heideggerian terms, how humans exist as) the context in which they arise. As Watsuji points out, for

Heidegger, human experience is a form of "transcendence" (*chōetsu*, 超越; Watsuji 1961, 12; *WTZ* 8:18).[32] The term "transcendence" is meant to indicate the contextual nature of human experience. Heidegger captures this contextual nature of human existence and experience by referring to the human way of being as "Dasein" (Dreyfus 1995, 14), which he explains is a way of "being-in-the-world"—the individual and the world are not separate, but rather, human existence is primordially the arising of humans together with and in the world. As Werner Marx explains, this means that the "environing world . . . is the unity of a referential context that bestows significance upon the relations of 'in order to,' 'whereto,' 'for,' and 'for the sake of'" (Marx 1971, 185). In other words, humans experience the world as having meaning and sense. This sense is not created ex post by humans who confront a random collection of unrelated and unidentifiable objects; instead, humans give meaning to the things and people they encounter because they are engaged in doing things with them or doing things together with them that are themselves meaningful. Watsuji explains,

> The usual distinction between subject and object, or more particularly the distinction between "the cold" and the "I" independently of each other, involves a certain misunderstanding. When we feel cold, we ourselves are already in the coldness of the outside air. That we come into relation with the cold means that we are outside in the cold. In this sense, our state is characterized by "ex-sistere" as Heidegger emphasizes, or, in our term, by "intentionality."[33] (Watsuji 1961, 3; *WTZ* 8:9)

Watsuji illustrates this in relation to a specific climatic phenomenon, "dryness." To experience "dryness," one does not need to be placed in air of a specific degree of humidity; rather, one must simply experience the mountain (landscape) of Aden in Yemen:

> The essential dryness of the desert is disclosed to the traveller by the dark and forbidding crag of Aden. Yet when this sort of thing has been said so many times of the desert, why should the traveller be made to feel such strangeness and wonder? It is because he has "lived" this dryness for the first time; and now, he understands dryness not as a determined atmospheric humidity, as indicated by thermometer or hygrometer, but as man's way of life.[34] (Watsuji 1961, 43–44; *WTZ* 8:48)

To experience dryness is not to be an object (a person) situated in a landscape with very low humidity like the desert. Rather, to experience dryness is to live in the desert, where the dryness of the air affects the landscape and how plants, animals, and humans live. As Stephan Käufer and Anthony Chemero explain, "Heidegger argues that the fundamental way we have and encounter our world is pre-cognitive and consists of skillful, familiar, disposed, purposive caring" (2015, 58). As humans we are always absorbed in (i.e., "care about") our world, and it is only when we step back from this absorption and adopt an abstract theoretical attitude that we can distinguish between our thoughts and feelings (the internal world) and the objects they are about (the external world). Watsuji adopts this phenomenological viewpoint.

For him, the context or world in which we primordially exist is a cultural context: culture is a set of meaningful activities in which our encounters with other humans and the objects, both natural and artificial always have inherent meaning.

How does culture function as a context from which meanings are derived? Imagine being handed an eight-inch-long piece of metal with multiple tines at the end. When we take hold of it, we know it is a fork and that it is used for eating because that is what we have learned by observing others who share our culture doing with similar objects. Today, it would be hard to find someone to whom one could hand a fork who would not know what it was. But one can imagine a time before mass communication and social media when a person from a culture that used primarily chopsticks could be handed a fork and have no idea what it was for. This is because that person's cultural context does not provide a meaning for a piece of metal eight inches long with tines. It is in this sense that culture discloses certain aspects of how humans experience the world: "In the context of the more concrete ground of human life, [transcendence] reveals itself in the ways of creating communities, and thus in the ways of constructing speech, the method of production, the styles of buildings, and so on. Transcendence, as the structure of human life, must include all these entities"[35] (Watsuji 1961, 12; *WTZ* 8:18). Thus human experience is ecstatic or transcendent in the sense that humans discover themselves within their cultural milieu. As humans, we "discover ourselves" (*jiko hakkensei*; 自己発見性; Watsuji 1961, 14; *WTZ* 8:20) as always already living in an environment that is inherently meaningful, that is, a world in which we generally understand what those around us are doing and what the meaning, use, and importance are of the objects we encounter.

It is important to note that culture is not the only context in which I experience the world and interpret it. Watsuji explains that some of our experience is specific to us—it is an experience of ourselves as an individual. In this case, our experience is constituted by our perception of the body (*shintai no jikaku*: 身体の自覚; Watsuji 1961, 12; *WTZ* 8:18), which takes up space and whose movements unfold in time. But since Watsuji is primarily interested in the social aspects of human existence that he believes European philosophy ignores, he focuses on the structures of human experience that are disclosed by studying cultural experiences.

Watsuji's phenomenological analysis differs from a purely psychological one because he emphasizes that we discover ourselves phenomenologically (as transcendence, ecstasis) in the concrete way that we do things (Watsuji 1961, 14; *WTZ* 8:20)[36] rather than through internal mental states alone. There is thus an objective or intersubjective element to phenomenological analysis that is lacking in a purely psychological one. For instance, Watsuji explains that we do not experience the cold of the air as a temperature of such-and-such degrees Celsius but rather as air that is "refreshing" or "bracing"—that is, cold based on a cultural standard (Watsuji 1961, 14–15; *WTZ* 8:20–21). Watsuji explains,

> Feelings or tempers are to be regarded not merely as mental states but as our way of life. These, moreover, are not feelings that we are free to choose of ourselves, but are imposed on us as pre-determined states. . . . One morning we may find ourselves "in a revived mood." This is interpreted in terms of specific temperature and humidity conditions influencing us externally and inducing internally a revived mental condition. But the facts are quite different, for what we have here is not a mental state but the freshness of the external atmosphere. But the object that is understood in terms of the temperature and the humidity of the atmosphere has not the slightest similarity with the freshness itself. This freshness is a state; it appertains to the atmosphere but it is neither the atmosphere itself nor a property of the atmosphere. It is not that we have certain states imposed on us by the atmosphere; the fact that the atmosphere possesses a state of freshness is that we ourselves feel revived. We discover ourselves, that is, in the atmosphere. But the freshness of the atmosphere is not that of a mental state, as is shown best by the fact that the morning feeling of freshness is embodied and expressed directly in our mutual greetings. We comprehend ourselves in this freshness of the atmosphere, for what is fresh is not our own mental state but the atmosphere itself.[37] (Watsuji 1961, 14–15; *WTZ* 8:20–21)

Experience is thus always "cultural" experience—we interpret our experiences of the world through our language, art, religion, customs, and so on (Watsuji 1961, 7; *WTZ* 8:13).

So now we understand the theoretical justification for Watsuji's interest in culture. Culture discloses certain aspects of human experience (phenomenological analysis) and human existence (ontological analysis). Our experience of the world is always mediated by culture, and the fact that culture has a history (temporal aspect) and is a response to the physical environment and the relations between people (spatial aspect) indicates that these temporal and spatial aspects are basic characteristics of human experience. From an ontological perspective, humans are in some sense individuals with their own private thoughts and feelings, and this consciousness unfolds temporally as a succession of thoughts and feelings. But they are also spatial because they belong to communities that are spread out in space and are made up of many individuals in innumerable relationships.

FROM METHOD TO CULTURAL MILIEU

This first chapter on Watsuji's *Climate and Culture* introduced the theory behind Watsuji's method of analysis. As we have seen, his method uncovers the fundamental structures of human existence that make us social beings. These structures are revealed through a study of the climatic nature of culture. Watsuji derives his method from Heideggerian phenomenology, but he corrects it by placing greater emphasis on the spatial nature of human existence, a modification in part inspired by his study of theories of culture and climate in German Idealism. Watsuji corrects the fault in Heideggerian phenomenology by choosing culture as the topic of phenomenological analysis because it is so clearly a form of social activity that is influenced by the environment—climate.

Having demonstrated that human existence is social and cultural precisely because of these universal features of human existence and experiencing, Watsuji now turns in *Climate and Culture* to describing how climate affects the way that people belonging to different cultures interpret the world around them. As we will see, Watsuji believes that our cultural milieu expresses a particular attitude toward society, our relations with others, and even the physical world in which we life.

Watsuji is also interested in explaining why there are many different cultures in the world. As we recall, the diversity of cultures is another spatial aspect of the phenomenon. The phenomenological method he chose has a tendency to universalize—that is, to generalize about the nature of human experience. After all, the phenomenological structures of human experience and the ontological structures of human existence are meant to be the same for all humans. And yet culture, which is made possible by virtue of these structures, is different everywhere one looks, even within the same locality. Moreover, these differences seem to lead to different philosophical, social, and political traditions. What causes this difference? This is what Watsuji addresses in subsequent chapters of *Climate and Culture*. The short answer, as we will see, is "climate." Climatic differences—geographic differences—result in cultural differences. The reason this is the case is because human existence is fundamentally spatial and temporal, and so human experience is shaped by the physical world around us as it changes through time.

In the next chapter, we will describe Watsuji's exploration of culture as a manifestation of the spatiality of human existence. At the same time, we will identify both Watsuji's tendency to acknowledge cultural pluralism and also to give Japanese culture a special place within the plurality of cultures.

NOTES

1. The author Natsume Sōseki recounts his alienating experiences in England in the preface to his *Theory of Literature* (Natsume 2010, 48).
2. Kuki Shūzō, Watsuji Tetsurō, Tanabe Hajime, Miki Kiyoshi, Nishitani Keiji, to name just a few.
3. There is an excellent French translation of the whole book by Augustin Berque (2011).
4. Watsuji interprets Herder's view as follows: "[What we have studied of Herder's climatic concept of spirit] is that it is based on a concept of nature that does not differentiate between nature and spirit, [and therefore] he greatly emphasized that each people is distinguished by its distinctive values."「ヘルデルの「精神の風土学」は、自然と精神とを区別しない自然の概念にもとづいて、個々の国民の価値個性を極端に力説したものである。」(*WTZ* 8:220). As Sonia Sikka explains, as a pantheist, nature and reality as a whole, as a manifestation of what Herder called "power" (*Kraft*), were the manifestation of God himself (2011, 224). Thus the identification of nature and spirit, of nature and God, meant that the values of each people were itself an expression of God.
5.「従つて我々は生活のあらゆる方面に實現せられた日本の文化を通じてそこに發露した日本精を捕へねばならない。これが日本精への通露である。」(1935, 21).
6.「生ける全體性」(1935, 22).
7.「日本民族としての主體的全體性」(1935, 22). As Dilworth, Viglielmo, and Jacinto Zavala explain, this essay, "a distillation of Watsuji's many volumes of historical research into the history of the Japanese ethical spirit," while it expresses nationalistic ideas, should only be considered "conservative and reactionary... when seen in an anachronistic light." What the essay attempts to express is "an astutely broad viewpoint put forth by Watsuji on both ultra-rightist and ultra-leftist biases," and it attempts to place "the debate in the larger context of Western liberal premises developed through the friction of the French Revolution and the reactive anti-bourgeois sentiments of the Marxists" (1998, 227–228).
8. For an excellent study of Herder's view in this regard, see Sikka (2011).
9.「... 個々の国民の姿をば、人類の究極目的への発展の単なる一過程として、ただ前後継起の秩序においてのみ見るのは、彼の極力排斥するところであった。それは並在の秩序において把捉せられなくてはならない。」
10.「彼は人類が多種多様な姿において地上に現われていながらしかも同一の人類であるということを観察した後に、この同一の人類の地上のあらゆる「ところ」において己れを風土化しているという点に論を導いて行く。まずアジアの草原におけるモンゴールや、沙漠にお

けるアラビア人や、世界の端のカリフォルニア（と言っても今は世界の中心になりかかっているあのカリフォルニアのことであるが）の土人などを、その生ける生活の姿において描写し、そうしてあらゆる国民がその土地と生活の仕方とによって性格づけられていることを、すなわち風土的であることを、示そうとする。」

11. On the relationship between culture and climate in Herder's philosophy, see Sikka (2014, 97–98).

12. Watsuji also cites Kant's criticism of Herder in *Idea for a Universal History with a Cosmopolitan Purpose* (*Ideen zu einer allgemeinen Geschichte in Weltbürgerlicher Absicht* [1784]) and *An Answer to the Question: "What is Enlightenment?"* (*Beantwortung der Frage: Was ist Aufklärung* [1784]).

13. On Herder's Spinozism, see Sikka 201, 95.

14. For similar interpretations, see Karl Ameriks (2009) at 50–51.

15. While Watsuji was critical of Kant's philosophy of history and culture, he did admire Kant's acknowledgment that human experience has certain universal forms (for Kant, sensibility and rationality; for Watsuji, space, time, and their interrelationship). Watsuji's view that human existence is both temporal and spatial and that these elements are expressed in the nature of human existence as betweenness (*aidagara*) is developed in part in conversation with Kant in Watsuji's *Ethics*.

16. There are different interpretations of the goal that Kant considers humanity to be aiming at. Allen Wood interprets Kant's approach in *Idea for a Universal History with a Cosmopolitan Aim* to be truly natural ends (*Naturzwecke*) rather than the actualization of God's intention (see "Kant's Fourth Proposition: The unsociable sociability of human nature" in Oksenberg Rorty and Schmidt 2009, 113–114). For a slightly different view, namely that Kant understood the purpose of nature to be the purpose of creation itself, see Eckart Förster (2009, 199).

17. For recent articles interpreting the significance of Fichte's essay, see Breazeale and Rockmore (2016).

18. Fichte wrote,

"Dies nun ist in höherer vom Standpunkte der Ansicht einer geistigen Welt überhaupt genommener Bedeutung des Worts, ein Volk: das Ganze der in Gesellschaft miteinander fortlebenden, und sich aus sich selbst immerfort natürlich und geistig erzeugenden Menschen, das insgesamt unter einem gewissen besondern Gesetze der Entwicklung des Göttlichen aus ihm steht. Die Gemeinsamkeit dieses besondern Gesetzes ist es, was in der ewigen Welt, und eben darum auch in der zeitlichen, diese Menge zu einem natürlichen, und von sich selbst durchdrungenen Ganzen verbindet" (Fichte 1978, 128).

In English,

"So, taken in the higher sense of the word, when viewed from the standpoint of a spiritual world, a people is this: the totality of men living together in society and continually producing themselves out of themselves both naturally and spiritually; which collectively stands under a certain special law that governs the development of the divine within it. The universality of this special law is what binds this mass of men into a natural whole, interpenetrated by itself, in the eternal world and, for that very reason, in the temporal world also" (Fichte 2008, 103).

19.「国民は神的なるものの自己開展におけるある特殊な法則の下に立っている。この特殊な法則をともにすることが、永遠の世界において、従ってまた時間的な世界において、人間の群れを一つの自然的な緊密な全体に結合させる。またこの根源的なものの発展の法則が、一つの民族の国民性と呼ばるるものを徹頭徹尾規定するのである。(Fichte, Schriften, VII, S. 381) かかる法則は、それがあるということはわかるが、しかしその下に立っている個人には決して概念的に明らかにされ得るものでない。国民あるいは民族がその統一を自覚するのは「歴史」によってである。共同の行動や苦悩、すなわち、支配者、土地、戦争、勝利、敗北等を共同にすること、それが人間の群れを民族として自覚させる。しかしこれなき場合にも、ドイツ民族のごとく、形而上的存在の力によって民族の統一の概念を保ったものもある。これはドイツの国民性の著しい特徴とせられている。しからば民族の特性は超歴史的の意義を持つことになるであろう。それは歴史的展開の内に具体化せられるが、しかしそれ自身の根拠を形而上的な精神的自然の内に有しているのである。フィヒテ自身はこれを風土として理解していないが、しかし我々の風土の問題はまさに形而上的な精神的自然の内に、従って彼自身のいわゆる「神的なるものの特殊法則」として、存するのである。」

20. "Spirit" means many things in Hegelian philosophy. Peter C. Hodgson has a very useful summary of the different levels on which "spirit" is used as a technical term: the spirit of the individual (*Geist*), the spirit of "a people or nation" (*Volksgeist*), the "world spirit" (*Weltgeist*), and "absolute spirit" (*absoluter Geist*) (Hodgson 2012, 6–7). Watsuji draws on the notion of *Volksgeist* in his discussion of Hegel's philosophy of cultural geography (Paetzold 2008, 167). For a discussion of the adoption of the term "spirit" by the Neo-Kantians in their philosophy of culture, see Luft (2015, 4, 21).

21.「個々の民族の全体性は直接的な自然性を現わす。それが地理的及び風土的規定である。かく規定された民族はそれぞれの精神生活の特殊な発展段階において存在し、その段階の中でのみ己れを把捉する。そこで人倫的精神が、「並在」及び「前後継起」の秩序における一定の規定の下に、個々の個体として自己を現わしたもの、それが民族だということになる。言い換えればそれは「特殊な民族としての精神」なのである。このような特定の民族精神はその特殊原理に規定された彼自身の現実の発展、すなわち「歴史」を持つのであるが、しかしそれは限定された精神であるというまさにその理由によって、普遍的な世界史に移って行く。」Watsuji is here interpreting what Hegel writes in his *Encyclopedia of the Philosophical Sciences in Outline* at §442–449 (Hegel 1990).

22. For a similar modern criticism and a review of similar criticisms by Hegel's contemporaries, see Bernasconi (2000).

23.「我々はヘーゲルのごとく欧州人を「選民」とする世界史を是認することができない。欧州人以外の諸国民を奴隷視するのはすべての人の自由の実現ではない。世界史は風土的に異なる諸国民にそれぞれその場所を与え得なくてはならない。」

24. For an explanation of the importance of actual concrete events in history to Hegel's theory of history, see Bubner (1991).

25. For a good explanation of the role of the idea of philosophy as the absolute in Hegelian philosophy, see Bubner (2003, Chapter 6, esp. at 129 ff).

26. It is important to note at the outset that Watsuji's interpretation of Heideggerian phenomenology is potentially problematic, especially for experts of Heideggerian philosophy. For examples of such a criticism, see Liederbach (2012) and Davis (2013).

27. For other works on Heideggerian ethics, see Olafson (1998) and Vogel (1994). For an interpretation of Heideggerian spatiality, see Dreyfus (1995, 128–162).

28. For useful interpretations of "betweenness," see McCarthy (2017) and Davis (2013).

29. 「ここに人間と呼ばれるのは単に「人」（anthrōpos, homo, homme, man, Mensch）ではない。それは「人」でもあるが、しかし同時に人々の結合あるいは共同態としての社会でもある。．．．人間を真に根本的に把捉するためには、個であるとともにまた全であるごとき人間存在の根本構造を押えなくてはならぬ．．．。」

30. 「．．．人間は単に一般的に「過去」を背負うのではなくして特殊な「風土的過去」を背負うのであり、…この特殊的実質としての「風土」は、単なる風土として歴史と独立にあり、その後に実質として歴史の内に入り来るというのではない。それは初めより「歴史的風土」なのである。一言にして言えば、人間の歴史的風土的二重構造においては、歴史は風土的歴史であり、風土は歴史的風土である。」

31. I am not using "ontological" and "phenomenological" in a technical sense. By "ontological" I mean that space and time are structures of human existence. By "phenomenological" I mean that space and time are forms of human experiencing.

32. On transcendence in Heideggerian philosophy, see Keller (1999) at 3. For an example of Heidegger's description of being-in-the-world as a form of Dasein's transcendence, see Heidegger (1996, 162).

33. 「．．．主観客観の区別、従ってそれ自身単独に存立する「我々」と「寒気」との区別は一つの誤解である。寒さを感ずるとき、我々自身はすでに外気の寒冷のもとに宿っている。我々自身が寒さにかかわるということは、我々自身が寒さの中へ出ているということにほかならぬのである。かかる意味で我々自身の有り方は、ハイデッガーが力説するように、「外に出ている」(ex-sistere) ことを、従って志向性を、特徴とする。」

34. 「アデンの陰惨な山は旅行者に対して沙漠の本質を「乾燥」として開示する。このことは沙漠について語る限り多くの人々の言い古したことである。にもかかわらず旅行者をして事新しく驚異を感ぜしめるのはなぜであるか。それは彼が初めて「乾燥」を生活したからである。乾燥は湿度計寒暖計によって示さるる空気の一定の湿度ではなくして、人間の存在の仕方だからである。」

35. 「．．．一層具体的な地盤たる人間存在にとっては、それは共同態の形成の仕方、意識の仕方、従って言語の作り方、さらには生産

の仕方や家屋の作り方等々において現われてくる。人間の存在構造としての超越はこれらすべてを含まなくてはならぬ。」

36. This distinction between psychology and phenomenology evokes the distinction Edmund Husserl makes between the methods of these two disciplines in his "Vienna Lecture" (Husserl 1970, 294–299).

37. 「このような気持ち、気分、機嫌などは、単に心的状態とのみ見らるべきものではなくして、我々の存在の仕方である。しかもそれは我々自身が自由に選んだものではなく、「すでに定められた」有り方として我々に背負わされている。... 我々がある朝「爽やかな気分」において己れを見いだす。これは空気の温度と湿度とのある特定の状態が外から影響して内に爽やかな心的状態を引き起こしたとして説明せられている現象であるが、しかし具体的体験においては、事情は全く異なっている。そこにあるのは心的状態ではなくして空気の爽やかさである。が、空気の温度や湿度として認識せられている対象は、この爽やかさそのものと何の似寄りも持たない。爽やかさは「あり方」であって「もの」でもなければ「ものの性質」でもない。それは空気というものに属してはいるが、空気自身でもなく空気の性質でもない。だから我々は空気というものによって一定のあり方を背負わされるのではない。空気が「爽やかさ」の有り方を持つことは取りも直さず我々自身が爽やかであることなのである。すなわち我々が空気において我々自身を見いだしているのである。しかしまた空気の爽やかさは心的状態の爽やかさではない。それを最もよく示すものは朝の爽やかな気分が直接に我々の間の挨拶として表現せられるという事実である。我々は空気の爽やかさにおいて我々自身を了解している。爽やかなのは己れの心的状態ではなくして空気なのである。」

Chapter 4

Watsuji's Three Climatic and Cultural Zones

Anti-essentialist and Deterministic Readings

CLIMATE AND CULTURE: SEPARATING ESSENTIALIST AND NON-ESSENTIALIST STRANDS IN WATSUJI'S THOUGHT

In the previous chapter, we described Watsuji's phenomenological method, the reason he adopted it, and the justification for applying it to a study of the relationship between culture and climate. Watsuji wished to capture both the temporal and spatial aspects of human experience but also correct the tendency he recognized in European phenomenology to place too much emphasis on temporality and the individual while neglecting spatiality and the social. Watsuji had not only theoretical reasons to draw out the spatial and social aspects of human existence; he also believed that Japanese culture placed greater emphasis on them. Indeed, the relationship between Japanese culture, nature, and the change of the seasons is a long-standing one which surges and recedes with the times (Arisaka 2017).[1] To make this link clear, Watsuji chose to investigate the relationship between climate and culture: climate as a geographic phenomenon is clearly spatial; and culture is spatial insofar as it is the expression of how humans relate to one another. Finally, Watsuji wished to bolster the importance of his observations about the spatial nature of human existence by connecting his analysis to a long line of German philosophers, including Kant, Herder, Fichte, and Hegel, who he believed recognized the importance of the spatiality of human existence. In so doing, he positioned his study as an important contribution to this tradition, and he elevated the importance of Japanese culture to a status on par with the modern societies of his day. In this chapter, we will examine how Watsuji connected his study of Japanese culture to this tradition by developing from his observations of Japanese culture a general theory of the relationship between climate and culture.

In *Climate and Culture*, Watsuji extends his analysis of the relationship between Japanese climate and culture to other cultures to demonstrate that the spatial element of human existence, and thus climate, are important for understanding every culture. Unfortunately, this kind of generalization can lead to problematic geographic determinism,[2] and it introduced elements of Japanese nationalism and chauvinism into *Climate and Culture* (Janz 2011, 176), elements which are carried over into his later work. Watsuji vacillates between considering culture something that is determined by nonhuman forces and something that is created through the interactions between human beings and between humans and their environment. When he swings to the first extreme, he lapses into geographic determinism; swinging to the other, he provides an account of culture that makes it highly contingent, the result of particular humans engaged in documenting and defining it.

As I explained in chapters 2 and 3, I do not intend to make a definitive judgment about Watsuji's political views or the politics that his cultural philosophy supports. Instead, I hope to identify in Watsuji's philosophy aspects that celebrate cultural difference and cultural dynamism and to separate them from aspects that can lead to cultural essentialism and chauvinism. I adopt this approach because I believe that the non-essentialist aspects of his cultural philosophy have resonance today (Bein 2017; Janz 2011). Thus my goal in this chapter will be to emphasize those aspects of Watsuji's analysis of climate and culture that support a dynamic and fluid account of culture that acknowledges diversity and the importance of intercultural interaction and avoids universalistic and essentialist tendencies.

THE THREE CULTURAL TYPES

In Chapters 2 and 3 of *Climate and Culture*, Watsuji provides examples of how human experience is influenced by culture and how cultural practices are influenced by climate, which are both a historical and a spatial phenomenon. Following the tradition of German romanticism and idealism studied in the last chapter, Watsuji identifies a limited set of climatic "types" and then demonstrates how these types influence the culture of the people who live in these climates. According to him, the three main climatic types (monsoon, desert, and meadow) play a constitutive role in the cultures that develop in regions of each type. As Watsuji puts it, climate gives rise to culture as a "mode of being of humans"[3] (*ningen no arikata*; 人間の有り方; Watsuji 1961, 40; *WTZ* 8:45).

We are not going to review in detail Watsuji's characterization of each of the three climatic types. Instead, we will focus on his understanding of the relationship between culture and climate that we have only sketched in outline in the previous chapter, deepening our understanding of how Watsuji understands the spatial and temporal aspects of both. According to Watsuji, culture is the response of a group of people to the conditions in the landscape in which they live (spatial aspect) that has developed throughout the group's history in the region (temporal aspect). This response influences how they interpret their experience in the world, which they then express in cultural ideals, philosophies, practices, and art.

SPATIAL ASPECTS OF CLIMATE AND CULTURE

The various climatic types are not just determined by the weather in a given region; Watsuji adopts a broader meaning of "climate" that incorporates the complete spatial environment in which a group of people live—that is, a landscape. He explains, "I use our word Fu-do [sic, 風土], which means literally, 'Wind and Earth,' as a general term for the natural environment of a given land, its climate, its weather, the geological and productive nature of the soil, its topographic and scenic features. The ancient term for this concept was Sui-do, which might be literally translated as 'Water and Earth' [水土]. Behind these terms lies the ancient view of Nature as man's environment compounded of earth, water, fire, and wind"[4] (Watsuji 1961, 1; WTZ 8:7). The landscape influences how we experience the world and how we think about the things and people we encounter.[5] As an example of this influence, Watsuji uses the phenomenon of "humidity." Humidity, he explains, is more than air saturated with a particular percentage of water; rather, it is a way of living—a form of human existence—of people living in a region with a higher level of moisture in the air. He writes,

> What I intended from the first by the word humidity was not simply a meteorological phenomenon but rather a principle governing man's spiritual make-up and acting as a dividing line in the matter of humanistic, intellectual or contemplative approaches to life between on the one hand the intensely strong-willed and practical way of life of the desert with its product of a faith in a stern god in man's likeness and, on the other, the highly emotional and contemplative attitude to life of the monsoon which created the belief that all life is one.[6] (Watsuji 1961, 204; WTZ 8:201)

Humidity is not just a physical feature of the environment; it denotes a way of responding to and going about in it.

Another example that Watsuji uses is the phenomenon of the cold. The cold is not something abstract such as the maximum or minimum temperature in a weather report. Rather, the cold is a set of specific, contextual experiences such as the feeling of being pierced by a cold wind or crowd around a fireplace or brazier for warmth. For those of us who live in cold climates, this is self-evident. For instance, when we check the weather report, we are not interested in the ambient temperature of the air but rather the "windchill" factor, which captures the feeling of cold, rather than the scientific measure of it. In other words, we do not experience climate as an objective phenomenon separate from us (Watsuji 1961, 4; *WTZ* 8:9–10). Rather, climate is experienced in the midst of our involvement in everyday life: we feel the cold wind while waiting at a bus stop, and so we huddle in the shelter to avoid its bite.

Climate is not solely something that we experience as individuals: it has a social aspect. And this is what culture is—ways that we have in common with others for feeling together the cold, the heat, or humidity and shared ways of responding to them. As Watsuji explains, "We feel the same cold in common"[7] (Watsuji 1961, 4; *WTZ* 8:10). Our cultural response to climate is not just evident in its external manifestations such as clothing or forms of shelter; it frames the way that we think about the world. According to Watsuji, people who have grown up in a monsoon region have a tendency to regard the natural world (and therefore the human world) fatalistically since they live in a place where the fight against nature will always result in the triumph of nature over humans (Watsuji 1961, 206; *WTZ* 8:203). Watsuji explains that the monsoon region is characterized by "the violence of nature. Humidity often combines with heat to assail man with violent deluges of rain of great force, savage storm winds, floods and droughts. This power is so vast that man is obliged to abandon hope of resistance and is forced into mere passive resignation"[8] (Watsuji 1961, 19; *WTZ* 8:25). Those who live in a monsoon area are defeated by nature, and so they become docile. But this is not a resignation to the threat that nature poses to life; instead, it is an acknowledgment of the overabundance of nature, which is full of life. This resignation of those in the monsoon region is therefore not the same as the resignation of those who belong to a desert culture, for whom nature is a killing force rather than a life-giving force (Watsuji 1961, 19–20; *WTZ* 8:25).

In contrast, those who live in the meadowlands where the climate is mild see the world differently. Watsuji explains,

> No doubt no-one could deny that in the course of the association between man and nature, natural characteristics come to be exemplified as features of man's life. When man first discovered himself standing in confrontation with nature—the world beyond him—man made nature's features his own. The bright and shadeless clarity and the aridity of Greece's "eternal noon" presently turned into a type of thinking in which man revealed his all. Nature's docility—the warm, humidity-free atmosphere, the tender pastures, the smooth limestone—presently

turned into the Greek style of clothing, with its sense of freedom and its carefree scorn of the need for protection against nature; it turned into, again, the nude contest, the love of the statue of the naked body. This does not mean that natural phenomena gave rise to distinctive effects on the soul of man as if it were a piece of blank paper, for man did not and could not live thus in isolation from his natural environment. The brightness of Greece's "eternal noon" was from the beginning the clarity of the Greek; the method in nature was from the first the rational inclination in the Greek. Hence the characteristics of nature should be understood as related to the spiritual make-up of those who live with that nature.[9] (Watsuji 1961, 203–204; *WTZ* 8:200–201)

Watsuji is proposing that our interactions with our environment—not our physical environment alone but also the modes of responding to it that have developed over time such as our manner of dress and abode—can affect the way we perceive, interpret, and structure our thoughts about the things with which we come into contact. This is why "music" for a middle-class European in the 1920s might mean classical music, for an American it could mean swing or jazz, while a Japanese might think of the drumming at folk festivals or *enka*, the popular music of the era.

Again, culture is not just limited to cultural practices and products but includes ways of structuring society. According to Watsuji, those who grow up in the desert tend to cooperate with those who are part of their in-group (Watsuji uses the term "tribe") while being hostile toward those from other groups who are in competition with the in-group for scarce resources (Watsuji 1961, 49–50; *WTZ* 8:54). Almost every culture places different value on insiders and outsiders, but the particular form that this takes—feelings, attitudes, and so on—is reinforced by the climate in which people live. Climate also penetrates how we think: those who grow up in hot places do not invent Santa Claus, nor do a fisher and a shepherd see nature in the same way (*WTZ* 8:217). As Watsuji explains, "The way of life and the mindset of each people forcefully penetrates their spirits"[10] (ibid.). Climate even affects our imagination: "Just as the particularity of 'place' (*tokoro*) signifies a particularity of mental structure, it also indicates the particularity of art and of the imaginative power of the artist"[11] (*WTZ* 8:201).

Of course, he does not go so far as to argue that everyone living in the same environment experiences the world in exactly the same way. Differences arise because a landscape has many features: different levels of humidity in different microclimates, flat and hilly areas, rocky and smooth regions, and so on.[12] Thus within the group of people who live on meadowland, a person who has grown up along a river or stream will have a subtly different way of interpreting the world than a person who has grown up on land without a waterway. This may manifest itself in its simplest form as a tendency to look

90   *Chapter 4*

for or identify particular kinds of wildlife around rivers that a relative without riparian experience might overlook.

A phenomenological analysis of climate reveals that it is a spatial phenomenon. But this spatiality does not just refer to the fact that climate is geographic and physical. Rather, the way that we experience climate reveals that humans are always experiencing the world in the context of a landscape. The way that we experience climate is not abstract or scientific—the cold is not an experience of air below 0 degrees Celsius but rather the cold wind that pierces our protective layers of clothing and causes us to greet others with "It's cold out there, keep warm!" Humans respond to the cold through cultural practices, creatively in music and art, and in the way that they reflect on the world and give it meaning. The fact that cultural practices are a response to climate indicates that culture is one way in which the spatial climatic dimension of human experience and existence is disclosed. However, culture provides evidence not just of the spatiality of human existence, but also of its temporal nature, to which we now turn.

TEMPORAL ASPECTS OF CLIMATE AND CULTURE

Although Watsuji emphasizes the spatial aspects of human existence and experience that are disclosed in the relationship between climate and culture, he does not wish to overemphasize space at the expense of time; this would be to simply commit the opposite error that Watsuji attributes to Heidegger. Rather, Watsuji acknowledges that climate and culture are also historical (temporal) phenomena. It is for this reason that he labels his theory of culture "historical-climatic" (*rekishiteki-fūdoteki*; 歴史的風土的). He writes, "Human existence possesses the particular structure of the historical-climatic. This particularity is revealed in the various types of climate (*fūdo*; 風土) that can be distinguished. Not only is climate historical-climatic from the get go, the various types of climate are at the same time types of history" [author's translation] (*KSZ* 8:161).[13] The three climatic "types" or "zones" that he identifies have a history—they emerged and evolved over time as people lived in a particular landscape and adapted to it.

Temporality, expressed as the history of a culture, is what allows cultures to change, to interact with each other, and to be exported to other regions with a different landscape. Watsuji explains,

> Naturally, historical influences can be carried over to other "places" (*tokoro*). For instance, the desert way of life that gave birth to the Old Testament took hold of Europe for a thousand years, while the very same desert [gave birth to] the Koran, which exerts a strong influence in present-day India. [These

examples] clearly illustrate that the particularity of "place" (*tokoro*) is not absolute.[14] (*WTZ* 8:201) [author's translation]

History is just as important as space (the physical environment) for shaping human experience. Indeed, the historical development of culture—culture's capacity to change and evolve over time—is proof that climate is not alone the sole cause of culture. Watsuji writes,

> I have attempted to interpret European culture in the light of its meadow climate. But I do not claim that this climate was the sole source of European culture. History and climate act as the shield and buckler of culture; the two are quite inseparable, for there is no historical event that does not possess its climatic character, nor is there climatic phenomenon that is without its historical component. So, if we can discover climate within a historical event, then we can also read history within climatic phenomena. All that I have attempted to do is to examine these two factors, while restricting my attention primarily to climate.[15] (Watsuji 1961, 116–117; *WTZ* 8:119)

We are now in a position to understand what culture is in Watsuji's *Climate and Culture*. Culture involves ways of thinking, of doing things, of creating and interacting that respond to the physical environment in which we live. Culture also changes over time because climate changes and people interact both within a culture and between cultures. Climate does not determine specific cultural practices; these practices are historically and spatially contingent: they are responses to objective aspects of the landscape, but they also evolve over time. In other words, cultural practices are nothing more than fortuitous manifestations of the spatial and temporal elements of climate. Finally, because our culture is climatic, climate affects how people interpret their experience of the world and perhaps even the experience itself.

We have seen in a general way that culture discloses both the spatial (climatic) and historical (temporal) nature of human existence and experience. In the next section, we will probe Watsuji's theory of culture and climate further to evaluate the degree to which the charge of geographic determinism is justified. The eventual goal of this probing will be to assess the positive and negative consequences of this theory, that is, the degree to which the problematic essentialism and nationalism with which it has been charged is warranted.

NONDETERMINISTIC ELEMENTS OF WATSUJI'S THEORY OF CLIMATE AND CULTURE

One of the goals of this chapter was to separate out the useful and interesting elements of Watsuji's theory of climate from the problematic ones. I contend that the former are those that first appeared in *Pilgrimages*. A less deterministic interpretation of Watsuji's *Climate and Culture* emerges when we read it in the context of his earlier work. The similarities between these two texts will help us to see what is innovative about *Climate and Culture*, namely the phenomenological method, while at the same time identifying what is shared between them, namely, a view of culture as flexible, malleable, and changeable—that is, an anti-essentialist notion of culture. In *Pilgrimages*, it is clear that Watsuji is creating Japanese culture—or at least a version of it. In light of this, it becomes easier to read *Climate and Culture* as a similarly inventive work that deploys new philosophical tools available from Watsuji's study of Heideggerian phenomenology.

As we recall, in *Pilgrimages*, Watsuji characterized culture as follows:

1. it is malleable and porous—open to influences from other cultures;
2. it is contingent—the meanings of objects and practices depends on the interpretation given to them by a cultural interpreter;
3. it is experiential—culture is not just objects and practices but also the feelings and emotions that they evoke;
4. it is social—the interpretation that we give to cultural objects and practices is influenced by the people in whose company we experience them.

A similar characterization of culture also emerges in *Climate and Culture*. As in *Pilgrimages*, Watsuji accepts that cultures interact and change over time. For instance, he describes the spread of messianic religions (Judaism, Christianity, and Islam) from the deserts to other climatic zones (Watsuji 1961, 52; *WTZ* 8:65; and *WTZ* 8:201). He continues to characterize culture experientially by describing it as a way of experiencing the world: those who share a culture share attitudes, ways of thinking, and ways of doing things. Finally, Watsuji delves in greater depth into the social nature of culture, which he uses to uncover the conditions for the possibility of a shared cultural life: the spatial and temporal nature of human existence.

However, we cannot ignore the essentialist and deterministic elements of Watsuji's study of the relationship between climate and culture. As we will see, Watsuji presumes that his standpoint is objective: despite his lack of cosmopolitan experience, he readily imputes to various cultures ways of feeling, thinking, and doing without letting people from those cultures speak for themselves. He finds support for his approach in the works of European philosophers that inspired him such as Herder, Kant, Fichte, and Hegel. However, Watsuji's failure to question the limitations of his own position as theorist and observer is what leads to many problematic generalizations and the tendency to regard climate as the primary factor in shaping culture (Berque 2011, 22; 2012, 289).

Is a non-essentialist reading of *Climate and Culture* warranted? There is evidence that Watsuji considered the "positive" features of culture listed previously to be key features of it: in his postscript to the 1948 edition of the book, he laments that he had not read Lucien Febvre's *La terre et l'évolution humaine* before writing *Climate and Culture*. As Augustin Berque points out, Febvre's work is avowedly anti-determinist (Berque 2011, 20),[16] and so the fact that Watsuji sees similarities between his work and Febvre's suggests that his principal intention is anti-essentialist and anti-determinist.

Febvre's approach to history and geography can be gleaned from *La terre et l'évolution humaine. Introduction géographique à l'histoire*, where he makes clear his rejection of geographic determinism:

> For a long time, we have considered human societies as appendices, so to speak, to the vegetable and animal worlds, [which are divided] into large climatic-botanical zones that are strictly dependent on meteorological phenomena. But these zones into which we have simply inserted humans as, so to speak, additions, are not meant to be tyrannical—they determine nothing: this bears repeating over and over and it is to be demonstrated in every possible way. [Author's translation](1949, 216)

I do not intend to simply assimilate Watsuji's view of the relationship between climate and culture to that of Febvre. But my interpretation of Watsuji's book will take its impetus from Watsuji's enthusiasm for the French geographer, and initially propose a non-determinist reading of *Climate and Culture*.

SIMILARITIES BETWEEN *PILGRIMAGES TO THE ANCIENT TEMPLES IN NARA* AND *CLIMATE AND CULTURE*

In this subsection, we will compare *Pilgrimages* and *Climate and Culture* with an eye to drawing out the similarities and parallels between the characterizations of culture in both books. To begin, Watsuji refers to many of the same cultures in both works. As we saw in Chapter 2, at the very beginning of *Pilgrimages*, Watsuji records his impressions of the Ajanta wall paintings, located in Aurangabad, India, and which date to between the second century BCE and 480 CE. Much of the description of the Indian personality in *Climate and Culture* reproduces Watsuji's similar description in *Pilgrimages* of the culture that created these impressive painting. In the earlier book, it is very clear that Watsuji was speculating about the Indians who created the paintings (*Pilgrimages*, 4), trying as best he could to imagine the character and emotional makeup of the artists. In light of the speculative approach in

Pilgrimages, it becomes easier to interpret Watsuji's treatment of India as an exemplar of a culture of the monsoon season as similarly speculative. Indeed, the evidence he uses to justify in *Climate and Culture* to sketch the Indian character is more or less the same as in *Pilgrimages*: for instance, the theory of transmigration (discussed in *Pilgrimages* via the *Jataka* tales [stories of the past lives of the Buddha]) and Indian art are topics in both books. Of course, there are also differences in the portrayals of Indian culture: in *Climate and Culture*, Watsuji engages in a lengthier discussion of the *Rig Veda* (Watsuji 1961, 27–32; cf Watsuji 2012, 60), and he provides a survey of classical Indian philosophy (Watsuji 1961, 32–36), two elements absent from *Pilgrimages*. He also introduces some entirely new material such as his discussion of modern applications of the doctrine of ahimsa (nonviolence) adopted by Indians to resist colonial domination, and which he uses to support his claim that monsoon culture tends toward docility and passivity (Watsuji 1961, 38).

In both books, Watsuji depicts Indian culture as dynamic: it evolves over time through interactions with other cultures. Recall, for instance, his discussion in *Pilgrimages* of the changes in Indian culture due to interaction with the Greeks, which included innovations in sculpture and theatre, eventually leading to the development of Japanese *gigaku* (伎楽), a form of mixed dance and theatre in which performers wear masks (Watsuji 2012, Chapter 10). In *Climate and Culture*, Watsuji makes similar observations about the transformations that result from intercultural exchange, although he now casts these as interactions between people from different cultural types (the meadowland in the case of the Greeks and the monsoon in the case of the Indian subcontinent). What makes intercultural exchange and cultural transformation possible, Watsuji explains, is the fact that we all share elements from every climatic and cultural zone. Thus Watsuji observes that as Buddhism traveled from India to China and Japan, it drew out of the latter the "Indian" aspect of their spirit (Watsuji 1961, 37).[17] Moreover, Watsuji recognizes the possibility of overcoming one's cultural tendencies, although doing so can be a slow process (Watsuji 1961, 38–39).[18] Interestingly, the precondition to overcoming these tendencies, Watsuji explains, is becoming aware of them and of their climatic nature (ibid.). The possibility of intercultural exchange and of self-conscious self-transformation are vestiges of the fluid notion of culture that Watsuji first adopted in *Pilgrimages* and that continued to influence his thinking in *Climate and Culture*.

Supporting the anti-essentialist reading of *Climate and Culture* is evidence in the text that Watsuji acknowledged that climate was not the sole factor that affects how people think about the world: for instance, social structure also plays an important role. In discussing the desert personality type, Watsuji explains that the people of the desert are influenced by their organization into tribes as much as they are by their physical environment. He notes,

> The livelihood of the tribe reflects this struggle against both nature and man. Man could not exist only by individualism. Since it is this unity of the tribe that in the outset renders possible the being of the individual, loyalty to the whole and submission to the general will are indispensable. And at the same time the fate of the individual depends upon the action of the whole. The defeat of the tribe spells the death of the individual. So every member of the whole must exert every last ounce of his strength and valour. A never-failing straining of the will, with never a moment's thought of yielding, is essential if man in the desert is to stay alive; he can afford no meek docility.[19] (Watsuji 1961, 50; WTZ 8:54)

The existence of a desert nomad depends on tribal organization and the opposition between tribes as much it does on the dry, arid, inhospitable desert. Thus climate alone does not determine culture—culture also emerges through interactions between people and the forms of social organization that they develop over time.

Similar reflections are to be found in the section of the text on the meadow region, the climate type that characterizes Europe. According to Watsuji, European culture is rooted in the Mediterranean landscape and Greek culture, which evolved and changed as it transported further from Greece. To illustrate this point, he uses the example of the spread of Greek crafts such as metalworking, cloth production, pottery, and so on, which brought economic success as they traveled further and further from their origin by means of regional trade (Watsuji 1961, 86–88; WTZ 8:89–90). He concludes on this point: "So this pattern of polis life, built more and more round a core of skilled technical labour, came to dominate the Mediterranean, and was to become a potent factor in guiding the destinies of Europe"[20] (Watsuji 1961, 88; WTZ 8:90).

Also, because Watsuji's concept of climate is not purely geographic but includes social and cultural elements, people can transfer a particular climatic-cultural outlook from one region to another through migration:

> Man in the desert has thus acquired a unique socio-historical nature. But at this point, we should remember that the desert is not just a land-mass itself, it is a very real socio-historical factor. So even if, in a spatial sense, man can leave behind the desert as a piece of land, he cannot leave it and its effects in the sense of its being a socio-historical entity. To be able to leave it, he would need to develop socially and historically into a different person. Even in the event of such development, he does not reject but in fact retains his past. If desert man chose out a site blessed with a rich supply of water and turned farmer, this would merely be the development of the man of the desert; it would not be the

development of, or transformation into, another person.[21] (Watsuji 1961, 50–51; WTZ 8:54–55)

Watsuji continues this theme by discussing the transportation of the desert culture to the Middle East, North Africa, India, and Europe as a result of the migration of Jewish and Muslim groups (Watsuji 1961, 51–56; WTZ 8:55–59). As well, the growth of Christianity, with its roots in Judaism, spread desert elements across the world. Of course, European Christianity involved a mixing of these original elements with those of the "meadow" climate, which introduced the softening influences of love that gave rise to the "meadowland" cult of the Virgin Mary (Watsuji 1961, 61; he returns to the subject at 112–113). He writes,

> The dialectic of the synthesis of humidity and dryness could be termed such in the matter of the structural connection of world culture. Again, the facts of cultural history can be interpreted in this light. For example, when Paul's Christianity, with its Jewish content, was growing up in the European world, although there was a rejection of the dryness of Judaism, the product of the desert, the moral passion of the prophets came to be more and more an integral part. And at the same time, in that the dampness that is not found in the desert became the feature of Christianity in Europe, the gentleness of the religion of love grew very strong. It would not be untrue to say that the worship of the Virgin Mary is much more of monsoon than of desert pattern. This characteristic, the synthesis of the humid and the dry, is not exhaustively explicable in terms only of historical development. It could be claimed that the latter is based, in the case of Europe, on the personality of the European; but when we call this personality European, we are already speaking in terms of climate. (Watsuji 1961, 61)

We see here the synonymy between human attitudes and ideas and climatic patterns: the transformation of religious ideals as they travel from the desert to other regions can be understood in terms of climate as the intermixing of climatic-cultural types.

As we have seen, Watsuji acknowledges that it is not only geographic climate but also social structure (such as the tribal organization of desert societies) shape human experience and ideas. And as people migrate, they both carry with them climatic patterns that evolve and change in new landscapes and through encounters with others. These patterns are embodied in culture, which is the dynamic and changeable form that relationships between people take; culture is not solely determined by geography and the natural environment. In other words, culture is both climatic *and* social. Watsuji writes, "I have attempted to indicate the structure of man of the desert. The desert is characterized by dryness and it is this dryness that first sets up the relationship of opposition and struggle between man and the world and, second, fosters the individual's absolute submission to the whole" (Watsuji 1961, 56; *WTZ* 8:54–55). A desert culture is as much a response to the social organization of desert nomads in tribes as it is a response to the harsh physical environment.

Finally, Watsuji emphasizes in *Climate and Culture* that it is possible for a person belonging to one climatic zone to come to understand how those from another zone think. There are two steps to this process: self-awareness, which can lead to an understanding of cultural difference. The first step in understanding the culture of others involves understanding ourselves, and climate can play an important role in this process: when we travel to an area with a new climate to which we are not accustomed, we learn things about ourselves that we could not have learned had we stayed at home. This self-understanding provides us the opportunity for insight into the lives of others who, though different from us, are perfectly adapted to their own landscape and climate. In this way, a person not raised in a desert climate can come to know what life in the desert is like because she has experienced the opposite—rain.

To illustrate the first step, which involves self-awareness, Watsuji explains how a person who has grown up in the desert can awaken to his own nature by experiencing intense rain: "His awakening to himself is usually realised through the agency of another. This being so, awareness of himself might perhaps be most forcefully effected in the case of the man of the desert if he were exposed to a long and steady downpour of rain"[22] (Watsuji 1961, 41; *WTZ* 8:45). At first it may seem puzzling that it is through an alien experience that we come to know ourselves. But Watsuji goes on to explain that alien experiences uncover both our own limits, limits of which we could not have been aware unless we experience new and different environments, and hitherto hidden aspects of ourselves that respond to the foreignness of rain. He explains,

> If climatic conditioning has affected every part of mankind and has given to each part its own peculiar merits it is just from this that we can be made conscious of our own weaknesses and learn from one another. This is again the means by which climatic limitation can be surmounted. Neglect of nature does not mean to surmount nature. This is merely lack of awareness within climatic limitation. However, climatic distinctions do not disappear as a result of the surmounting of limitations through awareness of them. The opposite is the case, for it is precisely by this recognition that their distinctiveness is created. In one sense, a meadow land may well be heaven on earth, but we cannot turn our own land, wherever it may be, into a land of the meadow type. We can, however, acquire the meadow character and with this our own typhoon character assumes fresh and broader aspects; for when we discover this Greek clarity in ourselves

and begin to nourish reason the significance of our own distinctive "perception" or "temper" becomes all the more vital. With this, the realisation of a suprarational reason sweeps over us with the force of one of our own typhoons.[23] (Watsuji 1961, 117–118; *WTZ* 8:119–120)

Experiencing climates and cultures different from our own help us to realize the limits of our own ways of thinking and our ability to learn new ways of thinking and living.

According to Watsuji, it follows from the fact that we come to know ourselves through new experiences that new experiences can also provide us insight into the cultures of others: if the rain helps the desert dweller understand what it means to be a man of the desert, it must be because the rain gives us insight into other ways of living and thinking. Thus a person not raised in the desert can also come to know the desert milieu by going to the desert. There, the nondesert dweller will come to know the desert concretely as a phenomenon of human existence *and* at the same time come to know that her native milieu is not the desert (Watsuji 1961, 41; *WTZ* 8:45–46). It is interesting that there is inherently a certain subjectivity involved in Watsuji's approach, but that it is at the same time mixed with objectivity in that it involves encountering difference and the other. Traveling in the desert,

> The tourist [who is not from the desert] lives a life of the desert only for a short term of his stay in the desert. He never becomes a man of the desert. His history in the desert is that of a man who does not belong to the desert. But just for that very reason he learns what the desert is, and understands the essential nature of the desert.[24] (Watsuji 1961, 41–42; *WTZ* 8:46)

Thus, climate does not alone create ways of being; we come to know what it means to be a "desert" person by experiencing the otherness of rain. Interactions with those different from us help us to understand the unique climatic aspects of our culture—social interaction creates a clearer sense of cultural uniqueness. To illustrate this, Watsuji uses the example of the Japanese expression "Everywhere that humans go they encounter green mountains" (*WTZ* 8:46).[25] This saying is self-evident for the nondesert dweller from a verdant mountainous landscape like that in Japan. But once such a person comes into contact with the desert, he is faced with the sinister rocky mountains of Aden in Yemen. And here, the fundamentally environmental and climatic nature of human existence becomes apparent because our emotional reaction of recoil brings into the foreground what we have, out of habit, considered life to be—verdant mountains—and at the same time, what we did not know was hidden with us—rocky desert crags. Watsuji writes, "Such a grassless and treeless crag is, in concrete form, dark and forbidding. This darkness is not essentially a property of the physical nature of the crag, but is nothing other than man's way of life. Man lives in relation to nature and sees himself in nature. He discovers a desire to eat in a fruit that seems tasty; he finds his own feeling of ease in a green mountain; and, in the same way, he sees his own ugliness in an ugly mountain. In other words, he discovers here a man other than of a green mountain"[26] (Watsuji 1961, 43; *WTZ* 8:47).

While in the next section on geographic determinism we will criticize Watsuji for claiming to be able to understand and grasp the essence of different cultures without having lived in them and without allowing members of those cultures to speak for themselves, we can see in his incorporation of an encounter with otherness into his description of how we become self-aware why Watsuji felt that despite being Japanese, he could provide some insight into the cultures of others. In some sense, Watsuji's concept of climate incorporates what Hans-Georg Gadamer would later term the "fusion of horizons"—the possibility that different people come to understand each other by discovering areas of shared understanding. For instance, in answering the question of why Christianity, which has its origin in the "desert" religion of Judaism, spread so readily in Western Europe, where the climate is of the meadow type, Watsuji explains that there are homologous elements between the climate of Northern and Western Europe and that of the desert: in Watsuji's view, the gloom and melancholy brought about by the grey skies and long winters of the North create an affinity for the harshness of the desert. He writes,

> Western Europe, responsive to the mystic, was from the very first the most fertile soil for Christianity. This was, of course, not the only area to which Christianity spread, but in no other did it plan its roots so firmly and deeply.... This complete spiritual conquest was only possible because Europe's agony of gloom responded to the terror of the desert. Probably no people accepted this wilful, personal one God as wholly as did the European; no one understood the wilful moral passion of the Old Testament prophets as well as he.[27] (Watsuji 1961, 112–113; *WTZ* 8:114–115)

For Watsuji, climate does not alone determine culture—that is, our way of thinking about and giving meaning to the world. We all have within us certain latent tendencies that can be drawn out in the right circumstances through the encounter with different landscapes and people of different cultures. Moreover, these latent tendencies make us interested in others: we can understand them because in doing so we come to understand a part of ourselves and also our own limitations.

When we read *Climate and Culture* after his earlier works such as *Pilgrimages*, we get the sense that Watsuji is primarily experimenting with

Heideggerian phenomenology in the later work, not necessarily changing his view about culture. Read in this light, Watsuji's concept of culture in *Climate and Culture* can be seen as a further development of the dynamic and flexible notion of culture in *Pilgrimages*. Seeing this continuity makes a non-essentialist, or at least a less essentialist, reading of Watsuji's analysis of the link between climate and culture more plausible. The interpretation and deployment of the phenomenological methodology in *Climate and Culture* is the real innovation of this work; in contrast, Watsuji's understanding of culture has not evolved that far.

However, there are also differences between the concept of culture in *Pilgrimages* and in *Climate and Culture*, which is characterized by universalistic elements not to be found in the earlier text. It is these elements that justify charges of geographic determinism against Watsuji. In the next section, we will explore the causes for the introduction of universalism and essentialism, which are to be found in Watsuji's interpretation of Heideggerian phenomenology. In *Climate and Culture*, Watsuji sought to identify space and time as transcendental structures of human experience and existence. Thus when he applies the phenomenological analysis to understand the relationship between climate and culture, the fact that space and time are transcendental, and hence universal, structures of human experience and existence tends to cast climate, which is the concrete manifestation of both space and time, as something universal and hence immutable. One might express this effect metaphorically by saying that Watsuji's somewhat Neo-Kantian interpretation of Heideggerian phenomenology has introduced scientific concepts of causality into his phenomenological analysis of climate and culture. In my view, this is likely due to a misinterpretation of the Heideggerian notion of phenomenology as a form of transcendental analysis, and it also disregards the radical things that Heidegger has to say about causality in *Being and Time* and in later works.[28]

DETERMINISTIC AND ESSENTIALIST ASPECTS OF WATSUJI'S THEORY OF CULTURE

In the previous section, we examined how one reading of Watsuji's theory of culture leads to the conclusion that climate does not rigidly determine culture: culture and climate interact over time, giving expression to just some of the infinite possibilities that can result from the interaction between humans and their landscape and between humans and other humans. However, Watsuji's tendency to universalize, motivated by his desire to identify universal structures of human experience and existence through his study of the relationship between climate and culture, can lead to both essentialism (the tendency to generalize about characteristics of a particular culture) and to geographic determinism (the tendency to see geographic or physical aspects of climate as determinative of culture).

This essentialism and determinism can be observed in three aspects of his analysis:

1.) the tendency to use the myth of Japanese culture as a model: culture is considered to be a character or spirit developed by a homogeneous group in isolation from other groups and with a shared history;
2.) the choice of the relationship between climate and culture as the phenomenon to be studied;
3.) the tendency to overlook alternatives to climate as a causal factor in the development of culture, for instance, overlooking the political nature of intercultural relations.

As we saw in the previous section of this chapter, Watsuji often acknowledges the fluidity and dynamism of culture. But this tendency also coexists with another tendency to regard cultures as insular—that is, as phenomena that are developed primarily by homogeneous groups with minimal influence from others. This results in part from Watsuji's unconscious use of a Japanese understanding of culture as a general notion of culture.

Watsuji's choice to study the climatic nature of culture in order to identify fundamental structures of human experience is itself something to question. As we will see, the alignment between cultural practices and climatic and seasonal phenomena is a common trope in Japanese culture, and to the extent that it is used as a general model of the relationship between climate and culture, it can lead to problematic essentialism and geographic determinism.

Finally, by concentrating on the relationship between climate and culture, Watsuji unfortunately overlooks other important influences on cultural development, for instance, political forces such as colonialism, economics, and so on. These elements are not entirely absent in *Climate and Culture*. For instance, Watsuji does allude to the spread of the meadowland culture of the Greeks and Romans through military conflicts such as the Punic Wars between Rome and Carthage (Watsuji 1961, 91–92). However, he has a tendency to reduce these wars to cultural and climatic factors. For instance, he attributes the Carthaginian defeat to Hannibal's inability to rival Rome's power, which resulted from its pursuit of an increasingly vast but unified empire (Watsuji 1961, 92–94). Watsuji ultimately attributes this Roman tendency toward unification to climatic factors, which he believes encouraged them to dominate nature and create a vast, unified empire (Watsuji 1961, 94–97). And while Watsuji sometimes indicates that he accepts the role of political factors in additional to cultural and climatic ones, he does not give them much of a causal role in his analysis. For instance, while Watsuji bristles at the chauvinistic presumptions of his European predecessors, especially Hegel, who considered European culture to be the apotheosis of world cultural achievement (*WTZ* 8:232), he elides as Hegel did the language of culture with the language of nation. As a result, political units such as the state or the nation are not distinguished from cultural groups, and so political factors that played a role in the analysis of Hegel and Watsuji are disguised as cultural analysis.

In the following subsections, we will examine the details of each of these three ways in which Watsuji slips from a non-essentialist view of culture into a problematic essentialism.

Japanese Culture as the Model for Culture in General

Watsuji has a tendency to use Japan as a model for cultures in general. Japanese often presume that their isolation as an island country (*shimaguni*; 島国) separated from China and Korea by an angry sea led to a unique form of historical and cultural development[29] (Hagland 1984; Crawcour 1980; Watanabe 1974). Unconsciously accepting this presumption, Watsuji imposes this model of culture on other climatic zones in Europe, the Middle East, Africa, and Asia. This tendency, part of the cultural baggage of a Japanese person of his generation, overlooks that Japan is not actually isolated either physically or historically from other parts of the world, as Watsuji's own study of the influences on Japanese Buddhist art in *Pilgrimages* attests.

Watsuji's use of Japanese culture as a model is apparent in his description of the development of Japanese culture in Part 2 of Chapter 3, which deals with the monsoon climate (Watsuji 1961, 133–154). In this section, Watsuji emphasizes Japanese uniqueness, stating that "Japan's climate is by far the most distinctive within the whole monsoon zone"[30] (Watsuji 1961, 134), and that "monsoon receptivity assumes a very unique form in the Japanese"[31] (Watsuji 1961, 135). One could object that identifying unique characteristics is consistent with Watsuji's goal of distinguishing three distinct climatic zones. But the words "uniqueness" and "distinctiveness" (*tokushusei*, 特殊性) do not appear as often (if at all) in Watsuji's description of the cultures of the other countries in the monsoon zone. Indeed, the comparisons he draws between Japan and the other monsoon cultures clearly favour Japan. For instance, while the Japanese are characterized by "a copious outflow of emotion, constantly changing, yet [concealing] perseverance beneath this change" (Watsuji 1961, 137–138), Indians are purely "receptive" and "resigned," lacking the "aggressive and masterful nature" (Watsuji 1961, 38) that characterizes the Japanese. The Chinese, closer culturally to the Japanese, have more vigor than Watsuji's description of South Asians, though he views them as leaning toward anarchy: the Chinese is "the man beyond the law, passive and resigned, yet at the same time teeming with unfathomable spite," characterized by "a regard for self-interest and a lack of emotion" (Watsuji 1961, 124–125).

In addition to modeling his general concept of culture on the Japanese idea of culture, Watsuji often takes as his starting point certain key features of Japanese culture and then goes in search of analogues in others. For instance, he identifies the "family" (i.e., 家) as the basic principle of Japanese culture (Watsuji 1961, 142; *WTZ* 8:142) and locates its roots in the unique climate of Japan, the "distinctive . . . fusion of a calm passion and a martial selflessness"[32] (Watsuji 1961, 143). He proceeds to describe the historical importance of the concept of "family" throughout the five periods of Japanese history (Watsuji 1961, 153–156) before searching for an analogue to this concept in the cultures of Greece (exemplars of the paradigmatic meadow culture) and the desert religions (Judaism, Christianity, and Islam). The correlate to "family" in Greek (and hence European) culture is the "polis"; in desert cultures, it is the "tribe" (Watsuji 1961, 140–141). Due to his imposition of the Japanese model of culture on other cultures, Watsuji does not consider the possibility that the Japanese concept of "family" has no analogue elsewhere. Nor does he question the uniqueness of the Japanese model, although one could easily trace the Japanese notion of "family" to the "five relationships" described in Chinese Confucianism (Tu 1985), thus making it an import rather than a feature endemic to Japan.

The tendency toward essentialism is also evident in more subtle ways. For instance, his identification of culture with "national character" or "disposition" (*kokuminteki seikaku*, 国民的性格; Watsuji 1961, 138; *WTZ* 8:138), which he defines as a form of "mental structure" or "spiritual structure" (*seishinteki kōzō*; 精神的構造) that affects how members of a culture interpret the world around them (*WTZ* 8:201), implies that cultures are homogeneous.[33] On this view, culture is the manifestation in cultural practices and artifacts of the spirit or the mental structure of people that dictates a particular approach to art, modes of production of objects, peculiar ways of seeing the world, and even religion (ibid.).

Watsuji's presumption that Japan is characterized by a single culture with a unique history developed as a result of physical isolation leads him to impose this notion of culture on other regions of the world. Doing so undermines his characterization of culture as malleable and dynamic, subject to influence through interactions with other cultural groups.

The Focus on the Relationship between Climate and Culture as a Source of Both Essentialism and Determinism

Watsuji used the myth of Japanese culture as homogeneous and unique as a general model of culture. Another tendency in Watsuji's study of climate and culture that led to essentialism is his focus on the climatic nature of culture. Watsuji's choice of the relationship between climate and culture as a phenomenon from which to derive the universal elements of human experience and existence betrays a Japanese cultural bias. For the Japanese, culture is closely linked to climate, and so studying the relationship between the two reveals many things about how the Japanese interpret the world. But the relationship between culture and climate is not as central in other cultures, and thus Watsuji's use of this relationship as a way of understanding how all humans experience the world has the potential to ignore other legitimate perspectives and other phenomena that may disclose something about the spatial and temporal nature of our lives.

Japanese often consider their culture to be particularly attuned to seasonal change. For instance, Watsuji illustrates the "dualistic" and "dialectic" nature of Japanese culture through the metaphor of the cherry blossom. He writes,

> The typhoon, while seasonal, is also unexpected and sudden; thus it contains the dual nature of the monsoon climate, which, at one and the same time, in the form of copious moisture blesses man with food and threatens him in the form of violent winds and floods, and on top of the passive and resignatory way of life that corresponds to this monsoon climate in general, there is a further distinctive addition in Japan—the distinctive duality of tropical and frigid zones, and the seasonal and the sudden. . . . Just like the changes of the seasons, the receptivity of the Japanese calls for abrupt switches of rhythm.[34] (Watsuji 1961, 135; *WTZ* 8:135–136)

In this passage, Watsuji uses climate as a metaphor for Japanese personality and cultural sensibility. This metaphorical use may be evocative for Japanophiles; but it is definitely not a strict application of the phenomenological analysis of climate Watsuji promised at the beginning of *Climate and Culture*. Remember, there, Watsuji had explained that human experience is both temporal and spatial. Thus humans, both individually but especially intersubjectively, exist in an environment—in a landscape—that influences their subjective experience. This subjective experience can be studied objectively as what Watsuji called culture—the clothing, food, social practices, philosophy, etc. of a group of people develop naturally to suit the environment in which they live. But the parallels Watsuji draws in the above passage are between Japanese climate and a generalization about Japanese personality, not climate and culture. It is using a phenomenon of climate—the short season of the cherry blossoms—as a metaphor for the changeable emotions

Watsuji associates with the Japanese (Watsuji 1961, 136–137; *WTZ* 8:136–138). Watsuji writes,

> Emotions can alternate with the unanticipated and abrupt intensity of a seasonal yet savage typhoon. This emotional power is not characterised by any tenacious sensation, but rather by a savagery akin to that of Japan's own searing autumn winds. . . . It is of deep significance and highly appropriate that this mood of the Japanese should be symbolised by the cherry blossoms, for they flower abruptly, showily and almost in indecent haste; but the blooms have no tenacity—they fall as abruptly and disinterestedly as they flowered.[35] (Watsuji 1961, 136; *WTZ* 8:136–137)

The Japanese temperament is "like" the typhoon or the cherry blossom. But this temperament is not an objectively observable response of the Japanese to the environment. Rather, it is a Japanese stereotype about the nature of Japanese "character" or "spirit." In other words, Watsuji's association of the cherry blossom with Japanese emotional tendencies displays a cultural bias on his part, not the result of a phenomenological study.

This generalization—the conversion of a Japanese myth about emotional character into an objective aspect of Japanese culture—is likely the result of the slippage from the study of "culture" at the beginning of *Climate and Culture* to a study of national "character" or "spirit," notions which Watsuji never defines in the book, but which were the subject of other research he undertook during this period, for instance, in two books on the history of Japanese spirit published in 1925 and 1935 and in a shorter essay titled simply "The Japanese Spirit" (*Nihon seishin*, 『日本精神』) published in 1934 (translated by A. Jacinto Zavala and David A. Dilworth in Watsuji 1998). This unexplained shift from phenomenological analysis to metaphysical conclusions is perhaps to blame for the introduction of apparent geographic determinism into Watsuji's philosophy. Cultural practices can be observed, as can landscape and geographic environment. The link between the two can also be studied, although the causal relationship between particular climatic phenomena and specific practices will remain elusive, especially given the phenomenological focus on how culture is experienced climatically (through responses to climate) and vice versa (climate is not an objective phenomenon but a way of humans living in a physical and social environment).[36] But how does one observe national "character" or "spirit"? Watsuji points to no objective phenomena that indicate it.

Moreover, the absence of a causal link between climate and culture is replaced by a stronger form of causation bordering on determinism in his analysis of the link between climate and "spirit." Indeed, in the second-last chapter of *Climate and Culture*, which focuses on climate and art, Watsuji emphasizes the necessity of particular ways of thinking ("ways of seeing the world" [*sekaikan*, 世界観] and "mental structures" [*seishinteki kōzō*, 精神的構造] [*WTZ* 8:201]) that develop in people who live in a particular natural environment. He writes,

> The bright and shadeless clarity and the aridity of Greece's "eternal noon" presently turned into a type of thinking in which man revealed his all. Nature's docility—the warm, humidity-free atmosphere, the tender pastures, the smooth limestone—presently turned into the Greek style of clothing, with its sense of freedom and its carefree scorn of the need for protection against nature; it turned into, again, the nude contest, the love of the statue of the naked body.[37] (Watsuji 1961, 203; *WTZ* 8:200)

In this passage, Watsuji posits a causal link between geographic environment and ways of thinking that would seem consistent with geographic determinism. However, in the rest of the paragraph, he tries to attenuate this apparent determinism by emphasizing that innate cultural tendencies also play a role. He writes,

> This does not mean that natural phenomena gave rise to distinctive effects on the soul of man as if it were a piece of blank paper, for man did not and could not live thus in isolation from his natural environment. The brightness of Greece's "eternal noon" was from the beginning the clarity of the Greek; the method in nature was from the first the rational inclination in the Greek. Hence the characteristics of nature should be understood as related to the spiritual make-up of those who live with that nature.[38] (*WTZ* 8:200–201)

Watsuji explains that people and their environment arise together as particular cultural practices. Greeks, he seems to argue, are not like leaves, whose characteristics are completely determined by their physical environment—they have a spirit that has always tended toward rationality.

However, the superficial resistance to determinism and causation in this passage is unconvincing: it is hard to understand exactly what this Greek "spiritual make-up," this tendency toward rationality, is meant to be if not some sort of essence incompatible with the phenomenological method laid out at the beginning of *Climate and Culture*. There, Watsuji was clear that "we find ourselves ... in 'climate'" (Watsuji 1961, 5). Human existence is "ecstasis"—we discover ourselves "on a plane which 'stands outside' (ex-sistere)" (Watsuji 1961, 12). We discover ourselves always already existing in a world that contains clothing, tools, and forms of shelter that are designed to keep out the cold or provide shelter from sun and heat (Watsuji 1961,

12–13). And while it is true that our environment imparts to us certain moods (Watsuji 1961), these are found as part of the concrete social environment in which we are always already living, not some spirit or essence transmitted to us that makes up our inner spirit or nature.

At the beginning of the book, Watsuji's view of history and its influence in shaping our self-understanding is more consistent with Heideggerian hermeneutics. History is a source of meanings—it is the world into which Dasein always already finds itself "thrown" and which it experiences as a mood or "attunement" (1996, 126–131; 1953, 134–140). But this does not mean that there is some "spirit" or essence that exists independently of the spatial (communal and physical) relations between people and between people and objects. To use Watsuji's example, we feel refreshed by a spring wind not because freshness is a mental state, but because the "atmosphere itself" is fresh (Watsuji 1961, 15). "Climatic character" in Chapter 1 is thus not an essence but the objective limits that climate and geography impose on human choices (Watsuji 1961, 15–16). These limitations and cultural responses to them are what make up the "climatic character" of "subjective human existence" (Watsuji 1961, 16).

In contrast, by the end of the book, climatic differences are now cast as "differences in spiritual make-up" (*seishinteki kōzō*, 精神的構造, Watsuji 1961, 204; *WTZ* 8:200). This spirit seems to be something that can live and move within individuals (Watsuji 1961, 205), for instance, as the creativity of the artist. Watsuji writes, "It is because his experience contains the order within nature that the artist is moved by the order in his experience"[39] (Watsuji 1961, 205). Thus cultural activity, rather than being merely the expression of the objective limitations on human subjective freedom, is now seen as the cause of an inner order within humans that finds expression in culture and art (Watsuji 1961, 205) and determines our destiny (*shukumei*, 宿命) as a people (Watsuji 1961, 207).

Watsuji Overlooks Factors Other than Climate that Influence Cultural Development

Watsuji's leaning toward geographic determinism is exacerbated by his tendency to overlook other forces such as politics that shape social practices. For example, he attributes colonialism in Southeast Asia to the interaction of cultures rather than the exploitation of political power relations. In his explanation of why Southeast Asia was easily dominated by European colonial powers, he blames the particular form that monsoon culture takes in that part of the world, which in his view led those living there to be completely submissive to nature. This submissiveness translated into a political docility, which facilitated their domination by colonial metropoles. As Berque notes

(2011, 66—fn. 9), this judgment is an instance of geographic determinism of the kind that Watsuji denied he would undertake at the beginning of his book. Moreover, it overlooks the political and economic forces that shaped colonialism. Just as cultures have histories, so too do power relations: but these are unaccounted for in Watsuji's study of climate and culture.

As we have noted above, here and there, Watsuji acknowledges the interpenetration and mutual influence of different cultures. But what he fails to do is to recognize that these interactions are not always politically neutral—sometimes, they involve a power differential that can be exploited by the dominant state. By emphasizing spatial climatic forces and de-emphasizing the history of political and economic forces, by limiting historical analysis to the history of particular cultures and by ignoring the form of their interaction (cultural exchange or colonial domination), Watsuji overlooks politics, which has also has a tremendous influence in shaping the world.

Another source of cultural essentialism in *Climate and Culture* is the elision between "culture" and "nation": Watsuji at times slips from the language of culture into the political language of nationhood and power. This is most obvious in the last chapter of the book, in which Watsuji shifts away from the dynamic and flexible notion of culture he adopted in *Pilgrimages* in favor of one in which culture is particular to a "nation." No doubt this language emerges in part because in the last chapter, Watsuji studies the cultural and historical philosophy of Herder, Kant, Fichte, and Hegel, who often consider culture "national" culture. This shift in *Climate and Culture* foreshadows Watsuji's espousal of Japanese nationalism in his later philosophy (Parkes 1997, 306).

THE ROOTS OF GEOGRAPHIC DETERMINISM IN WATSUJI'S INTERPRETATION OF HEIDEGGER

In the previous section I identified instances of geographic determinism and cultural essentialism in *Climate and Culture* that were potentially inconsistent with the phenomenological analysis of the relationship between climate and culture that Watsuji sets out as his goal at the beginning of the book. According to the phenomenological analysis, since climate is not the natural environment but rather a particular structure of the intentionality of the experiencing subject (Watsuji 1961, 2), then climate is not separate from the ways that we experience cold, hot, humid, and dry, and so it cannot be the causal determinant of cultural practices. Why then does Watsuji slip into cultural essentialism and geographic determinism? One answer may be found in the way that he interprets phenomenological analysis, or more precisely, the way that he interprets Heideggerian phenomenology. In this section, we examine to what degree these problematic aspects of Watsuji's analysis of the relationship between climate and culture originate in his interpretation and application of the phenomenological method. More precisely, we will see how it is possible for Watsuji to slip from characterizing culture as something dynamic and malleable to a generalization that can then be associated with the culture or "spirit" of a "nation." To confirm the correctness of our interpretation of Watsuji's phenomenological method, we will end this section with a short survey of the role of this method in his later work, especially his three-volume *Ethics* (*Rinrigaku*). To the degree that our interpretation of Watsuji's phenomenological method in *Climate and Culture* is consistent with his development and application of the method in *Ethics*, we will have some confirmation that it is correct.

In *Climate and Culture*, Watsuji emphasizes that human existence has a dual aspect: it is both individual and social (Watsuji 1961, 8). Humans "apprehend" (*jiko ryōkai*, 自己了解) themselves in climate in their "dual character of individual and social being"[40] (ibid.; see also Watsuji 1961, 12). Not only does human existence have the dual structure of individual and social, human existence is the relationship between these two, which in *Climate and Culture*, foreshadowing the centrality of this term in his later *Ethics*, Watsuji labels *aidagara* (間柄, "betweenness"). As individuals, humans experience climate bodily as a feeling of cold or warmth, and as societies, they experience climate as "ways of creating communities, . . . ways of constructing speech, . . . methods of production, . . . styles of building and so on" (Watsuji 1961, 12).

Watsuji purports to derive this theory of human existence phenomenologically, that is, by studying the phenomena of culture and cultural practices. These, we have seen, have a spatial aspect (they are climatic) and they have a temporal aspect (cultural practices have a history). Watsuji's phenomenological method seems to accord with Heidegger's, which also acknowledges that human existence (*Dasein*) as being-in-the world is both spatial and temporal because the world in which we live involves relationships with objects (spatiality) whose meanings are cultural and hence historically determined (temporality).[41] And in line with Heidegger, Watsuji acknowledges that the two aspects of human existence are not separate—we apprehend climate through bodily experiences of meteorological phenomena (Watsuji 1961, 4–5), but also in the culturally determined and historically emergent responses (rain is gloomy, the falling of cherry blossoms is melancholy; Watsuji 1961, 5) and ways to protect ourselves against the weather.

When one adopts this phenomenological method, it becomes very easy to slip into cultural essentialism. As we have seen, culture is a temporal phenomenon because it has a history. Moreover, culture, and therefore history, influence how we respond to our world—it constitutes a limit on our available responses (Watsuji 1961, 14). In this regard, too, Watsuji's notion of history is similar to that of Heidegger, for whom our thrownness into the world (*Geworfenheit*) places factical limits on available modes of life (Heidegger 1996, 144). As Dreyfus explains,

> The shared everyday skills, concerns, and practices into which we are socialized provide the conditions necessary for people to make sense of the world and of their lives. All intelligibility presupposes something that cannot be fully articulated—a kind of knowing-how rather than a knowing-that. At the deepest level such knowing is embodied in our social skills rather than in our concepts ... (Dreyfus 1993, 293–294). The shared practices into which we are socialized ... provide a background understanding of what matters and what it makes sense to do, on the basis of which we can direct our actions. (ibid., 296)

Once one accepts that culture provides the context of meaningfulness from which humans interpret their experience, it is only a short step to identifying this culture with the culture of a specific social group. Watsuji makes this step early on in *Climate and Culture*, where he writes that culture constitutes a "distinctive way of life" (*tokushuteki na shikata*; 特殊的な仕方; Watsuji 1961, 16). This distinctive way of life into which one is thrown consists of a "specific climatic past" with "specific content," namely, "the being of man in a given country at a given age"[42] (Watsuji 1961, 10). Thus when Watsuji explains that culture is historical, he means that it is the culture of a specific group with a specific content. Moreover, this content places limits on the possible self-understandings at which an individual can arrive (Watsuji 1961, 15).

Watsuji's tendency to equate culture with the culture of a specific group, especially a nation, was shared by Heidegger. In her study of Heidegger's moral and political thought, Sonia Sikka explains how Heidegger, too, essentialized cultures and identified them with a people (*Volk*) with a particular destiny. She points out that for Heidegger, "All historizing (*Geschehen*) is a co-historizing (*Mitgeschehen*) (BT 384), and destiny is therefore collective. The destiny of an individual participates in the destiny of a *Volk*, as it must if individuals are situated within the language, tradition, and concerns of a particular *Volk*. And Heidegger supposes that each *Volk*, like each individual, has a unique historical vocation, where the fulfillment of that vocation is also the fulfillment of its 'essence'" (2017, 143). In his attempt to identify a culture with the particular "spirit" of a nation, Watsuji adopts Heidegger's view.

What Watsuji's interpretation of Heideggerian historicality lacks is an appreciation for its two modes: one the everyday inauthentic mode in which we normally find ourselves, and the other the authentic historical mode in which we take choose to lead our lives in accordance with possibilities latent in our heritage (Heidegger 1996, 390–391; Dreyfus 1995, 328–333). As Heidegger explains, "Da-sein exists as futural authentically in the resolute disclosure of a chosen possibility. Resolutely coming back to itself, it is open in retrieve for the 'monumental' possibilities of human existence.... As having-been, Da-sein is delivered over to its thrownness. In appropriating the possible in retrieve, there is prefigured at the same time the possibility of reverently preserving the existence that has-been-there, in which the possibility grasped became manifest" (Heidegger 1996, 396–397). According to Heidegger, humans exist in the world in a particular time and at a particular place, and being thrown into the world "there" offers certain possibilities to Dasein and not others. But many of these possibilities are unquestioned: we act on them not because they represent considered choices about how to lead our lives, but simply because we have not taken the time to question them at all.

Watsuji does not distinguish authentic historicity from simple absorption in taken-for-granted social goals and meanings. When he identifies "social existence" (*shakaiteki sonzai*, 社会的存在) as the history of a specific society, he fails to see that the history of a specific society may be (is likely to be) inauthentic, covering over (like the history of Being that Heidegger describes in his work) more authentic and original ways of understanding the meaning of human existence. To be properly historical in the Heideggerian sense, a cultural self-understanding must be based on an acceptance that time, properly grasped, is "what makes ... existence primordially possible" (Heidegger 1996, 436). What he means is that while *existence* is necessarily temporal, and therefore that the structure of cultures as historical is therefore also temporal, nonetheless, specific cultures may not be based on an authentic notion of existence. Instead, they may mistakenly universalize or essentialize a particular cultural ideal.

Another problematic aspect of Watsuji's interpretation of Heideggerian phenomenology is his tendency to hypostatize the individual and the social—that is, to consider individuals and groups as "things" or "essences" that can be "dropped into time." Even in the first chapter of *Climate and Culture*, Watsuji interprets historicity as the "structure of social existence"[43] (*shakaiteki sonzai*, 社会的存在), the history of a group (*WTZ* 8:16). This "social existence" takes on a life of its own, continuing its existence even after the death of the individuals that compose it. Watsuji writes,

> No social formation could exist if it lacked all foundation in the space-structure of man, nor does time become history unless it is founded in such social being, for history is the structure of existence in society. Here also we see clearly the duality of human existence—the finite and the infinite. Men die; their world changes; but through this unending death and change, man lives and his world continues. It continues incessantly through ending incessantly. In the

individual's eyes, it is a case of an "existence for death," but from the standpoint of society it is an "existence for life."[44] (Watsuji 1961, 9–10; *WTZ* 8:16)

In this passage, it is clear that intersubjectivity, which Watsuji calls "social being" (*shakaiteki sonzai*, 社会的存在), has separate ontological status from that of the individual. Both social being and individual are transcendent in the sense of finding themselves always already in a world. But social being, unlike the individual, lives on even as individuals die, and in so doing, it is the basis of a persistent national "character" and "spirit" that survives the individual. For Watsuji, history displays continuity as the history of a society (*shakai*, 社会). In phenomenological terms, Watsuji seems to interpret Heidegger's concept of *being-with* as social existence, which is arguably only the "fallen" or "inauthentic" mode of this aspect of human existence (McMullin 2013, 109).

Hubert Dreyfus provides a very different interpretation of Heidegger's notion of historicity as found in *Being and Time*. According to him, history for Heidegger is simply a source of possible ways of being: "A culture's history," he writes, "[is a] source of . . . possibilities" (Dreyfus 1995, 328; see also McMullin 2013, 28). While it is true that individuals are limited by the history of the society into which they are thrown (their *facticity*), society is not some existent with a history—it is not a form of "historical being" (*rekishiteki sonzai*, 歴史的存在; Watsuji 1961, 10; *WTZ* 8:16) that limits human existence in the same way that the physical limitations of geography and physical environment do. Instead, Drefyus indicates that Heidegger sees history as a source of possibilities, some of which are simply taken for granted, but others which are unusual, having been abandoned by the mainstream. Individuals can choose these abandoned models if they like, thereby resisting collapse into the blandness of the "they." Dreyfus writes,

> A third kind of possibilities found in society are *marginal practices* that have *resisted leveling*. These can be practices that were central in past epochs, like Christian caring in the early Christian communities and absolute commitment at the height of romantic chivalry, or Greek mentoring of adolescent boys. These practices were once central (and presumably therefore banalized) but have now become rare and therefore are no longer what one normally does. They therefore offer fresh ways of responding to the Situation. (1995, 328–329) [emphasis in original]

Watsuji's reification of the social emphasizes the continuity of the group over time, whereas Heidegger's concept arguably emphasized discontinuity—history is a source of possibilities, none of which need necessarily continue into the future. Also, Watsuji's identification of historical being with social being seems to restrict the Heideggerian conception of historicity to inauthentic modes of historical being.

The reification of the group that I have pointed to in Watsuji's phenomenology becomes more evident in his later three-volume *Ethics*. There, we see the notion of ethics as a "study of human existence" (*ningen*) based on the idea that ethics must be developed out of the dual structure of this existence as individual-social. While in that work Watsuji tries to overcome the reification of the two poles—individual-social—the effort that he expends to do so reflects the difficulties caused by his approach to the relationship between the individual and the social in *Climate and Culture*.

Watsuji's interpretation of Heidegger's notion of the historicity of Dasein seems to presume the separate existence of the social, which is then "dropped into" time. In other words, Watsuji conceives the social as having a "social history." Indeed, this is clear in the later sections of *Climate and Culture*, where social existence is equated with the "spirit of a nation." The essentialism inherent in Watsuji's misinterpretation of Heideggerian phenomenology is compounded by the links he builds between his view and the philosophies of climate, history, and culture of Herder, Kant, and the German idealists.

THE TRANSITION FROM CULTURAL PHENOMENOLOGY TO ETHICS

Climate and Culture can be read as a midpoint in the development of Watsuji's theory of culture. In *Pilgrimages*, Watsuji conceived of culture as fluid and malleable: Japanese Buddhist art, often associated with Japanese culture generally, entered that country via Korea and China, which in turn transmitted the artistic and aesthetic sensibilities of Greece and India. In that book, Watsuji portrays culture as having a history—it changes and evolves over time—that involves constant interaction between societies.

Pilgrimages also casts Watsuji as cultural interpreter and *creator*. Much of the book involved his speculation about the emotions, societies, and aesthetic sensibilities of Japanese, Chinese, and Korean artists, nobles, and commoners who had been dead for 1,000 years. Watsuji used this speculation to describe the "Japanese disposition" of contemporary Japanese society, thereby creating both modern Japanese culture and reinforcing a sense of its continuity over a long period of time. For instance, at the end of that book, Watsuji strengthens the link between the traditional association of Japanese culture with nature and the expression of Buddhist compassion in Japanese Buddhist art. He wrote,

> The seedbed that produced these first manifestations of culture was none other than the tender nature of our island country. It is lovely, easy to feel comfortable in, elegant, and yet it possesses an unfathomable mystery just like any other natural environment. This environment, if we were to represent it in human form

must be that of a *kannon*—that *kannon* at Chūgūji. The sweet, luscious taste of taking in nature and being intoxicated by it is, I would argue, an undercurrent that runs through Japanese culture. The root of it, just as we saw in the case of the Chūgūji *kannon*, is the natural environment of this country. Take, for example, the delicate love for nature where we are keenly sensitive to the beauty of a drop of dew at the tip of a leaf, the tender embrace of nature where a man communes and becomes one with nature as he travels with nothing but the bare essentials, the intoxication we feel from each and every and very specialized sense, and the religious ecstasy from a playful heart—all these may seem to have nothing in common with this *kannon*. They are, however, very similar; the only minor difference is in where our attention is directed. The objects captured by that attention are varied but, underneath, the sentiments used while capturing them are nearly identical.[45] (Watsuji 2012, 184)

In *Pilgrimages,* Watsuji incorporates Buddhist art with its foreign influences into the orthodoxy of Japaneseness.

In *Climate and Culture,* Watsuji seeks to move on from simple description and creation of Japanese culture to a theory of culture by adopting Heidegger's phenomenological method. While in many instances Watsuji uses the method faithfully by uncovering how culture reveals both the temporal and spatial aspects of human experience and existence, at times, his search for a universal theory of culture creates a tendency to rigidify culture into something objective—the expression of a national character or spirit that persists and develops through time as individual members of the culture are born and die. It is this tendency to universalize and generalize that introduces a essentialism into his analysis that frequently manifests itself, especially near the end of the book, in a form of geographic determinism.

Climate and Culture was a reflection of the time in which it was written, which was marked by the struggle of Japanese intellectuals to find a place for their nation among the dominant powers of the world, which at that time were found either in Europe or its former colonies. Watsuji's search for a universal theory of culture, his tendency to generalize and reinforce cultural stereotypes, and his identification of culture with geographic regions reflected a similar well-established pattern in European (especially German) philosophy. He also followed their lead in mapping cultures onto political entities such as the nation. It is perhaps too simple to consider this as Watsuji's adoption of Japanese nationalism. For what we have seen in this chapter is that the sliding from "culture" to "nation" was to some degree inherent in the slippage between "culture" and "character" or "spirit," a slippage facilitated by the phenomenological method itself.

As well, some of the slippage in Watsuji's cultural theory was the result of his interpretation of Heideggerian phenomenology. Because of Watsuji's desire to emphasize two facets of human existence—the individual and the group—as equally constitutive, he occasionally separates the individual and the group and sets up each as a separate entity rather than staying true to the phenomenological insight that individual and group are merely existential modes of human being. We also noted that Watsuji picked up on an aspect of Heideggerian phenomenology that made it easy to identify culture with the culture of a specific nation. For both philosophers, the historicality of human existence points to the fact that the context in which humans always already find themselves and from which they derive the meanings of cultural objects and activities is delimited by the specific history of a group to which each person belongs: the context of historical possibilities in which Dasein always already finds itself thrown constitutes the reservoir of possible meanings that it can use to understand the world. And while one option was to acknowledge that cultural identity is complex and that individuals draw on many different cultures to give meaning to the world around them (Sikka 2017, 154), the bias in both Japan and Germany prior to the Second World War was to consider culture homogeneous, thus facilitating its identification with a nation or ethnic group.

The phenomenological method also facilitated the adoption of geographic determinism: if history is a specific history and if space is the particular landscape in which a specific group of people have lived, then there is a tendency to see this landscape as the cause of the history of this culture. And while Watsuji often tried to resist this tendency toward a rigid causal relationship between landscape and culture, he nonetheless fell into it on occasion.

In Watsuji's *Ethics*, he broadens his interest from culture to society in general. His phenomenological investigation of human existence in *Climate and Culture* led to the identification of two aspects of human existence—individual and group. While in that work the focus is on the life of the group as a set of cultural practices, in the later works, Watsuji focuses more on the nature of social life in general in order to describe a fundamental aspect of human existence, its *intersubjective* nature. The broadening of Watsuji's study from culture to intersubjectivity in general naturally led Watsuji to the topic of ethics, for as he explains at the beginning of *Ethics*, ethics is simply the study of human existence (*ningen no gaku toshite no rinrigaku*; 人間の学としての倫理学), in other words, ethics is the manifestation of the relationship between the individual and the group. A focus on ethics as the study of universal structures of human existence revealed through phenomenological analysis necessarily lends this ethics a universalist bent, which, as was the case in *Climate and Culture*, could easily slip into essentialism. Thus, the universalist *Ethics* is in some sense the result of the universalist tendencies that emerge in *Climate and Culture* as a result of Watsuji's adoption and interpretation of the phenomenological method.

One can also see vestiges of *Pilgrimages* and *Climate and Culture* in *Ethics* insofar as many of the examples that Watsuji uses in the later work to illustrate the dual structure of human existence as individual and social are drawn from cultural and social practices of the Japanese. However, what has disappeared in *Ethics* is what was already disappearing in *Climate and Culture*: an acknowledgment that Watsuji in some sense created Japanese culture. The result of this is that the cultural and social practices that Watsuji provides as evidence of the dual nature of human existence are not properly evidence—they are patterns that Watsuji himself as a key cultural interpreter first identified and labeled. He created Japanese culture, and then used what he had created as evidence of the universal structure of human existence. This problem inherent in Watsuji's philosophy becomes most obvious when one reads *Pilgrimages*, *Climate and Culture*, and *Ethics* together.

CONCLUSION

In this chapter, we have explored Watsuji's *Climate and Culture* in depth in order to identify the positive elements of his analysis of climate and culture that are still useful today. We then turned to the Heideggerian origins of his methodology and his deployment of the phenomenological categories of space and time. While he adopts the method of the early Heidegger, Watsuji sought in *Climate and Culture* to correct what he considered to be Heidegger's overemphasis on temporality at the expense of space: the relationship between climate and culture proved to be an ideal subject for illustrating the equal importance of both history (temporality) and climate (space) in shaping human social practices.

Many interpreters of Watsuji have been inspired by his notion of climate because it presupposes the inseparability between humans and their physical and social environment. One such thinker is French philosopher Augustin Berque, who engages creatively with Watsuji's notion of "climate" as an example of what he calls "la mésologie," which is the study of how human existence is rooted in a landscape or milieu (Berque 1990, 13, 32). This approach derives primarily from Berque's appreciation for the preface and first chapter of *Climate and Culture*, in which Watsuji demonstrates an innovative understanding of the spatial and intersubjective aspect of human existence (Berque 2011, 29).

But as we have seen, Watsuji's philosophy has a tendency toward cultural essentialism and geographic determinism, and the undercurrent of Japanese uniqueness in his work seems to support a problematic form of Japanese nationalism. Such interpretations of *Climate and Culture* are partly justified, but they overlook many aspects of Watsuji's theory of climate and culture that run counter to it. While an interest in Japanese culture and its uniqueness is definitely present in Watsuji's philosophy, including in *Climate and Culture*, Watsuji also acknowledged that Japanese culture, like all cultures, is open to influence from other regions. Watsuji thus accepted that cultures travel and infiltrate new areas which they transform at the same time that they themselves are transformed. Nonetheless, it is important to identify what aspects of Watsuji's method and analysis lead to determinism and essentialism. As we have seen, Watsuji overemphasized the role of geography in understanding culture at the expense of politics, economics, and sociohistorical conditions. He also had a tendency to apply the myth of the homogeneity of Japanese culture to all other cultures, which both overlooks the contested nature of Japanese culture and the heterogeneous and dynamic nature of cultures generally and made it more plausible that a single factor—geography—was the primary cause of cultural difference. Finally, we noted that in resisting what he considered to be Heidegger's overemphasis on temporality, Watsuji emphasized the social aspect of human existence to the point of reifying it. Once he falls into this trap, it becomes tempting to prioritize social cohesion and uniformity over the temporal aspects that favor heterogeneity and change over time.

Finally, a detailed study of Watsuji's *Climate and Culture* was warranted because it prepares the way for a better understanding of his later work, especially his three-volume *Ethics*. Through his study of culture in *Climate and Culture*, Watsuji realized the importance of intersubjectivity since culture is a set of practices that are done together with others and whose meaning is determined by interactions with others. The next step for him was therefore to examine the structures of human experience and through them the structures of reality that make the intersubjective world possible. And indeed, this is the focus of his later work until his death in 1960.

To finish with a word about the general theme of this book, from Watsuji, we learn that culture is a set of social practices that is rooted in both time and space. Culture is temporal because cultural practices have a history: they evolve over time and are passed on from generation to generation. Culture is also spatial because it is social and climatic—it is a series of practices that people do together and that are developed to respond to the environment in which people live (Bein 2017, 105). This was Watsuji's insight in *Climate and Culture*: spatial phenomena have an important role in determining how we experience the world—we experience ourselves in climate by participating in cultural practices that respond to it and are influenced by it. Due to the way that Watsuji examines culture as a set of social practices, groups (monsoon culture, prairie culture, desert culture) are the main object of study and individuals retreat into the background.

However, in the next three chapters, we will focus more on the relationship between individuals that is disclosed through cultural practices. Kuki Shūzō, the next subject of our study, was, like Watsuji, interested in Japanese cultural practices. He also recognized that these practices disclosed something about the intersubjective nature of human existence. But what he wished to explore was not the group ethos that culture expresses but rather the ethical obligations between individuals that are expressed through and give rise to these cultural practices.

NOTES

1. A typical example of the relationship that many Japanese see between nature and their culture is expressed by Umehara Takeshi in "Nationalism and Aesthetics." He writes, "In Japan we have the conviction, as a kind of backdrop to our worldview, that the mind that is symbolized [in Japanese art] and the nature that provides the symbols are in essence one and the same. Since humans and nature are manifestations of the same life, we have an implicit belief that the human psyche, however complex, is always expressed in natural form (2011, 1187).

2. Geographic determinism is the presumption that physical geography is the cause of particular aspects of society and culture (Berque 2011, 13–14; Mitchell 2000, 17). For an account of the social conditions in Europe and North America at the end of the nineteenth and early twentieth century that led to the popularity of geographic determinism, see Peet (1985) and Mitchell (2000).

3. Bownas has translated this as "a state of man," but I find this to be both anachronistic and inaccurate.

4. 「ここに風土と呼ぶのはある土地の気候、気象、地質、地形、景観などの総称である。それは古くは水土とも言われている。人間の環境としての自然を地水火風として把捉した古代の自然観がこれらの概念の背後にひそんでいるのであろう。」

5. As Steve Bein explains, for Watsuji, culture "does not simply carve out a space for itself in nature; it is always a response to nature—and not nature in the abstract, but always to a specific geohistorical context. . . . Climate is the lived-world, both of individuals and of collectives, and according to Watsuji—and to many existentialist thinkers—human existence is always existence in a lived-world" (2017, 105).

6. 「我々が初めに単純に「湿気」として言い現わしたことは、ただ単に気象学の問題とさるる現象ではなく、一方に峻厳な人格神の信仰を産んだ乾

燥な沙漠生活の極度に意志的実践的な生き方、他方にあらゆる生物の一であることを信ずる湿潤な地方の極度に感情的冥想的な生き方、そうしてその両者に対して人間中心的な知的静観的な生き方を区別せしめる精神的構造上の一つの原理である。」

7.「...我々は同じ寒さを共同に感ずる。」

8.「...湿潤が自然の暴威をも意味することである。暑熱と結合せる湿潤は、しばしば大雨、暴風、洪水、旱魃というごとき荒々しい力となって人間に襲いかかる。それは人間をして対抗を断念させるほどに巨大な力であり、従って人間をただ忍従的たらしめる。」

9.「かくのごとく自然と人間との交渉において自然の特殊性が人間の生活の特殊性となって現われることは恐らく何人も否定し得ないところであろう。人間が外界としての自然に対立するものとしておのれを見いだした時には、すでに人間はその自然の特殊性をおのれの特殊性としているのである。あくまでも晴朗な、乾燥のゆえに濃淡のないギリシアの「真昼」の明るさは、やがて現象が残ろところなくおのれをあらわにしているという思想となる。自然の温順さ、―――――湿気のない暖かい大気や柔らかな牧草や表面の滑らかな石灰岩は、やがて自然に対して自らを守るという趣の少ない解放的なギリシアの衣となり、裸体の競技となり、裸体像の愛好となる。それは自然現象が原因となって白紙のごとき人間の精神に特殊な結果を引き起こしたという意味ではない。人間はかつて周囲の自然から引き離された白紙の状態にいたことはない。ギリシアの真昼の明るさは初めよりギリシア人の明るさであり、ギリシアの自然の規則正しさは初めよりギリシア人の合理的傾向であった。だから自然の特殊性はその自然においてある人間の精神的構造に属する問題であると見られなくてはならぬ。」

10.「...それぞれの民族の生活の仕方と精神とが力強く子供の心に浸み込むことは言うまでもない。」

11.「「ところ」の特殊性が精神的構造の特殊性を意味するごとく、それはまた芸術の従ってまた芸術家の想像力の特殊性をも意味するのである。」

12. In his discussion of Herder, Watsuji writes, "That which can be said about the air [namely, that it unveils the key to understanding human existence] can also be said of water, sunlight, the shape and nature of the land, the flora and fauna, its products, food and drink, the way of life, the manner of work, clothing, leisure activities, and the various other forms of cultural production. All of this makes up the 'picture of climate' that reveals the life of all human beings. To discover 'climate' (*fūdo*), one must begin with the totality of the modes of everyday life" (author's translation). 「空気について言える事は、水、日光、土地の形性質、その土地の動植物、産物、食料や飲料、生活の仕方、動き方、着物、娯楽の仕方、その他種々の文化的産物の一切について言うことができる。それらはすべての人間の生の開示として、「風土の絵」を形成する。風土はこれらの一切を含む日常生活の全体の姿から見いだされねばならぬ。」(*WTZ* 8: 216).

13. Bownas translates this passage as follows, "Man's way of life has its own distinctive historical and climatic structure, the individuality of which is shown with the greatest clarity by climatic patterns governed by the limitations within a climate. Climate, essentially, is historical; so climatic patterns are at the same time historical patterns" (Watsuji 1961, 133–134).

14.「もとよりこれらは歴史的影響によって他の「ところ」にも移され得るものに違いない。たとえば砂漠生活の生んだ旧約聖書が千年にわたってヨーロッパ人を呪縛し、同じ砂漠から出たコランが現在のインドに強い勢力を持っているごとき、「ところ」の特殊性が絶対的のものでないことを示している。」

15.「我々はヨーロッパの牧場的風土からしてその文化を理解しようと試みた。しかしこの風土がこの文化の原因だというのではない。文化においては歴史性と風土性とは楯の両面であって、その一をのみ引き離すことできないものである。風土的性格を持たない歴史的形成物もなければ、また歴史的性格を持たない風土的形象もない。だから我々は歴史的形成物の内に風土を見いだすこともできれば、風土的形象の内に歴史を読むこともできる。我々は風土に視点を置きつつこの両方向の考察を雑然として試みたに過ぎぬ。」

16. For Febvre's critique of geographic determinism, see, for example, Febvre (1949, 74–79, 96, 216–222).

17. Compare with Watsuji's description of the influence of Gupta culture on China and Japan in Watsuji 2012 (67–68).

18. Compare Watsuji's description of the influence of Tang China on the Japanese court during the eighth century CE in Watsuji (2012, 82–83).

19.「かかる部族の生活はまさしく自然及び人間への対抗を反映したものである。人間は単にその個別態においてのみは生きることができぬ。部族の全体性が個別的なる生を初めて可能にする。従って全体への忠実、全体意志への服従は、沙漠的人間にとって不可欠である。が、それとともに全体的行動は人間の個別態における運命を左右する。部族の敗北は個人の死である。従って全体に属する各員はおのが力と勇気とを極度に発揮しなくてはならない。感情の温柔さを顧慮する暇のない不断の意志の緊張が、すなわち戦闘的態度が、沙漠的人間にとって不可欠である。」

20.「かくしてポリスの生活はますます人工的技術的な仕事を中心とし、それによって地中海を支配するに至った。この生活様式が特に「西洋的」としてヨーロッパの運命を定める有力な契機となっちるのである。」

21.「沙漠的人間はかくして社会的歴史的なる特殊性格を形成する。ここでは沙漠は社会的歴史的現実であって、単なる土地ではない。だから人間は単なる土地としての沙漠を空間的の意味において去ることはできても、社会的歴史的現実としての沙漠を同じ意味において去ることはできない。ここを去るためには人間は社会的歴史的に他のものに発展するを要する。しかしかかる発展においても人間は過去を捨て去るのではなくして保存するのである。沙漠的人間が水に豊かな土地に定着して農業的人間に転化するとしても、それはあくまでも沙漠的人間の発展であって他のものではない。」

22.「人間の自覚は通例他を通ることによって実現される。しからば沙漠的人間の自己理解は霖雨の中に身を置くことによって最も鋭くされるであろう。」

23.「風土の限定が諸国民をしてそれぞれに異なった方面に長所を持たしめたとすれば、ちょうどその点において我々はまた己れの短所を自覚せしめられ、互いに相学び得るに至るのである。またかくすることによって我々は風土的限定を超えて己れを育てて行くこともできるであろう。風土を無視するのは風土を超えるゆえんではない。それはただ風土的限定の内に無自覚的

に留まるに過ぎない。しかし限定を自覚することによってその限定を超えたからといって、風土の特性が消失するわけではない。否、むしろそれによって一層よくその特性が生かされてくるのである。牧場的国土はある意味では楽土であるが、しかし我々は己の国土を牧場に化することはできない。しかも我々は牧場的性格を獲得することはできるのである。そうしてその時には我々の台風的な性格は新しい生面を開いて来る。なぜなら我々が我々の内にギリシア的なる晴朗を見いだし、合理的なるものを充分に育て上げるときに、かえってよく我々の「勘」や「気合い」の意義が生かされて来るであろう。そうして超合理的な合理性があたかも台風のごとくに我々を咲きまくることをも自覚するに至るであろう。」

24.「旅行者はその生活のある短い時期を沙漠的に生きる。彼は決して沙漠的人間となるのではない。沙漠における彼の歴史は沙漠的ならざる人間の歴史である。が、まさにそのゆえに彼は沙漠の何であるかを、すなわち沙漠の本質を理解するのである。」

25. In his translation, Bownas substitutes an English proverb for the one Watsuji cites: "Every soil is the brave man's country." The Japanese original is 「人間到るところ青山あり」. Augustin Berque explains that this is a poem by the monk Gesshō (1813–1858) (Berque 2011, 88 fn. 41).

26.「かかる草木なき岩山は、具体的には物すごい、陰惨な山である。そうしてこの物すごさ陰惨さ は本来的に言えば物理的自然の性質ではなくして人間の存在の仕方にほかならぬ。人間は自然とのかかわりにおいて存在し、自然においておのれを見る。うまそうな果実においておのれの食欲を見、青山においておのれの心安さを見るように、物すごい山においてはおのれの物すごさを見る。言いかえれば非青山的人間を見いだすのである。」

27.「右のような偉大な文化的創造において己れを展開している西欧の特性は、神秘的なるものへの共鳴の地盤として、早くよりキリスト教の最もよき培養基となった。キリスト教が流れ込んだ地方は決して西欧にのみ限るのでない。しかも西欧におけるほど深くキリスト教が根を下ろした地方は他には見られない。 ... このように完全な精神的征服が何ゆえに可能であったのであろうか。それは陰鬱の苦悶がちょうど沙漠の恐怖と共鳴したからなのである。意志的人格的な唯一神を西欧人ほどよく受け容れたものはなく、また旧約の予言者たちの意志的倫理的な情熱を西欧人ほどよく理解したものもないであろう。」

28. Further exploration of the role of causation in Heidegger that is directly relevant to the subject of culture is possible through a study of Heidegger's notion of the circular nature of interpretation. The hermeneutic circle emphasizes the fact that every interpretation of the world is determined by the way that we are always already located in a context that gives meaning to the things and people we encounter. Revised interpretations are possible, but not by stepping outside the circle (Couzens Hoy 1993, 185–186). If Watsuji had faithfully accepted this aspect of Heigger's thought, he might have more diligently avoided giving the impression that culture is a direct response to one's environment, instead emphasizing the constant revision that goes on as humans interpret their world (Couzens Hoy 1993, 185–187).

29. For a study of the persistence of this view in modern Japan, see Yoshino (1992).

30. 「... 日本はモンスーン域中最も特殊な風土を持つのである。」(WTZ 8:135)

31. 「... モンスーン的な受容性は日本の人間においてきわめて特殊な形態を取る。」(WTZ 8:136)

32. 「...「家」としての日本の人間の存在の仕方は、しめやかな激性戦闘的な恬淡というごとき日本的な「間柄」を家族的に実現しているにほかならぬ。」

33. For a good critique of this notion of "character," see Febvre (1949, 144–147). He concludes, "Parler de l'influence du milieu géographique ou, plus précisément, de celle du climat sur le caractère des peuples, c'est vouloir expliquer le vide par l'arbitraire" (1949, 147).

34. 「...台風が季節的でありつつ突発的であるという二重性格は、人間の生活自身の二重性格にほかならぬ。豊富な湿気が人間に食物を恵むとともに、同時に暴風や洪水として人間を脅やかすというモンスーン的風土の、従って人間の受容的 忍従的な存在の仕方の二重性格の上に、ここにはさらに熱帯的 寒帯的、季節的 突発的というごとき特殊な二重性格が加わってくるのである。 ...四季おりおりの季節の変化が著しいように、日本の人間の受容性は調子の早い移り変わりを要求する。」

35. 「あたかも季節的に吹く台風が突発的な猛烈さを持っているように、感情もまた一から他え移るとき、予期せざる突発的な強度を示すことがある。日本の人間の感情の昂揚は、しばしばこのような突発的な猛烈さにおいて現われた。それは執拗に持読する感情の強さではなくして、野分のように吹き去る猛烈さである。 ...桜の花をもってこの気質を象徴するのは深い意味においてもきわめて適切である。それは急激に、あわただしく、華やかに咲きそろうが、しかし執拗に咲き続けるのではなくして、同じようにあわただしく、恬淡に散り去るのである。」

36. Watsuji notes that climate and culture cannot be separated in the phenomenological analysis. He writes, "I have attempted to interpret European culture in the light of its meadow climate. But I do not claim that this climate was the sole source of European culture. History and climate act as the shield and buckler of culture; the two are quite inseparable, for there is no historical event that does not possess its climatic character, nor is there climatic phenomenon that is without its historical component. So if we can discover climate within a historical event, then we can also read history within climatic phenomena" (Watsuji 1961, 116–117; WTZ 8: 119; for the Japanese, see *supra* note NOTEREF _Ref1822144 \h * MERGEFORMAT 15).

37. 「あくまでも晴朗な、乾燥のゆえに濃淡のないギリシアの「真昼」の明るさは、やがて現象が残るところなくおのれをあらわにしているという思想となる。自然の温順さ、―――湿気のない暖かい大気や柔らかな牧草や表面の滑らかな石灰岩は、やがて自然に対して自らを守るという趣の少ない解放的なギリシアの衣となり、裸体の競技となり、裸体像の愛好となる。」

38. 「それは自然現象が原因となって白紙のごとき人間の精神に特殊な結果を引き起こしたという意味ではない。人間はかつて周囲の自然から引き離された白紙の状態にいたことはない。ギリシアの真昼の明るさは初めよりギリシア人の明るさであり、ギリシアの自然の規則正しさは初めよりギリシア

人の合理的傾向であった。だから自然の特殊性はその自然においてある人間の精神的構造に属する問題であると見られなくてはならぬ。」

39. 「芸術家がその体験において規則正しさに動かされるのは、その体験が自然の規則正しさを含むからである。」(*WTZ* 8:202)

40. 「...個人的　社会的なる二重性格を持つ人間...」(*WTZ* 8:14).

41. Sikka explains, "Culture is a feature of Dasein's existence as being-with, not a property of objects. In *Being and Time*, Dasein imagines its future by drawing on its past, in terms of the heritage that has been handed down to it, which it can appropriate and revise in multiple ways (BT 383). What binds a culture together, on this account, is not a set of stable characteristics but the commonality of a shared history, on the basis of which the members of that culture relate themselves to a common future" (2017, 153–154).

42. 「ここにおいて人間は単に一般的に「過去」を背負うのではなくして特殊な「風土的過去」を背負うのであり、一般的形式的な歴史性の構造は特殊的な実質によって充実せられることになる。人間の歴史的存在がある国土におけるある時代の人間の存在となるのは、右のことによって初めて可能なのである。」(*WTZ* 8:16)

43. Bownas translates this as "the structure of existence in society" (Watsuji 1961, 10).

44. 「主体的人間の空間的構造にもとづくことなしには一切の社会的構造は不可能であり、社会的存在にもとづくことなしには時間性が歴史性となることはない。歴史性は社会的存在の構造なのである。ここに人間存在の有限的　無限的な二重性格も明らかとなるであろう。人は死に、人の間は変わる、しかし絶えず死に変わりつつ、人は生き人の間は続いている。それは絶えず終わることにおいて絶えず続くのである。個人の立場から見て「死への存在」であることは、社会の立場からは「生への存在」である。」(*WTZ* 8:16)

45. 「がこれらの最初の文化現象を生み出すに至った母胎は、我が国のやさしい自然であろう。愛らしい、親しみやすい、優雅な、そのくせいずこの自然とも同じく底知れぬ神秘を持ったわが島国の自然は、人体の姿に現わせばあの観音となるほかはない。自然に酔う甘美なこころもちは日本文化を貫通して流れる著しい特徴であるが、その根はあの観音と共通に、この国土の自然自身から出ているのである。葉末の露の美しさをも鋭く感受する繊細な自然の愛や、一笠一杖に身を託して自然に融け入って行くしめやかな自然との抱擁や、その分化した官能の陶酔、飄逸なこころの法悦は、一見の観音とははなはだしく異なるように思える。しかしその異なるのはただ注意の向かう方向の相違である。捕えられる対象こそ差別があれ、捕えにかかる心情にはきわめて近く相似るものがある。母であるこの大地の特殊な美しさは、その胎より出た子孫に同じき美しさを賦与した。わが国の文化の考察は結局わが国の自然の考察に帰って行かなくてはならぬ。」(*WTZ* 2:191)

Chapter 5

Kuki's Hermeneutic Approach to the Floating World

Iki *as the Living Form of Japanese Idealism*

Kuki Shūzō's most well-known work outside of Japan is surely his book *The Structure of Iki* (*Iki no kōzō*; 『「いき」の構造』). Its popularity is in part due to the subject matter—*geisha* culture and the relationship between a *geisha* and her lover—a theme that seems stereotypical as a representation of Japanese culture. Nonetheless, *iki*, which describes both an aesthetic sensibility and what Kuki considered to be an ideal form of ethical relationship, continues to be an important concept in modern Japan, including in *manga* (comics) and *anime* (animated films), artistic forms that are associated throughout the world with Japanese culture. For instance, in 2011, the manga *Showa Genroku Rakugo Shinjū* (*Descending Stories: Showa Genroku Rakugo Shinju*) appeared. It is the story of men and women involved in *rakugo*, a traditional form of comic Japanese storytelling. Historically, it was the domain of male storytellers, who portrayed men, women, boys, and girls in their performances. Yamada Tomoko, an authority on Japanese manga specializing in *shojo manga* (comic books for girls), describes the manga in an interview:

> *Rakugo Shinjū* is a dramatic story told with the traditional Japanese aesthetic of "Iki" ("style" or "flair"). People choose to die via double suicide rather than live separately (a very Japanese aesthetic). The story employs the Japanese traditional storytelling style of "rakugo." . . . Laughter is an important element, but there is a serious undertone to the drama of the people living in the world of the rakugo. (Toku 2015, 139)

While Watsuji's portrayal of Japanese culture focused on tradition—Buddhist statues and temples, the evanescent cherry blossom, and the close connection between Japanese culture and nature—Kuki chose an unlikely cultural subgenre to represent the essence of Japanese culture. In his view, the aesthetic of *iki* embodies a way of living together based on the traditional shared system of values of *Bushidō*, *Shintō*, and Buddhism. As the manga *Rakugo Shinjū* demonstrates, Kuki's choice of *iki* to represent Japanese culture has stood the test of time, unlike that of Watsuji, which seems increasingly anachronistic. Perhaps this is because *iki* expresses something about the relationship between lovers, something of universal interest, and yet it portrays this relationship in a distinctively modern way, as we will see in this chapter, which introduces the cultural philosophy of Kuki.

Kuki Shūzō (1888–1941) was a man of cosmopolitan experience, having studied philosophy for many years in Europe (1921–1929) after an elite education in Japan. Despite this experience, his philosophical treatment of culture was reactionary, a response to what he encountered overseas, where he observed that the scientific method was being deployed to study not just natural phenomena but all areas of social and cultural life. Kuki lamented this spread of the scientific worldview not only because of its consequences in Europe, but also because he regretted similar developments in Japan during the first-third of the twentieth century, when the whole country was engaged in a process of rapid modernization that was quickly obliterating the Japan that he had known in his youth.

Kuki's study of culture is influenced by both his cosmopolitan experience and his reaction against the Europeanization of Japan. On the one hand, he was interested in the latest European debate between those who favored a social scientific study of culture such as the Neo-Kantians and those who resisted it, such as the phenomenologists Edmund Husserl and Martin Heidegger, and proponents of life philosophy such as Henri Bergson.[1] On the other hand, to resist the negative influence he felt this modernization was having in his homeland, Kuki had to identify its effects, and this first required understanding what was unique about Japanese culture. Identifying what is unique about Japanese culture was an important step in preserving traditional Japanese values as a bulwark against the destructive forces of "modernization."[2] Kuki's revulsion toward modernization is expressed poignantly in a short essay called "Time Is Money," in which he writes,

> Despite my good intentions, it is difficult to conceive of the kind of attitude involved in constantly acting and speaking in accordance with the law of the "value of a dollar," an attitude which reduces everything to the level of money. To my taste, the most terrible slogan imaginable is "Time is money." However, it is true that today, this slogan has been adopted and revered in every part of the world. Born in the new world, it has victoriously invaded the ancient. In this circumstance, should we also say, "Ok, let's join the party?" No, our logic is different; instead, we will respond: we alone will take a different path. (*KSZ* 1: [101]) (author's translation)

Kuki also writes in the same essay that the traditional values of *Bushidō* (the way of the samurai), which placed little value on money and commerce, were still the foundation of modern Japanese culture. He explains,

> Until the revolution of 1868,[3] there were four castes [in Japan]: samurai, farmers, artisans and merchants. Our moral ideal was "the way of the samurai," which above all valued bravery, a noble spirit and generosity. The merchants, the bottom caste, suffered excessive disdain. To give a literary example, Tsurayuki,[4] a poet and critic of the tenth century, when writing about verses comprised of beautiful words that were inappropriate for the subject, compared them to a merchant dressed up in beautiful clothes. This disdain for merchants and for commerce is no doubt unjust from every point of view. However, I dare to praise our old caste system above all since it is the basis of the ideal of our country. And now that [the caste system] has disappeared, the ideal still survives. (*KSZ* 1: [100]) (author's translation)

This short essay clearly expresses Kuki's dual intentions in his study of culture: use modern European methods to study it, but with the goal of identifying and preserving traditional Japanese values and rejecting European modernity.

While Kuki's plan seems simple, methodological problems appear as soon as he puts it into effect. The European methodology he chose for studying culture was well adapted to the European context from which it emerged,[5] and therefore the method reflected the cultural and social transformation taking place there. But Kuki's goal was to use European methods to preserve old values that were quickly being supplanted by new ones in Japanese society. The use of a new philosophical methodology, hermeneutic interpretation, to study an aesthetic concept from the past introduced from the outset a fundamental methodological problem. The Heideggerian hermeneutic methodology that Kuki employs in *The Structure of Iki* was used by Heidegger to analyze contemporary culture, that is, the culture of everyday life (*die Alltäglichkeit*). However, Kuki used it to understand the ethics and aesthetics that characterized the relationship between a *geisha* and her patron as it existed at the end of the eighteenth and beginning of the nineteenth centuries, a cultural context far removed from the everyday life of the average Japanese person during the 1920s and 1930s when Kuki lived. Indeed, the relationship between a *geisha* and her patron was very different from the experience of most Japanese living in the period from which the concept of *iki* was drawn; farmers or artisans rarely, if ever, came into contact with the *geisha* who embodied the aesthetic of *iki*.[6] As a result of the difference in subject matter to which Heidegger and Kuki apply the hermeneutic method, Kuki modified Heidegger's method, which was unsuited to his study of Japanese culture.

One of the principal goals of the chapters on Kuki is to identify the similarities and differences between the hermeneutic method described by Heidegger in his early work and that employed by Kuki. A second task will be to explore how Kuki modified Heidegger's method and what consequences this had for each philosopher's portrayal of culture. Heidegger was interested in identifying the existential structures of actual (contemporary) everyday life. *Being and Time* was not really meant to prescribe cultural ideals; rather, Heidegger limited himself to pointing out where to find them (in the authentic aspects of our cultural heritage) and what the possibility of retrieving them tells us about the nature of human existence and experience. In contrast, Kuki did want to portray an ideal that would save Japanese culture from being overwhelmed by European modernization and scientific approaches. He knew what he wanted to explore—the relationship between a *geisha* and her patron—and so he had to choose a method that was suited to his task of uncovering some of the fundamental philosophical presuppositions of Japanese culture. Kuki was interested in identifying the existential structures of an idealized way of living that could in turn serve as an ideal model for Japanese life to combat Europeanization and problematic modernization.

Our task of characterizing Kuki's philosophy of culture and identifying the similarities and differences between it and that of Martin Heidegger will be spread over three chapters. In this chapter, I will provide a brief overview of *The Structure of Iki* in order to orient those who might be new to the text. The orientation will consist of a description of the hermeneutic method Kuki proposes to use and of his theory of culture. According to Kuki, Japanese culture is animated by the ideals traditionally embodied by *Bushidō*, Buddhism, and *Shintō*. These ideals are not just a set of concepts: according to Kuki, they frame the way that Japanese people experience the world and interpret this experience. In the first section of this chapter, we will describe the elements of *iki*, which is the concrete expression of these traditional Japanese ideals as lived by the *geisha* and her lover. We will then sketch the method that Kuki proposes to capture its content.

In chapter 6, we will provide a more rigorous analysis of both the hermeneutic method that Kuki uses and the concept of culture that emerges from it. When compared to Watsuji's early philosophy, Kuki's philosophy displays a greater mastery of Heidegger's method. He emphasizes the hermeneutic aspects of it, which focus on the interpretation that is always going on in the background of human activity and that constitutes the context on which we draw to give meaning to our lives (Moran 2000, 238). Kuki's understanding of space and time is thus closer to that of Heidegger for whom human existence is authentic care, a way of being in the world that is constantly oriented toward the creation of meaning (Heidegger 1996, 326). Kuki thus differs to some degree from Watsuji, who was more interested in a particular interpretation (culture as climatic) than in how culture functions as a process of interpretation. Kuki also depends on a less transcendental reading of *Being and Time*. For instance, Watsuji's notion of spatiality in *Climate and Culture*—spatiality as climatic existence—presupposes Heideggerian existential spatiality, which Watsuji turns to in his later work in which spatiality is interpreted as betweenness (*aidagara*).

Kuki is not an uncritical Heideggerian: he modifies the hermeneutic method slightly based on Bergsonian ideas in order to serve his purposes. As he explains in *Bergson au Japon*, the Japanese were introduced to Husserlian and Heideggerian phenomenology by means of Bergson's intuitionism. Indeed, Kuki writes that Husserl's notion of intentionality and Heidegger's idea of human existence as "being-in-the-world" are essentially to be understood as methods of intuition similar to those described by Bergson (*KSZ* 1: [90]). The result of seeing Heidegger through the lens of Bergson is that Kuki introduces into Heideggerian hermeneutics Bergson's hierarchy of values: for Bergson, that which is intuited is more authentic, closer to the reality of life, which is a dynamic flow of experiences. *Iki*, the sensibility of the *geisha* and of Japanese culture more generally, is in Kuki's view a sensitivity to nuances in relationships and a sensitivity to the nature of life as fleeting and vain. *Iki* is a Japanese idiom that Kuki believes captures Bergson's intuitionist method and his idea of life as élan vital—the flowing of life's force (*KSZ* 1: [92])

AN INTRODUCTION TO KUKI'S *THE STRUCTURE OF IKI*

Kuki's Hermeneutics of *Iki*

The subject of this chapter and the next is *Iki no kōzō* (*The Structure of Iki*), a book Kuki first published in 1930.[7] Beyond the topic, which is the life and aesthetics of Japanese *geisha* and their patrons, the work is interesting because Kuki couples a description of the *geisha*'s chic style with a description of her ethic, which he links with *Bushidō* (the way of the samurai), Buddhism, and *Shintō*. As he wrote in a short essay titled "Geisha," the ethical and the aesthetic are not separate. Rather, "The ideal [of the *geisha*] that we call 'iki' is at once ethical and aesthetic; it is a harmonious unity of the voluptuous and the noble" (author's translation) (*KSZ* 1: [107]). It is the combination of an "inviolable dignity and grace"[8] (Kuki 2004, 20) with coquetry (Kuki 2004, 19) in a way that frees the *geisha* from being anchored in the everyday world of pain and suffering (Kuki 2004, 23).[9]

The Structure of Iki sets out Kuki's understanding of culture: it is something that expresses the way of being of a people who share a way of life, a way of life that has ethical content expressed in its social and cultural practices such as dress, art, architecture, music, language, and behavior. His study of culture begins with an interpretation of the concept of *iki*, which both expresses a very specific kind of relationship (that between a *geisha* and her patron) while at the same time expressing something that he believes to be fundamental about Japanese culture: the combination of ethics with aesthetics. *Iki* is thus the "self-revealing of a particular historical culture"[10] (Kuki 2004, 14), and it corresponds to the "'being' of an ethnic group,"[11] namely the Japanese people (ibid.).

Kuki labels the method that he will use to study this concept "hermeneutic," which he describes in language drawn from the phenomenology of both Husserl and Heidegger (for an explanation of the relationship between hermeneutics and phenomenology, see Moran 2000, 234ff.). Before looking at the details, it is useful to describe in a general way what the method involves. Kuki says that his hermeneutics takes as its starting point the determination of the meaning of phenomena of consciousness, in this case, the phenomenon of *iki*. A "phenomenon of consciousness" (*ishikigenshō*, 意識現象), the object of study, has two aspects: an intensional structure and an extensional structure (Kuki 2004, 18). First, Kuki describes the "intensional structure" of *iki* (*iki no naihōteki kōzō*; 「いき」の内包的構造), which is itself comprised of three elements: coquetry (*bitai*, 媚態), pride and honor (*ikiji*, 意気地), and resignation (*akirame*, 諦め). These three elements are the "meaning" (*imi*, 意味) of *iki* as a phenomenon of consciousness, by which he means that they are its "semantic content" (*hyōchō*, 表徴). I think it is easiest to think of the intensional structures of *iki* as the attitude that the *geisha* who displays *iki* adopts toward the world and her experiences.[12] These experiences are "framed by" or interpreted through the *geisha*'s coquettish attitude, pride, and resignation.

After studying the intensional structures of *iki*, Kuki turns to its "extensional structures" (*gaienteki kōzō*, 外延的構造). To clarify the meaning of *iki* by means of its extensional structures means to examine how it is expressed as a "property of human taste" (*ningen no shumi no seishitsu*; 人間の趣味の性質; Kuki 2004, 25; *KSZ* 1:27). Taste is not a property of objects; it is a "mode of being" (*sonzai*, 存在; Kuki 2004, 24; *KSZ* 1:26). For instance, Kuki writes that a person who is *iki* lives within "particularized heterosexual being" (*isseiteki tokushu sonzai*; 異性的特殊存在; Kuki 2004, 24; *KSZ* 1:26), by which I think he means that *iki* is a taste or sensibility that exists between two heterosexual lovers, as distinguished from *jōhin* (high-class) and *hade* (flashy), which he says denote ways of "being in general" (*jinseiteki ippan sonzai*; 人生的一般存在; ibid.), that is, a taste or sensibility that can exist in many social relations, not just erotic heterosexual ones. The meaning of *iki* as a system of taste that expresses a particular way of being can be articulated by means of four pairs of terms: high-class versus low-class (*jōhin* vs. *gehin*; 上品-下品); flashy versus restrained (*hade* vs. *jimi*, 派手-地味); sophisticated versus unsophisticated (*iki* vs. *yabo*, 意気-野暮), and astringent (in the sense of understated) versus sweet (in the sense of actively expressive) (*shibumi* vs. *amami*, 渋味-甘味) (see figure 5.1). In each case, the meaning of *iki* is located somewhere between the extremes represented by the opposing pairs. For instance, *iki* is not the same as "high-class" because if a woman's taste is too superior, it is not alluring or coquettish. Kuki gives the example of a widowed woman of fifty years of age who has become a Buddhist nun: she is "high-class" (*jōhin*) and not *iki* because she is inaccessible—that is, unavailable for flirtation of the kind that characterizes *iki* (Kuki

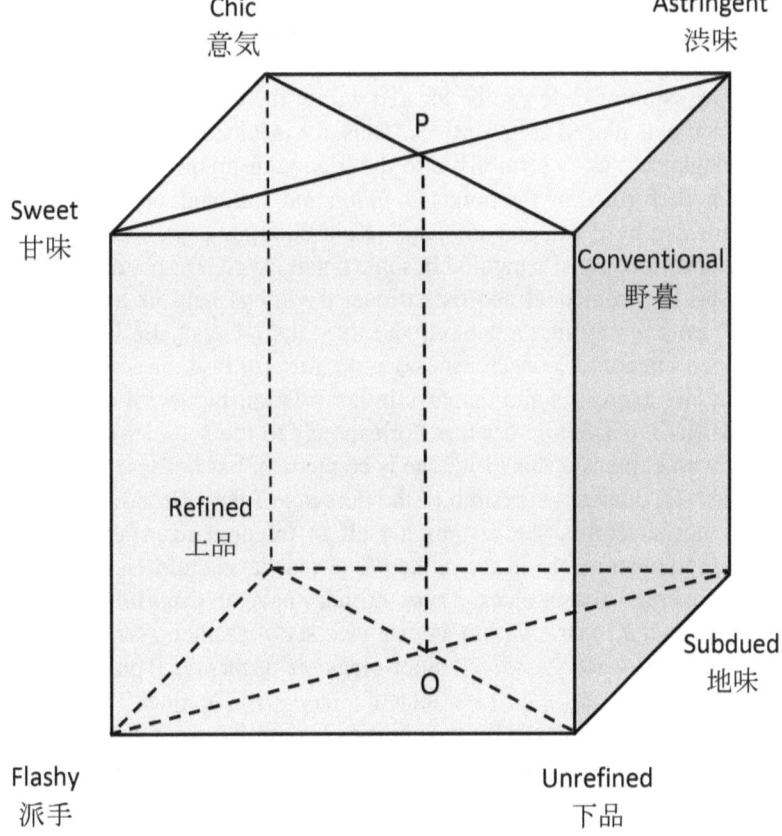

Figure 5.1 A System of Taste. *Source*: Author created.

2004, 25). On the other hand, not all flirtation is *iki*; vulgar flirtation is "low-class" (*gehin*). Thus Kuki concludes the following:

> When we consider how *iki* relates to *jōhin* "elegant, high class" and *gehin*, "crude, low class," we see why *iki* is commonly thought of as occupying the middle ground between *jōhin* and *gehin*. There are those who maintain that if a certain element is added to *jōhin*, we obtain *iki*, and if too much of it is added, we obtain *gehin*. *Jōhin* and *iki* both represent a positive value, but are distinguished by the presence or absence of this certain attribute. Moreover, this attribute is also shared with *gehin*, which represents a negative value. *Iki* is therefore viewed as signifying a middle ground between *jōhin* and *gehin*. (Kuki 2004, 26)

After identifying the pairs of opposites within which the extensional structure of *iki* is located, he reviews each pair, examining how *iki* is similar yet dissimilar to each of the opposing elements. Kuki depicts the four pairs of opposites by means of a cube of which each corner is occupied by one of the terms (high-class, low-class, flashy, restrained, sophisticated, unsophisticated, astringent, and sweet) (see figure 5.1). The various forms of extensional expression of taste can be located within the cube as a mixture of the various elements placed at its vertices. Thus, for instance, Kuki identifies *sabi* ("quiet elegance") as "a term given to the triangular prism which has on one side a triangle formed by the points O, *jōhin*, and *jimi*, and, on the other side, another formed by P, *iki*, and *shibumi*" (Kuki 2004, 33).

I have described Kuki's method in some detail in order to better understand what *iki* is. Its intensional and extensional meanings help us to understand that *iki* is both a way that a person who lives the *iki* aesthetic interprets the world (phenomenon of consciousness) and a form of taste or aesthetic sensibility that she expresses and displays in her relationships with others (Kuki 2004, 34). Its *intensional* structure corresponds to the subjective attitude of a *geisha* who expresses this taste: she is coquettish, but because of her pride and honor, she does not succumb to the pursuits of her patron. And because she does not succumb, she resigns herself to freedom from all permanent attachment to others—she is above the life of marriage, children, in short, the life of the average householder. These attitudes have an *extensional* structure in the sense that *iki* exists within an extended set of aesthetic sensibilities—a system of taste—such as *sabi* ("quiet elegance"), *miyabi* ("elegance"), *aji* ("witty"), *otsu* ("smart"), *kiza* ("affected"), *iropposa* ("coquet") (Kuki 2004, 33–34). Each of these aesthetic sensibilities is, like *iki*, a combination of the various tastes that form the vertices of the cube in figure 5.1. They are extensional because they constitute a particular taste that goes beyond a person's subjective attitude and is expressed in a certain way of being.

The last step in Kuki's analysis involves cataloguing ways in which *iki* as a phenomenon of consciousness is expressed objectively through ways of speaking, dressing, moving, holding one's body, and interacting with others that possess certain qualities: high-class yet alluring; not flashy, and yet not completely restrained; and so on. Kuki also describes various ways that *iki* can be expressed in art, architecture, textiles, and so on. Fujita Masakatsu explains the relationship between Kuki's discussion of these objective expressions of *iki* as a phenomenon of consciousness: art, architecture, the *geisha*'s way of speaking, dressing, and moving are only *iki* because they exist against the background of *iki* as a phenomenon of consciousness (Kuki 2004, 57). He notes that the various objective expressions of *iki* are not instances of the general concept of *iki*, but rather they express *iki* because they are experienced within a concrete relationship between people that expresses *iki* (Fujita 2002, 131). This is a very helpful insight because it points to the fact that what is being interpreted in *The Structure of Iki* is the interaction between a *geisha* and her patron, that is, a living relationship, not an abstract idealized one.

Iki as a Mode of Being: A Preliminary Indication of Kuki's Concept of Culture

What do we learn about Japanese culture from Kuki's analysis of *iki*? Culture is both a sensibility by which members of that culture give meaning to interactions with other humans and objects they encounter (*intensional* structure) and a way of being with others (*extensional* structure). In the case of the *geisha*, the taste or sensibility that is the *intensional* structure of *iki* is the set of attitudes (coquetry, pride and honor, and resignation) she adopts and that she uses to interpret the world. This sensibility is expressed in her deportment, dress, manner of speech, and so on. To be *iki* means to be coquettish, yet dignified and resigned. This sensibility is expressed by manners that are refined, yet not to the point of being distant—they are sensual in that they express a (heterosexual) flirtatious relationship.

But culture is more than just an attitude toward others: it is a way of being that is lived through certain kinds of relationships. The extensional structure of *iki* is a way of being that can be distinguished from and defined in relation to other ways of being:[13] the *geisha*'s way of living embodies a particular taste and sensibility that can be understood in relation to other such systems. The deportment of the *geisha* and her attitude have a place within a matrix of sensibilities and tastes. Thus culture is both an attitude toward the world and a particular way of being in the world.

While he derives *iki* from the specific relationship of a *geisha* and her lover, Kuki considers *iki* as going beyond this. He writes that *iki* also represents a "mode of being" (Kuki 2004, 34), "the manifestation of an ethnic group's past and present modes of being" (Kuki 2004, 14). It is the manifestation of a way of acting toward others, expressed in social actions, in the visual arts, architecture, manner of dress, and so on. While *iki* is not the only aesthetic in Japanese culture, Kuki believed that it expressed something fundamental about Japanese sensibility, something which a non-Japanese person would have difficulty comprehending (Kuki 2004, 55–56).

What makes *iki* a distinctive expression of Japanese culture while other sensibilities and forms of taste are not? It is the fact that a person who expresses *iki* and who adopts it as the frame through which she interprets her life and her relationships embodies ideals that have their origin in a set of traditional Japanese values represented by *Bushidō*, *Shintō*, and Buddhism. Thus for Kuki, culture is more than just the sum of shared ways of doing things; rather, culture expresses a way of living together based on shared values.

I think it is useful to consider this notion of *iki* as a phenomenon of consciousness as a sort of "worldview" (*Weltanschauung*) as Heidegger uses the term in *The Basic Problems of Phenomenology*. There, in his discussion of the historical origins of the term in Immanuel Kant's *Critique of Judgment* and in the writings of Goethe, Humboldt, and Schelling, he defines worldview as "a self-realized, productive as well as conscious way of apprehending and interpreting the universe of beings" (Heidegger 1982, 5); it is "interpretation of the sense and purpose of the human Dasein and hence of history" (ibid.).

Kuki described *iki* as the "manifestation of an ethnic group's past and present modes of being and . . . [the] self-revealing of a particular historical culture" (Kuki 2004, 14). Heidegger describes a worldview in a similar way:

> We grow up with such a world-view and gradually become accustomed to it. Our world-view is determined by environment—people, race, class, developmental stage of culture. Every world-view thus individually formed arises out of a natural world-view, out of a range of conceptions of the world and determinations of the human Dasein which are at any particular time given more or less explicitly with each such Dasein. (Heidegger 1982, 6)

Another way of thinking of Kuki's concept of culture is to draw an analogy between *iki* as an aesthetic sensibility and the aesthetic sense of the beautiful that Immanuel Kant describes in *The Critique of Judgment* (Kant 2000). According to Kant, aesthetic judgment has a subjective aspect: the feeling of pleasure in apprehending a beautiful object (5:189; 5:203–204). And yet it has an objective element because a claim that something is beautiful invites the assent of the community of judgment (5:212–213; 215–216; 237; 285; 292–293). *Iki* is not the equivalent of "the beautiful" in the Kantian framework. But it has both subjective and objective elements much like

Kant's idea of an aesthetic sense. On the one hand, it is a sensibility that an individual possesses: this is its *intensional* structure, which is the structure of a phenomenon of consciousness. On the other hand, it is a sensibility that is shared by a group and whose meaning can therefore be conceptualized in relation to other shared concepts of taste. This is the *extensional* structure of *iki*, which situates it in relation to the aesthetic of the refined, of the bawdy and vulgar, and so on. Moreover, to the extent that *iki* is the expression of the way of being of a people, its objective elements are agreed upon not by pure conceptual thinking but by (mostly unconscious) agreement between those who form part of the cultural community. As Kant explains in *The Critique of Judgment*, taste is not something that one learns by rote; one simply learns it by being in the company of those who already possess the shared aesthetic sensibility. To deploy it when one judges, one must take into account how the community of taste would judge (5:294). The "sensus communis" (common sense) on which aesthetic judgments are based, Kant explains, is "a faculty for judging that in its reflection takes account (*a priori*) of everyone else's way of representing in thought, in order as it were to hold its judgment up to human reason as a whole and thereby avoid the illusion which, from subjective private conditions that could easily be held to be objective, would have a detrimental influence on the judgment" (5:293–294).

We have now accomplished the first goal of this chapter, which was to describe the concept of culture that underlies Kuki's study of *iki*: *iki* is the expression of a sensibility shared by those who belong to and participate in Japanese culture that expresses itself on a subjective level as an attitude toward life, that exists on an objective level as one form that a system of taste can take, and that is expressed externally in various social practices and modes of interaction. Our next goal is to examine Kuki's method in detail and identify the influences on it. As we will see, these influences are primarily Heideggerian, but they also draw on the intuitive method of Henri Bergson. *The Structure of Iki* is innovative not only in the way that Kuki retrieves a past cultural understanding (*iki*) to present it as an ideal for modern Japan but also in his method of philosophical inquiry. The hermeneutic method Kuki describes may have its origins in the philosophy of Heidegger, but he modifies it by introducing spatial and relational concepts that were missing from the Heideggerian model.

KUKI'S HERMENEUTIC METHOD: ADAPTATION AND INNOVATION

Let us begin our detailed study of Kuki's hermeneutic method with the contrast he draws from the outset: the "study of *iki* cannot be 'eidetic,'" he writes, "it should be 'hermeneutic'" (Kuki 2004, 18). What does this contrast between "eidetic" and "hermeneutic" mean? A hermeneutic method, Kuki explains, places the investigation of *existentia* before the investigation of *essentia* (2004, 18): hermeneutics begins with understanding *iki* as a "phenomenon of consciousness" (*ishikigenshō*, 意識現象), which represents its existential (lived) dimension. Only then does the investigator turn to "objective expressions" (*kankyakuteki hyōgen*, 観客的表現) of *iki* in nature, art, manner of dress, and so on, expressions which represent its essential dimension. The terms "existentia" and "essentia" are used in Heideggerian philosophy. Kuki defines them in his book *Human Beings and Existence* (*Ningen to jitsuzon*, 『人間と実存』; Kuki 1939) as follows: a thing's essence is a "possible existence" (*kanōteki sonzai*, 可能的存在), which is not in time (*chōjikanteki sonzai*, 超時間的存在); while a thing's existence is its "actual existence" (*genjitsusonzai*, 現実存在), which necessarily takes place in time (*jikanteki no sonzai*, 時間的の存在) (Kuki 1939, 62).[14] The distinction between an eidetic method and a hermeneutic one is that the former is purely conceptual while the latter is experiential. Heidegger gives a good example in *Being and Time*: the statement "The hammer is heavy" is a conceptual statement; the experience "this hammer is too heavy" is an experiential one (1996, 157). To study *iki* conceptually would be to develop an abstract concept of its meaning; to study *iki* hermeneutically means to examine how it is experienced by the subject expressing it (*intensional* structures) and how it is expressed as a system of taste that is not purely conceptual but rather part of one's sensibility as a member of a culture.

To understand the difference between eidetic and hermeneutic analysis, it may be useful to sketch what an investigation of *iki* would look like using each form of analysis. An eidetic study of *iki* would begin with the end of *The Structure of Iki*, which catalogues objective expressions of *iki* in nature, in the behaviors and language of *geisha* and in art and architecture. Once we have a sufficiently accurate catalogue, the next step would be to find their shared "essence," which would involve identifying a concept that can encompass all of these objects and behaviors that express *iki*. Concretely, an eidetic method would involve taking specific instances of *iki* and then identifying (Kuki uses the term "intuiting") a general concept that expresses their common essence (*honshitsuchokkan*; 本質直観; Kuki 2004, 18; *KSZ* 1:13).[15] Kuki explains that he does not adopt this method for interpreting *iki* because the eidetic approach fails to achieve its goal: all that it manages to do is to derive a general concept of *iki* rather than grasp it as a living phenomenon (2004, 17–18), that is, it cannot capture *iki* as a way of being and experiencing of a specific group of people.

In contrast, the method that Kuki prefers is "hermeneutic," that is, it involves interpretation. What does interpretation mean in this case? As Ingrid Leman Stefanovic explains, in Heideggerian philosophy, the term "hermeneutic" is expanded beyond its usual application to textual interpretation "to include the fundamental activity whereby we seek to understand and interpret the holistic phenomenon of human experience of the world in general" (Stefanovic 1994, 62).[16] Studying *iki* hermeneutically requires investigating the way that *iki* as a phenomenon of consciousness gives meaning to the world of the *geisha* and specifically to her relationship with her lover. It is only once one has grasped *iki* as a phenomenon of consciousness—that is, understood its meaning as the *geisha*'s general attitude toward the world—that the hermeneuticist then turns to investigating its "objective expressions" (*kankyakuteki hyōgen*, 観客的表現), which, as we recall, was the starting point for the eidetic investigation. In contrast, the hermeneutic method permits one to grasp a phenomenon as it is (*sonzaietoku*, 存在会得), by which Kuki means the concrete (*gutaiteki*, 具体的), actual (*jijitsuteki*, 事実的) experience of it, how it presents itself (*KSZ* 1:13). In this case, he is interested in how the *geisha* experiences her world through the aesthetic sensibility of *iki*, which is then expressed for others to experience through the way that she behaves outwardly.

I mentioned in the previous section that there is some reason to think of *iki* as a phenomenon of consciousness as akin to a worldview held by the *geisha* (and by all Japanese, to the extent that Kuki thinks of *iki* as expressing the "being" of an ethnic group). We can now also see that the method he proposes to use to grasp it—the hermeneutic method—is well suited to uncovering a worldview because, as Heidegger says, a worldview is "not a matter of theoretical knowledge" but rather "a matter of coherent conviction." He writes,

> A world-view is not a matter of theoretical knowledge, either in respect of its origin or in relation to its use. It is not simply retained in memory like a parcel of cognitive property. Rather, it is a matter of a coherent conviction which determines the current affairs of life more or less expressly and directly. A world-view is related in its meaning to the particular contemporary Dasein at any given time. In this relationship to the Dasein the world-view is a guide to it and a source of strength under pressure. (Heidegger 1982, 6)

As we have seen, Kuki's hermeneutic method eschews the adoption of a theoretical perspective in order to grasp *iki* as a phenomenon of consciousness that frames the way that the *geisha* interacts with others in the world. Likewise, for Heidegger, a worldview eschews theoretical knowledge and captures something intuitively as if it were a memory, but that "determines the current affairs of life."

Charles Taylor contrasts the eidetic and hermeneutic methods by contrasting a conceptual with a "lived approach." He writes,

> [Heidegger's] aim is to show that grasping things as neutral objects is one of our possibilities only against the background of a way of being in the world in which things are disclosed as ready-to-hand. Grasping things neutrally requires modifying our stance to them that primitively has to be one of involvement. Heidegger, like Kant, is arguing that the comportment to things described in the disengaged view requires for its intelligibility to be situated within an enframing and continuing stance to the world that is antithetical to it, hence that this comportment could not be original and fundamental. (1993)

The *eidetic* mode of inquiry that Kuki rejects is the disengaged, neutral view described by Taylor. In contrast, the *hermeneutic* mode of inquiry is engaged in the sense that it describes the way that we experience things that forms the background to, the transcendental precondition of, abstract thinking about it.

We have explained the difference between eidetic and hermeneutic inquiries in a very conceptual and abstract way. A few examples might help to make the distinction more intuitive. Kuki uses the example of the scent of a rose. To understand the scent of a rose eidetically, one would try to define "the smell of a rose" by examining various instances of it from one's life. The goal would be to create a universally valid general concept of "the smell of a rose" that would be true for everyone (Kuki 2004, 17). To understand the scent of a rose hermeneutically as a phenomenon of consciousness, one must instead "grasp it as it is in its living form without destroying its actual concreteness."[17] The smell of a rose is experienced either as the memory of a rose we have smelled, or as the actual smelling of a rose; in either case, the smell is part of a context that includes all the other experiences that accompany the smell. Kuki explains,

> Bergson states that when we recall the past as we smell roses, it is not that the fragrance triggers the memory. Rather, we smell in the fragrance the memory of the past. Immutable object, such as the fragrance of roses, or, equivalently, general concepts that are universal for all men, do not exist in reality. Rather, there are individual fragrances having differing olfactory contents. According to Bergson, explaining experience by means of the combination of a general object, such as the fragrance of roses, and a specific object, such as a memory, would be much like trying to produce sounds specific to a language by arranging letters of the alphabet commonly used in many languages. (Kuki 2004, 17; *KSZ* 1:13)[18]

Another way that he explains the difference between eidetic and hermeneutic investigation is by contrasting a conceptual (*eidetic*) and experiential (*hermeneutic*) understanding of the relationship between God and the Trinity. Using an eidetic method, Saint Anselm derived from the three elements of God, Father, Son, and Holy Spirit, a general concept of a universal God that united them. In contrast, Roscelin[19] could not accept the generalized concept of God because he felt it was nothing more than a name for an abstract concept divorced from the reality of the Father, the Son, and the Holy Spirit. These, he believed, were three separate beings, and the concept of their unity in the Trinity was nothing more than a "name" (hence the label of "nominalist" that is affixed to him).[20] For after all, how can three separate beings be reduced to a single God except abstractly, that is, in name only. To bring us back to *iki*, Kuki suggests that if we adopt a hermeneutic approach to *iki*, we accept Roscelin's "nominalist solution" to the problem of universals, by which he means that *iki* should not be grasped as a universal concept that is intuited from specific instances of *iki*, but rather that we should grasp *iki* as the meaning of concrete ways of experiencing the world.

A hermeneutic study of *iki* requires that we grasp its meaning by examining the way that the patron interacts with the *geisha*. These interactions give hints of the system of attitudes that the *geisha* possesses, and which she expresses through her behavior, gestures, speech, mode of dress, and so on. Bergson's rose is the *geisha*, its scent is *iki*.

THE INFLUENCE OF BERGSON ON KUKI'S INTERPRETATION OF HERMENEUTICS

Thus far we have presupposed that Kuki's hermeneutic method was derived solely from Heidegger. However, as we will see in the next chapter, there are important divergences between both the method they employ and the conclusions they draw about the nature of culture. These differences may be attributable to the influence of Henri Bergson on Kuki's articulation of the hermeneutic method.

First, a historical note to explain why we are justified in identifying Bergson's influence on Kuki's hermeneutic method. While many scholars have rightly noted the influence of Heidegger on Kuki's method (Sakabe 1990, 78), Kuki's long sojourn in France also had a significant impact on his philosophy. Indeed, Japanese scholars have noted that Kuki had already begun drafting *The Structure of Iki* before reading Heidegger's *Being and Time*. As Takada Tamaki points out, Kuki probably met Heidegger for the first time shortly after the publication of *Being and Time* in April 1927, and Kuki returned to Japan in early 1929. In consequence, he probably had less than a year to actually study with Heidegger (Takada 2002, 140). But Kuki had already begun to draft a precursor text to *The Structure of Iki*, called

The Essence of Iki (*Iki no honshitsu*), in December 1926 (Fujita 2002, 117), well before the publication of *Being and Time*. Thus it is unrealistic to think that the method that Kuki uses in *The Structure of Iki* is solely based on Heideggerian hermeneutics. Indeed, the fact that Kuki uses examples from Bergson's work to illustrate his method suggest that the latter's philosophical method was also influential. For instance, Bergson's description of how a feeling pervades all of one's perceptions resonates with Kuki's description of how the attitude of *iki* (its intensional structure as a phenomenon of consciousness) pervades all of the *geisha*'s actions and the relationship between her and her patron. Bergson writes,

> For example, an obscure desire gradually becomes a deep passion. Now, you will see that the feeble intensity of this desire consisted at first in its appearing to be isolated and, as it were, foreign to the remainder of your inner life. But little by little it permeates a larger number of psychic elements, tingeing them, so to speak, with its own colour: and your outlook on the whole of your surroundings seems now to have changed radically. How do you become aware of a deep passion, once it has taken hold of you, if not by perceiving that the same objects no longer impress you in the same manner? All your sensations and all your ideas seem to brighten up: it is like childhood back again. We experience something of the kind in certain dreams, in which we do not imagine anything out of the ordinary, and yet through which there resounds an indescribable note of originality. (Bergson 1910, 8)

Bergson's description of desire and the way that it "permeates a larger number of psychic elements" resonates with the way Kuki describes how resignation (*akirame*), one of the features of the intensional structure of *iki*, takes hold of the *geisha*: "The sincerest heart," he writes, "callously betrayed often over time, is tempered by that repeated pain and ceases to pay attention to deceitful targets" (Kuki 2004, 21). This tempering, borne of experience, colors her actions, stealing her resolve to bravely remain free from permanent entanglements.

Later in *Time and Free Will*, Bergson also describes something similar to a worldview, but one which is personal to each individual and that "tinges" her sensations with her unique character. Bergson writes,

> The associationist reduces the self to an aggregate of conscious states: sensations, feelings, and ideas. But if he sees in these various states no more than is expressed in their name, if he retains only their impersonal aspect, he may set them side by side for ever without getting anything but a phantom self, the shadow of the ego projecting itself into space. If, on the contrary, he takes these psychic states with the particular colouring which they assume in the case of a

definite person, and which comes to each of them by reflection from all the others, then there is no need to associate a number of conscious states in order to rebuild the person, for the whole personality is in a single one of them, provided that we know how to choose it. (Bergson 1910, 165)

What Kuki considers a "phenomenon of consciousness" seems to be very close to what Bergson calls "the particular colouring" which all of a person's perceptions assume. The meaning of this coloring is the individuality of the self (the "fundamental self" [Bergson 1910, 167] or "deep-seated self" [ibid., 169] according to Bergson), which is our self as a "living thing" in a constant state of becoming (Bergson 1910, 231). It is, he writes,

> the whole of our most intimate feelings, thoughts and aspirations, with that particular conception of life which is the equivalent of all our past experience, in a word, with our personal idea of happiness and of honour. (Bergson 1910, 170)

Similarly, the experienced *geisha* is possessed by "the state of mind that has suffered through hard *ukiyo*'s tough and merciless tribulations and shed worldly concerns" (Kuki 2004, 22). This state of mind is maintained "as a possibility to the bitter end," indeed, this is what constitutes and sustains the idealism of the *geisha* (Kuki 2004, 22).

Finally, Bergson explains that the character of our fundamental self is expressed in all of the decisions in which we let this character manifest itself. The relationship between the fundamental self and its expressions are like "that indefinable resemblance . . . which one sometimes finds between the artist and his work" (Bergson 1910, 172). This seems to be much like the relationship that Kuki finds between *iki* as a phenomenon of consciousness and the objective expressions of *iki* in the way that the *geisha* moves, dresses, speaks, and so on. *Iki* is not just its natural expressions, but rather, its meaning is to be found in the very character, the very way of being of the *geisha*.

Kuki contrasted the hermeneutic method with the eidetic, the way of grasping *iki* as it is lived and experienced with a purely abstract and conceptual method of inquiry. Bergson also deplored abstract inquiry of this type when it came to seizing the fundamental character of what he termed the "deep-seated self." Bergson describes this abstract method as involving the artificial separation and labeling of psychic states, followed by the creation of general categories into which they can be fit. He contrasts the two methods thus:

> An attentive consciousness [would perceive] a living self, whose states, at once undistinguished and unstable, cannot be separated without changing their nature, and cannot received a fixed form or be expressed in words without becoming public property. [In contrast, an unreflective consciousness would] replace the

interpenetration of its psychic states, their wholly qualitative multiplicity, by a numerical plurality of terms which are distinguished from one another, set side by side, and expressed by means of words. In place of a heterogeneous duration whose moments permeate one another, we thus get a homogenous time whose moments are strung on a spatial line. In place of an inner life whose successive phases, each unique of its kind, cannot be expressed in the fixed terms of language, we get a self which can be artificially reconstructed, and simple psychic states which can be added to and taken from one another just like the letters of the alphabet in forming words. (Bergson 1919, 236–237)

There are clear links between Kuki's description of a hermeneutic method and the method that Bergson uses to grasp our "living self," eschewing abstract conceptions of human life.

INFLUENCE AND ORIGINALITY: KUKI'S HERMENEUTIC METHOD

In *The Structure of Iki*, Kuki demonstrates that Japanese culture is not defined by abstract ideas but rather by lived ideals. These ideals are derived from the traditions of *Bushidō*, Buddhism, and *Shintō*, but they are expressed concretely in the attitudes of the *geisha* toward life and in the form of relationship she chooses to have with others. The Japanese, like members of any culture, are sensitive to many aesthetics, including that prevalent in Europe. And yet the one that best expresses the mode of being of the Japanese is the one that is the concrete, lived expression of the ideals of their past and present. *Iki* is the aesthetic sensibility that expresses these ideals, and the fact that it continues to live on in modern Japanese art and culture—in manga and anime, for instance—demonstrates the profound insight that Kuki had into what it means to be Japanese.

In the next two chapters, we will examine in more detail how Kuki's philosophical expertise allowed him to modify Heideggerian hermeneutics to make it suitable for discovering and articulating the unique form of cultural expression and the source of cultural meaning that *iki* represents.

NOTES

1. In *Bergson au Japon*, Kuki explains the similarity he sees between the philosophy of Bergson and that of phenomenologists Husserl, Max Scheler, and Heidegger (*KSZ* 1: [88–92]). Note: page numbers in parentheses are as they appear in *Kuki Shūzō Zenshū*. The reason for them is that Volume 1 contains texts both in Japanese

language and European languages. Those in German and French are paginated separately from those in Japanese. The parentheses indicate this separate pagination.

2. Obama Yoshinobu gives an explanation of Kuki's choice of *iki* as a topic in a way that fits my explanation. He writes that there were two reasons for Kuki's interest in the topic. First, having spent a long period overseas, Kuki, like his contemporaries who had also studied abroad, sought a way to express to Europeans the important relationship between ethics and aesthetics in Japan. Second, being away from home gave Kuki the distance necessary to clearly see aspects of his own culture to which those living in its midst were blind (Obama 2006, 63). Of course, there have also been other explanations of his interest in *iki* and the aesthetics of the *geisha* that are more personal to Kuki; they depend in part on the fact that his mother, whom he loved and respected deeply, had been a *geisha* (Furukawa 2015, 223–224).

3. The Meiji Restoration, which returned political power from the samurai class to the emperor. The Restoration is also synonymous for many Japanese with the beginning of modernization and Europeanization of Japan, since many social, political, economic, and legal reforms were instituted during the reign of Emperor Meiji (1868–1912) (for a description of the reforms, see "The Early Meiji Revolution," Chapter 3 in Tipton 2008).

4. Ki no Tsurayuki (紀 貫之, 872–945) was a poet of the Heian period.

5. Here, I am thinking of the humanist tendencies that animated much of the Neo-Kantian study of culture and the social sciences, for example, in Herman Cohen's *Ethics of Pure Will* (*Ethik des reinen Willens* (1904)).

6. For a description of the world of the *geisha* during the Tokugawa period (1603–1868), see Teruoka (2000).

7. It first appeared in two parts in the journal *Shisō* in January and February 1930. It was published as a short book in November of the same year. There are two English translations: Nara (2004) and Clark (1997).

8. 気品気格 (*KSZ* 1:18).

9. 「「いき」は安価なる現実の提立を無視し、実生活に大胆なる括弧を施し、超然として中和の空気を吸いながら、無目的なまた無関心な自律的遊戯をしている。」(*KSZ* 1:22).

10. 「...歴史を有する特殊の文化の自己開示に外ならない。」(*KSZ* 1:8).

11. 「民族の生きた存在」(*KSZ* 1:8).

12. Dermot Moran refers us to Heidegger's lectures on the *History of the Concept of Time*, given in 1925, for a good discussion of his interpretation of intentionality and his critique of the concept in Brentano and Husserl (Moran 2000, 231). In the lectures, Heidegger discusses intentionality as "directedness toward objects" (Heidegger 1985, 62), which I think is helpful for understanding what Kuki means by "intensional structure."

13. Kuki explains that *iki* belongs to a "particularized heterosexual being" (*iseiteki tokushu sonzai*; 異性的特殊存在) whereas *jōhin* and *hade* (classy and flashy) belong to a "general human being" (*jinseiteki ippan sonzai*; 人生的一般存在).

14. Kuki is clearly using "essence" in the sense that Edmund Husserl does when describing the "eidetic reduction" that characterizes part of the phenomenological

method. Kockelmans describes the eidetic method as follows: "Eidetic phenomenology . . . explores the universal a priori, without which neither I nor any transcendental ego whatsoever is imaginable. And since every eidetic universality has the value of an unbreakable law, eidetic phenomenology explores the all-embracing laws that prescribe for every factual statement about something transcendental the possible meaning of that statement. . . . [To be truly scientific, the phenomenologist must] go back to the apodictic principles that pertain to this ego as exemplifying the *eidos* 'ego'" (1994, 265).

15. This idea of intuiting the essence refers to "eidetic reduction," part of Edmund Husserl's phenomenological method, especially as set out in *Ideas* (the *Stanford Encyclopedia of Philosophy* entry on Husserl cites: *Experience and Judgment*, sec. 87). While eidetic reduction is part of Husserl's phenomenological method (Stefanovic 1994, 70, quoting Seamon 1982, 121), Kuki finds this approach to be essentially analytical, since it aims at forming an "abstract general concept" of which the concrete phenomenon is only a part (Kuki 2004, 17; *KSZ* 1:12). You can find Kuki's analysis of ideation and the process of free variation by means of which one intuits the essential meaning of a phenomenon in *Human Beings and Existence* (1939, 73–75).

16. Husserl used the term "phenomenon" in this holistic, contextual sense as well. For instance, he writes in *Phenomenology*, "When we are fully engaged in conscious activity, we focus exclusively on the specific things, thoughts, values, goals, or means involved, but not on the psychical experience as such, in which these things are known *as* such. Only reflection reveals this to us. Through reflection, instead of grasping simply the matter straight out—the values, goals, and instrumentalities—we grasp the corresponding subjective experiences in which we become 'conscious' of them, in which (in the broadest sense) they 'appear.' For this reason, they are called 'phenomena'" (cited in Kearney and Rainwater 1996, 15) [emphasis in original].

17. 「... 事実としての具体性を害うことなくありのままの生ける形態に於いて把握すること...」 (*KSZ* 1:12)

18. 「ベルクソンは、薔薇の匂を嗅いで過去を回想する場合に、薔薇の匂が与えられてそれによって過去のことが連想されるのではない。過去の回想を薔薇の匂のうちに嗅ぐのであると云っている。薔薇の匂という一定不変のもの、万人に共通な類概念的のものが現実として存するのではない。内容を異にした個々の匂があるのみである。そうして薔薇の匂という一般的なものと回想という特殊なものとの連合によって体験を説明するのは、多くの国語に共通なアルファベットの幾字かを竝べて或る一定の国語の有する特殊な音を出そうとするようなものであると云っている。」 (*KSZ* 1:13) The examples Kuki uses are from Bergson (1910, 161–162).

19. Roscelin of Compiègne (*c.* 1050–*c.* 1125), a French nominalist philosopher.

20. For a detailed explanation of Roscelin's nominalism, see Erismann (2008, 5).

Chapter 6

Kuki and Heidegger
The Method for Interpreting Culture

In order to appreciate Kuki's theory of culture, it will be useful to understand the hermeneutic method he uses to capture what is unique about Japanese culture.[1] In chapter 5, I indicated that this method is not purely Heideggerian as it integrates elements of Bergson's intuitionist approach. There have also been suggestions that Kuki was influenced by the concept of intuition in Husserl's phenomenology (Fujita 2002). For Kuki, culture is a system of taste that, like a worldview, frames the way that we understand ourselves and our world. But according to Kuki, this system is not purely worldly: from time to time, we catch glimpses of the absolute, something that has no place in Heideggerian philosophy. The worldview that Kuki labels *iki* depends on recognizing the manifestation of the absolute in the aesthetic sensibilities of the *geisha* and her lover and in the art and architecture that express *iki*. It is in these moments in which we intuit the infinite that we grasp the importance of choosing to live an ethical life and can make a real choice.

Heidegger's phenomenological ontology firmly grounds human existence in this world: human existence is Dasein as being-in-the-world (*In-der-Welt Sein*). How can Kuki use a hermeneutic method inspired by Heidegger that does not acknowledge a tenet fundamental to the latter's philosophy? As we will see, Kuki only adopts limited aspects of the Heideggerian hermeneutic method. First, he accepts that humans exist in a world *that is inherently meaningful*, and therefore that this existence involves a process of constant interpretation: as Hans-Georg Gadamer explains, "Understanding . . . is . . . the *original form of the realization of Dasein*, which is being-in-the-world" (2103, 260; see also Couzens Hoy 172) [emphasis in original]. Second, he accepts that a consequence of the fact that human existence involves interpretation is that hermeneutics has an important historical element: the context of meanings in which we each exist in the present is rooted in possibilities of the past (Couzens Hoy 178). What he does not accept is Heidegger's analysis of the ontological structures of human existence (temporality and spatiality) that make human existence as a process of interpretation possible. Kuki does accept the fundamental importance of time and space for constituting human existence; but he insists that our ability to access the absolute implies a "metaphysical" dimension to human existence. The intuition by means of which we experience the absolute and the possibility of acting on what we learn through this intuition requires Kuki to conceive of the relationship between possibility and necessity, and hence Heideggerian temporality, in a radically different way. This reinterpretation is undertaken in many of Kuki's works including *The Problem of Contingency*.

Since Kuki's method is not purely Heideggerian, it will be useful to disentangle the Heideggerian elements woven into it in order to better appreciate how he creatively modified the hermeneutic method to serve his own purpose. In this chapter, our aim is to understand Kuki's idea of culture by identifying the originality of his hermeneutic method. And this in turn requires us to begin with Heideggerian hermeneutics in order to better compare and contrast Kuki's hermeneutic method with it.

THE ORIGINS OF HERMENEUTICS IN HUSSERL—"TO THE THINGS THEMSELVES!"[2]

Kuki is very clear at the beginning and end of *The Structure of Iki* that he is using a hermeneutic method, and throughout the text, he adopts Heideggerian terminology. In order to better understand Kuki's interpretation of Heidegger, and in particular, his application of the hermeneutic method to his study of Japanese culture, it is useful to examine Husserl's phenomenological method, particularly as he applied it to culture. Within Husserl's approach, one can already recognize what appealed to Kuki about the phenomenological study of culture, namely, that it takes as its starting point intersubjectivity, something that is missing from the transcendental methodology of the Neo-Kantians who dominated the social and cultural sciences in the early part of the twentieth century, but also something which Kuki found lacking in Heidegger's philosophy.

As Heidegger explains in *Ontology: The Hermeneutics of Facticity*,[3] Husserl's great insight was that the object of philosophy is the flow of experience, and so to understand it, one must bracket all theoretical approaches, including naturalistic ones, through what he called "reduction." Heidegger describes the phenomenological method as follows: "Phenomenology is a *method of inquiry* that explores objects as they appear clearly and only in so far as they do so" (1923, 72) [emphasis in original]. Paul Ricoeur explains that when practicing Husserlian phenomenology "one occupies oneself only with the pure appearing" without "pronouncing . . . on the ultimate ontological status of the appearing" (1967, 10). As Dermot Moran explains, "The reduction allows the true structure of intentionality to be understood, now stripped of naturalistic misconceptions" (2000, 160). Husserl himself described what is involved in carrying out a phenomenological investigation by means of phenomenological reduction in his Vienna Lectures of 1935:

> We wish . . . to consider the surrounding life-world concretely, in its neglected relativity and according to all the manners of relativity belonging essentially to it—the world in which we live intuitively, together with its real entities [*Realitäten*]; but "we wish to consider them" *as* they give themselves to us at first in straightforward experience, and even [consider] the ways in which their validity is sometimes in suspense (between being and illusion, etc.). Our exclusive task shall be to comprehend precisely this style, precisely this whole merely subjective and apparently incomprehensible "Heraclitean flux." Thus we are not concerned with whether and what the things, the real entities of the world, actually are (their being actual, their actually being such and such, according to properties, relations, interconnections, etc.); we are also not concerned with what the world, taken as a totality, actually is, what in general belongs to it in the way of a priori structural lawfulness or factual "natural laws." We have nothing like this as our subject matter. Thus we exclude all knowledge, all statements about true being and predicative truths for it, such as are required in active life for its praxis (i.e., situational truths); but we also exclude all sciences, genuine as well as pseudosciences, with their knowledge of the world as it is "in itself," in "objective truth." (1970, 156) [emphasis in original]

Husserlian phenomenology investigates the nature of reality from the point of view of experience just as it is, unbiased by any theory about what it is that we are experiencing (Gadamer 246, 259). "Intuition" is the mechanism whereby phenomena are grasped just as they are. As Ricoeur explains, "intuition is to be the ultimate for all constitution" of phenomena (1967, 19).

While Husserl brilliantly captures the importance of intentionality for understanding the nature of human experience,[4] Heidegger and Kuki were critical of the fact that Husserl's method did not recognize the importance of the everyday world as the basic context in which we find meaning. Husserlian phenomenology may have called us to begin philosophical inquiry with this context by bracketing theoretical suppositions about it. But what Husserl did not do was seriously question why everyday existence is so fundamental to human experience and a proper subject of philosophical inquiry. Thus in his 1923 lectures, Heidegger criticized Husserl's philosophy as being insufficiently radical: all that it aims at is establishing a firm philosophical foundation for the sciences (1923, 32–33)[5] without questioning what the method of philosophical inquiry that Husserl adopts tells us about more basic questions such as what it means to be human, or more specifically, what the human mode of existence is.

Husserl's second error was to fail to stay true to his initial insight that phenomenological inquiry must begin with everyday life. The most obvious instance of this failure is that phenomenologists begin by focusing on something that originates outside us—the stream of experiences: Husserlian phenomenology is a kind of epistemological inquiry into the nature of our experience that leaves the realist presumptions about the existence of an external world unquestioned. Thus, according to Heidegger, most phenomenologists forget to ask if epistemological questions of this kind have any true philosophical meaning (1923, 73). A "true" phenomenological inquiry, writes Heidegger, is one which explores the possibility of phenomenology understood as clear and direct access to the things themselves (1923, 74), not one that simply presupposes the propriety of the standpoint from which the inquiry is undertaken.

Thus Husserlian phenomenology is not sufficiently radical to ask the questions that Heidegger and Kuki are interested in asking. We can recast their concern in a way that is of importance to the theme of this book: culture. Husserl presumed that all forms of group life, including cultural life, ultimately have a universal structure that is revealed through the phenomenological reduction (Moran 2000, 181). Husserl explains this in the following way:

> *I* am the one who performs the epochē [phenomenological reduction], and, even if there are others, and even if they practice the epochē in direct community with me, [they and] all other human beings with their entire act-life are included, for me, within my epochē, in the world-phenomenon which, in my epochē, is exclusively mine. The epochē creates a unique sort of philosophical solitude which is the fundamental methodical requirement for a truly radical philosophy. In this solitude I am not a single individual who has somehow willfully cut himself off from the society of mankind, perhaps even for theoretical reasons, or who is cut off by accident, as in a shipwreck, but who nevertheless knows that he still belongs to that society. I am not *an* ego, who still has his *you*, his *we*, his totally community of cosubjects in natural validity. All of mankind, and the whole distinction and ordering of the personal pronouns, has become a phenomenon within my epochē; and so has the privilege of I-the-man among other men. (1970, 184) [emphasis in original]

For Husserl, the intersubjective world (of which culture is a part) is constituted within my experience as an experience of the possibility of other experiencing subjects who collectively experience the same world. As Joseph Kockelmans explains, through phenomenological reduction

> an ego community as a community of monads is constituted in the sphere of my ownness, which in its communalized intentionality constitutes the one identical world for everybody. In other words, my transcendental subjectivity is gradually expanded into a transcendental intersubjectivity or community, which in turn is the transcendental ground for the intersubjective value of nature and the world in general. (*Par. Lect.,* 35 [35]) (1994, 25–26)

As we can see, Husserl's phenomenological approach is not useful for exploring culture as a process of giving meaning to the world in which we exist together. Instead, intersubjectivity is the experience of a community of monads experiencing a shared world whose meaning remains unquestioned. Thus Husserlian phenomenology fails to thematize the context of meanings in which I live for the most part. It is precisely this dissatisfaction to which Heidegger points and for which he devised the hermeneutic method. As Gadamer points out, Heidegger is able to demonstrate through his "hermeneutic of facticity" that humans always exist in the midst of a process of interpretation from which they cannot stand completely clear (2000, 281). As Dermot Moran summarizes, "Heidegger understood phenomenological clarification as always working against a background of that which resists illumination" (2011, 83).

HEIDEGGER'S PHENOMENOLOGICAL METHOD—THE HERMENEUTICS OF FACTICITY AS FUNDAMENTAL ONTOLOGY

Heideggerian Hermeneutics: Grasping the Context of Meaning in which Our Experience of the World Is Rooted

Husserl's phenomenology sought to examine the world from the point of view of experiences untainted by theories about the nature of those experiences. Even culture—the intersubjective world—was to be studied from the point of view of the individual's experience and reconstituted as a world that others experience *as I do* (Gadamer 248–249). Heidegger wished to question into the presuppositions of this method—that is, what it assumes about the nature of human existence and the nature of experiencing. In other words, Heidegger sought to articulate the understanding of existence that operates in the background of daily life. As Hubert Dreyfus explains, the method that Heidegger must use thus "cannot be a Kantian transcendental analytics nor a

Husserlian eidetic science." Rather, it must be a hermeneutic method "practiced on the background of an horizon of intelligibility in which the ontologist must dwell" (1995, 22). Heidegger thus develops a method to question into the context of meanings in which we go about unquestioningly in everyday life. This method he calls "hermeneutic."

If we have any associations with the term "hermeneutic" at all, it is with the study of religious texts such as the Bible. The most well-known proponent of a hermeneutic approach to the Bible was Friedrich Schleiermacher,[6] but the hermeneutic method soon spread to other areas of study including history, as exemplified in the work of Wilhelm Dilthey.[7] For Heidegger, hermeneutics does not take a text as its starting point. Instead, the goal of Heideggerian hermeneutics is to provide a method for humans to understand themselves by uncovering the self-understanding within which they are always already operating. He writes that "through the hermeneutic [method], a method takes shape that provides humans (*Dasein*) the possibility of becoming or being in a state of understanding [themselves]" (1923, 15). Why would Heidegger use the term "hermeneutics" for this method? Because he conceives of human existence as always involving a sort of interpretation (or process of interpretation): our actual concrete factual existence (*Faktizität*) is a process of ongoing self-interpretation (*Auslegung*) (1923, 15). How can this be? Because at any moment, a human being always understands him- or herself as being in the process of becoming that which he or she imagines him- or herself to be: a baker, a smith, an assistant manager of a car dealership, a mother, a father, a partner, and so on. In Heidegger's words, "Dasein . . . exists always as a process of becoming who he is" (1923, 17). Hermeneutics, then, is a method for human beings to come to understand a fundamental possibility within human existence: the possibility of understanding themselves as a process of ongoing interpretation (1923, 15–17).

Traditional hermeneutics aimed at uncovering the meaning of God or Christ's words; Heideggerian phenomenology aims at uncovering the truth of what it means to be human: we are constantly interpreting who we are—we live in a world constituted by meaningfulness. In *Being and Time*, Heidegger explains this in the following way: we encounter objects in the world *as* inherently meaningful. We do not just encounter an assemblage of sheet metal, rubber, and glass and then deduce or infer that it is a car. Instead, we discover the object made up of these materials *as* a car. Heidegger explains,

> The "as" constitutes the structure of the explicitness of what is understood; it constitutes the interpretation. The circumspect, interpretive association with what is at hand in the surrounding world which "sees" this *as* a table, a door, a car, a bridge does not necessarily already have to analyze what is circumspectly interpreted in a particular statement. Any simple prepredicative seeing of what

is at hand is in itself already understanding and interpretative (1996, 149). . . . Things at hand (objects encountered as objects rather than in the process of using them) are always already understood in terms of a totality of relevance. This totality need not be explicitly grasped by a thematic interpretation. Even if it has undergone such an interpretation, it recedes again into an undifferentiated understanding. This is the very mode in which it is the essential foundation of every, circumspect interpretation. (1996, 150)

The world is inherently meaningful; we do not first encounter a world of meaningless objects and then assign meanings to them after the fact. Thus human existence is characterized by a kind of "going about in a meaningful world." As Hubert Dreyfus explains, Heideggerian hermeneutics is a method that "lays the basis for all other hermeneutics by showing that human beings *are* a set of meaningful social practices and how these practices give rise to intelligibility and themselves can be made intelligible" (1995, 34). "Hermeneutic phenomenology," he goes on to write, "is an interpretation of human beings as essentially self-interpreting" (ibid.).

Thus for Heidegger, culture constitutes a set of social practices that provide possible meanings for each person as she interprets herself. These practices come to us from the past simply as the factual background of our existence, and so Heidegger calls this existence in the midst of a set of preexisting, meaningful social practices "facticity." This aspect of Heideggerian hermeneutics is present in Kuki's hermeneutic of *iki*: he considers his contemporaries to be acting within a system of meaning, which for him is a system of taste, and whose origin he wishes to uncover. But Heideggerian hermeneutics does not just stop with an acknowledgment of the fact that human existence is a process of constant self-interpretation: culture and cultural practices are capable of pointing to something about the mode of being of human existence, and through a hermeneutic inquiry, this mode can be uncovered. As Dreyfus explains, the practices that constitute a culture "contain an interpretation of what it means to be a culture" (1995, 15), and a hermeneutic methodology can uncover what this interpretation is. This aspect will also feature in Kuki's study of Japanese culture: for Kuki, culture is a form of being of an ethnic group (2004, 58) that cannot be understood by means of an "eidetic method" that simply creates a general concept of culture from the specific cultural practices and objects that express it (2004, 55).

Two Aspects of the Culture of Everyday Life (Facticity): The Culture of Today and the Culture of the Past

There are various ways of approaching the interpretation of social and cultural context. In this subsection we examine two: the culture in which we are unquestioningly absorbed in everyday life and the interpretation of the historical culture from which our present self-understandings are derived. These are both aspects of culture that play a role in Kuki's theory: he seeks to understand modern Japanese culture, but he considers this understanding to be the embodiment of a system of taste that originates in the past, specifically the end of the eighteenth and beginning of the nineteenth centuries (roughly from the *Meiwa* era [1764–1772] to the *Bunka* and *Bunsei* eras [1804–1830]), and that reflects a set of ethical ideals from that time. As we will see, Heidegger's hermeneutic method is an excellent tool for Kuki precisely because it reveals the relationship between the present and the past as disclosed in the current cultural and social practices.

To return to Heidegger, culture is a set of present cultural practices, and so one way to grasp it is as something in which we are already immersed, already absorbed. Heidegger points out that most of the time, we do not take the trouble to look into what our everyday ways of doing things tell us about what it means to be human. Rather, we simply engage unreflectingly in the everyday world in everyday ways. In his 1923 lecture, Heidegger gives various names to these unreflective modes of going about in the world: it is engaging with the "public" (*Öffentlichkeit*), with "what people are saying" (*das Gerede*), in short, with average everyday life (*Durchschnittlichkeit*) (1923, 31, 48, 85). For the most part, when we are absorbed in everyday modes of being, we do not realize that the process of living in accordance with established social and cultural practices is only one possibility open to us. Rather, social and cultural practices are a set of unquestioned practices "out of which" humans live and which describe "how" we live for the most part (1923, 31).[8]

Heidegger's hermeneutic approach to understanding the ontological structures of how we exist in the present (i.e., how we are the "here," the "da" of Dasein) suggests that we should try to uncover the meaning of the various orientations that we tend to take when going about in our social and cultural context. Doing this necessarily points us to the past, which is the source of the various taken-for-granted orientations that for the most part we unquestioningly adopt in everyday life. As Heidegger explains, "The way in which an era (what happens to be the present at any given time) looks at the past (a past way of being or its own past way of being) is an indicator of how the present is in relation to itself, how it is its own here and now" (1923, 36). Culture is not just something in which we are unquestionably absorbed most of the time: it is how we view our cultural heritage and the meanings we give today to our past.

Heidegger notes that when we turn to the past in order to understand the present, it is all too easy to take a wrong turn and to forget that what we intended to do was to study our present and past culture in order to understand something fundamental about how humans experience the world. If we forget the purpose of a phenomenological inquiry as a hermeneutic of facticity, we may become fascinated by cultural products and practices such as art, literature, religion, ethics, society, science, and economic activity (1923, 36). If we take this as the starting point for our approach to cultural history, we will focus on the "style" of a given culture (*Stil der Kultur*; 1923, 36 and 38), becoming caught up in describing it and tracing its evolution. Another wrong turn involves studying culture as if it were a kind of living organism with a soul that evolves throughout history (*Kulturleben, Kulturseele* 1923, 36). Both of these mistaken approaches to the history of culture adopt a universal standpoint outside of culture from which to study the many cultures we find throughout the world. Indeed, historians of culture are often involved in comparative cultural history precisely because they misunderstand that the point of studying culture and its history is to understand what it means to have a culture or to have a history (Heidegger 1923, 38–39).

Heidegger's hermeneutic approach to the past is much different than that of comparative cultural historians. Rather than being fascinated by the style or soul of a culture, we should look for a set of cultural meanings into which we have been thrown at birth (facticity). In this way, we can uncover a basic stance that our culture has taken toward human existence and the world and that limits how we think about what it means to be human. Heidegger believes that philosophers should undertake a historical inquiry with the goal of uncovering some of these fundamental orientations; indeed, he does this very thing in his own work, focusing on the philosophical tradition of which he was a part—the European tradition. Through such a study, he uncovers the origins of this tradition in Greek philosophy (Heidegger 1923, 41; Gadamer 257), and he concludes from this that the Greek conception of what it means to be human and what these other things are that surround us (i.e., what it means to be in general) is decisive for the self-understanding of those who share his culture. Thus, a hermeneutic investigation of the history of philosophy, as Heidegger conceives it, reveals that the enduring theme of the European philosophical tradition since Plato is an inquiry into what it means to be human, even if this theme is not always explicit (1923, 40).

We have now identified two primary ways in which culture plays a role in Heidegger's philosophy. First, culture can be understood as the ways of doing things and thinking about things that we adopt unthinkingly in our everyday lives: the opinions, attitudes, and unquestioned social practices of our taken-for-granted world. However, we can also be interested in the history of our culture. This can occur in two ways. One way is as a historical study of our present-day culture as expressed in the history of art, literature, and music. If we take this path, we uncover the cultural style or spirit of a given culture or cultural period, and thereby gain an understanding of present culture as the end point of this history. A second mode of historical inquiry is hermeneutic: we can examine the history of a society's self-understanding as embodied in its philosophy in order to identify the kinds of general inquiries toward which it is oriented. This last form of inquiry is specific to a given culture insofar as a philosophy develops in a particular geographic region (e.g., Europe or the Christian world) and has a traceable historical development.

Kuki's approach to Japanese culture, as expressed in *iki*, uses the second mode described above. Though it is true that *iki* constitutes a system of taste involving three elements (coquetry, brave composure, and resignation), Kuki is not simply interested in capturing the "style" or "spirit" of the everyday world. Or rather, this "style" or "spirit" operates within a deeper set of meanings that is their source: Buddhism, Shintō, and *bushidō*. Moreover, the ideals expressed within each of these traditions are not abstract concepts; rather, they are embodied concretely in ways of interacting with others—that is, they are deeply embedded in the Japanese way of relating to others. It is for this reason that Kuki spends so much time in *The Structure of Iki* describing the movements, voice, and attitudes of the *geisha* as she interacts with her lover.

Heideggerian Hermeneutics of Culture as Fundamental Ontology: Uncovering the Fundamental Interpretation of Being within which Humans Operate

We have identified three ways in which Heidegger believed that humans can engage with the cultural world. First, the world is inherently meaningful—it is a context with cultural meaning. Second, our culture has a history that is revealed as a style or a soul. Third, we can investigate the presumed self-understanding within which a group of people operate and out of which their present self-understanding has emerged. However, Heidegger identifies one final way in which humans can study their existence: they can inquire into the ontological presuppositions of everyday life and uncover the modes of human existence that these cultural forms presuppose.

Thus the next step in the inquiry into human existence is to uncover the existential structures of human being that make these various ways of being in the world possible (1923, 65–66). This next step proceeds phenomenologically as an inquiry into the existential characteristics of human being, namely time and space (1923, 66). Hermeneutically, the inquiry continues by asking how humans can exist as understanding (Gadamer 264).[9]

We have now finally established what the hermeneutic method is meant to achieve in Heidegger's philosophy. The inquiry into what it means to be human which is at the center of Heidegger's early philosophy requires us to inquire into the way that humans exist in a social and cultural context. Because this context is social and cultural, it is the source of meaning in our lives—it is the social meaning associated with being a doctor that makes certain people strive for that career; it is the social meaning of being good at sports that makes others pursue excellence in football, hockey, or baseball. Hermeneutics is the study of interpretation, and so if being human means being immersed in a meaningful context, interpretation is the proper tool not only for understanding what these social and cultural meanings are but also for uncovering the presuppositions that make it possible for the context to be meaningful in the first place. Of course, the meanings that are given to us by our social and cultural context are not systems of belief. As Dreyfus explains, for Heidegger, "There are no beliefs [about our world] to get clear about; there are only skills and practices. These practices do not arise from beliefs, rules, or principles, and so there is nothing to make explicit or spell out. We can only give an interpretation of the interpretation already in the practices" (Dreyfus 1995, 22). Indeed, it is because we are involved in our context by the things we do, the method for understanding the context and how it functions must be hermeneutic, not theoretical or eidetic, but a form of study that ensures that the enquirer remain immersed in the world she seeks to understand (ibid.).

While Kuki does not undertake this last step of Heidegger's hermeneutics as the ontology of facticity in *The Structure of Iki*, he does provides hints in the book about some of his ontological commitments, including his views about the importance of relationships to others (the priority of intersubjectivity) and about temporality as a fundamental aspect of human existence. As I mentioned at the beginning of this chapter, temporality has a phenomenological dimension—it makes everyday experiencing possible; but it also has a metaphysical dimension—East Asian time is transcendent and circular (Kuki 1998b).

KUKI'S HERMENEUTIC INTERPRETATION OF JAPANESE CULTURE

So now we are set to understand what Kuki's hermeneutic method is by comparing it to the method described by Heidegger, from whom at first glance he seems to have adopted it. In fact, Kuki's method is both original and eclectic, drawing on the notion of intuition as it features in both Husserl's phenomenology and Bergson's intuitionist philosophy.

As we have seen, in *The Structure of Iki*, Kuki seeks to uncover a basic worldview that he believed shaped the way that the Japanese understand what it means to be human and how we ought to relate to each other. This worldview is not a set of images—what Heidegger derides as an "object-sphere" that blinds the viewer to the process of giving meaning (1977, 123)—but rather a basic aesthetic sensibility—a kind of taste that expresses a particular way of going about in the world. In his view, it can be found through a study of Japanese art and architecture, but also in emotional responses to and ways of interacting with others. Moreover, *iki*, the phenomenon that Kuki believes embodies this unique Japanese way of being, has a history that leads back to an era just before the influx of European culture into Japan. The goal of his hermeneutic method is to expose the meaning that animated a past period of Japanese culture in order to set it up as a continuing source of meaning for modern Japan that could resist the influx of foreign influence.

As we saw in the previous chapter, Kuki's hermeneutic method involves interpreting a phenomenon from two points of view: as a phenomenon of consciousness (*ishikigenshō*, 意識現象) (the intensional structure; *naihōteki kōzō* [内包的構造]) and as a part of a system of taste (the extensional structure; *gaienteki kōzō* [外延的構造]). Once this hermeneutic interpretation is complete, we can then study the specific objective expressions (*kankyakuteki hyōgen* [観客的表現]) of *iki* in Japanese culture. Kuki's method does not allow one to begin with a concept of *iki* obtained by generalizing from its various objective expressions: this would be an *eidetic* approach. Rather, we must take a hermeneutic approach, which involves first questioning the *existentia* of *iki*[10] in order to grasp *iki* as a "comprehension of being" (*sonzai-etoku*; 存在会得) (Kuki 2004, 18; *KSZ* 1:13); only once this is achieved can we turn to a study of its essence through an examination of specific expressions of it.

This method seems to fit with a number of elements of Heidegger's hermeneutic method. *Iki* corresponds to the attitude of the *geisha* toward the world that functions as a framework for interpreting it. Like Heidegger, who derided the approach favored by historians and sociologists, Kuki does not want to study *iki* from a comparative perspective, nor does he begin with the art, architecture, or other cultural objects or practices in order to generalize about the essence. Instead, he seeks to uncover the presuppositions of the way that the Japanese people understand what it means to be a human living in society with others as expressed in the aesthetic sensibility of *iki*. However, in *The Structuer of Iki*, Kuki does not explicitly take the final step that Heidegger does in his phenomenological ontology: he does not study the ontological presuppositions of this mode of being—that is, what the distinctive ethics of the *geisha* can tell us about the temporal and spatial structures of human existence. As a result, Kuki does not inquire into what makes the interpretative framework of *iki* possible. However, as I mentioned earlier, he does hint at his views about the nature of existential structures such as temporality (Kuki posits both a phenomenological and a metaphysical dimension to time; 1998b) and about the form of ethical relationships, which he believed ought to be modeled on the relationship between the *geisha* and her lover (Mayeda 2012).

Iki is the way in which the *geisha* faces the world, namely with resignation, pluck, and a coquetry that maintains the distance between herself and her lover. This is really an expression of her attitude, an attitude which enframes the world and gives it a context in which to interpret it. However, *iki* does not just describe a state of consciousness, it is a phenomenon of consciousness: it is not the state of feeling resigned, but rather the meaning of the various ways in which the *geisha* behaves, dresses, speaks, moves, and so on. In this regard then, Kuki's hermeneutic is true to Heidegger's because the interpretation that is uncovered as *iki* is a way of being absorbed in the world, which Heidegger was careful to distinguish from a state of mind (*ein Akt im Bewußtsein*) (1923, 102). Kuki's method does not simply uncover the psychology of the *geisha* but truly captures her concrete way of being.

In "Bergson in Japan," Kuki confirms that his real goal is not a phenomenological ontology but rather using European philosophical ideas in order to identify what is essential to the Japanese philosophical outlook. He writes,

> Now why do we [Japanese] have an instinctive aversion to Utilitarianism? Why did Kant exert such a great influence in Japan? Why is Mr. [Henri] Bergson so highly esteemed in Japan? People often make the puerile criticism of [the Japanese] that we are nothing other than skilled "imitators." When one civilization encounters another, a reciprocal influence is only natural. However, accepting an idea is not imitation: the outcome [of the encounter] is simply incorporation [of ideas] by choice. And the way in which the choice is made always reveals the spontaneity and activity characteristic of the choosing subject. (*KSZ* 1: [90–91])

Kuki's hermeneutic method is thus meant to uncover the meaning of a specific Japanese worldview. However, he does not want to interpret any old worldview—he wishes to describe one that embodies ideals that he thinks were essential to Japanese culture and which should continue to animate it. Here, Kuki's method picks up on what Heidegger says at the end of *Being and Time* about identifying authentic possibilities that exist within one's heritage and choosing to pursue them as one's own possibilities.

It might be tempting to presume that because Kuki did not pursue a phenomenological ontology and identify the fundamental structures of human existence disclosed by the mode of cultural existence he labels *iki*, he misunderstood the Heideggerian method. Such a presumption would be inaccurate;[11] instead, Kuki adopted that aspect of the hermeneutic method required to identify something fundamental about Japanese culture as a point of resistance against the encroachment of European cultural and scientific views into Japan during the period in which he wrote. The method he uses to do this fits with certain aspects of Heideggerian hermeneutics: he accepts that a culture contains traces of a philosophical outlook inherited from the past that can be recovered and reappropriated, and he considers culture to function like a worldview, furnishing those who live with it an interpretation that gives meaning to various experiences. In *The Structure of Iki*, Kuki was not yet interested in uncovering the ontological structures of the Japanese way of being. However, as we will see in the next chapter, he turned to this task in later works such as *The Problem of Contingency*.

Elements of Intuitionism in Kuki's Method

It is easiest to appreciate what Kuki adopted from Heidegger's hermeneutic method by identifying the new elements that he incorporates into it. Other scholars have noted the influence of Husserl on Kuki's method in *The Structure of Iki*. Fujita Masakatsu argues that when one compares the language of earlier drafts of *The Structure of Iki*, it is clear that he at first intended to use Husserl's phenomenological method (2002, 120–121). For instance, the concluding chapter of *The Essence of Iki* (*Iki no honshitsu*, 『「いき」の本質』), one of these earlier drafts, includes a reference to Husserl's *Phenomenological Psychology* as Kuki explains that grasping *iki* as a form of ethnic experience means to grasp it "intuitively" (*chokkan suru*, 直観する). Kuki thus invokes Husserl's claim that the phenomenological method goes "to the things themselves," that is, things as they are given in "intuition" (*Anschauung*) (Moran 2000, 9).

Fujita explains that the shift to the Heideggerian term "hermeneutics" was a question of timing: when *The Structure of Iki* was finalized, Kuki had only recently come into contact with Heideggerian philosophy, and he was particularly influenced by Tanabe Hajime's summary of it in the first Japanese-language article on the subject published in 1924 and based on Heidegger's lecture "Ontology: The Hermeneutics of Facticity" of 1923 (Fujita 2002, 122–124). In his essay Tanabe describes Heidegger's phenomenology as being more suited than that of Husserl's to grasping life in its concreteness. It is evident that this characterization of Heidegger's method influenced Kuki's interpretation of the hermeneutic method, which he describes as being able to grasp *iki* as a "concrete, factual, and specific 'comprehension of being'" (Kuki 2004, 18).

Another obvious influence on Kuki's method is Bergson's intuitionism. Indeed, in his *Lectures on Contemporary French Philosophy* (1981), Kuki quotes Bergson's comment that "either metaphysics is nothing but a conceptual game, or else, if it is to be a serious spiritual enterprise, it must transcend concepts to arrive at intuition" (2003, 104 [author's translation]; Kuki 1981, 305).[12] Moreover, Kuki's distinction between the eidetic and hermeneutic methods makes use of language reminiscent of Bergson. In *The Structure of Iki*, Kuki deplores the static "eidetic" methodology that "first analyzed objective expressions of *iki* and then sought general characteristics from this domain," a method that he says "failed to grasp the ethnic specificity of *iki*, even in the area of objective expression" (2004, 18). In "The Philosophy of Intuition," an essay in *The Creative Mind*, Bergson criticizes the scientific method in similar terms:

> Ordinary knowledge and scientific knowledge, both destined to prepare our action upon things, are necessarily two visions of a kind, although of unequal precision and range; what I wish particularly to say, is that ordinary knowledge is forced, like scientific knowledge and for the same reasons, to take things in a time broken up into an infinity of particles, pulverised so to speak, where an instant which does not endure follows another equally without duration. Movement is for it a series of positions, change a series of qualities, and becoming, generally, a series of states. It starts from immobility (as though immobility could be anything but an appearance, comparable to the special effect that one moving body produces upon another when both move at the same rate in the same direction), and by an ingenious arrangement of immobilities it recomposes an imitation of movement which it substitutes for movement itself: an operation which is convenient from a practical standpoint but is theoretically absurd, pregnant with all the contradictions, all the pseudo-problems that Metaphysics and Criticism find before them. (Bergson 2007, 104)

He contrasts this abstract method, which would study *iki* from the point of view of its many instances, with a method that would force the philosopher to start with the phenomenon of *iki* as it is lived. He describes this intuitive, embodied method as follows:

> Intuition doubtless admits of many degrees of intensity, and philosophy many degrees of depth; but the mind once brought back to real duration will already be alive with intuitive life and its knowledge of things will already be philosophy. Instead of a discontinuity of moments replacing one another in an infinitely divided time, it will perceive the continuous fluidity of real time which flows along, indivisible. Instead of surface states covering successively some neutral stuff and maintaining with it a mysterious relationship of phenomenon to substance, it will seize upon one identical change which keeps ever lengthening as in a melody where everything is becoming but where the becoming, being itself substantial, has no need of support. No more inert states, no more dead things; nothing but the mobility of which the stability of life is made. A vision of this kind, where reality appears as continuous and indivisible, is on the road which leads to philosophical intuition.
>
> ... It is not necessary to transport ourselves outside the domain of the senses and of consciousness. (Bergson 2007, 104–105)

Kuki begins his hermeneutic study of the meaning of *iki* with an investigation of *iki* as a phenomenon of consciousness of the *geisha*. He thus begins as Bergson's intuitive method prescribes with the consciousness of a living being—the *geisha*. In the next chapter, we will explore in greater detail the similarity between Kuki's philosophical method and Bergson's intuitive method. For now, we will have to satisfy ourselves with indicating the possibility that Kuki's interpretation of Heideggerian hermeneutics is based on the similarities he sees between it and Bergson's intuitive method.

KUKI'S CONCEPT OF CULTURE: *IKI* AS THE MEANING OF A JAPANESE WORLDVIEW

In *The Structure of Iki*, Kuki uses the Japanese term for "culture" (*bunka*, 文化) interchangeably with that for "people" (*minzoku*, 民族). Nara translates the word "minzoku" by "ethnicity," presumably since the word is meant to refer to specific people, namely the Japanese. While it might be tempting to take this as an indication that Kuki presumes that culture is national culture, one has to remember the context in which Kuki undertook his study of *iki*, namely the recovering of a possibility within historical Japanese culture that could counter the Europeanization and modernization of Japan during the Taishō and early Shōwa periods prior to the Second World War. In this regard, he adopts a stance somewhat similar to Heidegger's. Both philosophers were critical of the increasing use of the presuppositions and objectifying standpoint of the natural sciences as a general framework for understanding human existence and human relations (Heidegger 1977). Of course, Kuki naturally identified this reductionist framework with Europe, and his motivation for distancing himself from it was in part motivated by the need to resist European colonial and imperial expansion.

The culture that Kuki is interpreting is not the culture of everyday Japanese life. Thus it does not correspond to culture in the first sense that Heidegger uses it, that is, to denote the views, attitudes, and assumptions of inauthentic everyday life. Indeed, this is obvious because Kuki has chosen to interpret the culture of *iki* which was not associated with modern Japan but with a period of the long-past Tokuagawa period.[13] Moreover, it is a term associated with a period that one normally associates with the decline of the *geisha* culture (Teruoka 2000).

However, Kuki's use of the term "culture" does seem to jibe with the second sense in which Heidegger uses the term "culture," namely to designate the style or spirit of a specific era. For instance, Kuki writes that a phenomenon such as *iki* "is the self-expression of the past and present of a given people; it is nothing other than the historical self-disclosure (*jikokaiji*) of a characteristic of their culture" (*KSZ* I:8).[14] This meaning, he goes on to write, "as an expression of the way of being of that people, will naturally take on the characteristic complexion of their concrete [historical] experience" (*KSZ* I:8).[15] This resembles very closely the description that Heidegger gives of Scheler's approach to culture, which sees in "art, literature, religion, ethics, society, science and economic enterprise . . . forms of the expression of an vital cultural life (cultural soul), that is, as the objectification of the subjective" (1923, 36).

However, unlike the attitude of the cultural historians and comparative cultural theorists that Heidegger deplored in his 1923 lectures, the method that Kuki adopted was hermeneutic, not scientific. He did not seek describe Japanese culture as a series of cultural developments, nor did he characterize Japanese culture by contrasting it with other world cultures as Watsuji did in *Climate and Culture*. Instead, he sought to identify the meaning of important elements of Japanese culture that had their origins in the ideals of *Bushidō*, Buddhism and Shintō. He identified the meaning of these ideals by studying the sensibility and attitude of the *geisha* of the late Tokugawa period which characterizes her way of going about in the world, including her interactions with others, which in turn provide a unified set of meanings expressed in many aspects of Japanese art, architecture, language, and modes of comportment.

In *Being and Time*, Heidegger considers culture to be a source of possible ways of understanding ourselves—it is "heritage" (*das Erbe,* 1996, 383). Kuki's exploration of Japanese culture in *The Structure of Iki* as the mode of being of a cultural group (Kuki 2004, 18) similarly seeks to capture historical possibilities latent within Japanese culture: the values of *bitai* (coquetry, which combines voluptuousness with nobility (*KSZ* 1: [107]), *ikiji* (the bravery of the samurai), and *akirame* (Buddhist resignation). For Kuki as for Heidegger, society is at a crossroads—it can take up the possibilities of this heritage or it can reject them. Indeed, Heidegger makes it clear that it is only once a people (or a person) truly accepts that it has a choice to make—that is, that it has faced its ultimate possibility, the finitude of death (1996, 383, 385)—that it is truly able to choose. However, when a possibility is taken up from one's heritage, it becomes that group's (or person's) destiny (*Geschick*). Hubert Dreyfus explains this last "mode" of being for humans (authentic existence) as follows:

> In this mode Dasein finally achieves individuality by realizing it can never find meaning by identifying with a role [such a lawyer, a father, a lover, a victim, etc.]. Dasein then "chooses" the social possibilities available to it in such a way as to manifest in the style of its activity its understanding of the groundlessness of its own existence. (1995, 27)

162   Chapter 6

The subtle difference between Kuki and Heidegger's approach to culture is in two regards. First, Kuki does not trouble himself with distinguishing authentic and inauthentic modes of being. While Heidegger points out that most of us do not make real choices because we are lost in the everyday modes of being that involve seeking "comfort" (*das Behagen*) and "taking things easy" (*das Sichdrücken*) as others (*das Man*) do for the most part, Kuki considers Japanese culture to be a set of inspiring ideals—it is Europeanization and modernization that are the dangers, not collapsing into everyday life. This is a potential weakness in Kuki's cultural philosophy: while *The Structure of Iki* sets out an ideal that he thinks exists within Japanese culture, it would be helpful for Kuki to identify the everyday, ordinary, "unauthentic" (*uneigentlich*) way of life in which the Japanese are absorbed. Doing so might make it clearer how Kuki is suggesting that Japanese society (or individuals) should change in order to live up to the ideal.

Second, Heidegger seems to believe that a group can take up an authentic possibility handed down to it by its heritage without explicitly knowing the origin of this possibility (1996, 385). Indeed, the history of European philosophy, according to Heidegger, is the history of the forgetting of a particular understanding of what it means to exist and recovering the truth of being requires significant philosophical work. In contrast, Kuki's culture of *iki* is found very much in plain sight in the aesthetic sense of the Japanese; indeed, it is one of a set of aesthetic sensibilities that he is able to conceptualize through his cube of opposites (see figure 5.1 in the last chapter). Moreover, the Japanese aesthetic is thematized directly in Japanese art that Kuki describes in his other writings such as "The Expression of the Infinite in Japanese Art" (Kuki 1998). Admittedly, in *The Structure of Iki*, Kuki depicts this aesthetic by means of a form of relationship that is far from typical for the average Japanese person: that between a *geisha* and her lover. And yet there is a self-consciousness involved in iki that does not seem essential in Heidegger's notion of authentic culture: *iki* is a self-conscious attitude that the *geisha* develops over time and which colors the way that she interprets the world.

CONCLUSION: CULTURE AS THE REDISCOVERY OF *IKI*

As Paul Ricoeur explains, all philosophy is in some sense historical:

> It can be said that every philosophy is an interpretation of the history of philosophy, an explication of its contradictions, and a justification of its possible unity by the suprahistorical sense of the philosophical activity or the philosophical

intention. . . . [The] obligation to philosophize, specifically engenders a history on the reflective level, a history of signification, because it is the development of its own sense. (1967, 83)

Kuki's method for studying culture is hermeneutic in the sense that he identifies an interpretation that he believes gives the world meaning to the Japanese. It is an interpretation in the sense of an orientation, a taste, a way of being, not a concept. Moreover, Kuki's method is hermeneutic because it roots this way of being in a history, thereby uncovering for the Japanese their "own sense" of how their distinctive outlook on life developed. He does not undertake a critique of the interpretation he uncovers because he is concerned about providing a self-understanding that can resist the encroachment of European science and culture. But as we will see in the next chapter, the understanding he uncovers, because it includes a particular view about the nature of human relationships, has profound ethical implications. In this regard, Kuki's rediscovery of a Japanese way of being makes up for the apparent lack of an ethics in Heidegger's philosophy.

NOTES

1. All translations of Heidegger 1923 in this chapter are the author's.
2. This was Heidegger's slogan for phenomenology (Heidegger 1962, 58).
3. We focus in this chapter in particular on this early lecture for two reasons. First, because as Fujita Masakatsu explains, it influenced Kuki's description of the hermeneutic method that he employs in *The Structure of Iki*; Kuki did not attend Heidegger's lecture in the summer of 1923, but his colleague, Japanese philosopher Tanabe Hajime, did, and his description of what he learned in an article entitled "A New Shift in Phenomenology" (1924) influenced Kuki (Fujita 2002, 122–126; see also Furukawa 2015, 224). Second, I rely on this lecture because already by the time of *Being and Time*, Heidegger had begun to be critical of the hermeneutic method (see, for instance, his lecture *Einleitung in die Philosophie* [Wintersemester 1928/29], *Gesamtausgabe*. II. Abteilung: Vorlesungen [Frankfurt a.M.: 1996]).
4. As Paul Ricoeur explains, in *Ideas I*, Husserl conceives of intentionality in a way that recognizes that humans are always already in a world. He writes, "Chapter Two [of *Ideas I*] contains the study of the intentionality of consciousness, that remarkable property of consciousness to be a consciousness of . . . , an intending of transcendence, a bursting out towards the world" (1967, 16).
5. Here Heidegger is referring to the eidetic reduction by means of which the "sense" or "concept" of a thing is extracted from specific concrete instances of it (Ricoeur 1967, 146).
6. See, for example, Friedrich Schleiermacher, *Hermeneutik und Kritik mit besonderer Beziehung auf das Neue Testament* (Berlin: F. Lücke, 1838); cited in Heidegger 1923 at 13.

7. See, for example, Wilhelm Dilthey, *Gesammelte Schriften*, I. Band: *Einleitung in die Geisteswissenschaften*, 9. Auflage (Stuttgart: B.G. Teubner Verlagsgesellschaft und Göttingen: Vandenhoeck & Ruprecht, 1990), originally published in 1883.

8. Heidegger specifically refers to "culture" and the study of culture as a *mistaken* means of inquiring into the nature of human existence (1923, 30).

9. Heidegger writes, *"Als was* ist . . . in den genannten Auslegungsweisen das Dasein für es selbst da, und welches ist der Seinscharakter der Weise dieses So-daseins?" (1923, 66).

10. Kuki uses the Latin term "existential" (*KSZ* I:13).

11. Kuki wrote many texts about Heideggerian philosophy. Indeed, the distinction that Heidegger draws in *The Basic Problems of Phenomenology* between philosophy as worldview and philosophy as phenomenological ontology is mentioned at the very beginning of "Heidegger's Philosophy" (Kuki 1939, 218).

12. "Ou la métaphysique n'est que ce jeu d'idées, ou bien, si c'est une occupation sérieuse de l'esprit, il faut qu'elle transcende les concepts pour arriver à l'intuition" (104).

13. Many explanations have been proposed for why Kuki chose *iki* as his theme. Obama suggests that he wished to choose a term that came from a "different" or "outsider" world in order to better bring in to focus the tension between possibility and necessity that would become a theme in his later work, *The Problem of Contingency*. For in the world of the *geisha* as Kuki describes it, one can experience true freedom in the sense of being not bound to love another, and yet one is bound to this freedom as the destiny of a *geisha*. Both books, Obama argues, thematize the problem of how to live in the face of destiny of this kind (Obama 2006, 67–68; see also Furukawa 228; see also the mention of possibility and necessity in *The Structure of Iki* (Kuki 2004, 23; *KSZ* 1:22).

14. 「... 一の意味または言語は、一民族の過去および現在の存在様態の自己表明、歴史を有する特殊の文化の自己開示に外ならない。」

15. 「一民族の有する或る具体的意味または言語は、その民族の存在の表明として、民族の体験の特殊な色合いを帯びていない筈はない。」

Chapter 7

Kuki Shūzō's Concepts of Culture and Society

The Intuition at the Heart of Ethics

KUKI'S CONCEPTS OF CULTURE AND SOCIETY

As we have seen, Kuki's philosophy was heavily influenced by Martin Heidegger. However, whereas culture does not play a central role in *Being and Time*, appearing only as the context of inauthentic everyday life or as heritage in Heidegger's discussion of authentic historicity (1996, 51–52, 395–396), Kuki takes culture as his starting point, uncovering in it possibilities—ways of being—that embody the ideals of the Japanese people and their traditions (Kuki 2004, 14, 17, 58, 60). However, in his study of *iki*, Kuki does not elaborate on what it would mean for an ethnic group (*minzoku*, 民族; Kuki 2004, 14; *KSZ* 1:8) to live in accordance with the possibilities—the ideals—that are manifest in their specific mode of being. The goal of this chapter will be to elaborate on what Kuki means by "culture" and to demonstrate what it means to take up the ideals that characterize it.

According to Kuki, Japanese culture is expressed in a shared taste or sensibility called *iki*. But this is more than just a shared aesthetic sense: it also embodies the values of the Japanese people (Kuki 2004, 59–60) that are expressed in Japanese fashion, art, architecture, and other social and cultural activities. For instance, Kuki begins his lecture "The Expression of the Infinite in Japanese Art," given at Pontigny, France on August 17, 1928, with a reference to Okakura Tenshin's (岡倉 天心, 1862–1913) *The Ideals of the East: With Special Reference to the Art of Japan*, in which Okakura wrote, "The history of Japanese art becomes the history of Asiatic ideals" (Okakura

2007, 13; quoted in Dilworth et al. 1998b, 207). Kuki goes on to explain how Japanese art expresses that culture's ideals:

> What rapport does Japanese art, as an element of the spiritual life, have with the infinite? The plane of action in the spiritual life is time. Man, enclosed in time, aspires to be liberated from time. Thus, he searches for the eternal—for truth, morality, and beauty. (Dilworth et al. 1998b, 216)

Kuki adopted Okakura's view that art expresses an ideal, and most of his philosophy aims at explaining what this ideal is. The ideal is initially sketched in *The Structure of Iki*, which also provides hints as to its source. We will follow the elaboration of these views in his later works in order to understand his idea of Japanese culture and the role that it serves in Japanese society.

While *The Structure of Iki* hinted that Japanese culture is an expression of an ethical ideal, Kuki did not elaborate in that text on how the aesthetic of *iki* and the consciousness it represents were maintained throughout the ages and came to be shared by the Japanese. Also, since Kuki admits that people who are not Japanese can learn to understand *iki*, this raises a question about the universality of ethnic consciousness and how it is possible for non-Japanese people to acquire it. Kuki states that people acquire ethnic consciousness through their "inner sense" (*naikan*, 内官) (Kuki 2004, 55–56); indeed, even foreigners who were not raised in Japanese society can come to understand *iki* in this way. What is this "inner sense"? Although Kuki did not answer such questions directly in *The Structure of Iki*, he addresses them in his later philosophy, and it is our task in this chapter to summarize his answers and evaluate how effective they are at explaining Kuki's understandings of the nature of Japanese culture and the social relations it embodies.

As we shall see, Kuki believes that *iki* expresses some fundamental ethical ideals underlying all of Japanese culture, ideals which have their origin in Buddhism (resignation; *akirame*, 諦め), *Shintō* (nature; *shizen*, 自然) and *Bushidō* (brave composure; *ikiji*, 意気地) (Kuki 1939, 310; see also Kuki 2004, 60).[1] These ideals are experienced as "the call of conscience from within man's heart" (Kuki 1966, 194), which occurs in the rare moments when a person has an intuition of the universal totality of which all things are each a part. Such intuitions occur only from time to time in unexpected and surprising ways. When they do arise, Kuki believes that it generally during chance encounters with others (Kuki 1966, 194–95) in relation to whom one has an ethical relationship like the relationship between a *geisha* and her lover described in *The Structure of Iki*. In these chance encounters, conscience calls to us as "destiny" (Kuki 1966, 195), a kind of intuition in which one transcends everyday time and comes into contact with the infinite as the experience of the end of all mundane samsaric life (Kuki 1966, 196), that is, nothingness understood as the emptiness of all dharmas (Kuki 1966, 191).

Kuki's answer that Japanese culture expresses a set of ideals that has its origin in an intuition of nothingness leaves many questions unanswered. In this chapter, we will try to provide a more detailed explanation of how Kuki understands the mechanism whereby a shared culture is developed and transmitted. We will also trace the philosophical roots of his view in the European philosophy that interested him, especially the concept of time in the phenomenology of Martin Heidegger and the notion of intuition in French "Life Philosophy" (*Lebensphilosophie*), especially that of Henri Bergson and Maine de Biran.

A Puzzle: If Culture Is Experienced Intuitively by Each Individual, How Can It Be a Shared Culture?

The central problem that Kuki faced in his philosophical study of culture is how something like an aesthetic sensibility such as *iki* can express a shared culture. Throughout most of *The Structure of Iki*, Kuki focuses on *iki* as a "phenomenon of consciousness," which tends to suggest that *iki* is experienced by individuals. But he also clarifies that this phenomenon of consciousness is shared by all Japanese people, and that it can even be acquired by non-Japanese who have not been immersed in Japanese culture. This clearly suggests an intersubjective aspect to the phenomenon.

Adding to the puzzle about how *iki* expresses an intersubjective phenomenon is the fact that Kuki describes the means by which one acquires the sensibility of *iki* as an "inner sense" (Kuki 2004, 56). What is this inner sense? How can an individual have an inner sense of something that is a shared phenomenon of consciousness? What is the relationship between an individual's inner sense and this shared sensibility? We will try to expose Kuki's answers to these questions and thereby gain an understanding of the role of the individual and others in his concept of culture.

There are various ways that one could approach the study of what Kuki calls the "inner sense." A sociologist might investigate how individuals are taught to recognize and express this culturally shared form of consciousness that gives meaning to its many outward expressions in art, fashion, architecture, and so on. Through such a study, the sociologist could discover that the process of acquiring this sense is deliberate, or perhaps that it is a form of "cultural capital" that Pierre Bourdieu demonstrated was unconsciously transmitted to children immersed in a particular environment.[2] In contrast, a biologist might search for organic, chemical, or physical causes of the shared aesthetic of *iki*. For instance, neuroscientist Antonio Damasio writes that "cultural activity began and remains deeply embedded in feeling" (2018,

15–16), which he defines biologically as portrayals of "the organism's interior—the state of internal organs and of internal operations" (102). One can also imagine psychological explanations and so on. However, the approach that Kuki chooses is different: it is both intuitive and metaphysical.[3] Kuki's intuitive approach is similar to that employed by Henri Bergson and other French philosophers, for whom intuition is a means for individuals to get in touch with their "deep-seated self." Moreover, the approach is "metaphysical" because what one gets in touch with, according to Kuki, is the nature of nothingness (*mu*; 無) (Kuki 1966, 192; *KSZ* 2:255).

What I suggested in the two previous chapters is that Kuki's hermeneutic method is in part derived from Bergson's intuitive one, and that Kuki has sought to transpose Bergson's notion of the "deep-seated self" or "fundamental self" (Bergson 1910, 167–172) into the cultural realm: a person who has internalized the sense of *iki* has somehow connected with her fundamental self. This fundamental self, which one accesses through the inner sense or intuition, is how individuals know what is and is not *iki*. However, there are also points in *The Structure of Iki* when Kuki suggests that this fundamental self is not purely individual but rather possesses some intersubjective aspect. An example is in a passage in which Kuki draws a parallel between the individual's experience of *iki* and artistic expression. He writes

> Artistic objectification of lived experience need not be a conscious endeavour, since artistic impulses often work unconsciously. Yet this type of unconscious creation is nothing less than an objectification of lived experience. That is to say, *personal or social experience* freely and unconsciously selects formative principles and completes self-expression in art. The same can be said about natural forms. Physical movements and other natural forms are often created in the unconscious. Whatever the case may be, the objectified expression of *iki* can be understood only if its understanding is based on *iki* as a phenomenon of consciousness.[4] (Kuki 2004, 57) (Emphasis added)

Here, Kuki indicates that artistic expression involves both an individual artist's personal "lived experience" (個人的体験) and a form of "social experience" (*shakaiteki taiken*, 社会的体験): the art he or she produces is an objective expression of a person's concrete experience, some of which is individual and some of which is intersubjective.

In another passage, Kuki also goes back and forth between the fundamental self as individual and as shared. He notes that while *iki* is the taste of a people (i.e., a group), to apprehend it requires something like a *sens intime* (a concept he adopts from the philosophy of Maine de Biran) (Kuki 2004, 55; *KSZ* 1:73). A group may have some common reference points; but does it have a *sens intime*? Probably not if Kuki is using "sens intime" like Maine de

Biran, who employs the term to refer to an individual's capacity to intuit the self: one's *sens intime* is the faculty by means of which one becomes aware of those perceptions that one "actively" produces oneself, which Maine de Biran contrasts with perceptions that are produced externally and are felt through the senses of sight, hearing, touch and taste (Maine de Biran 1834, 17; 1841a, 22; 1841b, 5). Thus we are left with a puzzle: what is the relationship between the self that intuits *iki* and the intersubjective culture of which *iki* is the fundamental mode of being?

This question is not answered in *The Structure of Iki*. But answering it is the task of the rest of Kuki's philosophy, which one could characterize as a search for the metaphysical structure of a collectivity's *sens intime*. In order to understand the solution he proposes, let us first describe it, then examine what ideas drawn from European philosophy influenced Kuki's theory.

Kuki's Proposed Metaphysical Solution to the Puzzle: Intuition as Individual Intuition of the Universal

The *sens intime* to which Kuki refers appears to give a person access to an experience that is intimate to each one of us and yet which is universal in the sense that it can be accessed by any individual, whether Japanese or non-Japanese. The best explanation of this appears to be that what is accessed through this *sens intime* is universal, but that accessing the universal is easier if one belongs to a culture whose very being expresses the universal in their cultural practices and daily interactions. Japanese culture is just such a culture in Kuki's view. We thus see that for Kuki, culture is the expression of something universal through social practices that represent the way of life of a group, the Japanese people. Other cultures can also express this universal, but Kuki finds that they rarely do so as effectively as Japanese culture. As Kuki puts it, "*iki* has no place in Western culture as a certain meaning in its ethnic being" (Kuki 2004, 59).

Kuki's explanation of what one experiences through the *sens intime* is contained in many texts. We will concentrate primarily on what he says at the end of *The Problem of Contingency*. However, since we began our study of Kuki with an examination of *The Structure of Iki*, we will first review the hints he provides there about the universal that we access through this intimate experience before moving on to the impetus of this experience, which is the chance encounters analyzed in detail in the later text.

At the end of *The Structure of Iki*, Kuki explains that *iki* expresses something "that our soul once saw" (Kuki 2004, 60). This is a reference to Plato's theory of knowledge as recollection, for instance, as developed in the *Phaedrus* (249 c; cited in Kuki 2004, 91, fn. 203). Kuki's allusion to Plato suggests that what is involved in experiencing *iki* is intuition—some inner sense like Platonic recollection. Indeed, what Kuki likens to *anamnesis* (Plato's term for this theory of recollection) or a *sens intime* he also refers to as "intuition" (*KSZ* 1: (89)), a term which Kuki uses in the same sense as Henri Bergson and which Bergson contrasts with the method of analysis of which he is critical (Bergson 2003, 100). However, whereas what is recalled in Plato's theory of *anamnesis* is an "abstract universal," in the case of *iki*, what is intuited is destiny and freedom as expressed concretely in Japanese culture. Kuki writes,

> We cannot allow coquetry to take the form of *iki*, unless we as a people possess an unclouded vision of our destiny and an unabated longing for freedom of soul. We comprehend and understand completely the core meaning of *iki* only when we grasp its structures as a self-revelation of the being of our people.[5] (Kuki 2004, 60)

Thus the universal to which we have access through intuition is not an abstract idea or concept but rather something concrete: the possibility of human spiritual freedom embodied in a specific set of cultural practices (Kuki 2004, 60).

Of course, it may seem strange that Kuki considers this ideal of freedom to be expressed in the culture of the *geisha*: How can she realize freedom when her relationships with patrons are contractual? And how does the aesthetic of the *geisha* express this freedom? Kuki admits that it may be difficult to recognize the aesthetic of *iki* as the expression of an ideal of freedom.[6] But he explains that the flirtations of the *geisha* are not in pursuit of a permanent relationship: she will never be completely united with her patron or lover, nor does she desire to be. Indeed, through all of her past disappointments in love, the *geisha* has learned that a permanent relationship is impossible. However, if she accepts the impossibility of permanent relationships and resigns herself to reality, she will be freed from her attachment to the material world. Kuki writes, "*Iki* contains the sense of *resignation* to fate and the freedom from attachment based on that *resignation*"[7] (Kuki 2004, 22).

How is resignation essential to being free? Having repeatedly experienced disappointment in love (Kuki 2004, 21), the *geisha* realizes that this world is *samsara*, a world of suffering. And through this realization, she is no longer bound by impossible dreams. Kuki explains,

> In short, *iki* arises from the "world of suffering" in which "we are scarcely able to keep afloat, carried down on the stream of *ukiyo*." *Resignation* or *disinterest* in *iki* represents the state of mind that has suffered through hard *ukiyo*'s tough and merciless tribulations and shed worldly concerns; in other words, the state of mind that is free of grime, unclinging, disinterested, and free from obstacles, and that has removed itself from any egotistical attachment to reality.[8] (Kuki 2004, 22)

As we see, Kuki associates the *geisha*'s resignation to the impossibility of love and consequent freedom from attachment to her lover with the Buddhist view of liberation as detachment from worldly desire.

While the relationship between a *geisha* and her lover might be sensual, playful and passionate, in Kuki's eyes, this is not incompatible with Buddhism despite the common association of Buddhism with renunciation and asceticism. Kuki insists that coquetry can also express resignation (*akirame*), the third intensional element of *iki*, because unlike the ideal of marriage, the *geisha* and her lover must accept the impossibility of their love. Why not just give up in the face of this impossibility? Kuki explains that the impossibility of the relationship also discloses the *geisha*'s freedom: thus her worldly fate (the impossible love) is the manifestation of her freedom from attachment to this fate. Kuki writes:

> *Akirame*, the third distinguishing characteristic [of *iki*], is not incompatible with coquetry. . . . Because it does not achieve the hypothetical final objective, coquetry remains faithful to itself. Consequently, it is by no means irrational for coquetry to embody *akirame* in attempting to reach the final objective; *akirame* forces the fundamental state of being of coquetry to reveal itself. Unifying coquetry with *akirame* means that fate forces us to return to freedom and that positing of this possibility is determined by necessity. In other words, affirmation is reached by way of negation.[9] (Kuki 2004, 23)

The *geisha* is free precisely because the fulfillment of the relationship is impossible. And it is the necessity of this impossibility that assures this freedom. This necessity, Kuki writes, is fate.

The ethics of *iki* is thus somewhat similar to that of Emmanuel Levinas: ethics requires the maintenance of the independence of the subject, which in turn necessitates the impossibility of the complete unity of two people. To put this in more Levinasian terms, one person cannot ever expect to completely understand the other: the other's subjectivity is always partly hidden from us (Levinas 1987, 30–31; Derrida 1978, 108). Kuki expresses a similar idea. He explains that the ethics of the *geisha* embodies a state of detachment in which she boldly maintains her independence:

> When "a loving pair, thought to be *sui*," lose the spirit of lightheartedness and stylishness "because of the capricious spirit of an unrequited love" over time, they would have to find a way to excuse themselves. They would have to explain why they have fallen prey to a situation wherein "the deeper they are in love, the closer they are to *yabo* ['boorish']." When the affair is "a free-spirited flirtation, like a lotus leaf floating freely on the water," it is still in the domain of *iki*. When "a couple becomes inseparable, *yabo* rules." Their relationship has left the

domain of *iki* far behind. A woman may become an object of ironic ridicule when her love can be seen in such a light: "how *yabo* she is, living a life in the samurai quarters, hardly the place for a woman with *iki* like hers."[10] (Kuki 2004, 23)

By accepting her separation from others, the *geisha* can realize ultimate liberation.

Kuki makes the link between the *geisha*'s resignation and Buddhist liberation explicit by linking the fact that she is alone and unattached with the Buddhist concepts of "transmigration" and "transience," and by linking the freedom she experiences through this detachment with the Buddhist principles of "emptiness" and "nirvana." According to Kuki, the Buddhist principle of the transmigration of the soul from one existence to another expresses the idea of differentiation and difference—the soul is continually sheathed in a different body as it transfers from a being that has died to a different new one. However, the possibility of being free from this cycle of constant death and rebirth is "nirvana": one achieves ultimate freedom through not being attached to the attractions of the samsaric world. Kuki explains,

> *Iki* contains the sense of *resignation* to fate and the freedom from attachment based on that *resignation*. Two views of life and the universe undoubtedly lie behind this definite moment in *iki*, both serving to intensify and purify it. One is especially Buddhist, with its regard for *ruten* "transmigration" and *mujō* "transience" as forms of differentiation, and for *kūmu* "emptiness" and *nehan* "nirvana" as principles of equality.[11] (Kuki 2004, 22)

Thus we see that *iki* expresses a fundamental Buddhist concept: in this world, try as we might, we will only remain separate from others; but if we recognize the emptiness of this seemingly separate self (i.e., if we stop seeking to unify ourselves with others and thereby stop bumping up against the reality that we cannot do so), we unexpectedly become capable of recognizing our unity with others as the possibility of freedom from attachment. We see expressed here Kuki's model for the relationship between *iki* as an experience intuited by an individual and *iki* as the intuition of the universal: only individuals recognize instances of *iki*, but the recognition of it is at the same time a recognition of something eternal expressed in the aesthetic, a sort of ethical ideal.

As we can see, in *The Structure of Iki*, Kuki already hints at the fact that life of the *geisha* and the aesthetic of *iki* that she embodies expresses a Buddhist ethical ideal. This ideal accepts the possibility that each of us can be free: that is, it expresses a universal ideal. But what is not explained in that early text is the kind of specific experiences that allow individuals to intuit something that is universal. Nor does *The Structure of Iki* describe either the status of what is intuited or what we specifically experience that makes us understand our inherent freedom. Kuki hints at the link between *iki* and Buddhist ethics in *The Structure of Iki*. However, he only fully elaborates the Buddhist concept in his later work on contingency, whose purpose is not only to explain why encounters between the *geisha* and her lover are able to provide her insight into an ethical ideal, but also to give more detail about what this experience consists of.

CHANCE AND THE ETHICAL INTUITION OF FREEDOM

One might wonder why Kuki takes up the theme of contingency. In the essay "The Feeling of Surprise and Contingency" (*Odoroki no nasake to gūzensei*; 『驚きの情と偶然性』), Kuki describes the general existential structures of human existence that make the specific experiences described in *The Structure of Iki* possible. The *geisha*'s intuition of her freedom through resignation is a specific instance of a more general kind of intuition that is available to us all through the feeling of surprise. Kuki explains what is involved in surprise:

> The feeling of surprise is a feeling that is aroused when one encounters something by chance. The contingent thing breaks through one's solitude. [In contrast,] faced with something that falls within the range of one's experience, i.e., faced with something commonplace, one does not feel surprised. One is surprised only by something that is outside of one's own experience, something that is not commonplace.[12] (Kuki 1939, 163–64) (Author's translation)

What causes one to be surprised is the fact that one encounters something so entirely different from oneself that one is shaken to the foundations: all one's assumptions and ideas are inadequate for capturing the experience one has had.

Surprise is an experience that can cause us to question our assumptions about ourselves and the adequacy of our knowledge. Moreover, surprise "is aroused when one encounters something by chance." Thus the link between *The Structure of Iki* and *The Problem of Contingency* comes into view. If the feeling of surprise is a feeling that frees us from our everyday views such as those about love as the pursuit of an eternal bond with another, then the contingent encounters which cause these surprises must play an important role in the ethics of the *geisha*, who is liberated from such conventional views. This is what Kuki explores in *The Problem of Contingency*.

We will not review in detail the whole of Kuki's study of contingency explained in his very technical book on the subject.[13] Instead, we will focus on the last part of the text in which Kuki explains the link between contingency as that which gives rise to surprise and what we discover through surprise, which is our freedom. He also deals in the last chapter with the ethical consequences of these experiences, which is in some sense a description of Kuki's general ethics of which the ethics of the *geisha* described in *The Structure of Iki* is a specific cultural instance.

Kuki begins the last chapter of *The Problem of Contingency* by contrasting two different ways that we can react when surprised by a chance discovery or a contingent event: we could try to understand what has happened (i.e., take an analytical scientific approach), or we could try to make what we encountered a basis for action, that is, take a practical ethical approach and respond to and take responsibility for what we have encountered. Of course, it is the latter approach that the *geisha* takes and which is expressed in the aesthetic of *iki*.

Let us look first at the scientific approach that according to Kuki does not lead to an understanding of our inherent freedom and consequent ethical obligation. When we take this approach, we try to make sense of unusual or new experiences by comparing them to experiences that we already understand. The whole of scientific exploration is precisely of this nature: the advancement of science depends on the discovery of new creatures or new natural phenomena that we simply encounter by chance, but which we then try to fit into a universal system of knowledge. Such an approach to chance encounters does not give rise to ethical responsibility.

The scientific approach is based on judgments of the kind "this x is like y," for example, "this new kind of snail is like this kind of snail that I have previously encountered and classified." To explain why this approach to new encounters has no ethical dimension, Kuki points out the kind of attitude toward the world that is inherent in it, an attitude that kills the ethical possibilities of the encounter by trying to incorporate it into a system of knowledge of which one is oneself master, and which consequently does not recognize the needs or perspectives of others.

To make this problematic feature of the scientific approach clear, Kuki describes scientific judgments from the point of view of sameness and difference, which he then links to the ethical categories of "you" and "I." When we encounter a new kind of snail, the scientist either recognizes it as an example of a species that she already knows or else discovers that it is different. To capture this process, Kuki uses a slightly unfamiliar terminology: the system of existing knowledge to which the new snail is being compared Kuki calls the "I" (because it is the system of knowledge that *I* already possess), while the snail being categorized is "you" (because the snail is something outside of the observer that she encounters). Employing this terminology, Kuki describes the scientific judgment that fits the new snail into the existing system of knowledge about snails as a judgment "that incorporate into the 'I' the 'you' that I encounter." The ideal of scientific judgment is thus to "concretely identify the *you* exterior to me within the internal system of identity of the *I*"[14] (Kuki 1966, 193) [emphasis in original]. This may seem somewhat obscure, but what Kuki means is that when a scientist discovers something unknown and so "external" to the existing system of knowledge, her approach toward the object is to try to find a place for it within the system. This attitude does not express an ethical ideal because ethics depends on there being a "you" separate from the "I" to which I owe some obligation; if all that exists is the "I," what need is there for practical ethics?

Kuki contrasts the scientific approach and the unappealing ethical stance it implies with an intuitive approach. When we intuitively experience the contingent in its immediacy, we accept that what is encountered resists incorporation into a general system of knowing; what we intuitively experience constitutes a limit on our own knowledge. Why is the recognition of one's limits necessary for ethics? According to Kuki, it is because ethical action involves the pursuit of non-selfish ends. When by chance the plea of a poor person on the street touches us, we are jolted out of our selfish circle of self-concern and find within us an immediate sense of responsibility. Kuki expresses this as a form of limit on the self: personal goals can be achieved entirely within our comfort zone by applying our system of knowledge, but ethical goals are different because they are set by the needs of others—we can strive to achieve them, but we may not be capable of doing so completely.

Kuki clearly has in mind here ideals or goals that are religious or mystical in nature. For instance, he uses the example of Christian revelation, which sets up an ideal of good and light which is unachievable by humans on this Earth but toward which those who believe in God must strive. He quotes Hatanō Seiichi's *Philosophy of Religion* (1935):

> There must be some point in our march or on our journey that we come up against a divine reality that dominates us through its absolute power and decrees that here is the limit that human power and ingenuity cannot surpass because they are only human. In the case of the revelation, this takes place by an unexpected pull toward the light, truth, and happiness: a life that no humans can resist, in which all desires and dislikes become unimportant, and the human personality offers itself up without the power to refuse. (32–33; quoted in Kuki 1966, 173) (author's translation)

To act ethically, we must let contingency (the "unexpected pull toward the light") completely permeate our actions. In so doing, we confront our limits, and in the same moment, we intuit reality expressing itself within us as the pull of the ethical ideal, whose achievement is impossible ... an "end without end" ... a goal that can never be completely achieved.

Kuki characterizes this kind of ethical ideal in terms of the categories of "contingency" and "necessity." We realizes our ethical responsibilities through a chance encounter that reveals to us that action is necessary—we are compelled to it from the bottom of our hearts.. The encounter that can have this effect is one that somehow demonstrates to us that that we are necessarily limited, that is, truly contingent in a fundamental sense. Thus, a chance encounter with ethical significance is really a combination of contingency and necessity, which Kuki calls "contingency-necessity" (Kuki 1966, 168–176, 193–196): we encounter another in need by chance, and when we do so, we recognize that if we take on the challenge of responding to this need, we set ourselves a task that is endless from a human point of view since its full achievement is beyond our power. Thus, Kuki explains, in ethics, contingency enters into a relationship with necessity (the demand the ethical ideal makes on us), but in so doing, establishes its "true character" of contingency in the sense that one encounters the limits of one's human powers (Kuki 1966, 195). He concludes,

> Surprise can be introduced into the moment of a chance encounter by giving rise through the creation of the future of an "end without end." And when we emphasize the surprise at the totality of contingencies that constitutes any given future, this gives rise to the correlation "contingency-necessity" in which contingency thereby becomes truly contingency. This is the meaning of finite existence, and at the same time, it is its salvation. The words of the *Doctrine of the Pure Land*, "If one realizes the power of the Buddha's vow [to save all beings], no encounter will have occurred in vain," essentially come down to this. "The encounter" is the chance that *you* meet *me* in the present. The phrase "will not have occurred in vain" means my future possibility of interiorising the you who conditions me [limits me]. The infinite possibility that approaches the impossible becomes reality in contingency, and this contingency creates yet a new contingency which develops towards necessity. In this development is the salvation of man: in the desire to make the salvation of the Buddha one's destiny.[15] (Kuki 1966, 195–196)

When we meet another by chance, we can treat them as an object to know and investigate them scientifically in order to integrate them into our system of knowledge. But another possibility is to recognize (to our surprise) the ethical nature of the encounter and allow the chance meeting with another to give rise to an infinite ethical obligation. When we react in this way, each chance encounter is the initiation of an ethical obligation, and so the encounter will "not have been in vain." In recognizing this obligation, one "interiorises the other" in the sense of taking up one's ethical obligation as the basis for action. But in the encounter, one also recognizes one's limits—one must set aside the pursuit of selfish goals and place the salvation of the other ahead of personal and petty desires and pursuits.

In Kuki's view, the scientific approach treats the world as dead: it is full of objects to be encountered and incorporated into a static system of universal knowledge. In contrast, the ethical approach is "alive": thanks to the present encounter, we abandon our absorption in the everyday world and resolve that each meeting with another not be in vain. This means pursuing the ideal of saving all beings from the world of suffering. In so doing, we make the other's salvation our own destiny (Kuki 1966, 196), one which we cannot fulfil in our lifetime, but toward which we must strive nonetheless.

In *The Problem of Contingency*, Kuki explains how one can discover freedom in destiny: freedom comes from recognizing that the ultimate impossibility of one's worldly existence is the possibility of realizing that one is nothing other than ultimate reality manifesting itself in phenomenal existence (Kuki 1966, 195–196). To put this in Buddhist terms, Kuki maintains that we discover in the limits of the samsaric world that we are not bound by these limits because we are an expression of reality itself. This is what Kuki means when he quotes the *Pure Land Discourse*, which states "If we realize the power of the Buddha's [vow to liberate all beings], nothing happens in vain":[16] If we realize our power to liberate others, then every encounter, rather than being a limit, is an opportunity, a possibility, to actualize the power to liberate in order to save others.

THE INFLUENCE OF FRENCH PHILOSOPHY AND HEIDEGGERIAN EXISTENTIAL PHENOMENOLOGY ON KUKI

In this section, we will briefly look at the role of European philosophy in Kuki's work. The purpose will be to shed more light on how Kuki understood the nature of culture, and in particular, how he thought it was possible for individuals to experience the meaning of a phenomenon of consciousness such as *iki* which expresses something that can be shared by all Japanese people and even some non-Japanese who have immersed themselves in Japanese culture. Earlier in this chapter and in the previous one we have already alluded to the fact that Kuki's concept of a phenomenon of consciousness, introduced in *The Structure of Iki* to characterize the intensional structure of that form of aesthetic sensibility, can be accessed intuitively through something like Maine de Biran's *sens intime* or Henri Bergson's "metaphysical intuition." However, Kuki characterized *what* one intuitively experiences in phenomenological terms using Heidegger's philosophy. For instance, the notions of possibility and fate that play such an important role in Kuki's *The Problem of Contingency* borrow from Heideggerian notions of possibility and impossibility in his analysis of the existential structure of human existence as being-toward-death (*Sein-zum-Tode*) in *Being and Time*.

In this section, we will examine the similarity between Heideggerian notions of possibility and necessity and those used by Kuki. We will also learn what French philosophers Maine de Biran and Henri Bergson wrote about the kinds of intuition that were a model for Kuki's intuitive access to the deep meaning of culture as the being of an ethnic group. As we will see, for Maine de Biran, intuition is the method for understanding our true self as an expression of the Divine. Henri Bergson takes up this idea but gives it a secular orientation: through intuition, we experience "l'élan d'amour" (a powerful love) whose origin is Divine, but which forms the basis for everyday ethical rules embodied in nonreligious social and cultural practices. Kuki's notion of culture as something mundane expressed in Japanese art and in certain kinds of relationships (like that of the *geisha* and her lover) whose meaning can be described phenomenologically but which individuals must intuit in order to truly acquire, is very similar to the notions of intuition of both Maine Biran and Bergson. We will begin with a short overview of the Heideggerian influence on Kuki before ending the chapter with a consideration of the impact of Bergson and Maine de Biran on his work.

Heidegger's Influence on Kuki's Notions of Contingency, Necessity, and Fate

Kuki insists that *iki* expresses the ethical ideal of freedom: those who accept this ideal eschew certainty and instead accept that life is a world of possible goals and relationships that will never be completely fulfilled. Many scholars have noted that his view about the role of freedom as acceptance of possibility was influenced by Heidegger's philosophy, in which he characterized "being-toward-death," a fundamental existential structure of human existence (Dreyfus 1995, 311) as "maintaining existence within possibility" (Furukawa 2015, 238–240; see also Takada 2002, 161). The possibility of death is simply the possibility of no longer existing (Heidegger 1996, 262; Dreyfus 1995, 311). Facing up to this possibility is an existential structure of human existence because Heidegger believes that at the moment of dying (and whenever we face this possibility authentically), we realize most clearly that the nature of our existence is to be in the world: we are not first and foremost individual, self-sufficient, and self-contained beings, but worldly beings (Heidegger 1996, 291; see also Dreyfus 1995, 311).

Kuki contrasts *iki* and the ideal of freedom it embodies with what is not *iki* and which involves attachment to the everyday vulgar world. This contrast mirrors Heidegger's discussion of authentic and inauthentic attitudes toward death (Heidegger 1996, 260). Humans act authentically when they accept that their life is finite: they live life with an understanding that the *possibility* of their death is its defining feature (Heidegger 1996, 261), and that therefore they will never fully realize their plans. As Hubert Dreyfus writes, one lives authentically when one accepts "Dasein's essential structural nullity, viz., that Dasein can have neither a nature nor an identity, that it is the constant impossibility of *being* anything specific" (1995, 312). When Kuki describes this authentic existence as living within possibility, he means the opposite of what your parents meant when they said your "life is full of possibilities!" Your parents likely meant that you could realize these possibilities, but Kuki is encouraging you to live within possibilities that will never be realized, like the relationship between a *geisha* and her lover that can never be depended upon. The possibility of death is the possibility that no further realization in actual life is possible. Thus, Heidegger says that "death as something possible is not a possible thing at hand or objectively present, but a possibility-of-being of *Da-sein*" (Heidegger 1996, 261). Facing up to the possibility of death does not require one to brood on death or seek it out; Heidegger states that we must not try to actualize death or tame it, reducing it to our own terms, but rather that "in being-toward-death this possibility [of death] must not be weakened, it must be understood *as possibility*, cultivated *as possibility*, and endured *as possibility* in our relation to it" (Heidegger 1996, 261). Here, Heidegger uses the term "possibility" in much the same way as Kuki uses the terms "chance" and "contingency," which open up the possibility of recognizing our infinite ethical responsibility to others.

When Kuki moves from his specific study of *iki* to his more general study of the role of possibility and necessity in human existence, he tries to insert the chance for redemption into the scheme. Without this possibility, he could not maintain that the life of the *geisha* or anyone who lives in accordance with *iki* is pursuing an ideal. Thus in *The Problem of Contingency*, the possibility of the impossible is transformed into the "end without end," in the sense of the "goal which one must pursue without it every being fully achieved." He now shifts from simply talking about the importance of living within possibility to conceiving of this defining feature of human existence as "contingent-necessary": each thing is contingent because its existence will necessarily come to an end. Kuki writes, "Contingency means the possibility of nothingness"[17] (Kuki 1966, 185) and also,

> In contingency, we find a deep penetration of nothingness into being. This is why contingency is a fragile existence: the contingent has only a weak and tenuous existence in the here and now, all chances contain within them in principle the destiny of death and collapse.[18] (Kuki 1966, 187)

Like Heidegger, Kuki believes that living with one's face turned toward the possibility of nothingness is essential: it is authentic existence. And like

Heidegger, he does not think that this means living in dread of death, but rather living with a profound questioning in one's core, which Kuki identifies with Milinda's question, "Why?" (Kuki 1966, 187), or with the *geisha*'s resignation and brave composure in the face of the impossibility of achieving her goal of love because all things come to an end.

However, while Heidegger does not derive an ethics from his description of authentic being-toward-death, Kuki does: he believes that at certain times in one's life, chance encounters give one insight into one's death, the possibility of nothingness, but that this is at the same time a glimpse of the absolute (Kuki 1966, 176). It is, he says, a glimpse of destiny: "In the midst of existence, one of the possible elements of disjunctive possibility emerges to disturb it; thrown like a die, it is destiny"[19] (Kuki 1966, 176). Here, too, one can see the similarity between Kuki's characterization of destiny and Heidegger's; but one can also see a difference. For while destiny for Heidegger, as for Kuki, lifts one out of absorption in everyday existence and allows one a glimpse of what it truly means to be human, for Kuki, destiny not only jolts us into reality but also discloses to us the ethical obligation that accompanies the recognition of the absolute.

First, let us point out the similarity between Kuki's treatment of fate in *The Structure of Iki* and Heidegger's discussion of this in *Being and Time*. In that text, Kuki identifies the *geisha*'s fate as the reality that her love is impossible (Kuki 2004, 22–23). However, by accepting this fact and resigning herself to it (*akirame*), she affirms her freedom: freedom from attachment to the world and from absorption in a permanent relationship in which two lovers become one. Similarly, in *Being and Time*, Heidegger writes that fate (1996, 261) is the call of death which liberates us from our absorption in the everyday world of "the They." He explains,

> The more authentically Da-sein resolves itself, that is, understands itself unambiguously in terms of its own most eminent possibility in anticipating death, the more unequivocal and inevitable is the choice in finding the possibility of its existence. Only the anticipation of death drives every chance and "preliminary" possibility out. Only being free *for* death gives Da-sein its absolute goal and knocks existence into its finitude. The finitude of existence thus seized upon tears one back out of endless multiplicity of possibilities offering themselves nearest by—those of comfort, shirking and taking things easy—and brings Da-sein to the simplicity of its *fate*. This is how we designate the primordial occurrence of Da-sein that lies in authentic resoluteness in which it *hands itself down* to itself, free for death, in a possibility that it inherited and yet has chosen. (Heidegger 1996, 383–384)

Thus for Heidegger, fate is the certainty of death, and once we accept this fate, we make authentic choices rather than simply being absorbed into the assumptions of the everyday world and passively accepting the choices that are made for us. As Dreyfus explains, "Dasein must arrive at a way of dealing with things and people that incorporates the insight gained in anxiety that no possibilities have intrinsic significance—that is, that they have no essential relation to the self, nor can they be given any—yet makes that insight the basis for an active life" (1995, 316).

In *The Problem of Contingency*, Kuki deepens and generalizes the analysis of fate that he sketched out in *The Structure of Iki*. One's fate is in some sense contingent because one is thrown into the world accidentally at a particular time and place: one does not choose to be born, one does not choose the circumstances into which one is born, and therefore one does not choose one's destiny, which is death. However, fate also involves necessity if one accepts that where one happens to be thrown in time and space is the manifestation of some hidden purpose. Kuki quotes Schopenhauer, who writes, "No matter how contingent the unfolding of things appears to be, fundamentally it is not so. Rather, all these contingencies are actually contained within a deeply hidden necessity whose tool is itself contingency"[20] (Schopenhauer 1913, 228; quoted in Kuki 1966, 170). He goes on to explain that the original contingency, the moment we are thrown into the world, can also be seen as the manifestation of necessity understood as absolute reality, which consists of all possible contingencies (Kuki 1966, 179). Thus destiny, Kuki writes, is contingency and necessity at the same time, which he describes as "contingency-necessity" (Kuki 1966, 168, 195).

As we have seen, Kuki develops this idea in Buddhist terms by explaining that if one accepts that one's samsaric existence is also the manifestation of *nirvana* understood as the possibility of liberation for all beings, then the apparent random and irrational character of the actual world takes on the character of necessity as the expression of this fundamental truth (Kuki 1966, 195–196).

The Influence of French Philosophy on Kuki: The Intuitionism of Maine de Biran and Bergson

Many scholars have emphasized the influence of phenomenology, especially Heideggerian existential phenomenology, on Kuki. While this is undeniable, to understand how his thought differs from the phenomenologists and to appreciate his originality, we must examine the French philosophy that influenced him such as that of Henri Bergson and Maine de Biran. Both of these French philosophers championed the role of intuition in our lives as a counterweight to the growing influence of scientific rationality that had emerged since the eighteenth century and culminated in the application of scientific approaches to the study of culture and society by some Neo-Kantian scholars. No doubt Kuki's adoption of a phenomenological mode of analysis as opposed to the Neo-Kantian analysis of society and culture drew him toward the French philosophers. Indeed, he writes in "Bergson in Japan," "[t]o philosophize is to place oneself within concrete reality through an effort of intuition." Thus Bergson was a foil to the Neo-Kantians, opposing himself, according to Kuki, to Kant's "clear distinction between the matter of knowledge and its form," favoring intuition over rational analysis and concepts (*KSZ* 1: (89)).

In addition to being a good foil to the Neo-Kantians, French philosophy applied the intuitive method directly to ethics, the topic of interest to Kuki, who sought to describe *iki* as the embodiment of the ethic of the *geisha*, and who in *The Problem of Contingency* described the role of intuition in accessing the absolute. As we will see, both Maine de Biran and Bergson were interested in the intuition that spurs us to act altruistically and morally, and which Bergson also considered to be the basis of the ethical rules and habits that are inculcated in us through culture and society.

Maine de Biran

The philosophy of François-Pierre Gonthier Maine de Biran (1766–1824) is not often studied by North American philosophy students nor even by Europeans. He was a "spiritualist philosopher" (Nicolas 1858, xxxix; Meacham and Spadola 2016, 12) who was interested in understanding what the "je ne sais quoi" is that causes matter to move and to think (Maine de Biran 1834, 24). He was spiritualist in the sense that he was a critic of the naturalist philosophers, foremost among them, Étienne Bonnot de Condillac (1715–1780) (Maine de Biran 1834, 27). While the naturalists sought a psychological explanation of the inner life of the human mind—that is, they sought to understand its nature by examining its outward manifestations—Maine de Biran felt that it was only through inner reflection and meditation—that is, by examining one's "spirit," that one could truly understand this life (Maine de Biran 1834 30, 36; Dunham 2006, 181–182; 186–187). He critiqued psychology as follows,

> Of course, one cannot deny the usefulness or legitimacy of scientific study. But philosophers must not follow the example of the naturalists and lose from sight the proper subject of study by imagining that they can shed light on and perfect the science of the facts of the soul or of the "I" through transforming psychological ideas and notions into images that represent from outside that which can only be perceived from within, and which vanish and dissipate in the light of the external world. (Maine Biran 1834, 28; see also Maine de Biran 1859, 189–190) (author's translation)

What does one discover through this inward study of the self? Maine de Biran believed that through reflection, it was possible to discover within oneself the work of God, which alone is the active principle that creates the movement and activity of the material world. He wrote, "all created and finite substances are passive, and the human soul is no exception, neither in regard to the foundation of their being nor the foundation of their ideas and inner notions, which have been carved into them by the hand of the Creator himself" (author's translation) (Maine de Biran 1834, 40). The soul is ultimately what is free; the material of the body alone is subject to necessity, to fate (Maine de Biran 1834, 45). But the soul as a merely thinking thing is not itself some substance or force that moves the body (Maine de Biran 1834, 47). To think of the soul as a thinking thing or a mental substance is to abstract from its fundamental nature, which is that the soul is the primal experience of the "I" (Maine de Biran 1834, 52).

Maine de Biran elaborated on this primal experience of the self in his essay "Essai sur les fondements de la psychologie," where he writes of it in the following way,

> Properly speaking, man cannot perceive or know anything except in so far as he is conscious of his own personal individuality, i.e., that his own existence is a fact for him in so far as he is an "I." The sense of the "I" is thus a primal fact of knowing and, as we will prove subsequently, it does not depend essentially on any impression received through the external senses. The [sense of the "I"] is not associated with any changeable modifications or accidents despite being associated with every [thought], but rather [this fact] inheres exclusively within a particular inner sense. It is in this sense that it is a primitive fact of the "sens intime." (Maine de Biran 1859, 141) (author's translation)

The sense of the self is a primitive fact of one's experience that accompanies every sensation and every thought (Maine de Biran 1859, 142, 149, 152). He criticizes Kant, whose analysis he considers to be only abstract rather than concrete and reflective (Maine de Biran 1859, 167). Here, one sees the same criticism of Kant that Kuki noted in his preference for Bergson over the philosopher from Königsberg, who "was two neat in his separation of the matter of knowing and its form" (*KSZ* 1: [89]). Indeed, Maine de Biran says that the problem with Kant is precisely the "thick line of demarcation that he draws between subject and object, between form and matter," a distinction that Maine de Biran considers to be no more than a logical distinction (Maine de Biran 1859, 168) rather than a phenomenological one because it is not a distinction based in experience. Thus while Kant separated experience and its form, Maine de Biran unifies the two. He writes, "By demonstrating that all reflective ideas and supposed inner substances (*innées*) are nothing but the primitive facts of consciousness analyzed and expressed in its various types, we will have also demonstrated that these ideas have a single origin since the *I* or the individual's personality is indivisible"[21] (Biran 1859, 248; see also 251) (Author's translation).

The great innovation of Maine de Biran that interested subsequent philosophers, especially phenomenologists, was his identification of the *sens intime* with the will, which he describes as a "sense of effort" or "force" (*sens de l'effort*) (Maine de Biran 1859, 208) that constitutes a "primitive fact" of the *sens intime* (Maine de Biran 1859, 215). The *sens intime*, he writes, is "indivisible and instantaneous"—there is no gap between willing and the sense of myself—it is always clear that it is I who wills. The will is an active force. When we perceive external objects through sensation, we are passive: we receive the transmission of impressions without having to actively reach out to grasp them (Maine de Biran 1859, 211). But in the case of the *sens intime*, we exert an effort or force, and this is what causes our body to move in a particular way (Maine de Biran 1859, 211). He describes this *sens intime* as follows,

> The exertion of the effort or the ability to start and continue a given series of movements or actions is a fact of the *sens intime* that is as evident as the fact of our existence. There is no foreign force to which this exertion is necessarily subordinate. (Maine de Biran 1859, 214) (author's translation)

Interestingly, Maine de Biran does not consider as separate the willing and the physical action that results. He explains that "neither one of the terms in the fundamental relation [i.e., the force that is the primitive fact of the *sens intime* and the muscular activity it generates] is constituted as necessarily depending on impressions coming from outside [of me]" (author's translation) (Maine de Biran 1859, 216). The experience of willing is simply the physical actions of the body that I cause (Maine de Biran 1859, 223). He writes,

> The primitive fact of the *sens intime* is nothing other than the desired effort, inseparable from the organic resistance or muscular sensation that *I* have caused. This fact is thus a relation in which there are two distinct terms that are not separate. In order for them to be separate ... it would require that the action that is immediately exerted from the centre on the motor nerves be accompanied by a particular internal perception that is distinct and separate from the muscular sensation. But in that case, the same internal perception would consist of another relation that is itself [even] more intimate with the hyperorganic force exerted by the centre and the nerves on which it immediately acted. This nervous inertia would thus replace the muscular inertia, and so nothing would have changed the character of the primitive fact. (Maine de Biran 1859, 216) (author's translation)

There are thus two elements to willing—my effort of will and the "living resistance" of the body that is felt as muscular contraction and movement as my will is put into effect (Maine de Biran 1859, 217). But these are not truly separate (Maine de Biran 1859, 223, 245, 247).[22] Indeed, according to Maine de Biran, "The supposition that there is an inner substance is the death of [philosophical] analysis" (Maine de Biran 1859, 247). For in presupposing such a substance, all that we have done is climbed up the chain of causation until we reach a point that we do not understand and which there "remains floating in the void" (Maine de Biran 1859, 247). He adds that "once we leave behind the absolute (i.e., the sense of the self or *sens intime*), we have lost our foundation: we end up outside of both internal and external experience where the innate ideas are to be found" (author's translation) (Maine de Biran 1859, 249). One's inner sense cannot be separated from the experience of it (ibid.).

Now, Maine de Biran links his reflections on the nature of the self to the topic of interest to Kuki: ethics. According to Maine de Biran, if one is not conscious of one's self in an immediate way as a being capable of choosing and willing, then one is simply acting on instinct without truly knowing oneself. Indeed, Maine de Biran does not really think that a person who has not reflected on him- or herself in this way can really know anything at all: for perception, Maine de Biran says, is precisely "distinguishing oneself from all objects of representation or of external intuition" (Maine de Biran 1834, 59; 1859, 248).

Moreover, without distinguishing between oneself and external objects, one cannot make moral judgments, which depend on the distinction between the judging subject and its attributes. Without a sense of self, there is no will separate from actions and movements of the body: one identifies with the "successive modifications" of the body that we perceive (ibid.). Without a sense of self, one cannot really deploy one's intelligence (1834, 60). One notes here the similarity between what Maine de Biran says about judgment and what Kuki wrote. Kuki emphasized that judgment involves the absorption of the other into the self. We can see here that this is a modification of the idea of Maine de Biran that to judge, one must start from the self and understand all of our experience of the external world in relation to this self. Thus Maine de Biran believed that we have two sets of faculties: an active internal faculty and a passive external one (Maine de Biran 1834, 61). Without the internal faculties, we have no sense of ourselves, and without this sense, there is no moral person (Maine de Biran 1859, 234). He describes the importance of the internal faculty to morality as the capacity within us to do both good and bad. He wrote,

> We carry within us the source of good and bad, of favourable or unfavourable destiny. Oh, is this invisible and mysterious agent of life that operates within us but is beyond our control not like destiny? We will always be subject to its

laws, although what appears to be necessary (fated, *fatum*) in the physical world is transformed into predetermination in the moral? (Maine de Biran 1859, 18) (author's translation)

Indeed, we see here that Maine de Biran ties the notion of morality to chance and fate, which he considers to be two sides of the same coin. Life expresses itself as the rules of nature in the physical world, but as a drive toward some predetermined fate when seen from the point of view of consciousness. Here, we see in Maine de Biran's thought the duality of life as necessary but also contingent, perhaps the forerunner of Kuki's similar notion of contingency-necessity, which is the unified dual nature of the existential structure of human existence as both finite (the possibility of death) and yet infinite (the possibility of realizing the ideal of making each moment an opportunity to save all beings).

In his philosophy, Kuki is inspired by Maine de Biran's notion of the inner sense that we have of ourselves and its essentially moral nature. What is this sense? Maine de Biran describes it as follows:

Humans are conscious (have an internal perception) of themselves as active and free beings, or causes—virtual forces—that are capable of initiating the movement of their bodies without being carried away or constrained by any other natural force. They perceive or sense the existence of an "I," of a person who is free and intelligent.

. . .

Understood in this way, humans are more than merely animal; they do not only live and sense as do animals, but they also have an internal perception of their fundamental life and of the sensations that affect them. They not only have physical relations with beings around them, but they perceive and understand these relations and can either adapt to them or defy them to a certain point. They can intensify them, extend them, vary them by virtue of their active force which itself overcomes the bonds of destiny. (Maine de Biran 1834, 87–88) (author's translation)

This interior sense, as we have already seen, Maine de Biran classifies as an intuition. He distinguishes it from affectivity (*affection*), which is how external things are sensed or "affect" us (Maine de Biran 1834, 90; see also his work on habit). Through our interior sense, we come into contact with life expressing itself through us as the freedom to choose and to act, and even to "overcome the bonds of destiny."

This intuition of our true self is also the capacity to experience God, according to Maine de Biran. From time to time, that is, by chance and contingently, we glimpse the Divine that is the source of our active capacities. He writes,

The Spirit blows where it will, we cannot awaken within us the sense of our Sovereign or love for Him in the same way that we can conceive of (or remember) the idea of Him in exercising our ability to act freely. We have no idea the means that God uses to inspire us or to reveal to us internally what he communicates to us and that intimately unites us with him. Divine insight is not given to every soul, nor to the same soul constantly and at all times. Sometimes, the insight seizes us suddenly and causes us happiness up to Seventh Heaven, but in the next instant it abandons us and leaves us to fall back to Earth with all our weight. It is here, and here alone, that Divine action explodes within the human soul. (Maine de Biran 1834, 161) (author's translation)

While it is clear that Maine de Biran has solely the Christian model of divine inspiration in mind, the fact that God manifests himself through chance and uncontrollable instances reminds us of Kuki's insistence that it is also only on occasion that we catch a glimpse of the absolute. Also, Maine de Biran differs from Kuki in that for the former, it is only through inner reflection that one comes to know oneself, whereas for Kuki, it is through chance encounters with others that one sees who one truly is.

Maine de Biran clearly inspired Kuki to identify intuition as the means by which we come to know the essence of ourselves and our culture, the source of the ideals that motivate us. One could perhaps see Kuki's moral philosophy as to some degree a substitution of phenomenology and Buddhism for the pure intuitionism and Christianity of Maine de Biran. Maine de Biran did not go into very much detail about the relationship between social and cultural norms and individual morality: his model was really one of individual revelation and inspiration. It is no doubt for this reason that Kuki turned to Bergson. For as we will see, Bergson does examine the role of the social—that is, our interactions with others—in motivating us to act. But rather than adopting a purely sociological explanation for why we act, Bergson sees at the root of everyday social pressure and social conformity an inspiration of the Divine that, like the role of the Divine in Maine de Biran, is the true underlying impetus for all of human action.

Henri Bergson—Adding the Social Dimension

While Maine de Biran focused primarily on the inner sense as an expression of the Divine, Bergson examined the degree to which our external social life is also an expression of the Divine or absolute. In this subsection, we will study the social dimension that Bergson added to the intuitionism of Maine de Biran, and which contributed to Kuki's study of cultural and social practices as the expression of the absolute. As we shall see, Bergson acknowledges that most moral rules are simply social *mores*—habits and customs. However, we adhere to them not just because they are inculcated in us, but also because from time to time, the Divine is injected into them as they are reinvigorated by the inspiration of mystics who directly experience God.

Bergson's model of the relationship between the individual and society was organic. He writes,

> When we reflect philosophically [on the nature of society], we might compare it to an organism of which the cells, joined by invisible links, subordinate themselves to one another in a conscious hierarchy and which naturally bend to a discipline that might require that a part sacrifice itself for the greater interest of the whole. Of course, this is only an analogy, because a society comprised of individual wills is different from an organism that must obey necessary laws. But once these wills become organized, they imitate an organism, and within this more or less artificial organism, habit plays the same role as necessary [laws] in the works of nature. (Bergson 1932, 9; see also 12) (author's Translation)

Individuals feel moral obligations because we have in some way internalized the requirements of this larger organism, society (Bergson 1932, 10, 18–19). It is internalized because the language we speak is necessarily social, and even in one's most private moments, we find ourselves talking to ourselves and so reinforcing our attachment to society (Bergson 1932, 13–14). Indeed, all aspects of daily life remind us of our social context: family life, our profession, attending to the tasks of daily life like going shopping, going for a walk or even staying at home—all exhibit the stamp of the social nature of our existence (Bergson 1932, 16). The main point that Bergson is making through the organic metaphor and the fact that social obligation is internalized by individuals is that ethical action is not motivated by reason alone (Bergson 1932, 19, 26).

But while society inculcates morality in us through social pressure (Bergson 1932, 68), this is not its only source. And despite the use of the organic metaphor to describe the relationship between the individual and society, Bergson does not think that moral obligation in human societies is the result simply of instinct or of some necessary natural law (Bergson 1932, 22–23). Another source, it turns out, is emotion: the "force of love" ("l'élan d'amour";[23] Bergson 1932, 67). Sometimes, we act not because of social pressure but out of altruism or a recognition of the humanity of others. Bergson believes that this is the result of some sensation or emotion, some feeling that motivates us: "It cannot be doubted that new emotion is the origin of great artistic creations, of science, and of civilization in general. This is not solely because emotions are stimulating, but because they stimulate our intelligence to exert itself and our will to sustain it" (Bergson 1932, 32) (author's translation). Now these emotions Bergson divides into two kinds: one is caused by an idea or a representational image and is not profound—they are "within the bounds of our intellect"; the second is "supra-intellectual," since it is not generated by ideas or representations, and it is this kind of emotion that stimulates artistic and scientific endeavor (Bergson 1932, 33, 45–46, 69). Mediocre art might stimulate us in the first sense—in a banal and everyday manner. But a true masterpiece touches us deeply because it leaped forth from the soul of its creator and then disturbed our own (Bergson 1932, 34). This is the kind of emotion that Bergson believes is at the root of moral obligation:

> No simple speculation would create [in us] a sense of obligation or anything that resembles it. No matter how sublime the theory, I could always say that I do not accept it. And even if I were to accept it, I would still maintain that I was free to act as I wish. But if the atmosphere of emotion is present, if I have breathed it, if the emotion has penetrated me, I will act in accordance with it, transported by it. I am not in this case constrained by necessity, but rather I am motivated by an inclination that I do not wish to resist. (Bergson 1932, 35) (author's translation)

Having explained the relationship between the individual and society to be like that of an organism in which the individual adopts the imperatives of the group, Bergson goes on to explain the role of religion, which he says "reinforces social obligations" (Bergson 1932, 12). Religion does not win any converts simply because of the rationality and consistency of its doctrines; it does so via the emotion that it causes to well up in us (Bergson 1932, 35). Those who are inspired by religion are really inspired by an emotion or feeling that "emanates from an emotion . . . born from the act of the creator" (Bergson 1932, 38–39). The religion that inspires great moral actions is simply the welling up of life within us: life expressing itself (Bergson 1932, 66).

Having found two sources of morality: social obligation and emotional impetus, Bergson then makes a number of observations about the two that recall Kuki's characterization of the relationship between everyday life and the life that manifests itself in surprise as experience of the absolute. Bergson's description of the difference between our experiences of the everyday world and of the absolute world of the creation could almost be mapped onto Kuki's description of the difference between samsara and nirvana in Buddhism. He writes,

> Viewed from without, the study of the activity of [everyday] life in each of its creations would be infinite: one will never be able to definitively describe the structure of an eye like our own. But what we consider the totality of the means employed is in reality nothing but a series of obstacles that have been overcome: the acts of nature are simple, and the apparent infinite complexity of

the mechanism that it seems to have created bit by bit to create vision is nothing other than the unending interaction of opposing [forces] that have overcome each other to allow the exercise of [the eye's] function to emerge. (Bergson 1932, 39) (author's translation)

One can look at nature and see it simply as an infinitely complex set of contingent interactions. But from the point of view of the creator and the soul that communicates with it, nature is simply the expression of freedom—the overcoming of obstacles (Bergson 1932, 20631). He explains later in *The Two Sources of Morality and Religion*, "That which, seen from the outside, can be disassembled into an infinity of interrelated pieces coordinated linked the one to the other, may seem from the inside as a simple act like the movement of our hand, which we experience as indivisible" (Bergson 1932, 79) (author's translation).

Bergson then goes on to make the same point that Kuki made at the end of *The Problem of Contingency*, namely, that the continual unfolding of cause and effect seems to be animated by a principle of heterogeneity—thing A causes different thing B (Bergson 1932, 39, 80). But this same reality can also be a manifestation of the principle of homogeneity—it is an expression of a unified life, a single absolute living thing (ibid.):

Where our analysis, which is external [to the experience] discovers positive components in ever greater numbers such that, by virtue simply of their number, they seem surprisingly to be more and more linked one to another, [in contrast], an intuition that transports us into [the experience] would realize these simply as obstacles that have been overcome rather than as a combination of elements." (Bergson 1932, 79) (author's translation)

What he means by this is that the social and natural world can be seen as an infinite number of physical and chemical effects; but this very same material world can be experienced as an obstacle to be overcome in order to express the imperatives of life (ibid.).[24]

To get back to the theme that interested both Kuki and Bergson, ethics could be considered analytically and rationally as a series of obligations arising out of social necessities. But one can also understand ethics and moral obligation as the expression of life in which "there is still obligation, but in which this obligation is the force of an aspiration or élan, the very élan that resulted in the creation of the human species. . . . In this case, the motivation is the direct effect [of this élan], and not simply the result of the [social] mechanisms that it has put in place provisionally at a given time" (Bergson 1932, 40, 67) (author's translation). Like Kuki, he expresses this in terms of contingency and necessity:

> The instinct [that is the source of profound moral obligation] gave way provisionally to a set of habits, each of which was contingent, and whose only necessity was their tendency toward the preservation of society. . . The necessity of the whole, which we experience through its contingent parts, is what we call moral obligation in general. The parts are in fact only contingent in the eyes of society; for the individual, in whom society has inculcated certain habits, each part is as necessary as the whole. (Bergson 1932, 40) (author's translation)

Morality, viewed from the point of view of everyday life, is a series of historically established contingent social rules that we absorb through social interactions and make into our habits of life. But viewed from the point of view of absolute reality, morality expresses life itself, and our inmost nature, too, is an expression of this life. Bergson explains,

> The religious foundation of morality . . . deals with mystical experience. By this we mean the mystical experience that is immediate and beyond all interpretation. True mystics simply open themselves to the flow that envelops them. Sensing something better than themselves within themselves, they are sure of themselves and so demonstrate their greatness as men through their actions. [In this regard], they surprise those for whom mysticism is only a vision, transportation or ecstasy. What they have allowed to flow within them is a descending flux that seeks to touch others through them: they experience this desire to spread what they have received to others as the power of love (*l'élan d'amour*), a love which each [mystic] impresses with the mark of his personality. (author's translation) (Bergson 1932, 69; see also 157)

Thus morality does not simply express itself in the everyday world of habits and social rules; rather, these facts emanate from and are periodically recalibrated against the absolute expressed through the mystic (and potentially through all of us) (Bergson 1932, 69).

Finally, Bergson introduces the ideal element of morality, an ideal for which we strive but never completely achieve. In this regard, too, Bergson's ethics, aimed at an ideal, is like Kuki's in that it is an "end without end" (Kuki 1966, 195–196). Bergson writes that a "mystical society that would encompass the whole of humanity and which would proceed, animated by a common will, toward the eternal recreation of a new humanity, will obviously never be realized in the future any more than it has existed in the past among human societies that existed organically like the society of animals. The pure aspiration is a limiting ideal, like a bare obligation" (Bergson 1932, 59). The insights of the great mystics who remind us of the ideal are "deposited in the memory of humanity," liable to being remembered as Plato's forms (29).

Each of us can access this insight by being inspired by those mystics or the stories about them (ibid.).

EVALUATING THE SUCCESS OF KUKI'S SOLUTION TO THE PUZZLE OF THE INDIVIDUAL AND INTERSUBJECTIVE NATURE OF ETHICAL EXPERIENCE

We began this chapter by considering the fundamental puzzle at the heart of Kuki's philosophy: How could the morality of the Japanese, expressed through a culturally shared phenomenon of consciousness like *iki*, be understood intuitively by individuals and yet be a shared sense? Kuki did not draw on East Asian sources to answer this question, although his answer is a classic instance of the East Asian philosophical model, which posits the unity of immanence and transcendence. For instance, in Confucianism, human morality is the expression of universal harmony, and the authority of the emperor is the expression of the Mandate of Heaven. In Chinese Buddhist philosophy, the unity of all beings can be grasped by individuals who pursue the way, find a teacher, and learn to live as an expression of this unity. But instead of drawing on such sources, Bergson tried to find a European paradigm that would express the same idea after a few modifications.

The philosophy that Kuki drew on to express his understanding of Japanese ethics expressed as a shared moral ideal through cultural and social practices was the life philosophy (*Lebensphilosophie*) of Maine de Biran and Bergson. He was also inspired by the phenomenological outlook of these two philosophers, especially their emphasis on the importance of studying concrete experience and consciousness in order to understand this life that is expressing itself through and as us.

Kuki's interest in the phenomenological bent of Maine de Biran and Bergson in turn led him to the phenomenology of Husserl and Heidegger. The advantage of their phenomenology is that it provided Kuki with a method of inquiry and a congenial understanding of the relationship between the individual and the social. In *The Structure of Iki*, Kuki employed Heidegger's phenomenological and hermeneutic method in order to uncover some of the fundamental structures of Japanese ethnic being by studying the meaning of a cultural phenomenon, *iki*. He also drew on Heidegger's examination of the existential structures of human existence in order to express in existential terms the basic insight of the unity of transcendent (or absolute) and immanent, replacing this unity with the unity of necessity and contingency, expressed in moral terms as the unity of fate and chance.

Traditional East Asian philosophy emphasized that each individual should, through self-reflection and self-study, discover how he or she is an expression of the infinite. To express this in modern European terminology, Kuki drew on French spiritualism (Maine de Biran) and vitalism (Bergson), which accepted that one could, through intuition, discover one's true self, which is the expression of God. He expressed this in secular terms by examining how the *geisha* and her lover express the moral ideal that one finds within oneself, and in so doing, drew on Heidegger's secularized version of the fall and redemption in *Being and Time*.

NOTES

1. In *The Structure of Iki*, Kuki only mentions the relationship between *akirame* and Buddhism and *ikiji* and *bushidō*. *Bitai* (媚態), the third intensional element of *iki*, is not explicitly related to nature (*shizen*) or Shintō.
2. Kuki suggests that "the experience and critical knowledge that *iki* embodies [may be] socially inherited rather than individually acquired" (Kuki 2004, 22).
3. Kuki refers to Bergson's "metaphysical intuition" in his essay, "Bergson au Japon" (*KSZ* 1:(89)).
4. 「体験の芸術的客観化は必ずしも意識的になされることを必要としない。芸術的衝動は無意識的に働く場合も多い。しかしかかる無意識的創造も体験の客観化に外ならない。即ち個人的または社会的体験が、無意識的に、しかし自由に形成原理を選択して、自己表現を芸術として完了したのである。自然形式においても同様である。身振その他の自然形式は屡々無意識のうちに創造される。いづれにしても、「いき」の客観的表現は意識現象としての「いき」に基礎附けて初めての真に理解されるものである。」(*KSZ* 1:76–77)
5. 「人間の運命に対して曇らざる眼をもち、魂の自由に向って悩ましい憧憬を懐く民族ならずしては媚態をして「いき」の様態を取らしむることは出来ない。「いき」の核心的意味は、その構造がわが民族存在の自己開示として把握されたときに、十全なる会得と理解とを得たのである。」(*KSZ* 1:81)
6. For a critique of using *geisha* culture as the ultimate expression of human freedom, see Mayeda (2006, 144–145).
7. 「…「いき」のうちには運命に対する「諦め」と、「諦め」に基づく恬淡とが否み得ない事実性を示している。」(*KSZ* 1:19)
8. 「要するに「いき」は「浮かみもやらぬ、流れのうき身」という「苦界」にその起原をもっている。そうして「いき」のうちの「諦め」従って「無関心」は、世知辛い、つれない浮世の洗練を経てすっきりと垢抜した心、現実に対する独断的な執着を離れた瀟洒として未練のない恬淡無碍の心である。」(*KSZ* 1:23)
9. 「媚態はその仮想的目的を達せざる点に於て、自己に忠実なるものである。それ故に、媚態が目的に対して「諦め」を有することは不合理でないのみならず、却って媚態そのものの原本的存在性を開示せしむることである。媚態と「諦め」との結合は、自由への帰依が

運命によって強要され、可能性の措定が必然性によって規定されたことを意味している。即ち、そこには否定による肯定が見られる。」(*KSZ* 1:21-22).

10. 「「粋と云われて浮いた同士」が「つい岡惚の浮気から」いつしか恬淡洒脱の心を失って行った場合には「またいとしさが弥増して、深く鳴子の野暮らしい」ことを託たねばならない。「蓮の浮気は一寸惚れ」という時は未だ「いき」の領域にいた。「野暮な事じゃが比翼紋、離れぬ中」となったときには既に「いき」の境地を遠く去っている。そうして「意気なお方につり合ぬ、野暮なやの字の屋敷者」という皮肉な嘲笑を甘んじて受けなければならぬ。」(*KSZ* 1:22)

11. 「ともかくも「いき」のうちには運命に対する「諦め」と、「諦め」に基づく恬淡とが否み得ない事実性を示している。そうしてまた、流転、無常を差別相の形式と見、空無、涅槃を平等相の原理とする仏教の世界観...背景をなして、「いき」のうちのこの契機を強調しかつ純化していることは疑いない。」(*KSZ* 1:21)

12. 「...驚きという情は、偶然的なものに対して起こる情である。偶然的なものとは同一性から離れているものである。同一性の圏内に在るものに対しては、あたり前のものとして、驚きを感じない。同一性から離れているものに対して、それはあたり前でないから驚くのである。」(Kuki 1975, 163–164)

13. For such a detailed review, see Mayeda (2006, 2012, 2016).

14. 「判断の本質的意味は邂逅する「汝」を「我」に深化することでなければならない。我の内的同一性へ外的なる汝を具体的に同一化するのが判断の理念である。」(*KSZ* 2:256). Translation by the author.

15. 「「目的なき目的」を未来の生産に醸して邂逅の「瞬間」に驚異を齎すことが出来る。そうして、一切の偶然性の驚異を未来によって強調することは「偶然——必然」の相関を成立させることであって、また従って偶然性をして真に偶然性たらしめることである。これが有限なる実存者に与えられた課題であり、同時にまた、実存する有限者の救いでなければならぬ。『浄土論』に「観仏本願力、遇無空過者」とあるのも畢竟このことであろう。「遇う」のは現在に於て我に邂逅する汝の偶然性である。「空しく過ぐるもの無し」とは汝に制約されながら汝の内面化に関して有つ我が未来の可能性としてのみ意味を有っている。不可能に近い極微の可能性が偶然性に於て現実となり、偶然性として堅く掴まれることによって新しい可能性を生み、更に可能性が必然性へ発展するところに運命としての仏の本願もあれば人間の救いもある。」(*KSZ* 2:259–260). Translation by the author.

16. "In contemplating the Power of the Buddha's Primal Vow, I realize that no one who encounters it will pass by in vain" (*kanbutsuhonganriki gumukukasha*; 観仏本願力 遇無空過者; *Jodoron: Discourse on the Sutra of Eternal Life and Gatha of Aspiration to Be Born in the Pure Land*, composed by Vasubandhu, translated into Chinese by Bodhiruci, translated into English by David Matsumoto, online: http://web.mit.edu/stclair/www/Vasubandhu.html)

17. 「偶然は無の可能を意味する。」(*KSZ* 2:247) Translation by the author.

18. 「偶然においては無が深く有を侵している。その限り偶然は脆き存在である。偶然は単に「この場所」にまた「この瞬間」に尖端的な虚弱な存在を繋ぐのみである。一切の偶然は崩壊と破滅の運命を本来的に自己のうちに蔵している。」 (*KSZ* 2:249) Translation by the author.

19. 「賽の目の如くに投げ出された離接肢の一つが実存の全幅をゆり動かしながら実存の中核へ体得されるのが運命である。」 (*KSZ* 2:235) Translation by the author.

20. "So sehr auch der Lauf der Dinge sich als rein zufällig darstellt, er es im Grunde doch nicht ist, vielmehr alle diese Zufälle selbst, τα εικη φερομενα, von einer, tief verborgenen Notwendigkeit, ειμαρμενη, umfaßt werden deren bloßes Werkzeug der Zufall selbst ist."

21. Maine de Biran actually states that the individual personality is "one." But to avoid confusion, I substituted "indivisible." See also his comments at pp. 276–278 about the nature of the unity and indivisibility of the self.

22. Maine de Biran does of course recognize that not all movements of the body have their origin in the will. Some are simply instinctual (Maine de Biran 1859, 225). He explains that "when the centre moves [the body] by its own proper initial action, these movements take on a different character from spontaneous instinctive [actions]. Indeed, this spontaneity is not yet the will or the exertion of effort but rather immediately precedes it. . . . But once [the will takes over] the power [to control the body], it exerts this power by itself creating the movement" (Maine de Biran 1859, 227–228).

23. Bergson defines "élan" as "that mysterious property of the functioning of life" (Bergson 1932, 79).

24. Bergson writes later, "Life is the effort to obtain certain things from brute matter; instinct and intelligence, viewed in their completed state, are two means of using a single tool to achieve this: in the first case, the tool is part of a living being, in the second, it is the tool of something inorganic that had to be invented, fabricated, and which we had to learn to use" (author's translation) (Bergson 1932, 81).

Chapter 8

Nishida

Who I Am and Who You Are

It is common to regard society and culture as separate from us. We realize that we are part of a society, but only in the sense that we belong to a collection of individuals who participate in certain shared social, cultural, and political institutions. In fact, many of us think of our membership in a society as amounting to little more than sharing cultural practices such as the slang that we use, the foods that we like, or the clothes that we wear, all of which are influenced by what others around us do.

More important to our identity than our shared social practices is our belief that there is an "I" that is ultimately separate from society. We assume this is the case because our thoughts and ideas, feelings and memories are not generally experienced by others—they are private—and so we believe that they represent who we truly are.[1] Certain approaches to sociology reinforce this view of the separateness of the individual and society. For instance, in *The Rules of Sociological Method*, Emile Durkheim writes that a "social fact," his term for the subject matter of sociology, consists of a "category of facts with very distinctive characteristics: it consists of ways of acting, thinking, and feeling, external to the individual, and endowed with a power of coercion, by reason of which they control him" (Durkheim 1964, 3). In other words, the social is a set of "ways of acting, thinking and feeling" that are imposed on the individual from outside and therefore separate from them. In less technical terms, Durkheim describes the "social" as "the collective aspects of the beliefs, tendencies, and practices of a group" (ibid., 7). Implicit in this is approach is an opposition between "I" and "we."

Nishida demonstrates that it is wrong to think about the relationship between "I" and "we" (self and society) in these terms. We are wrong both about who we are as individuals and about what the world around us really is, including who other people are. Before the division into "I" and "we" there is a fundamental unity between us all. In this regard, Nishida shared similar concerns to many of his contemporaries. For instance, Max Scheler wrote that social experiences (experiences of those other than me) are just as integral a part of the experience of each individual as her private experiences (consciousness of oneself, conscience, etc.), and as such, they are an important part of who we are as individuals. As Scheler writes,

> An individual person *and* a collective person "belong" to every *finite* person. Both factors are essentially necessary sides of a concrete whole of person and world. Thus individual and collective persons can be related to each other *within* every possible concrete finite person, and the relation of one to the other is experienceable.[2] (Scheler 1973, 522) [emphasis in original]

Nishida believed that our usual tendency to assume a split between the individual and the group, the self and the social, is incorrect, and he sets out in his philosophy to dispel this erroneous belief. To do so, he begins by pointing out that our everyday way of thinking of ourselves as the collection of our thoughts and ideas, feelings and memories, is wrong; we are much more than this. According to Nishida, each of us as an individual is in some way the manifestation of the productive activity of the whole world. If we look closely at our experience in a critical way, Nishida believes we will discover that our thoughts, ideas, and feelings are actually the expression of something that does not originate in our everyday sense of self. Nishida describes this as follows: the "existential self discovers the self-transforming matrix of history in its own bottomless depths" (Nishida 1987, 84).[3] In simpler terms, he writes, "that we are the individual self-expressions of the world" (Nishida 1998c, 58). In other words, each of us is a manifestation of the self-transformation of the creative world; each of us is an expression of the world as a dynamic activity (Nishida 1987, 64).[4]

In addition to addressing our misconceptions about who we are as individuals, Nishida also explains who the others around us are. Here, too, Nishida believed that our everyday assumptions about others, like our assumptions about who we are as individuals, are mistaken. The world is not just "outside" of us—outside of our thoughts and feelings—nor is society simply a collection of individuals. Like Scheler, Nishida emphasizes that the distinction between "I" and "You," while habitual, is merely derivative: it derives from a more basic relationship between the individual and others.[5] Echoing Scheler, Nishida writes that "our self does not have its origin in the individual ... rather, its origin is communal consciousness (*kyōdō ishiki*, 共同意識)." In other words, "The individual is born from society" (*NKZ* 6:348).[6]

Nishida presents a dialectical conception of the social: the social forms the individual, but likewise, individuals form the social. For instance,

Nishida writes that communal consciousness, as the context in which the individual emerges, "determines what is situated within it (*oite aru mono*, 於てあるもの), but what is situated in [the context] likewise determines the context" (*NKZ* 6:350–351).[7] Thus those around us who form part of the social context in which we exist as individuals are not simply other individuals like us; they are also an integral part of the creative activity of reality that gives rise to individual experience. Thus, contrary to our everyday assumption, our private thoughts and feelings and our individual experiences do not have their sole origin in an inner self separate from others.

In this chapter, I will examine in more depth who Nishida thinks we are as individuals, who these "others" are with whom we interact, and what the society and culture are in which these interactions take place. Throughout, my focus will be on how Nishida's ideas about individual, other, and group should inform how we live our lives. In other words, I examine the moral and ethical implications of Nishida's theory of society.

WHO WE ARE AS INDIVIDUALS

If we really are nothing but our ideas, feelings, desires, hopes, and fears, we would be forced to think of ourselves as very passive beings because we do not actively choose to have most of these thoughts (Nishida 1987, 92). Indeed, we have all had the experience of thoughts that come unwelcome and unbidden to disturb our peace of mind. Nishida encourages us to abandon this everyday view of the self as passive and realize that we are not just defined by our thoughts: we have the capacity to be truly active. Nishida expresses this by saying that we can be "consciously self-expressive" (Nishida 1987, 92; *jikohyōgenteki*, 自己表現的 [*NKZ* 11:426]): we have a capacity to think (*shii* [思惟]), to choose (Nishida uses the term to "will" [*ishi*, 意志]), and to express ourselves in an active way that goes beyond mere passive acceptance of our habitual thoughts and feelings.

To realize this active, creative capacity, we have to sincerely investigate who we truly are.[8] According to Nishida, all of our thoughts, both active and passive, are actually the manifestation of the creativity of the world as a whole.[9] As David Dilworth explains, for Nishida, "truly personal awareness begins from an active intuition of one's own contradictory embodiment of individual historical existence; it develops into a religious insight into the simultaneous revealment of self and world" (1987, 5). We can come to realize that this is who we truly are through a process of self-discovery by using a capacity that Nishida calls "active intuition" (*kōiteki chokkan*, 行為的直観). This term refers to thoughts that are not clouded by everyday patterns of thought and feeling; it is a kind of seeing that sees through our everyday patterns.[10] As Robert Carter writes, "It is only by forgetting the surface or ordinary self that deep Self is enabled to emerge at all" (1997, 105). "Active intuition," Nishida writes, "means to see things from a standpoint transcending that of the preconceived conscious self" (Nishida 1987, 85).[11] When our actions and choices are rooted in active intuition, they reflect who we truly are, and so our actions and choices can be actual manifestations of the world as creativity—they manifest "the creative world in the very depths of the active self" (Nishida 1987, 85; see also ibid., 92 and Nishida 1998e, 78).[12] Carter explains that "'action intuition' serves as epistemological notice that seeing, intuiting, perceiving and sensing are not to be conceived of in purely intellectual terms" (1997, 104; see also Maraldo 2017 at 205–206 and 217–218). Nishida writes,

> The self is active by reflecting the world and is simultaneously reflected by the world in that same interaction. I refer to this structure of interaction between self and world as active intuition, which is always an expressive act having both active and passive aspects to it. . . . All our historical behaviour [i.e., behavior rooted in active intuition] is always thoroughly expressive in this sense. (Nishida 1998e, 83)

In summary, Nishida's philosophy encourages us to abandon our unreflective view of who we are and inquire more deeply into our true nature. We have the tendency to think of ourselves as our thoughts and feelings, and because others cannot easily access this inner mental life, we conclude that we are separate from others: although we live in society, society is not fundamentally a part of who we are. Nishida demonstrates that this tendency to identify with our thoughts and feelings is simply a habit. In fact, we are integrated into our world in a much more fundamental way: our thoughts and feelings—indeed, all of our experiences—are actually a manifestation of the world as a whole which is acting creatively in each moment. We are a part of the life all around us; we are not separate from it.[13]

How to Lead Your Life to Realize Your True Self

Having exposed us to who we truly are as individuals, Nishida suggests that we should live our lives in a way that allows us to realize our true selves (Carter 1997, 136–137). At various points in his philosophy (especially at the beginning and at the end of his life), Nishida casts the path to self-knowledge as a religious path: it is a spiritual life (Nishida 1987, 85). Such a life involves not just responding emotionally to religious inspiration, but instead involves making a real, reasoned choice (Nishida 1987, 93). In other words, being spiritual means to make rational choices that are based on an accurate understanding of who we truly are. The emotional fervor that we sometimes associate with being "spiritual" or "religious" is not necessary for the self-reflection that Nishida regards as truly spiritual. As Nishida explains, "Only a volitional, a consciously active individual person can be religious" (Nishida 1987, 93, 94).[14] We must make a rational choice to live spiritually. We must live in and from our true self, which is identical with the absolute, the dynamic creative power of reality.

Throughout his work, Nishida occasionally described in explicitly religious terms the kind of sincere spiritual inquiry that he proposes; but in doing so, he also emphasized that a spiritual inquiry can be philosophical. For instance, in his first published book, *An Inquiry into the Good*, after devoting three-quarters of the book to philosophy, in Part IV, Nishida turns to his early ideas about religion. There, he makes it clear that religion and philosophy are not opposed to each other. For instance, in the preface to the first edition, he writes that his consideration of religion is the "consummation of philosophy" (Nishida 1990, xxx). As we can see, for Nishida, philosophical inquiry is not separate from the spiritual life. It is therefore not surprising that in his philosophical works, he often explains the process of discovering who we truly are in religious terms. In doing so, he drew primarily on Buddhism and Christianity, the two religions that he studied most thoroughly. For instance, in his last published work, he wrote that through the process of self-discovery, we come face-to-face with God within ourselves "as God's own mirror image and opposite"[15] (Nishida 1987, 93).

We are truly human when we are truly spiritual, and we are truly spiritual when we discover who we truly are and then act in a way that accords with what we discover (Maraldo 2017, 155; Dilworth 1987, 39; Carter 1997, 145). As we set out in the previous section, according to Nishida we are not merely reactive beings whose emotions, instincts, and habits respond to things that happen to us from "outside" ourselves and over which we have no control (Nishida 1987, 92). Rather, the human world is truly creative—it moves "from the created to the creating" (Nishida 1987, 94). It is through creation that we truly become the self-expression of the world understood as the self-expression of the absolute or God. Nishida writes, "The more the self is a consciously active individual, the more it faces God. It does so as an absolute individual. The self faces the limit point of God, the absolute One, at the limit point of its own being as a sheerly individual self-determination of the historical world"[16] (Nishida 1987, 95; see also Nishida 1998e, 88). How does one lead one's life in the way that Nishida advocates? What is he really asking us to do?

Some have proposed that Nishida exhorts us to follow the path he himself followed—that is, Zen meditation under the instruction of an awakened teacher.[17] However, Nishida is clear that philosophical inquiry is itself a spiritual path that can lead to true self-discovery. Religion simply provides the language to express the spiritual realization to which he wishes each of us to awaken. For instance, he explains that reality is dynamic and creative, "having the form of self-affirmation through self-negation, that transforms itself by expressing itself within itself"[18] (Nishida 1987, 73). This philosophical description, he goes on to write, can be expressed in the language of religion. He continues, "The absolute's self-expression may be understood in religious language as God's revelation, its self-transformation as God's will"[19] (ibid.). Thus while the journey that Nishida exhorts us to undertake is spiritual in a certain sense, it can be undertaken as a form of philosophical inquiry. Of course, the journey can be explained by analogy to religious terms drawn from Buddhism and Christianity. But what is important is to inquire into the true nature of the self; becoming a Buddhist or a Christian is not per se important, according to Nishida.

To describe the result of Nishida's own philosophical inquiry into the nature of the individual, the next section contains a short introduction to a concept central to Nishida's philosophy, *basho* (space). This concept will help to explain what Nishida means when he says that the true self is the self-expression of absolute reality in itself. While the language is philosophical, it is important to keep in mind that Nishida conceives of the process of self-inquiry as spiritual. This will help to contextualize his very abstract discussion of the logic of *basho*. And it will also help to understand that the dense philosophical language describes something very concrete—the nature of our conscious experience.

The Role of *Basho* and Dialectic in Nishida's Conception of the Self

The concept of *basho* or "space" plays a central role in Nishida's philosophy starting in the late 1920s. *Basho* is a term that Nishida uses to refer to the condition for the possibility of all human experiencing and to express who we truly are.[20] How can these be the same thing? As we have already explored, Nishida believes that each individual is fundamentally an expression of the dynamic activity of the world as a whole. Thus we are each a "space" (*basho*) where the world can express itself dynamically.[21] When we consider this from the point of view of the individual, this space is a necessary condition for the world that we experience to manifest itself.

Dialectic also plays an important role in Nishida's middle and late philosophy. A dialectic usually involves the opposition of two terms such as "self" and "other," "being" and "nothingness," "life" and "death." The relationship between these two terms can be static or it can be dynamic. For instance, life is constantly in a process of dying, and dead things are constantly being incorporated into the living. Thus all humans die, but their dead bits decay and become integrated into the material out of which new life is built. Nishida considers that the dynamic process of reality depends for its dynamic movement on the opposition of two terms. Often, he describes this opposition as one between "self" and "other." At other times, he considers the opposed terms to be "nothingness" and "being" or "many" and "one." To give an example, in his essay "The World as Identity of Absolute Contradiction," written in 1939 near the end of Nishida's life, he describes reality as follows: "The world is an identity of absolute contradiction in that it moves incessantly in the form of its contradictions and yet does not move insofar as it remains identical with itself" (Nishida 1998c, 56). Later in the same essay, he describes the creativity that characterizes both the world and each individual as a part of the world in terms of the dialectic between the "one" and the "many" and the "individual" and the "group." He writes,

> The various activities (intellectual, artistic, moral) of our individual selves are not to be conceived of by first positing these individual selves and then predicating their relationships with their environments as grammatical subjects. They must be rendered from the standpoint of being individuals of the self-formative historical world as the contradictory identity of the one and the many. These activities can be adequately rendered only in terms of the various kinds of co-originating relationships obtaining between the self as *poiesis* and the world. (Nishida 1998c, 69)

According to Nishida, the world as dynamic, active experience is the manifestation of activity that takes place in a space or place (*basho*). This activity results from the interaction between opposed terms in a dialectical relationship. We will explore this more below.

First, let us examine the concept of *basho*, which is so central to Nishida's philosophy and to his understanding of the mechanisms by which each person as an individual is a possible place for the manifestation and self-expression of the world as dynamic activity. It is difficult to know whether to translate *basho* as "space" or as "place," because both ideas are important to understanding what Nishida means when he uses the term.[22] Let me address both aspects of *basho*.

Basho has the connotation of "place" because Nishida conceives of it not as physical or geometric space but as the location where the individual encounters his or her true self.[23] As we will see, this encounter leads to an important philosophical insight since it allows us to understand the nature of the place where reality manifests itself dynamically. The encounter with one's true self thus has metaphysical consequences. But Nishida's metaphysics also has important epistemological implications since the encounter of the self with the absolute is the source of all of our experience. Using language with Heideggerian resonance, Andrew Feenberg describes what happens in the "place" of *basho* as the "giving of givenness" (Feenberg 1999, 35).[24] This conveys a good sense of the epistemological significance of *basho* as the source of experience.

Basho is not an abstract place; it is concrete. Nishida writes, "The individual, volitional self is something neither merely transcendent nor merely transcendental. It exists as a self-determination of the concrete place of the contradictory identity of objectivity or subjectivity"[25] (Nishida 1987, 96). What is concrete about this place? *Basho* is concrete because what is unfolding in that space (*basho*) is the actual world that is developing dynamically before us and of which we are ourselves a dynamic expression.[26] Thus Nishida writes, "The true individual arises as a unique, momentary self-determination of the absolute present"[27] (Nishida 1987, 96). He quotes the words of Zen Master Linji, the founder of Rinzai Zen, who wrote that "in this mass of red flesh there abides the True Man of No Rank: he constantly exists and enters through your own face"[28] (ibid.). In the depths of the self, one finds concrete reality—"this mass of red flesh" that makes up "your own face"—as that which is universal—the "True Man of No Rank." In the terminology of his middle work (1927–1933), Nishida writes that place (*basho*) is that wherein the universal takes place.[29]

Basho is not just a concrete "place": it is also a term that indicates the transcendental preconditions of experience,[30] that is, it refers to the conditions for the possibility of all human experience. It is to these transcendental qualities of *basho* that Nishida refers when he describes *basho* as the "apriori of aprioris" (Nishida 2015, 52; *NKZ* 4:21). To understand what Nishida means by this, it is useful to begin with Immanuel Kant's explanation of how we experience things since Nishida's approach is developed in some of his texts as a modification of Kant's framework.[31] As we will see, for Kant, the transcendental preconditions of experience are located in the subjectivity of the individual. But for Nishida, the *basho* that functions as a transcendental precondition of experience is located not only in the subjectivity of the individual but also in our true self, which is the whole of reality expressing itself through us. Thus *basho* as a precondition of our subjective experience has an element of objectivity that derives not from the abstract universality of Kant's notion of subjectivity, but from the concrete universality of absolute reality that expresses itself actively as all of us.

Let us begin with Kant's explanation of experiences that appear to come from "outside" us such as the seeing of a red flower. According to Kant, when we see a red flower, two "systems" are in play. One system is that of our senses (our eyes, in this case) which Kant calls "sensibility" (*Sinnlichkeit*, Kant 1965, A51/B75). The other system is our "understanding" (*Verstand*, Kant 1965, A51/B75)—our internal system for processing and identifying the sensations that the eye perceives as a flower. Kant believes that to see something and recognize it as a red flower, our eyes must first receive data from the outside world. Then this data must be processed by our understanding in order to identify the pure sense data received by the eyes as a red flower (ibid.).

Nishida has a very different view. Experience does not require two systems; it just involves one. In his early work, Nishida called this single source "pure experience" (*junsui keiken*, 純粋経験), which he described as direct experience before there is either an object that is known (the red flower) or a subject that knows (the "I") (Nishida 1990, 3). In his middle work, he describes this kind of pure experience in Kantian terms as the "apriori of aprioris," or again as the "pure activity" (*junsui katsudō* (純粋活動) rather than "pure experience") of consciousness (Nishida 2015, 55; *NKZ* 4:26). He calls this experience "activity" because experience is always being produced in every moment; it is never still.

So where does *basho* fit into this scheme? Nishida explains that that which generates this pure experience cannot itself be known (Nishida 2015, 56; *NKZ* 4:26). However, we do know something about it—it is the source or wellspring of all of our experience. Given that it is the source of all experience, it must be an infinitely deep wellspring since it must contain all possible experiences within it (ibid.). Just as an actual spring requires an opening from which the water wells up, the infinite wellspring of activity—the source of all our experience—presupposes an opening or place in which it occurs. This constant opening, which is a precondition to experiencing, is what Nishida comes to refer to as *basho*, "place" or "space." Nishida writes,

> That which is must be located in something. Otherwise, it would be impossible to distinguish between that which is and that which is not. Logically, it must be possible to distinguish between the terms of a relation and the relation itself, and likewise to distinguish between that which unifies the relation and that in which the relation is located. Even in regard to acts, the "I," considered as the pure unity of activity, there must something that contains within it the opposition of the "I" and the "non-I" and establishes within itself the "phenomena of consciousness" in order for it to be possible to think of the "I" and the "non-I" as opposed to each other. Following the language of [Plato's] *Timaeus*, I call [this container], which one must also consider as the receptacle of ideas, "space" (*basho*).[32] (Nishida 2015, 213; *NKZ* 4:208)

While Kant assumed that two systems were necessary for us to experience something—a system for "intuiting" experience and a system for giving it the form necessary for us to recognize it as an experience of a particular object or idea, Nishida identifies only one system. This system is a place where experience "wells up" or "springs from." Because this experience is not reducible to systems of perception and cognition of specific human beings, *basho* refers to any place where experience happens rather than being a feature of the subjective experiencing of each individual. Put another way, each of us experiences the world because the world is a place (or many places) where experiencing is happening as concrete dynamic activity.[33]

As I indicated earlier, *basho* also has the connotation of "space." This refers to the fact that the place where experience takes place must be open and empty so that experiences can occur. Imagine that you want to watch a film. In order to do so, you need both a space for it to be shown (your computer screen, a blank wall on which it can be projected, etc.) and enough time to watch it. Thus to experience the film, both space and time are necessary—they are the necessary preconditions of all experience. The spatial aspect of *basho* as emptiness or openness refers to preconditions in a similar way, except that these are preconditions for *every* experience, not just for the specific experience of watching a film. These preconditions are often labeled "transcendental" preconditions by philosophers in order to capture the idea that they are logical and not merely physical or material prerequisites. *Basho* is the transcendental precondition for experience because the space that it creates is the condition for the possibility of every experience.[34]

As Kant noted and many subsequent philosophers have maintained, there are two essential preconditions to all experience—time and space.[35] Similarly, Nishida conceives of *basho* as being an opening or space that has two dimensions, one temporal and the other spatial (Nishida 2003b, 106; *NKZ* 6:361).[36] The world or our experience thus unfolds temporally and spatially in the "space" (*basho*) of experiencing.[37] This may seem somewhat obscure, but when both Kant and Nishida refer to space and time as transcendental preconditions for experience, they simply mean that our experience always appears to be happening somewhere—that is, in space—and at some time—in the present, which is part of the apparent continuity of past, present, and future.

The difference between Kant and later European philosophers who adopt his approach to epistemology such as J. G. Fichte and F. W. J. Schelling and Nishida is that Nishida conceives of experience as an activity that is generated in a sense independently of each individual (while at the same time including each individual's experience), and so time and space are not the forms of *subjective* sensibility as they are for Kant, but rather forms with an objective aspect that is independent of any individual's experience. As Maraldo explains, "Awareness is not a property belonging to an individual self, not a property belonging to a greater whole" (2017, 335). As I mentioned earlier, according to Nishida, "pure experience" or basic experiencing is simply an activity that preexists the division into subject and object. This is why for Nishida the transcendental preconditions of experience are not the subjective forms of the sensibility of any given individual human being.[38] Instead, the preconditions of experience are the forms that experiencing in itself take, separate from any single perceiving subject. Another way to put this is as follows: while all experience appears to take place in both space and time, *basho*, the place where experience arises, is not itself located in space and time. It is spatial in the sense that it is the place where temporal and spatial experience takes place: it is spatial in the transcendental sense because it is an opening or a clearing with both geometric *and* temporal aspects.[39] But it is not itself in space and time.

As we have seen, *basho* is spatial in the sense that it is empty and therefore able to give "room" for experience to unfold. The two ways in which it is "empty," or the two dimensions of the opening that *basho* allows, are time and space. It is for this reason that the world of activity that unfolds around us is both spatial and temporal. Let me explain briefly what these spatial and temporal aspects refer to.

Our experience is spatial because it is contextual—that is, the activity of our experience unfolding all around us is a world in which multiple objects and people coexist simultaneously. As Nishida writes, the world of dynamically unfolding experience is "a world of spatial determination, an order of simultaneous coexistence" (Nishida 1987, 98). Bernard Stevens notes the importance of "others" and environment to Nishida's notion of experience. He writes,

> In effect, I and You always find themselves in the I-You relationship in specific situations, within a field or environment, which is itself made possible by the absolute nothingness [*basho* of absolute nothingness] from which it originates. The relational material that unites I and You and their environment is a self-determination of absolute nothingness. (Author's translation) (Stevens 2005, 94)

The world of our experience is a "field of relationships" or an "environment" in which I am in a relationship with other humans and other objects. Thus "space" in the sense of "environment" is a transcendental precondition for any experience. These ideas, which Nishida developed in his texts written around the middle of his career such as "I and Thou" (Nishida 2003b), are later joined with the temporal notion of historical development in Nishida's conception of the "historical world" that he emphasized in his later philosophy. As we will see later in this chapter, the idea of the "historical world" captures the way in which Nishida conceives of experience as consciously active, unfolding itself as the activity of humans (and others) in the world (Maraldo 2017, 207).

Our experience is not just spatial and environmental; it is also temporal because it takes place now along the continuum of time from past to future.[40] In his early philosophy, Nishida thought of time somewhat like Henri

Bergson as a kind of unending flow of experience as captured by Bergson's concept of *durée* (Bergson 1950). In *An Inquiry into the Good*, Nishida writes that while there is only one consciousness, it is temporal because it is unfolding over time:

> There is always a certain unchanging reality at the base of the mind [i.e., a single consciousness]. This reality enlarges the development of consciousness from day to day. The passage of time is the continuous change of the unifying center that accompanies this development, and this center is always "the present." (Nishida 1990, 61)

However, while Bergson focused on the individual's perception of time, Nishida considers experience to be unfolding independently of individuals and yet through them. Thus in his later work, he is careful to indicate where he differs from Bergson by shifting from the notion of pure experience to that of the "historical world," which better evokes the idea that the world of our experience is not just the unfolding of the experience of an individual human being, but rather, the unfolding of all experience of the "historical world," the world of all "consciously active humankind"[41] (Nishida 1987, 98).

Nishida explains how his notion of time differs from that of Bergson in his lecture "The Historical Body," where he writes that while "Bergson's position . . . is close to my own; . . . his philosophy considers the world subjectively, and thus it does not adequately thematize the creative historical world, either" (Nishida 1998b, 50). Nishida captures this concrete element, or rather, the fact that experiencing is the activity of something other than each individual, when he writes that experience simply arises as the self-determination of each moment: experience "arises from and returns to non-being" (Nishida 1998a, 32; see also Nishida 2003b, 95–96)—it simply occurs as the active present, as the "the indeterminate determination of non-being," or as "the self-determination of a dialectical universal"[42] (Nishida 1998a, 33).

Thus the place in which experience occurs (*basho*) is a space or opening with both a temporal dimension and a spatial dimension. The temporal aspect is the dynamic aspect of consciousness, while the spatial aspect is the existence of multiplicity within consciousness—the fact that our consciousness unfolds as a concrete world of interaction with other humans and nonhumans. Or in technical philosophical terms, the world has a noetic dimension, which is temporal, and a noematic dimension, which is spatial (Nishida 1998a, 30).

Before leaving the topic of *basho*, a fundamental concept in Nishida's philosophy, one last step will be useful. We have seen that each individual is a place (*basho*) for the unfolding of experience in the spatial and temporal world.[43] What, then, is the process of self-consciousness which Nishida thinks is so important for realizing what each of us truly is? As we have seen, the process of coming to know our true self is the process of understanding the real world as creative activity. In *The System of Self-Consciousness of the Universal*, Nishida writes that this kind of self-consciousness is consciousness in which "a self . . . sees without a seer" (Nishida 2005, 197; see also 207). What he means by this is that seeing as one's true self is seeing without the self-consciousness of the "I" that accompanies the "seeing" (ibid.).[44] *Basho* is the place where the self is confronted with itself,[45] and it is a space in the sense that it is an opening in space and time in which the real world realizes itself as a moment of self-consciousness. Nishida explains,

> For objects to be known by me they must be immanent in me; I must be the topos [*basho*] in which these things are situated. In this sense then I am utter nothingness with respect to things and merely reflect them. Yet, insofar as I know things, these things must be determined by me; what is in the self must be what is determined by the self. The self knows by determining and reflecting its content within itself. One can say that by making itself nothing it determines being. This is the sense in which self-consciousness can be said to be the self seeing its own content in itself. Further, this self-conscious determination must form the foundation for all knowing. (Nishida 2005, 194; *NKZ* 5:431)

So *basho* is a way of describing this condition for the possibility of self-consciousness and also consciousness in general. It is an empty place (transcendental precondition) where the meeting of self and reality can take place as self-consciousness; and it is an empty space in the sense that it is an opening where experiencing, which is both spatial and temporal, can occur. *Basho* is empty because it is devoid of the everyday sense of self that peers out of the world. As Nishida explains, "The self's determining itself [as the expression of the universal—the real world] is the self seeing the nothingness of its self, the disappearance of the seen self, the inability any longer to see noetic determination" (Nishida 2005, 200). This is the standpoint of the "expressive universal" (Nishida 2005, 202)—the universal expressing itself. This "nothingness of its self" that expresses itself as the true self is the condition for the possibility of all consciousness, and this is what is indicated by the term *basho*.

We have taken a short detour to explain *basho* and its role in consciousness and self-consciousness in order to demonstrate that Nishida's exploration of who "I" am is meant to disrupt everyday notions of who I think I am. Who I truly am is a space or place (*basho*) in which the world experiences itself.[46] I now turn to Nishida's explanation of who the "others" are who feature in all of my experience.

While we have already seen some of the ways in which dialectic places an important role in Nishida's philosophy, we will develop the notion of dialectic more fully in Nishida's explanation of who the others are that share this world with me. We have already seen a number of quotes in which Nishida explains reality in terms of a dialectical movement. For instance, he wrote that "one can say that by making itself nothing [the self] determines being" (Nishida 2005, 194). Here, he is describing a dialectical relationship between "being" and "nothingness" that is the source of the activity of human experiencing. When we experience something, there is no sense of the "I" that experiences—there is just the experience of the red flower. Thus in a sense the self has "made itself nothing" at the same time as the experience ("being") of the flower manifests itself. Rather than exploring the role of dialectic at this point, we will first look at who the "others" are in the world, since the way that Nishida describes the relationship between "self" and "other" is inherently dialectic.

WHO ARE THE OTHERS?

The others around us are other selves: others like us. In what way are they like us? It is true that other living beings are like us because they are separate biological entities that share similar biological processes. But Nishida is not interested in this kind of explanation, since in his view this is not the most important or basic way in which others are like us. For the philosopher, others are far more than other biological beings; they are, like us, the self-expression of the creative, historical world.[47] Nishida writes that while "the historical world is usually understood one-sidedly as a world of spatial determination, an order of simultaneous co-existence," in reality, the "historical world includes the consciously active humankind" (Nishida 1987, 98). He thus emphasizes that from a philosophical point of view, what is distinctive about others is that they are conscious and active, and therefore, they are part of the self-expression of the active world unfolding around us as experience. But more than this, understanding who others are from a philosophical perspective can lead to insight into who we ourselves are, since both I and the other are the self-expression of the world. In *An Inquiry into the Good*, Nishida makes this point when he writes that the consciousness of other people is important not only as a recognition of the otherness of others but also as an acknowledgment of one's own consciousness—one's true self—as identical with the universe.[48]

The relationship between the self and others is a paradigmatic example of a dialectical relationship in Nishida's philosophy. The dialectic exists at two levels because each individual is in a relationship with something other than him- or herself in two senses. In one sense, who I am is defined by others because my sense of who I am depends on being recognized as an individual by others. As we will see, Nishida describes this in a very technical way; but in fact, this kind of dialectical relationship between "You" and "I" is common in everyday life. When you complain to your romantic partner, "You don't really see me for who I am!" or when you say that you are looking for a romantic partner who "Really lets me be who I am," you express the frustration with and desire for recognition by others.

The dialectical relationship between self and other exists in another sense that is more fundamental to Nishida's explanation of who we truly are, which is an expression of absolute reality. This relationship—that is, the relationship between my everyday self and my "true" self—is dialectical because my everyday self depends on something that is not within my control. This is easiest to understand when one considers Nishida's religious explanation of who we are, that is, when he says that we realize who we are when we come face-to-face with God (aka "the absolute" in nonreligious language). Who I am in my core is thus God, whom I cannot control, expressing him- or herself through me.

I have just touched on the role of dialectic in Nishida's understanding of the self and the other to remind us about the central place that dialectic has in his philosophy. Indeed, it is his dialectical interpretation of reality and of the relationship between myself and others that makes his investigation original. However, since our primary purpose in this chapter is to understand who the others are, I turn now to two ways in which Nishida explains this.

In the following, I will examine both one of the early ways in which Nishida explains who the "others" are around me, which is based on the concepts of "I" and "You" and the dialectical relationship between them. I will then briefly look at how Nishida explains otherness in his later philosophy, which he does in terms of the "historical body." This is a way of speaking of the world as the body of the absolute expressing itself as the historically situated culture and society of which each of us is a part.

The Other in the Dialectic of "You" and "I"

Nishida's first thorough attempt to explain who the "others" are with whom we share our world is in his essay "I and You" (「私と汝」; *NKZ* 6) written in 1932. He begins the essay with a reminder that the world in which we live is active and dynamic. This dynamism is the result of the activity that is evident all around us. In this essay, Nishida describes this activity in terms of a relationship between individuals and their environment (*NKZ* 6:346–347). This interaction consists in the individual acting on or affecting the environment, and the environment acting on or affecting the individual (ibid.; see also *NKZ* 6:355). Indeed, in a fundamental sense, this is what Nishida means when he characterizes the world as a world of dynamic activity—we have an effect on the world and the world affects us (Nishida 1987, 52).

As we have seen, the environment with which each individual is connected is not just a world of objects, the material world described by science (Nishida 2003b, 99; *NKZ* 6:348). Rather, it is a living world that is dynamic and unfolds itself as the expression of the absolute universal. Nishida refers to this dynamic world as a "historical world" in order to distinguish the active world from the passive, static world of scientific objects (*NKZ* 6:349, 417). The historical world unfolds as an actual society that evolves and changes. Nishida writes, "Our self is not born in the individual. . . . [Rather,] it originates in communal consciousness (*kyōdō ishiki*, 共同意識), as we see in the case of many primitive peoples. In other words, the individual is born from society"[49] (ibid.).

Nishida then goes on to explain what the relationship between individual and society presupposes: a universal pure activity that acts as and through the activity of individuals interacting within society. Nishida writes,

> When seen from the point of view of the relationship between an individual and the environment, the determination (*gentei* 限定; here Nishida means the process of acting and changing) can be understood as the self-determination of an infinitely large environment which encompasses all things. The moments of time can likewise be understood as the centre of the self-determination of an infinitely large circle. It follows that that which in its turn determines temporal succession, the passing of one instant to another, must be something which encompasses this infinitely large circle: in other words, a circle without an edge—the universal universal.[50] (*NKZ* 6:357)

Nishida goes on to write that it follows that this infinitely large circle without an edge contains an infinite number of self-determining circles, and so the infinite circle has an infinite number of centers throughout it. These infinite centers are the individuals who are active as the self-expression of the universal universal—the circle without edge (*NKZ* 6:358). Thus the pure activity of the universe expresses itself as the infinity of individual beings of which it is composed.

To summarize, the individual and the social are not opposed to each other in Nishida's philosophy. Rather, social activity (interactive activity) is primordial. The condition for the possibility of this activity is activity in general—the activity of the absolute universal—which expresses itself as the specific interactions of each individual with others in society. Nishida writes that "in this sense, all things that are located in the self-determination of the eternal now are of the order of active things that are determined by the environment which is self-developing. . . . The vast current of life is in this sense . . . socio-historic life"[51] (*NKZ* 6:368).

Although we have seen that for Nishida, social activity is primordial and therefore the world conceived of as the interaction of separate individuals is an abstraction from this primordial activity, we have not yet examined what Nishida believes the nature of the relationship between "I" and "You" to be. It turns out that the relationship is one of reciprocal action—"I" act and affect "You"; "You" act and affect "Me" (*NKZ* 6:416). But what is the nature of this reciprocal action? Other philosophers have suggested that "I" knows "You" because in my interactions with others, I can analogize between my consciousness and the consciousness of others. Still others think that the relationship between "I" and "You" is a sort of unification of the two (Hollywood movies often take this view, in that they tend to portray true love as the perfect synchronicity between two people). But Nishida does not think that this is the correct approach. Instead, he says that we come to know the other in the fact that "You" answers "I" (Nishida 2003b, 124; *NKZ* 6:392; Nishida uses the word ōtō 応答, which I have translated as "answer"). The paradigm of "call and answer" emphasizes that the others whom I encounter in the world are other "I's" separate from me (Nishida 2003b, 414–415), although they are also I's with whom I can interact and whose answers I can experience myself.

Why does Nishida use the paradigm of call and answer? It is because the relationship of "call and answer" is one that recognizes the absolute difference between two individuals. He writes,

> The "I" and the other are not simply unified even though the "I" knows the thoughts and feelings of the other. The consciousness of "I" and the consciousness of the other are absolutely separate. The "I" is completely unable to know the consciousness of the other in the sense that the consciousness of the "I" cannot become the consciousness of the other.[52] (*NKZ* 6:393)

The other is thus another center of the self-expression of the universal. However, "call and answer" does not entail a complete separation of "I" and "you" because when I hear the answer of another, I am conscious of them—I experience their response. Thus in some sense, the other is within me (*NKZ* 6:394). The relationship of "I" to "you" is thus dialectic: when "I" experience "you," I experience within me the possibility of something completely different than me—another subjectivity that limits my subjectivity. This dialectic is actualized in the concrete encounter between "I" and "you."[53] Nishida writes, "In the midst of this dialectical determination [of 'I' and 'you'], the other which ['the "I"'] sees in herself is not a simple other but rather takes on the character of a call by 'you'"[54] (*NKZ* 6:397). In other words, when I interact with others by calling to her and the other answers, I do not simply interact with others as the objectification of the other. The other must choose to respond; she is not forced to do so by my call.

As I noted earlier, when we explore the nature of the relationship between "I" and "you," we also learn something about ourselves. Nishida emphasizes that the structure of the relationship between "I" and "you" indicates something about the nature of the individual's relationship to himself. As we have seen in our examination of Nishida's concept of the individual, at the root of the individual is the absolute universal expressing itself. Thus at the root of our self is something that we cannot determine and control; in fact, we are only the expression of this absolute universal (*NKZ* 6:399). The relationship between "I" and "you" has a similar structure, because in this relationship there is something that "I" cannot control: I can only experience "you" through the other's answer—I cannot experience "you" through unifying with or becoming the other. What I experience when I experience you is your expression of your experience *as your experience which is not my experience*—I experience the other's answer, not her actual experiencing (*NKZ* 6:405). It thus follows that the "I" is co-originary with the "you." Nishida writes, "The individual is determined solely in the gaze of [another] individual. The "you" must exist as the "I" is born"[55] (*NKZ* 6:401; see also 406–407).

As I noted at the beginning of this section on who the "others" are in the world around me, the activity that constitutes who I am has a dialectical structure: it is characterized by a relationship between two opposites that interact dynamically. Nishida's characterization of the relationship between "I" and "you" has a dialectical structure in two senses. In the more ordinary sense, I am in a relationship with many other human beings. My relationship with them is dialectical because these others are in some sense "opposed" to me—they are able to have private experiences that I cannot access, and they sometimes act in ways that I do not like and cannot control. Yet at the same time, who I am depends on being recognized as an "other" by those around me (Stevens 2005, 94). Thus my everyday relationships with others are dialectical in structure because who I am is constituted by recognition by others who are not me and vice versa.

There is also a more fundamental way in which I am in a relationship with otherness. As we have seen, each of us is the self-expression of absolute reality. This means that, in some sense, I am in my very being the expression of something that is outside of my control. In practical terms, this is why most of my experience cannot be controlled: it either appears to come from outside of me, or else it consists of thoughts and feelings that I do not consciously choose to have. At the very base of my self is something that I have no control over—the generation of experiences that constitutes the display of absolute reality (Maraldo 2017, 335–336). Thus in a fundamental sense, who I am is actually generated by a dialectical relationship between my everyday self as an individual and who I truly am—absolute reality. As Nishida explains, "The self is one with what is absolutely other. This means that the self recognizes within itself the absolutely other [while at the same time] seeing itself within it. The true way in which death is-and-is-not life is to be found there where the [self] cannot think the absolutely other, and yet [the absolutely other] nonetheless constitutes the 'I' as 'I'"[56] (*NKZ* 6:378). It is in this way that the self can be understood as the dialectical movement of the self-determination of absolute nothingness (ibid., 380).

To summarize, in Nishida's first complete attempt to characterize who the "others" are in his essay "I and You," he expresses two important points. First, one cannot have any experience at all without there being something that is separate from the apparent self (my everyday sense of self): this is the absolute universal which is expressing itself as all experience. The relationship between the self and the absolute is a dialectical relationship because the wellspring of all of my experience is just experiencing itself, and it is a wellspring whose outflow I cannot control. Second, the relationship between "I" and "You" has a similar dialectical relationship to the relationship between the self and the absolute. I know you through my social interactions with you—that is, through language and other forms of communication. This knowing is not a unification of "I" and "you," but rather it has the same dialectical structure as all experience because I cannot force you to answer, nor can I answer for me: I am completely dependent on the other choosing to respond. In this way, others are both necessarily constitutive of each individual, yet at the same time, are fundamentally separate from and opposed to others. I now turn to Nishida's characterization of "others" in his later philosophy.

The Other in Social and Cultural Terms: Nishida's Concept of the Historical Body

In Nishida's later philosophy, he explains who others are in terms of what he calls the "historical body." He adopts this approach in order to give a description of what I and the world are in terms of embodied existence (Maraldo 2017, 207). One might think that "embodied existence" refers to a scientific view of understanding who we are since the term "body" evokes biology or physics. But Nishida is interested in the *historical* body: he is interested in our bodily existence as manifest in the things that humans do and the things that they produce through time—he is interested in our cultural and social existence. Indeed, he writes that "the content of the historical world's self-transformation is culture"[57] (Nishida 1987, 117). In what sense is human existence embodied? Nishida says that we are embodied because our fundamental purpose is to produce and create: we produce the society and culture in which we exist.

However, the relationship between individuals and society is not one way. Rather, we produce society and culture, but in turn, society and culture produce each individual as an embodied creative person. Thus the embodied nature of our existence that Nishida describes shows us something about the nature of our relationships to other people. As Nishida explains,

> The various activities (intellectual, artistic, moral) of our individual selves are not to be conceived of by first positing these individual selves and then predicating their relationships with their environments as grammatical subjects. They must be rendered from the standpoint of being individuals of the self-formative historical world as the contradictory identity of the one and the many. These activities can be adequately rendered only in terms of the various kinds of co-originating relationships obtaining between the self as *poiesis* and the world. (Nishida 1998c, 69)

In other words, by focusing on the activities that humans are involved in, we can learn something about the relationship between individuals and the culture and society of which they are part. What we learn, Nishida thinks, is that the individual is foremost to be understood as embedded in a series of relationships with its environment: it is only an abstraction to think of individuals as separate from the culture and society of which they are a part. Fundamentally, "The body exists at the very time and place where it is a function of the historical world, the world that is creative and formative" (Nishida 1998b, 51).

The approach to understanding the world as the historical body, a process of creative production that occurs in a social and cultural environment, helps us to understand who the others are around me. They are, along with me, sharing in a process of creating our culture and society. This is a primary form of relationship. Nishida writes, "As the many individuals comprising the self-expressive historical world, we are created-and-creating transformative elements of the world's own self-expression"[58] (Nishida 1987, 98; see also Nishida 1990, 151, 154). In other words, others, like me, are expressions of the world expressing itself throughout history in a bodily—that is, social and cultural—form.[59]

Earlier, we saw that in the middle period of Nishida's philosophy, he explained the nature of the relationship between myself and others in a fairly abstract way in terms of "call and answer"—that is, in terms of the form of the relationship between us. But now, Nishida wants to look at this relationship from the point of view of what we produce together, which are communications (poetry, novels, etc.) and things (machinery, consumer goods, and agricultural products) that are necessary for the performance of our cultural and social practices. A shift toward the historical body thus signifies a switch from the very abstract concept of activity in Nishida's middle philosophy to more concrete and embodied forms of activity. It also allows Nishida to explain the form that the relationship between "I" and "You" takes in terms of the function that individuals serve in the whole (Nishida 1998b, 45). To put this in a less obscure way, it allows us to look at actual cultural and social products and to learn from these who we ourselves and others are.

What we learn about who we are and who the others are is that we are social and cultural beings in the sense that our actions both create our communal existence as a social and cultural existence, and our actions are in turn formed by the activity of the historical world, which is a social and cultural world. As Nishida writes,

> The historical world is a world in which the making of things is in turn made by that which it makes, and so the world is a continuing creative process.... *It is a world in which that which is made makes that which makes;* it is a creative world. (Nishida 1998b, 48) [emphasis in original]

> [...]

> The historical world is something creative, and therefore our world is creative. Our humanity consists in the fact that we are active as parts, as elements, of that created world. Because we have bodies we can be said to make things as elements of the historical world. And our very life and our true self exist in the place that becomes a creative subject as an element of the historical world. Human activity in such a sense is nothing other than production. And production is something bodily. (Nishida 1998b, 51)

So others are a fundamental part of who we each are as an individual. Why? Because our fundamental nature is to be active and productive—we have an embodied existence. And this embodied existence is historical because its content consists of the historically emergent cultural and social practices of the society in which we live. Who are the others in terms of the historical body? They are loci of the productive activity of the social and cultural world.[60] In the next chapter, I explore how Nishida thinks that we should live as social and cultural beings of this kind.

OVERCOMING OUR EVERYDAY NOTION OF SELF: RECOGNIZING OUR FUNDAMENTAL CO-ORIGINATION WITH OTHERS AS THE ACTIVITY OF CULTURAL PRODUCTION

In this chapter, we have examined Nishida's concepts of the self and the other. According to him, who we truly are is far different than who we think we are in our everyday life. We are at our base expressions of absolute reality—the concrete world—unfolding and expressing itself as each of us. However, the concrete world is not just a world of individuals; it is a truly cultural and historical world, a historical body, to use Nishida's terminology (Maraldo 2017, 207). Thus the relationship between the self and others is fundamental and constitutive of who we each are. In more abstract terms, we depend on others to constitute who we are. This is clear from the fact that my sense of self is dependent on recognition by others, just as others' sense of themselves is dependent on my recognition of them. Nishida considers the form of this relationship to be one of "call and answer." In bodily terms, each of us acts and creates in a way that produces and defines the culture and society of which we are a part, yet at the same time, this individual creative activity takes its shape and meaning from cultural and social practices.

Although Nishida's investigation of who we all are is philosophical, he often casts this philosophical investigation in religious terms. Thus each of us is charged to investigate in philosophical terms who we are, but at the same time, this philosophical investigation is also spiritual in a general sense, in that it underlies the spiritual search described in many religions such as Buddhism and Christianity.

In the next chapter, we will develop how Nishida thinks that we ought to live our lives as beings whose existence is itself the expression of the absolute and an expression of the relationship between the self and others. This will require a more in-depth analysis of what culture and society are, as well as an exploration of the moral and ethical duties that arise from our cultural and social existence.

NOTES

1. Nishida discusses this mistaken view in his essay "I and You" (*Watashi to nanji,* 『私と汝』) (Nishida 2003b, 99; *NKZ* 6:347).

2. Scheler goes on to explain that both the individual and collective experiences of the individual are co-originary. He writes, "In our view . . . all persons are, with *equal* originality, both individual persons and (essentially) members of a collective person" (1973, 524) [emphasis in original].

3. 「我々の自己の奥底には、何處までも歴史的に自己自身を形成するものがあるのである。」(*NKZ* 11:416).

4. 「私は我々の自己の存在とは如何なるものであるか、意識作用とは如何なるものなるかを論じた。矛盾的自己同一的世界の自己表現面的規定として、個物的多の一々が自己の中に世界の自己表現點を含み、自己表現的に自己自身を形成する所に、我々の自己の存在があるのである。」 (*NKZ* 11:391). "In the position I am articulating, the self is to be understood as existing in that dynamic dimension wherein each existential act

of consciousness, as a self-expressive determination of the world, simultaneously reflects the world's self-expression within itself and forms itself through its own self-expression" (Nishida 1987, 64).

5. On this point, see Tremblay (2007).

6. 「我々の自己は個人から始まるのでなない。多くの原始民族に於て見られる如く共同意識から始まるのである。個人は社會から生れると云つてよい。」(*NKZ* 6:348)

7. 「…環境が「於てあるもの」を限定し、逆に「於てあるもの」が環境を限定すると云ふことであり…」(*NKZ* 6:350–351)

8. Krummel describes Nishida's approach to acquiring self-knowledge as follows: "The true self lies where the abstract self, the substantialized ego serving as the subject of consciousness, is negated" (2015, 172). In other words, sincere investigation requires looking past our identification with the subject of our everyday conscious life and revealing what lies within it as its creative source.

9. While I am relying here primarily on Nishida's later work, the idea that the self is creative and an expression of the creativity of the world is to be found throughout his writings. For instance, in *An Inquiry into the Good*, published in 1911, he writes that "the unifying power called the self is an expression of the unifying power of reality; it is an eternal unchanging power. Our self is therefore felt to be always creative, free, and infinitely active" (Nishida 1990, 76–77).

10. In *An Inquiry into the Good*, Nishida had not yet developed the language of "active intuition." Instead, he speaks of "reflection" as a means of discovering our true selves. He describes this process of reflection as follows: "Self-consciousness arises through reflection, and the reflection of the self is the activity that in this way seeks the center of consciousness. The self is nothing other than the unifying activity of consciousness" (Nishida 1990, 162; see also 170).

11. 「私の行為的直觀と云ふのは、何處までも意識的自己を越えた自己の立場から物を見ることである。」(*NKZ* 11:417). In "On the National Polity," Nishida explains what he means by active intuition as follows, "Our self, as something both made and making and as a creative element of the creative world, intuits the Idea in the form of active intuition; and this intuition is a manifestation of eternal life" (Nishida 1998e, 87). Using more philosophical terms, David Dilworth explains that for Nishida, active intuition is an act originating in our true, "self-conscious" selves, in which "the contradictory identity of transcendent and immanent planes" intersect (Dilworth 1987, 39). Nishida himself uses philosophical language to explain that intuition (as opposed to intentional consciousness) is a situation in which the "plane of the 'self (as object)' [is] absorbed into the 'self (as subject)'" (Nishida 2005, 209). By this he means that there is a merging of noesis (knowing) and noemata (what is known) such that the ordinary self-conscious self is recognized as an expression of the universal. John Krummel explains that for Nishida, active intuition is "the self intuit[ing] the world's self-expressive forms" (Krummel 2015, 121). This means that active intuition is in fact a sort of "dialectical interactivity between human self and world, whereby we see things by working upon them, and as we work upon our environment our self-awareness is in turn shaped" (Krummel 2012, 48). Peerenboom writes that active intuition "entails an expression of both the particular and the universal/whole in the concrete immediacy of religious experience" (1991, 164). He also explains

the negation of the everyday self and the affirmation of the self-as-world as follows, "Active intuition of the self is a reflection and expression of the whole. . . . By negating themselves, each particular [individual] is able to overcome the subject/object split and directly experience the whole through, and as, a network of interrelations" (ibid.).

12. 「我々の自己の根柢には、何處までも意識的自己を越えたものがあるのである。これは我々の自己の自覺的事實である。」(*NKZ* 11:417). For Dilworth's explanation of the role of "act" in Nishida's philosophy, see Dilworth 1987 (18, 24 and 29). An individual's *self-conscious* act "reflects the world itself as a unique coincidence of every transcendent and immanent plane of historical co-origination. It is radically transformative as a monadic vector of the world's self-expression" (ibid., 20). Feenberg sees "active intuition" (*kōiteki chokkan*) as "the form of awareness that belongs to subjects engaged in mutual interaction" (1999, 37).

13. John Krummel describes the individual as "the expressive focal point . . . of the world, its momentary self-determination. The self is a self-expressive element of the world forming itself in self-expression" (Krummel 2015, 121). Maraldo explains that "the embodied self [is] a historical practical body (歴史的実践的身体), through which the world manifests or expresses itself" (2017, 207).

14. 「... 何處までも意志的なるもの、唯一的に個なるものにして、始めて宗教的と云ふことができる。」(*NKZ* 11:428).

15. 「... 逆對應的に神に接する ...」(*NKZ* 11:427). In earlier works, he gives an example from other religions. For instance, in *An Inquiry into the Good*, he says that the realization of our true self and fusion with God is called "kenshō" in Buddhism ("seeing into one's nature" 見性) (Nishida 1990, 145). However, this "seeing into one's nature" is not some special kind of experience—it is rather a seeing of the "unity of pure experience" that is always "at the base of our consciousness" and that is the "one great intellectual intuition" that is both the base of individual consciousness and the base of the universe (Nishida 1990, 164; see also 166). For Dilworth's interpretation, see Dilworth (1987, 37).

16. 「...個なれば個なる程、絶對的一者に對する、即ち「に對すると云ふことができる。我々の自己が神に對すると云ふのは、個の極限としてである。何處までも矛盾的自己同一的に、歴史的世界の個物的自己限定の極限に於て、全體的一の極限に對するのである。」(*NKZ* 11:430).

17. Many have interpreted Nishida's philosophy as an articulation of his "Zen" experience; see Nishitani (2016, 37–38), Dilworth et al. (1998, 3), Yusa (2002, 49–75; 2014, 12), Heisig (2012, 20), and Stevens (2005, 117).

18. 「矛盾的自己同一的世界が自己の中に自己を表現し、自己自身を表現することによつて自己自身を形成して行く。」(*NKZ* 11:403).

19. 「かゝる絶對者の自己表現が、宗教的に神の啓示と考へられるものであり、かゝる自己形成が宗教的に神の意志と考へられるものである。」(*NKZ* 11:403).

20. Dilworth lists a number of terms to translate *basho*: "place," "field," "matrix," "medium," and "world" (1987, 15). Carter translates it as "the place of unification" (1997, 102). I find that Nishida uses the term in the sense of the "dharmadhatu" or "hokkai." For a discussion of the "dharmadhatu," see Kang-Nam Oh, "Dharmadhātu: An Introduction to Hua-yen Buddhism" *The Eastern Buddhist* 12(2) 72–91 (1979).

21. Maraldo writes that for Nishida "this ultimate *basho* [the *basho* of absolute nothingness] is to serve as the foundation of both world and self as they interact" but also that "it functions as an uncommon kind of self-negating foundation that forms or performs self and world rather than lying at their ground" (2017, 121).

22. Other translations include "place" (Heisig 2012), "topos" (Yusa 2014), and, alluding to Platonic terminology, "chora" (Krummel 2015).

23. To use the language of his earlier philosophy, it is a place where noesis confronts noema, even though "there is neither noesis nor noema in the self-consciousness of absolute nothingness" (Nishida 2005, 212).

24. Feenberg writes about the concept of "nothingness," which Nishida, according to Feenberg, considers to be the foundation of experience. He writes, "The only way I can make sense of [Nishida's] concept of nothingness is as an attempt to grasp the first-person standpoint from the first-person standpoint itself, an attempt that leads to its depersonalization and identification with the given in its givenness. As such, first personhood loses the character of a present-at-hand thing in the world and becomes a horizon that cannot be directly thematized" (1999, 35).

25. 「我々の個人的自己即ち意志的自己は、主語的有でもない、述語的有でもない。主語的方向と述語的方向との矛盾的自己同一的に場所の自己限定として、生起するのである。」(*NKZ* 11:431). Bernard Stevens writes that *basho* is what makes it possible for consciousness to become self-conscious by providing a place where both the knower and the known are produced and the true self is reflected and sees itself (Bernard 2005, 88).

26. In "The System of Self-Consciousness of the Universal," Nishida writes that our thoughts and experiences are the self-expression of reality itself: "As the universal determines itself, i.e., as topos determines topos, its occupants become things that determine themselves, and having finally become active, leave the domain of that universal. To say that the universal determines itself or that the topos determines itself is to say that life determines itself" (Nishida 2005, 201; *NKZ* 5:442). He writes something similar in his essay "Basho," where it states that "consciousness is the self-determination of the universal" (*NKZ* 4:212). As Maraldo explains, *basho* "is a universal field, sphere or "place" within which manifestation takes place" (2017, 336). Dilworth writes that the "final *basho* of nothingness is paradoxically the fullness of the existential present. It is the only concrete *basho*" (1987, 16).

27. 「真の個人は絶対現在の瞬間的自己限定として成立するのである。」(*NKZ* 11:431).

28. For a discussion of this quote from Linji, see Dilworth (1987, 39).

29. John Krummel uses the very helpful term "implaced" to translate *oitearu mono* (於いてあるもの) (Krummel 2015, 24).

30. See also Krummel (2015, 58, 60). Krummel writes of *basho* that it is a "root concept" in Nishida's philosophy which, "as the most concrete level of reality-cum-experience, he takes ... to be the grounding immediacy that embraces all the contradictory planes involving self and world, whether in terms of the epistemological subject and its object, the grammatical subject and its predicates, or the determining act of consciousness (noesis) and its determined object (noema). Nishida takes all such dichotomizations to be implaced within this place as hence irreducible to the merely ideal or the merely real" (ibid., 60).

31. Stevens (2005, 46).

32. 「有るものは何かに於てなければならぬ、然らざれば有るといふことと無いといふこととの區別ができないのである。論理的には關係の項と關係自身とを區別することができ、關係を統一するものと關係が於てあるものとを區別することもできる筈である。作用の方について考へて見ても、純なる作用の統一として我といふ如きものが考へられると共に、我は非我に對して考へられる以上、我と非我との對立を内に包み、所謂意識現象を内に成立せしめるものがなければならぬ。此の如きイデヤを受取るものとも云ふべきものを、プラトンのティマイオスの語に傚うて場所と名づけて置く。」(*NKZ* 4:208)

33. Dilworth explains why Nishida's view is incompatible with Kant's. He writes that for Kant, "the unconditioned can in principle never appear" (1987, 13). Nishida would retort, "and yet here it is as this experiencing!"

34. As Wargo has explained, *basho* can be understood to some degree as transcendental in the sense of being a context for or giving rise to the possibility of both Nishida's epistemology and metaphysics. Nishida does use the term "transcendental" when he refers to the self that expresses itself as the universal—our true self (Nishida 2005, 204). He writes, "Transcending the conscious self and attaining the transcendental self is not simply a matter of transcending the intellectual self, but rather must be a transcendence in the noetic direction of the acting self" (ibid., 205).

35. Kant explains that time and space are "subjective condition[s] of sensibility" (A26:B42; A34:B50). Thus space is the "form of all appearances of outer sense" (ibid.), that is, the condition for the possibility of sensing objects outside of ourselves, while time is the "*a priori* condition of all appearance whatsoever" (A34:B50), both inner and outer.

36. He writes that the absolute universal is determined spatially as a sphere of bodily activity limited by encountering other bodies (the material world) and temporally as the infinite current of activity unfolding in the present (ibid.).

37. Here, I am thinking of the Heideggerian concept of *Lichtung* or "clearing." However, I do not interpret *Lichtung* as subjectively as Hubert Dreyfus, who interprets the term "clearing" to mean that "things show up in the light of our understanding of being" (Dreyfus 1995, 163). Nishida's sense of space as clearing is a clearing that does not presuppose a subject that understands (i.e., a subject of an intentional act). He writes in "The System of Self-Consciousness of the Universal" that in religious experience, "form is seen as void and void as form," that is, it's a "state in which there is neither a seer nor that which is seen" (207; *NKZ* 5:451). Feenberg also argues for a similarity between Heidegger's notion of *Lichtung* or "clearing" and Nishida's concept of *basho* that is absolutely empty (Feenberg 1999, 36).

38. For just one of the many places where Nishida notes this, see Nishida (2015, 141) (*NKZ* 4:127), where he writes, "Self-awareness is not established in time; it's time that establishes itself in self-awareness" (「併し「時」に於て自覺が成立するのではなく、自覺に於て「時」が成立するのである。」 Here, "self-awareness" (自覺) refers to something similar to what Nishida called "pure experience" in his early philosophy (see Tremblay 2007, 61).

39. "The creative world has the form of a contradictory identity. Spirit is temporal and matter is spatial. Time and space, spirit and matter, contradict each other,

signifying separate domains. But the concrete world itself is temporal and spatial at the same time. The creative world is this kind of temporal-spatial world that unifies contradictory and separate dimensions" (Nishida 1998b, 53).

40. He writes that "Being situated in time means that what appears is unified [in experience] by means of temporal relations such as "before/after" and simultaneity" 「時に於て現れるものが前後とか同時とかいふ如き時の関係によつて統一せられると云ふことでなければならぬ。」(*NKZ* 4:325).

41. 「歴史的世界は人間を含んだ世界でなければならない。奮き言表を似てするならば、主観客観の相互限定、その矛盾的自己同一的の世界でなければならない。」(*NKZ* 11:434) Stevens makes a similar point (2005, 96).

42. There have been many interpretations of Nishida's concept of *basho*. Wargo (2005) understands *basho* to be a "mechanism for solving . . . the 'problem of completeness' of epistemological and metaphysical schemes" (121). By this, he is referring to Quine's view that ontology is determined "once the overall conceptual scheme has been established" (ibid., 119). Wargo does not think that *basho* is a conceptual scheme. But he does think that it is a sort of context or category that can then be deployed in epistemology and ontology (ibid.). He writes, "Basho is intended to serve as a tool to solve the problem of completeness. This problem centers on the fact that no theory attempting to give an account of the whole of experience can be complete unless it includes an exposition of its own possibility" (ibid., 118). In other words, *basho* is, like a conceptual scheme, something that creates the possibility of Nishida's theory of knowledge and metaphysics.

43. Stevens provides a similar interpretation (2005, 88).

44. Nishida writes, "Since the ultimate self cannot at all be seen noetically, the noematic plane of this self must have the meaning of an objective determination with respect to the noetic determinations of all seen selves" (Nishida 2005, 199; *NKZ* V:438). In other words, the true self is a self that is not seen by the everyday "I" that knows (noesis). Rather, such knowing is the expression of the knowing of the real, objective world itself (for a good explanation of this, see Feenberg 1999, 30; unfortunately, Feenberg gives a psychological interpretation, but this is understandable given that he is discussing Nishida's early work, which was influenced by William James). This is why Nishida develops his logic as the logic of the predicate—at the root of noesis (everyday knowing) is something objective (the noematic). Nishida writes, "Since the self-determination of the universal is a determination of the noematic plane of the self that truly sees, its topos necessarily determines the noetic" (Nishida 2005, 200; *NKZ* 5:439–440).

45. As Krummel writes, *basho* is "a place transcending and enveloping the self, as that wherein the self knows itself in its self-mirroring" (Krummel 2015, 62). Maraldo writes that "the self-reflecting structure of self-awareness describes what we might call the nature of reality for Nishida" and that "the most concrete and inclusive whole or "place" envelops and is reflected in all beings, in self and world and all differentiations of reality" (2017, 327).

46. Nishida (2005, 197–199; *NKZ* 5:435–439).

47. A similar interpretation is given by Stevens (2005, 94).

48. "To acknowledge another personality is to acknowledge one's own" (Nishida 1990, 171).

49. See note NOTEREF _Ref32933666 \h * MERGEFORMAT 6.
50. 「かゝる限定を個物と環境との關係から見れば、それはすべてを包む無限大の環境の自己限定と考へることができるであらう。時の瞬間といふ如きものは無限大なる圓の自己限定の中心と考へることもできる。而して更に瞬間から瞬間に移る時間的系列を限定するものは、かゝる無限大の圓を包むもの、即わち周邊なき圓と考へねばならぬであらう、一般者の一般者といふことができる。」(*NKZ* 6:357)
51. 「かゝる意味に於て、永遠の今の自己限定として之に於てあるものは、すべて働くものの意味を有し、自己自身を限定するといふ環境から限定せられる、即ち大なる時の流に於てあると云ふことができる。 ...併し生の面に即しては、社會「歷史的生命と考へられる。」(*NKZ* 6:368)
52. 「私が他人の思想感情を知ると云つても單に私と他人とが合一すると云ふことではない、私の意識と他人の意識とは絕對に他なるものでなければならない。私の意識は他人の意識となることはできないといふ意味に於ては、私は絕對に他人の意識を知ることはできない。」(*NKZ* 6:393)
53. For a similar interpretation, see Stevens (2005, 94).
54. 「かゝる辯證法的限定に於ては私に於て見る他と考へられるものは、單なる他ではなくして汝の呼聲の意味を有つてゐなければならない。」(*NKZ* 6:397)
55. 「我々の自己は自己自身の底にかゝる絕對の他を見ることによつて自己であるといふ意味に於て、それは私を生むものでなければならない。」(*NKZ* 6:601)
56. 「...自己が絕對に他なるものと一であると云ふことでなければならない、自己の中に絕對の他を見、絕對の他の中に自己を見ると云ふことでなければならない。絕對に他なるものとは考へることのできないものである、而もそれが私をして私たらしめるものであるといふ所に、眞の死卽生の意味があるのである。」(*NKZ* 6:378)
57. 「而して歷史的世界のかゝる絕對現在的自己形成の內容が文化...」(*NKZ* 11:456).
58. 「我々の自己は、かゝる世界の個物的多として、何處までも作られたものたると共に何處までも作るものである、世界の自己表現的形成要素である。」(*NKZ* 11:433).
59. R. P. Peerenboom characterizes Nishida's understanding of the relationship between myself and others as follows, "Nishida does conceive of the universe as a matrix of interrelationships. But each node in the matrix, each particular, each provisionally individual self, is a 'self-expressive individual of a self-expressive world'" (Peerenboom 1991, 163).
60. Dilworth explains that "the Nishidan world creates its own space-time character by taking each monadic "act of consciousness" as a unique position in the calculus of its own transformations" (1987, 18). Carter writes that for Nishida, "each existent, and particularly each self-consciously aware existent is a unique perspective on the world, and yet the world as a whole is mirrored in each and every self-consciously aware existent" (1997, 110).

Chapter 9

Nishida's Views on Morality and Culture

The Moral Individual and the Moral Culture

According to Nishida, we should lead our lives in a way that recognizes that each of us is an expression of absolute reality, which is constantly dynamic and creating the world that we experience. But what is this world and what does it mean in concrete terms to live in a way that is consistent with our true self as an instance of the self-expression of the world? In this chapter, we will explore Nishida's answers to these questions by studying his views on the relationship between the individual and society and their implications for ethics and morality.

We will begin by a description of Nishida's view that our lives are the expression of the dynamic activity of absolute reality as captured in his notions of the "historical body" and the "historical world," terms that he used in his later philosophy. We start here in order to make more accessible to the reader the language that Nishida uses in his essay "The Logic of the Place of Nothingness and the Religious Worldview" (Nishida 1987) in which Nishida addresses the topic of interest to us: how an individual can lead a moral life and how cultures can become aligned with the morality inherent in the absolute reality of which they are a reflection. As we have seen, our lives are the expression of the dynamic activity of absolute reality (Nishida 1987, 92). The term "historical body" captures the concrete nature of this dynamic activity, which is manifest in human life as a process of creative production. But this activity is not just bodily in the sense of being purely material: it can also express absolute reality through moral action.

We will examine Nishida's concept of morality in a variety of contexts. First, we will look at the examples he draws from religions such as Christianity, Judaism, Buddhism, and others. We will then turn to other contexts to emphasize how aspects of modern culture, such as science and art, can also express the same ideals that are embodied in religion. We will then turn to morality in general to explain Nishida's notion of the moral life. The examples of religion, scientific inquiry, artistic creativity, and morality are all illustrations of how human activity can be true to our nature as expressions of absolute reality. At the end of the chapter, we will also explore some of the political consequences of his views, expressed in his idea of a "world culture," and engage some of the critiques that have been leveled against them.

How should we lead our life once we adopt a self-aware view of the context in which we arise? Nishida believed that the precondition for leading a moral life is that each person live as the dynamic nature of absolute reality (Carter 1997, 137). Because our lives are social and cultural, societies and cultures should also change and evolve both internally and through interactions with others so that cultural and social practices align with the self-expression of the world. Because cultures are constantly evolving and changing (they are *historical* bodies, according to Nishida), to live morally does not just involve conforming to present cultural beliefs, values, and practices. Rather, our cultures and values should be shaped by making choices that reflect the dynamic process of absolute reality. Through this process of change, cultures and societies can come to express the universal process of the unfolding of the historical body, though each will naturally unfold this reality in a different way.

THE HISTORICAL BODY AND THE HISTORICAL WORLD AS THE CONTEXTUAL UNFOLDING OF ABSOLUTE REALITY

As we explored in the last chapter, Nishida believed that our true self is the creative activity of absolute reality. In the middle period of his philosophy, he began to explain what this creative activity consists of in social terms by introducing a "You" with whom "I" am constantly interacting. The relationship between "I" and "You" is more fundamental than the notion of the individual "I" cut off from others, whom I think I am in everyday unreflective life. In his later philosophy, he explains the relationship between "I" and "You" in terms of the "historical body," that is, in terms of the embodied existence which forms the context in which we are always living. This existence is embodied in the sense that humans are constantly involved in creative activities such as communication (Nishida considers language to be a form of creative activity), the production of material objects (buildings, clothing, art, poetry, etc.), and scientific experimentation. Human existence is "historical" because this creative activity is shaped by the social context in which we live, which has evolved over time.

To truly live in a way that reflects who we are, we must interact with other beings who have the same nature as us. As Nishida writes, "The human-historic world is the world of the mutual determination of objectivity and subjectivity, of the contradictory identity of the transcendent and the transcendental. In these terms the historical world is a living world, a self-creative world, expressing itself within itself" (Nishida 1987, 98). When I face another person, I perceive her as a conscious person like me, capable of thinking and feeling (Nishida 1987, 103). But this consciousness—my consciousness of the other and her consciousness of me—does not have its origin in either one of us. Instead, this mutual consciousness of oneself and of the other is a form of "mutual interexpression" (Nishida 1987, 103). As Nishida explains, this mutual interexpression "is neither the self becoming the other nor the other becoming the self; the other simultaneously creates the self and its own self-expression" (ibid.).[1]

Nishida says a bit more about interexpression in "The World as Identity of Absolute Contradiction" (1998c). There, he explains that interexpression both affirms our individuality (our separation from others) and denies it. For instance, when we interact, we cannot use a solely private language of our own devising; we must use the forms of communication of our shared culture. Thus, when we communicate, we end up negating our individuality to some degree because our communication must use an objective, shared form in order to be meaningful to others (Nishida 1998c, 60). At the same time, the objective social world is negated because it is expressed through individuals, each of whom has his or her own unique way of using language and of doing things. Indeed, such unique forms of expression are the basis for the continued evolution of language—each new person uses language in surprising and unique ways that "negate" previous linguistic practice to some degree. But at the same time, these new ways of speaking are the evolution of the same language.

Nishida writes about this kind of relationship in the area of biology. He emphasizes that when an individual organism interacts with its environment, in some sense, it loses itself in its environment, but in doing so, the environment is shaped by the organism's interaction with it. Nishida explains,

> The physical world may . . . be thought to appear in our bodily movements and yet transcend them in the direction of the universal. Thereby, the individual subject negates itself and becomes the environment. . . . But, contrary to this, the more that individuals are independent the more the world becomes a living world. In the biological world, there is already a true movement from environment to subject, from the one to the many. Here, the environment becomes subject through its self-negation as environment . . . [through] the transformation of environment into organism. (Nishida 1998c, 63)

When individual organisms act, they do so as part of their environment. Likewise, when individuals express themselves, they must do so as part of a social world, and they must use its paradigms of communication. The contrary process is also at work. The environment is negated and expressed through the acts of the individual organism; likewise, society expresses itself and creates itself through the acts of individuals. Nishida summarizes, "Each monad that forms the world expressively becomes a perspective of the world's own self-expression. The world thus infinitely transforms itself through self-expression" (Nishida 1998c, 64).

Why do we fail to recognize that our true nature is actually determined by the context or environment in which we are embedded? According to Nishida, it is because we have a tendency to retreat into our minds and think abstractly rather than living actively in the world outside of our heads. Because we habitually live in our heads, we tend to forget that we are embodied beings intimately involved in mutual relationships of interexpression with others. When individuals merely think abstractly and do not act (e.g., by expressing themselves in language or by making physical objects), the world that they conceive "loses its contradictory identity and becomes the mere plane of consciousness" (Nishida 1998c, 65). In turn, others become objectified and are perceived as separate from the self that is thinking and experiencing (ibid.).

Thus, for Nishida, self-consciousness (as opposed to self-awareness) is really a form of abstraction from the creative and dynamic relationship between individuals and the world. When we make choices to act on the basis of this purely abstract thought construct, we overlook some important aspects of human existence. Far better, Nishida believes, that we should act from a position of self-awareness in which we recognize our relationship to our environment. In order to more fully develop Nishida's ideas about the relationship between self and other, it will be necessary to explore what the "environment" is to which we belong. One aspect of this environment is human society. And as we will see, societies are embodied—that is, take concrete form as the culture of distinct groups.

What Is Society? Embodied Social Existence

In everyday usage, we say that we live together with others in a "society." What is this social existence? We tend to think of it as simply the collective activity of a group of individuals producing and creating, choosing and expressing. But Nishida has a different view: society is not just the collection of the acts of individuals. Instead, social activity, like the activity of individuals that we explored in the last chapter, is also a manifestation of the creative, productive activity of the absolute manifesting itself as world. As Nishida writes, "Our life is social in character in the sense of being a creative element of history" (Nishida 1998b, 52). In other words, our social life is the expression of the historical body just as is the case with our creative and productive activity as individuals.[2] So "social" does not just mean "a group of individuals." Instead, the social is itself an expression of the absolute; but it is an expression of the absolute by a group of people.

In "The Historical Body," Nishida writes about societies as being like a "species." Nishida here adopts the biological term, but without a technical, biological definition. Since he was writing in the first half of the twentieth century, Nishida's understanding of biology is a bit archaic. So rather than criticizing his concept of species, let us look more closely at what he meant by considering a society a species. Using the biology of his day, Nishida explains that a species consists of organisms who share a common type of cell: dogs are made from dog cells, monkeys from monkey cells, etc. (Nishida 1998b, 52). But there is more to his concept of species than this. A species is also characterized by a particular pattern of responses to the outside world. Thus "A certain species achieves definite form by the way it acts and according to the pattern of its acts" (Nishida 1998b, 52). So animals of the same species are unified by a similar way of acting or behaving in response to the same stimulus.

What does it mean for a society to be a species? The totality of humanity is divided into societies, and these societies are species that are unified by both sharing similar physical characteristics (Nishida refers to "race";[3] Nishida 1998b, 52) and similar kinds of creative acts such as language (ibid.) and "productive output" (ibid.), by which he means particular styles of dwelling, of clothing, laws, customs, etc.[4] Nishida writes, "Various species—that is, various patterns of cultural development—appear. Just as there are different species in the biological world, so too there are different historical species in the human historical world. These historical species are the foundations of historical bodily existence and are creative processes" (Nishida 1998b, 53). These "patterns of cultural development" have a dialectical structure because they involve individuals shaping their environment and also being shaped by their environment (Nishida 1998e, 81).[5]

When Nishida refers to a society as a "species," he is really referring to different cultures[6]—different forms of creative activity. These cultures, Nishida explains, are actually manifestations of the historical world that are produced through the individual creative acts of individuals who belong to that culture (Nishida 1998c, 59; 1998e, 78; Feenberg 1999, 38). Every individual belongs to some species or culture. Thus the historical world has a dual, self-contradictory structure—it is composed of individuals, but these individuals create products that reflect their species, that is, their culture (Nishida 1998c, 60, 66).[7] Nishida explains this as follows, "Our self is born historically-bodily—it is both created and creative. A people functions as a self-developmental force of the historical world, mediating the development of the historical world" (Nishida 1998e, 78).

Societies are in no way static in Nishida's conception. While members of a given society have shared cultural preferences, over time, they necessarily borrow and share with each other[8] because societies produce goods and language that are "public" and can be adopted by those from other societies: "The things that have been produced by the Japanese move the Japanese people. But because Japanese goods and cultural resources are public things they also may become goods and resources for the Chinese people. Chinese goods and resources are historical products for the Japanese people. The historical world develops through its own creative action in this way" (Nishida 1998b, 53). Nishida's observation about the relationship between different cultures demonstrates that he was describing a process of social development which is universal in the sense that it involves intimate and frequent cultural interactions between diverse societies. It would be an exaggeration to say that Nishida had recognized what we today call "globalization," but he had something of this nature in mind.

Nishida was not merely interested in describing what a society is and how it relates to the individuals who shape and form it and who are in turn shaped and formed by it; he also wanted to articulate the ethical consequences of recognizing this relationship. Ethics was of interest to Nishida from the very beginning of his career. Indeed, in *An Inquiry into the Good*, much of the latter part of the book is devoted to how we should live our lives once we have realized who we truly are. In the next section, I examine Nishida's ethical views in more detail in so far as they are related to his explanation of the nature of social existence.

HOW SHOULD WE LIVE AS SOCIAL BEINGS? NISHIDA'S VIEW OF ETHICAL AND MORAL LIFE

There have been many articles written that suggest that Nishida's concept of society and the role of culture in it leads to a problematic form of nationalism. As well, his ranking of Japanese culture at the head of world cultures as an ideal form of culture is rightly considered chauvinistic (Maraldo 2017, 159–177). But rather than starting from these preconceptions, I would like to explore in some detail what Nishida actually wrote in regard to how we ought to live and what the role of society should be in this life. In this way, the reader can draw her own conclusions. Of course, we will take up some of the critiques of Nishida later in the chapter.

We will examine two aspects of Nishida's writings that shed some light on his ideal of ethical life. First, we will examine what Nishida saw as the similarities and differences between the Judeo-Christian tradition and Buddhism. Doing so will serve two purposes. As we saw in chapter 8, Nishida considers human existence to be spiritual at its root since our true self is really the self-expression of absolute reality, which Nishida also names "God." The second purpose of looking at Nishida's use of Judaism, Christianity, and Buddhism is to illustrate what Nishida thought that ethical and moral life consists in. This will be achieved by examining the aspects of these specific religions that he considered to be manifestations of the spiritual life that he advocated.

Second, we will examine in some depth Nishida's first well-known work, *An Inquiry into the Good* (*Zen no kenkyū*). As I mentioned, that work contains a very clear articulation of the ethical obligations that arise from a realization of Nishida's understanding of spiritual enlightenment. Moreover, these initial ideas remained active throughout Nishida's career even if his framework for articulating them changed significantly.[9] Thus a study of this early text can help to shed some light on the rather complex dialectical and spatial (*basho*) structure that he identified as the nature of human and social experience in his middle and late period (see chapter 8 for a discussion of *basho*). The language of *An Inquiry into the Good* is quite simple and straightforward, and this simplicity may also help to clarify the complicated picture painted by Nishida's later works.

Finding the True Self: Examples from Christianity and Buddhism

According to Nishida, living an ethical life and making good moral choices requires living in constant recognition of our true self as the self-expression of absolute reality. Of course, rather than living in this way, most of us live our lives according to our habits, our perception of social and cultural expectations, and our likes and dislikes. Why is our daily life so at odds with our true nature? Is Nishida wrong to think that we are capable of living in a way that reflects who we truly are? Nishida addresses this issue through an exploration of various religions. To each, he gives his own unique interpretation in order to draw out from them the kernel of truth that they contain, that is, the way in which each religion expresses something about how to live one's life in accordance with our true natures. As we will see, according to Nishida, Christianity and Judaism express the true self ultimately as the denial of the everyday self: the truly religious person embodies God as a prophet and God lives through her. In Buddhism, the individual similarly gives up on petty everyday hopes and fears, but the transformation is not external but internal: the Buddhist ideal is that of the bodhisattva whose life becomes aligned with the self-expression of the absolute as the world of concrete reality.

Nishida acknowledges that human existence is physical and material; invoking a common trope of early modern philosophy, he calls these its "animal aspects" (Nishida 1987, 92).[10] However, our existence also has a spiritual dimension, which is our ability to express ourselves, to make choices, and to create things. This spiritual dimension is not just something individual; rather, each person's expressions and acts only manifest their true self when they express the absolute that is constitutive of each individual. Most of what the ordinary person expresses and wills is merely his own hopes and fears— "fleshly lusts and sorrows" (Nishida 1987, 92); but humans are capable of expressing and willing something that reflects who they are in a more fundamental way.

Although Nishida considers acting from the ground of our true selves as the moment when we are truly active as "individuals," this notion of individually is ironically contrary to what we tend to think of as our "self," which we primarily associate with our likes and dislikes—that is, with the animal aspects of our nature. According to Nishida, our most profound self is not these habits and tendencies but what he calls "absolute negation": at the base of our existence, what we truly are is a "coming face-to-face with the absolute."[11] We can express our everyday hopes and fears, or we can come face-to-face with the absolute and express this instead. Humans have the capacity to express the absolute, or to use Christian terminology, we can express God.[12] Nishida writes,

> The human self as an individual is the self-negation of the absolute. But the more it is consciously self-forming through its own dynamic expression—that is, volitional and personal—the more it discovers its own absolute negation in its bottomlessly contradictory depths, and thus faces an absolute One—faces God as God's own mirror image and opposite. At the very root of our individually we always face the absolute face of God, and stand in the dimension of decision between eternal life and death. It is in that radical dimension of existential decision that the religious question opens up for us. (Nishida 1987, 93)

Nishida puts the choice we face in Christian terms—we can live in accordance with our everyday hopes and fears, or we can live as Christ living through us. He recalls what St. Paul says, "It is no longer I who live, but Christ who lives in me" (Nishida 1987, 93; quoting Galatians 2:20). Of course, it is important to remember that to live in this way, humans must make a choice. This is because, to use the Christian terminology, humans are fallen—they reject God in their very being, as illustrated in the story of Adam eating the apple in the Garden of Eden in disobedience of God (Nishida 1987, 97). But this inherently sinful nature is also capable of choosing to obey the will of God (ibid.).

Nishida interprets Mahayana Buddhism in a way that mirrors the Christian concept of the fallen and originally sinful nature of humans. In his view of Buddhism, the equivalent of original sin is to be found in our everyday deluded thoughts. Nishida points this out when he draws the parallel between the fall of Adam and a passage in *The Awakening of Faith in the Mahayana*, attributed to Asvagosha:

> The fall of Adam who ate of the fruit of the tree of knowledge of good and evil, in disobedience to God, is nothing other than an expression of the existence of mankind as God's own negation. The paradox of God's own negation is also behind the phrase of *The Awakening of Faith in the Mahayana*: "A thought suddenly arises."[13] Humankind is bottomlessly self-contradictory. (Nishida 1987, 97)

Although our minds share in Buddha-nature, deluded thoughts can still arise. According to Nishida, this is because at the base of the self, the absolute is the dialectical movement of opposites within the space (*basho*) of absolute nothingness (see chapter 8 on the role of dialectic and *basho* in Nishida's philosophy).

To further explain how Nishida thinks we should live, he goes beyond drawing parallels between a particular interpretation of Christianity and Buddhism[14] and turns instead to distinctions between various religions. Thus, he contrasts his interpretation of Judaism with his interpretation of Christianity in order to emphasize what he means by the spiritual nature of human life. He characterizes the prophets in the Old Testament as examples of individuals who transcend their everyday concerns and compulsions *externally* by becoming prophets who "spoke the will of God" to others (Nishida 1987, 99). In contrast, for Nishida, Buddhists seek transcendence *inwardly*. Thus when a Buddhist realizes her true self, she does not become a mouthpiece for the absolute; instead, she realizes herself as always already the self-expression of the absolute (Nishida 1987, 111). Nishida writes

> [In the case of] transcendent transcendence [as in Judaism] . . . the self, as the self-expression of the absolute, hears [the] commandments [of God] and must obey by negating itself. He who obeys lives, and he who disobeys is plunged into eternal fire. [In the case of] immanent transcendence, conversely, the absolute embraces us. It pursues and embraces us even though we are disobedient and try to flee. It is infinite compassion. . . . It is absolute love. (Nishida 1987, 99; see also ibid., 110)

As we recall, for Nishida, transcendence and immanence both exist in the "true self"—the true self is realized when the individual (the immanent) comes face-to-face with the absolute (the transcendent), and this realization is expressed concretely as making a choice: while human life is inherently the negation of the absolute in each moment, we have the choice to act in accordance with the absolute. This is how we should understand our duty as humans from the point of view of immanent transcendence that characterizes Nishida's interpretation of Buddhism and Christianity. In contrast, the adoption of the transcendent transcendence of Judaism would mean that ethical action involves the individual denying the self-contradiction within him (the coexistence of sinfulness and the absolute; the meeting of the individual and the absolute face-to-face as mirror images) and instead becoming the mouthpiece of the absolute—of God (Nishida 1987, 104; see also Nishida 1998a, 22).

To put this more starkly, in Nishida's interpretation of Judaism, the individual denies in order to become the mouthpiece of God. In contrast, in Buddhism and Christianity, God/the Buddha denies himself (i.e., his divinity in the case of God, or his transcendence of samsara in the case of the Buddha) and appears in human form to use *upaya*—various skillful human means—to help humans to be free (Nishida 1987, 100).[15] God becomes human by becoming love (Nishida 1987, 100–101); the Buddha remains in the human world out of compassion. So for Nishida, the world is a world of the "infinite compassion" of the absolute rather than a world governed by "the Lord of ten thousand hosts" (Nishida 1987, 103).

We live our lives as social beings by being located in a specific cultural environment. But we do not act ethically simply by following the cultural mores of our day or adopting its current values. Rather, what is essential is to understand how to distinguish between those values that truly reflect who we are as human beings from those that do not. Nishida's investigation of Christianity, Buddhism, and Judaism is a way of illustrating how a set of shared values—a "culture" in Nishida's sense—can contain within it a kernel of truth that reflects our true nature, and which can therefore be a beacon for making moral choices. He finds such a kernel within Christianity and certain forms of Buddhism: in Christianity, it is God's love that should inspire moral action (Nishida 1987, 100–101), while in the case of Buddhism, it is Buddha's compassion that should guide our actions (ibid.). This kernel must become actualized in our choices; in this way, the transcendent and the immanent, which exist in constant tension, can express themselves dynamically through our lives. We will begin to develop what this means in practical terms through a study of Nishida's early work *An Inquiry into the Good*.

Acting from the Ground of Our True Selves: Ethics through the Lens of Nishida's Early Philosophy

Nishida's ideal of ethical behavior is that we live in a way that acknowledges our true self and expresses the true nature of reality as the dynamic self-expression of the absolute. This is an ideal which extends throughout his philosophy.[16] To develop what this means in more concrete terms, we will examine *An Inquiry into the Good,* Nishida's first published philosophical work, where he explains some of the ethical implications of his explanation of the nature of our self and our consciousness.[17]

In concrete terms, Nishida's exhortation to live our lives by seeking our true selves (Nishida 1998c, 72) is a call to decrease the influence of our everyday habits and our biological imperatives (Nishida sometimes calls them "animal" imperatives) on us, thereby making room for our choices and actions to manifest what the world as the dynamic expression of the absolute itself expresses. How do we do this? Nishida says that we do it by opening our eyes to see the world and opening our ears to hear the world (Nishida 1987, 107). This means to give up living in the abstract world of self-consciousness in which the individual and the world are presumed to be separate (ibid., 104) and instead to live in the world of direct experience that is constantly unfolding itself, unmediated by our everyday thoughts and feelings.

What is entailed by living with "open eyes and open ears"? When we emerge from our internalized world of desires and hopes, thoughts and feelings, we recognize that we have more options for living our lives than we thought. And we come to see that these choices are not restricted to the choices of individuals conceived in the normal way in our everyday life. In the modern world, we tend to think that the choices that express who we are in the most fundamental sense are those which reflect our private hopes and wishes. But for Nishida, choosing to pursue these internalized goals is really a failure to choose because they involve choosing after one has separated oneself from the rest of the world and retreated into our habits and patterns—they are based on shrinking ourselves to the internal life of our thoughts and feelings. When we act on the basis of our inner thoughts and feelings, we act on the basis of our "small" self—our merely self-conscious self, rather than our reflective, true self. Nishida writes in *An Inquiry into the Good*, "That which we speak of as the internal, subjective spirit is a highly superficial and feeble spirit, an individual fancy. In contrast, great, deep spirit is the activity of the universe that is united with the truth of the universe. Such spirit of itself accompanies the activity of the external world, and it does nothing but act" (Nishida 1990, 78). In this passage, Nishida makes it clear that to act from the ground of our true selves—that is, as historical selves using the terminology of his later work—we must act in a way that expresses the universe as a whole expressing itself. The superficial hopes and interest, Nishida says, must be eradicated in order to live like this. He describes how to act in this way:

> The true unity of consciousness [that is our true self] is a pure and simple activity that comes forth of itself, unhindered by oneself; it is the original state of

independent, self-sufficient consciousness, with no distinction among knowledge, feeling, and volition, and no separation of subject and object. At this time our true personality expresses itself in its entirety. Personality therefore is not found in mere reason or desire, much less in unconscious impulses; like the inspiration of a genius, it is an infinite unifying power that functions directly and spontaneously from within each individual. . . . And as I discussed in the section on reality, if we assume that phenomena of consciousness are the only reality, then our personalities are the activity of the unifying power of the universe. In other words, our personalities are the particular forms in which the sole reality—which transcends the distinction between mind and matter—manifests itself according to circumstances. (Nishida 1990, 131)

Acting from our "true personality," to use the terminology of Nishida's early philosophy, means to not act selfishly as an individual separate from others, but rather to act in a way so as to realize the sincere desires of other people (Nishida 1990, 134).

In his later writings, Nishida draws from Buddhist texts to help explain what he means. For instance, he refers to the Prajnaparamita teaching "Having No Place wherein it abides, this Mind arises" (Nishida 1987, 95).[18] He quotes the Tang Dynasty Chan Master Panshan Baoji (盤山寶積, 720–814 CE), a student of Zen Master Mazu Daoyi (馬祖道一, 709–788 CE), who wrote,

> It is like waving a sword in the air. It is not a question of striking anything. It does not leave any trace as it cleaves the air. Nor does the blade break off. If our mind is like this, each thought is freed from knowing through concepts or ideas. The whole mind is Buddha, and the whole Buddha is oneself. Oneself and Buddha are not two. This is the true enlightenment. (Nishida 1987, 95; quoting *The Mirror of Orthodoxy* (『宗鏡錄』 Ch. *Zongjing lu;* Jp. *Shūgyōroku*)

Acting in a way that reflects our true selves means to act from the activity of the waving sword without any preconceived idea of striking anything. Freed from having its trajectory determined by thoughts, the sword simply acts as swords are meant to do.

Now, this view might seem to lead to moral relativism because whatever random path the sword happens to take would turn out to be the path it was "meant" to take. But this is not the case. Many forces in the world act on the sword and must be taken into account when swinging it: for instance, it would be unsafe and unwise to swing it near children or in an enclosed space. Thus moral action is not simply arbitrary action. We must choose in a way that is in harmony with the actual conditions of the world. And as we have seen, the true state of the world is the world expressing itself as the historical body and manifesting itself in both social/cultural existence and individual existence, which exist in a mutual, dialectical, creative relationship.

In *An Inquiry into the Good,* Nishida explains that we must actualize our "true personality." This means to live unselfishly and to observe the conditions of the world around us with open eyes so that we can act for the best in a way that accords with these conditions. This "true personality" is the true self that is in accord with the absolute reality of which it is an expression Nishida sees a parallel between his approach and that which Kant advocates when he writes that "Two things fill the mind with ever new and increasing admiration and awe, the oftener and more steadily we reflect on them: the starry heavens above me and the moral law within me."[19] Nishida understands these words to mean that ethics is the expression of the divine actualizing itself through us when we allow it to do so. And this expression occurs as the moral law, which, as we will see, Nishida understands to be the social and cultural mores of our time that, like us, are expressions of the absolute.

In the next section, we will explore in greater detail the role of society and culture in guiding our moral life. In this way, we will make Nishida's exhortation to live as who we truly are more concrete.

EXPRESSING OUR TRUE SELF IN SCIENCE, ART, AND MORALITY

What are the practical consequences of living from the source of our true self? First, as we have seen, it means to recognize ourselves as the expression of the world all around us (Nishida 1987, 107). Nishida alludes to how this occurs in three realms—science, art, and morality (Nishida 1990, 78; 1998c; 1998e, 87). The perspective from which Nishida approaches these domains is the following: we should find within science, art, and morality ways of acting in each of these fields that reflect the nature of reality as the expression of the absolute. While this may seem abstract, it is not meant to be: to ground science, art, and morality in the reality of the world as an expression of the absolute simply means to start from everyday experience (Nishida 1998b, 38). This means that rather than approaching these subjects by thinking about them in an abstract way, we must start by grasping "what the actual everyday world really is prior to such abstractions" (ibid., 38–39). These are the modes of inquiry that we should pursue and promote since they bring us and others to a better understanding of the world and ourselves as we truly are.

What is the role of culture and society in this approach? Generally, when we adopt a scientific perspective, we either tend to think abstractly about cultures and societies, reducing them to a few characteristics that we wish to study, or else we generalize about them in order to derive general rules about how they function. But Nishida believes that the everyday world is the expression of the absolute and that therefore the everyday world as a social and cultural world is also an expression of the absolute. The term he uses to indicate this is "historical body" living as the "historical world." Nishida explains:

> The real world is the world in which we are actively involved—the concrete world in which we are living in that active involvement. To live means to be actively involved; and to be actively involved means to be transactionally productive. Thus, the real world is the world of production. It is the world in which we are made by making. In a word, it is the historical world. (Nishida 1998b, 40–41)

The social and cultural world are simply facets of the historical world expressing itself: they are the expression of the world manifesting itself creatively as concrete social relations, cultural practices, and the making of cultural products. Morality is the most obvious form that social and cultural life takes, and we will examine Nishida's view of morality shortly. To begin, however, we should sketch his views of science and art to demonstrate that society and culture are not different in kind from them: rather, science, art, and morality are all three modes of expression of our true selves manifesting itself in the everyday world of creative activity.

Aligning Science with True Reality

Science, if undertaken from a world-historical perspective, must take as its starting point the world as a world of production. In the case of the study of the human body, for instance, this means studying the human body "in relation to [the] entire world" as it is involved in creating things and being created by them (Nishida 1998b, 47). "Our first understanding of the physical body," Nishida writes, "comes from an existential act of productive work—through the human being's actually using tools and making things" (ibid.). Nishida's view of scientific inquiry takes this as one of its starting points: science is productive activity because it involves experimentation. However, even scientific reasoning, if oriented in a particular way, can reflect the true reality of the world as a dynamic world of complex interactions. To take this perspective, the scientist must always keep in mind that "the world is a living world, and in one aspect it moves itself; that is, in the world there is the aspect of the world moving itself in and through itself" (Nishida 1998b, 48). For instance, the human body "has its being in bodily existence through its functions which are related to that aspect of the self-moving world, functions that various parts of the body have in relation to the world's movement" (Nishida 1998b, 48).

Scientific inquiry can reflect the true nature of ourselves and the world as absolute reality expressing itself as the historical world. Nishida gives the example of Galileo as a scientist whose style of thinking "takes place in the historical world" (Nishida 1998c, 68) and who understood that the world expresses who we truly are as the expression of "contradictory identify of the many and the one" (ibid., 66). If scientific inquiry is truly creative, the scientist herself expresses its creative activity. He explains Galileo's perspective as follows,

> To see things in the transformational structure of active intuition signifies to see things in the form of the contradictory identity of the many and the one. It . . . means to see things in their concrete logic. As individual selves, we see things in the forms of individuality of the world. This was the ground of Galileo's standpoint that conceived of the processes of things from the relation among concrete individuals in their concrete relational situations. This kind of seeing in the style of Galileo entails that we see the world from within the world, as the very individuals of the world that has the form of a contradictory identity. As Leibnizian monads, we simultaneously express the world and are the world's expressions. (Nishida 1998c, 66)

Science reflects its world-historical nature when it acknowledges the relational nature of the physical and biological worlds and eschews abstract theoretical perspectives. What distinguished Galilean science from that of Galileo's predecessors was his mathematical approach (Cohen 2005, 20). Admittedly, a mathematical approach seems abstract. But what Galileo attempted to capture through mathematics was the relationship between moving objects, that is, the dynamism of real moving systems. As H. Floris Cohen explains, Galileo's study of free fall involved a mathematical analysis of the relative motion of bodies and testing the mathematical ideal against the reality of bodies falling in order to make his model approach reality as closely as possible (20–21). Galileo was thus conducting science as the reflection of the dynamic world in two ways: through creative experimentation and by recognizing the dynamism of physical systems.

Nishida provides another example of a scientific approach that is grounded in the nature of reality as everyday experience in "That Which Underlies Physical Phenomena," one of the essays that form a part of *From the Acting to the Seeing*. Nishida finds a parallel between his dialectical conception of space in a modern scientific view, which conceives of space as a "field of forces" (*chikara no ba*, 力の場). On this view, the objects of the world are naturally in relation to each other, rather than being separate objects contained in an empty space that form relationships to other objects after the fact (*NKZ* IV:48–49; for an interpretation of this point, see Tremblay 2015, 76–77; see also Nishida 1998b, 49–50).

The very process of scientific inquiry also manifests its rootedness in the world as historical body, a world of productive and creative activity. Nishida gives the example of experimental science, which he believes is productive and creative in the same way that the world itself is (*NKZ* 8:326). In his view, scientific experimentation is similar to the creativity of the artist (Maraldo 2017, 212). For example, he cites the insights of Niels Bohr and the principle of uncertainty, which Nishida considers to be a rejection of the view that "the activity of an experimental observer did not affect and was irrelevant to the world of matter which was governed by immutable physical laws" (Nishida 1998b, 49) in favor of a view in which "the experimental observation is integral to the physical effect produced" (ibid.). Nishida uses this as an example of the dialectic nature of the historical world in which the subject (the observer) both creates effects in the phenomenal world and is in turn created as an observer by the activity.

Aligning Art with True Reality

Nishida explains that art can express the nature of reality as the form of contradictory identity; it does so when art does not merely express "private fantasy" nor retreats into "quiescent absorption in objects" (Nishida 1998c, 69). Art, like all human action, should be the creative expression of reality manifesting itself as the absolute. It achieves this goal when it is intuitive and creative. In *Art and Morality*, Nishida emphasizes the commonality between art and morality—both are expressions of "the objective world of the same pure will" that is the creative source of human life (1973, 168).

In his essay on Goethe's poetry, Nishida explains that good art—art that expresses the absolute expressing itself as the dynamism of reality—must both express this dynamism, which he describes as the flow of time from the past into the future, and its absolute nature, which he expresses as "eternity," the "backdrop" to the flow of time. He writes,

> It may be that all of culture is shaped by history against the backdrop of eternity, but this is especially so in the case of art. In much the same way, Michelangelo's "unfinished sculptures" and Rodin's statues were hewn out of blocks of marble; great art is a relief carved out of the marble of eternity. In comparison with the more personal things of life, such a background may seem rather impersonal, but the personal is not a question of matter as opposed to form, but of where and

how something is given shape. Absent the backdrop of eternity, there is nothing personal. (2011, 659)

Art is the creative activity of the individual. In this activity, the artist has the possibility of expressing the impersonal—the backdrop of eternity—through the highly personal creative process. In this situation, the artist should not be guided by abstract ideas or conceptions, but simply align with reality expressing itself. John Maraldo explains this by contrasting art as it is commonly conceived and art that expresses the absolute:

> [Art] is commonly regarded as the activity of an artist who first conceives a work and then carries it out through bodily actions, producing a more or less durable artifact, a more or less repeatable event. In the usual view, the creative impulse begins in the individual's mind and ends in a work perceptible by others, in a process described variously by aesthetic theories. Whether the aesthetics interprets the particular work as the embodiment and therefore the revelation of the artist's intention, or as a cultural product whose meaning is ascertained only by outside observers and participants, the work as a work of art is the creation of human subjectivity. In contrast to this commonplace view, Nishida envisions the artist not as an entity who simply pre-exists the creation of the artwork, but as someone who intuits the world by transforming it—a process that creates not only a work but the artist and a newly emergent world as well. Artist and work form mutually and are reflected in one another. (2017, 209)

When one looks at Nishida's calligraphy, one can see in his brush strokes what he was trying to express in his philosophy of art. His writing is devoid of embellishment, and he uses a style of writing that one might consider monotonous if the strength of the line were not as dynamic as it is. His calligraphy clearly does not involve the steps that one normally finds in a manual on calligraphy for beginners: there is no consideration of the categories of shapes that the various kanji fit into, nor is there any self-conscious manipulation of the stroke to create a pleasing variety of thin and thick lines. Nishida's brush is simply the movement of inked brush on paper by a body aligned with breath. Nishida's own art is the expression of his philosophical conception of art.

Aligning Morality with True Reality

A world-historical morality must be rooted in a "historical-formative imperative" (Nishida 1998e, 91). This means that it must have a universal aspect to it (Nishida 1998e, 91),[20] and yet it must be concrete, by which Nishida means that it must be anchored in a particular society or culture (Nishida

1998e, 84). The universal aspect of morality is expressed in Immanuel Kant's categorical imperative that we must act in a way that accods with a maxim of action that we could rationally defend as a universal law to guide all actors in a similar situation—formulated in a less abstract way, the imperative requires us to act in a way that treats all people as ends in themselves rather than as a means to our own selfish ends. The imperative explains how an individual must relate to others, and so it reflects the dialectic that is at the root of the productive creativity of the historical world. As Nishida explains, "Kant's kingdom of ends—his concept that the moral law requires a person always to treat another person as an end, never as a means—already presupposes this form of the moral practice of the personal self. Implicit in Kant's formulation is the dialectical fact that the many are always constituted in reciprocal mediation with the one" (Nishida 1998e, 84). However, what Kantian philosophy lacks in Nishida's view is a root in an actual culture which can give abstract morality concrete content (Nishida 1998e, 84).

What would be the appropriate root for a moral theory? Nishida does not answer this question in a purely parochial manner by pointing out moral systems anchored in small communities or even in national cultures. While he acknowledges that the concrete content of ethical life has historically been provided by specific cultures or societies,[21] he points out that a global society is also capable of providing the content required of true world-historical morality (Nishida 1998e, 85, 92). Thus Nishida points out how the Kantian kingdom of ends takes on different forms in different cultures. It is embodied in Confucianism, which expresses the kingdom of ends formally as the practice of humaneness (*ren*, 仁) and concretely through the Five Relationships (ruler-ruled; parent-child; husband-wife; elder-younger; friend-friend). The kingdom of ends is also expressed in the Japanese idea that the nation is a family with the emperor, a manifestation of the divine, at its center (Nishida 1998e, 86, 91).

Second, acting morally means grounding our actions in compassion, which requires that we be completely sincere (ibid.). For Nishida, acting sincerely means that we must act simply and straightforwardly without seeking to achieve our own petty goals. We must not be bound by "biological instinct" or by our "own rational determinations" (ibid., 111); we must live straightforward lives in the "ordinary" and "everyday" world (ibid., 110 and 112) and not try to "press the self forward"[22] by acting from the perspective of egoistic subjectivity (Nishida 1998c, 70) or on the basis of selfish motives (Nishida 1990, 143). In *An Inquiry into the Good*, Nishida explains that we ought to act like an innocent child (Nishida 1990, 133; see also Nishida 1973, 167),[23] sincerely and without using others for our own ends.

Nishida uses the artist as an example of how to act sincerely in a way rooted in one's true personality. He writes,

> When does the true personality or originality of the painter appear? Insofar as the painter intends various things in his or her consciousness, we cannot yet truly see the painter's personality. We first see it only when, after long years of struggle, the painter's skills mature and the brush follows the will. The expression of personality in the moral realm is no different from this. We express personality not by following temporary desires but by following the most solemn internal demands. This is diametrically opposed to self-indulgent decadence and, contrary to what one might expect, it is an endeavor of difficulty and pain. (Nishida 1990, 134)

To act sincerely and tap into the source of one's true personality, one must set aside one's personal predilections, desires, everyday hopes and fears and express through oneself the world expressing itself.

To achieve such sincerity and to act morally, one must be disciplined. However, the discipline should not be imposed externally so as to reform our recalcitrant, selfish selves. Instead, the process of discipline involves unleashing one's true self (Carter 1997, 138), not binding it through rules and ritual. Nishida writes,

> Our deepest demands and greatest goals unite automatically. While internally we discipline the self and attain to the true nature of the self, externally we give rise to love for our fellow humans and come to accord with the supremely good goal—good conduct that is perfect and true. From one angle, such perfect good conduct appears exceedingly difficult, but from a different angle, it is something anyone must be able to do. Morality is not a matter of seeking something apart from the self—it is simply the discovery of something within the self. (Nishida 1990, 144–145)

Thus when, through disciplined searching, we discover what is universal within ourselves—when we realize that we are the manifestation of the historical body, to use the language of later Nishida philosophy—we are naturally willing to realize the greatest good in all of our activities, no matter how small their scope (Nishida 1990, 145).

In addition to actualizing a universal world-historical imperative in our lives as compassion and sincerity, living a moral life also requires living in the absolute present (Nishida 1987, 113). Nishida means this in a common-sense way: we must take care of what is really going on in front of us right now (ibid., 113). Moreover, we must deal with what is at hand with a consciousness that we and the world are self-expressions of the absolute. As Nishida points out, when our mind truly understands the world and we make real choices, they express the world itself. He writes,

> The foundation of the human self's practical morality does not lie in the imperatives of syllogistic logic. The self is born, acts, and dies in this historical world. As a unique individual of this historical world, our self expresses the world of the absolute present. In the absolute present, it embodies an infinite imperative as self-determination of the absolute present—that is, it embodies the self-formation of the historical world. Therefore, as a creative element of the creative world, it also forms the historical world. Moral practice must be historically formative in this sense. The self's expression of the world is a self-expressive form of the world in its historical formation. Herein lies the foundation of truly practical morality. (Nishida 1998e, 83)

When we act, we must act from the source of creativity and activity that we share with the historical world: the real world unfolding all around us of which we are only a part.

To illustrate how we are to live, Nishida uses examples drawn from Japanese culture. Why? Because he sees in Japanese culture an expression of the creativity that also characterizes the creative and dynamic nature of the world as the self-expression of the absolute through the individual.[24] He writes, "The Japanese culture of pure feeling has 'the form of the formless, the sound of the soundless.' It is very much a symbolic culture. It is, like time, a formless unity. Such a culture of formless emotion is, like time, creative. It is, like life itself, developmental. It receives various forms but, at the same time, gives a certain form to them" (Nishida 1998a, 31). What stands out for Nishida about Japanese culture as a culture of feeling is its spontaneity (Nishida 1998a, 31). By this, he does not mean that Japanese people are impulsive. Rather, he means that Japanese art is expressive in the same way that the world is expressive.

Such expression has both a subjective and an objective aspect to it (Nishida 1998a, 30). For instance, the Japanese concept of *mono no aware* (物の哀れ, "the experience of the impermanence of things") is precisely the "*aware* of things"—it is not an individual's impulsive response, but rather a particular expression of an objective "modality of pure feeling" that can be felt when we interact with an object that expresses impermanence (ibid.). Also, Japanese feeling expresses the universal form *formlessly* (Nishida 1998a, 31–32). By this, Nishida means that it does not express this flow of feeling in purely rational terms (Nishida 1998a, 34), but rather as something "infinitely dynamic" (ibid.).

Nishida illustrates why this process of acting as the self-expression of the world involves engaging in the present with common everyday occurrences by pointing to the Zen saying that "The willows are green, the flowers are red." He says that a common misunderstanding of this phrase is that it expresses a "naturalism" or "sensationalism" (prioritization of the senses); but what it really expresses is the idea that our true mind is the expression of the world unadulterated by our thoughts and feelings.[25] Nishida explains, "While positivistic science regards the actual as thing, Buddhism (which thinks in such dialectical terms) sees it as mind. Western scholars often consider the Zen saying that 'the willows are green, the flowers are red' to be directly a statement of naturalism or sensationalism. But it is actually a subtle dialectical idea from the opposite standpoint" (Nishida 1998a, 27). Thus according to Nishida, for Buddhists, living in recognition that the world is an expression of the absolute means living simply with an unmediated acceptance of the "actual" or "real" world as an expression of our true selves.[26] Willow trees and flowers are not simply objects that we sense (the standpoint of physics), but rather they have a subjective dimension as the expression of our true selves (ibid.), and they also have an objective dimension, since these willows and flowers are the world expressing itself.[27]

Nishida explains in more detail in "The World as Identity of Absolute Contradiction" what he thinks Zen Masters mean when they exhort people to live in the world of the "ordinary and everyday." First, Nishida explains that this does not mean that a simple life is preferable to a more elaborate one. Rather, what is important is to recognize that life is the self-expression of the world (Nishida 1990, 143; 1998c, 71). It also does not mean that all things participate in some transcendent universal whole, or in a state of "non-differentiated oneness" (ibid.). One ought not to live in some blissed out meditative state: there are still choices to be made based on the actual circumstances in which a person finds herself.

Further explanation is found in *An Inquiry into the Good*, where Nishida explains that expressing the self that reflects the true nature of reality means responding to what is actually going on in front of us without letting our everyday desires and passions get in the way. He writes,

> Each individual's true self is the system of independent, self-sufficient reality appearing before that person. In this way, the sincerest demands of each and every person necessarily coincide at all times with the ideals of the objective world the person sees. For example, however selfish one might be, if one has any degree of sympathy, the greatest demand is certainly to give satisfaction to others after securing one's own satisfaction. If we assume that the demands of the self are not limited to carnal desires but include idealistic demands, then we must by all means speak in this way. The more selfish we become, the more we feel anguish at blocking the personal desires of others. Contrary to what one might think, I believe that perhaps only someone devoid of personal desire can

obliterate the personal desires of others without losing peace of mind. To fulfill the greatest demands of the self and to actualize the self is to actualize the objective ideals of the self—that is, to unite with objectivity. (Nishida 1990, 134)

When one "steps out of the way" by setting aside selfish desires and everyday concerns, one sees the objective world as it truly is, and so one can act in response to the situations one beholds and meet the needs of others.[28] One feels directly what others feel; one laughs and cries with others together as one (Nishida 1990, 175).

Living in this way is to live with an intimate understanding of the fragility of life. Or to put this another way, it is to live with an awareness that reality is unfolding itself as the appearance but also the disappearance of each and every being and thing. Nishida expresses this idea in religious terms by exhorting us to act "eschatologically," by which he means that "God's decision [must] coincide with mankind's decision" (Nishida 1987, 101; see also Nishida 1998e, 83). Here, Nishida draws a parallel between what he is expressing and Pascal's "roseau pensant" ("thinking reed") (Nishida 1987, 113)—like Pascal, one must think recognizing the fragility of our existence. We must act as if our everyday self is dead (ibid.).[29] We must act truly selflessly (ibid., 102), by which Nishida means that we must act as if our everyday self, governed by lust and hope and fear, is dead. As Nishida writes, "The relation between God and mankind is always to be understood as dynamically interexpressive based on the principle of self-negation" (ibid., 103).

In *An Inquiry into the Good*, Nishida also refers to Plato's explanation of love in the *Symposium*, where he writes that love "is the feeling that arises when that which is lacking tries to return to its original, perfect state" (Nishida 1990, 135; quoting *Symposium* 191D). He goes on to explain that to act for the good means to allow one's self to merge with the universe. In such a situation, it is possible to act as the expression of the universe. Nishida writes, "At that point we can say that things move the self or that the self moves things, that Sesshū painted nature or that nature painted itself through Sesshū. There is no fundamental distinction between things and the self, for just as the objective world is a reflection of the self, so is the self a reflection of the objective world" (Nishida 1990, 135).

As we have seen, the moral life according to Nishida is a profoundly spiritual life. But this is a spirituality that is not to be found in abstract beliefs, but rather through becoming attuned to what the everyday world around us is constantly expressing: it is creative, but also destructive; the absolute is not hidden, it is there before your eyes in willows and flowers. This world is our true selves, and once we exert ourselves in order to realize this, we can manifest the love and compassion that the world expresses. This love and compassion are not simply feelings toward others. Rather, love and compassion mean doing what needs to be done in each concrete situation that arises before us. It means to act in unity with the creative activity of the world, and so to act informed by how the world is actually being presented to us right now. Artists can live in this way; but so can the rest of us, whether we work in a factory, an office, indeed, in any workplace in the modern world. The key is to act sincerely in recognition of who we truly are as the expression of the absolute.

EXPRESSING OUR MORAL AND ETHICAL OBLIGATIONS IN SOCIETY

As we have seen, Nishida believes that we have a duty to actualize our true selves in our moral and ethical decisions. In this section, we will explore how this duty manifests itself at the social and cultural level. As we have already explored, community and our relations with others are the source of who we are rather than being opposed to our true nature: cultures, like individuals, are reflections of absolute reality. To act morally, we must use the forms of our social and cultural existence to express ourselves—however, we should only align ourselves with those aspects of culture that truly reflect reality. This means that we have a responsibility to create and promote cultural and social development such that every culture can fulfill its potential to express absolute reality. But because not every culture nor every aspect of a given world-historical culture reflects this reality, we must clarify what Nishida believes our moral obligations are in this case.

Nishida believed that his concept of the historical world is expressed in many cultures, not just Japanese culture (Nishida 1987, 117; 1998a, 36). However, it is best expressed in cultures that become aware (self-aware) that their foundation is in the creative process that characterizes the historical body.[30] Every culture has the potential to discover the creative process at its foundation. Indeed, Nishida describes the worldwide process of each culture discovering this creative process at its root as a "common inter-civilizational project" that each culture should undertake (Nishida 1998e, 82).[31] As Maraldo explains, "The problem that Nishida addressed was how individual nations, peoples, or cultures could interact as equals and mutually determine themselves in the global world" (2017, 174). This undertaking has a spiritual aspect, for as we have seen, the process of becoming self-aware is fundamentally spiritual. Thus Nishida writes that when a nation is "conscious of its own worldhood as a unique world, it has a religious significance as a concrete identity of the transcendent and the immanent, the immanent and the transcendent" (Nishida 1998e, 80; see also 88). Nishida considered Japanese culture to be an example of a culture that expressed the unity of the transcendent and the immanent that characterizes a world-historical culture

(Nishida 1998e, 86). Indeed, he considered it to be particularly apparent in the unique forms of Buddhism that developed in Japan (Nishida 1987, 102), and he also saw it expressed in Japanese society and culture more generally (Nishida 1987, 112).

What did he see in Japan? He saw in its religion and in some aspects of its culture a recognition that everyday life is spiritual—life is the self-expression of the absolute. In the poems of the *Manyōshū* (a poetry collection compiled during the Nara period [719–794 CE]), the *Tale of Genji* (*Genji monogatari*, written in the early eleventh century CE), and the poet Bashō's haiku, Nishida saw a reflection of Shinran's Pure Land Buddhism (Nishida 1987, 112). What does Nishida mean by saying that Japanese society and culture express the kind of creativity that characterizes the essence of reality? In "The Forms of Culture of the Classical Periods of East and West Seen from a Metaphysical Perspective" (Nishida 1998a), he explains that Japanese culture is a culture of feeling—human emotions and responses directly express the absolute and eternal (Nishida 1998a, 30). In this way, the emotional nature of Japanese culture mirrors Nishida's notion that reality is the self-expression of the absolute and eternal self.

In "On the National Polity," Nishida also sees indications that Japan is a world-historical society in the Shintō roots of Japanese culture and the identity of the polity with the emperor, whom the Japanese considered to be divine. He saw in this identity a realization that everyday life—cultural and social activities—are unified with the divine.[32] He writes,

> "The line of Emperors unbroken for ages eternal" is, for us Japanese people, an absolute fact in the sense of being a world-historical development that has formed itself. From such a standpoint, all things are things of the Imperial household; all affairs are affairs of the Imperial household; all things have a public character—and therefore we can speak of a Japanese family that takes the Imperial household as its center. However, this is not a family in a private sense; it is a nation in the strict sense, as the identity of immanent and transcendent and in the form of a world-historical development. (Nishida 1998e, 86)

While Nishida's description of Japanese culture as a world-historical culture is clearly chauvinistic,[33] it is important to recognize that Nishida was not saying that Japanese culture was unique in its ability to express the absolute; rather, he chose to extoll Japanese culture because he felt that it expressed aspects of the philosophy he was articulating. Indeed, Nishida was also critical of Japanese culture, explaining that "the Japanese spirit has been too insular; its sense of the ordinary and everyday . . . superficial, and vainly self-confident" (Nishida 1987, 112). He thus hoped that Japan, like every culture, would take a religious turn and help to express a global culture (Nishida 1987,

120; 1998d). Such a culture must have its roots in the spirituality Nishida expresses. But in making this assertion, he did not mean that Japanese culture should itself become global culture. Instead, he wrote that the Buddhism he saw best expressed in Japanese Mahayana Buddhism should contribute "to the formation of the new historical age" and reflect a religion that evolves "in the direction of the immanently transcendent rather than the transcendently immanent" (Nishida 1987, 121).

In his early works, Nishida was more explicit that every culture necessarily expressed aspects of the historical world as a dynamic world of creation (Nishida 1998a, 36). He explained that a plurality of cultures rather than a world monoculture is essential for the realization of a world culture as a truly historical culture. He wrote, "The world's cultures are, of course, essentially plural. They cannot be reduced to unity for the reason that, when they lose their specificity, they cease to be cultures. Consequently, the process of development of an authentic world culture from the standpoint of authentic culture cannot be a merely abstract advance in a single direction" (Nishida 1998a, 36). Similarly, in "Fundamental Principles of a New World Order," he wrote that

> this basic principle of world-within-the-world world formation does not negate the uniqueness of each nation and people; indeed, it does precisely the opposite.... For the world to become concretely one, each nation and people must in every respect live its own historical life. Just as in the case of an organism, the unity of the whole requires the healthy functioning of the parts, and vice versa.... By this I do not mean that each nation exists merely "for itself." In today's world situation the world must become one in every respect, and yet each nation must maintain its own national identity. (Nishida 1998d, 75)

In Nishida's view, there is a multiplicity of world-historical societies that interact with each other throughout history (Nishida 1998e, 95).

As Brett Davis explains, Nishida's concept of culture has two aspects: multiculturalism and openness to cultural difference. He writes,

> A true world of worlds (*sekaiteki sekai*) would thus be neither a monocultural fusion, which would abolish cultural difference, nor a relativistic dispersion, which would reify assertions of uniqueness; rather, it would be a multicultural conversation, where cultures maintain and develop their uniqueness only by way of opening themselves up to ongoing dialogue with one another.... This opening up involves not only a willingness to critically appropriate valuable aspects of other cultures, but also a movement through self-negation, that is, a willingness to call into question, rethink, and in some cases abandon aspects of one's cultural tradition. (2006, 218)

What Nishida imagined was that each nation would, within its social and cultural resources, find a model for what the world should be like—a "world-principle" (Nishida 1998d, 76)—and that this principle could then be the basis for cooperation among nations. However, rather than achieving his goal, Nishida recognized that, by plunging itself into the Second World War, Japan and the rest of the world had adopted a worldview that was based on the cultural and social views of Western Europe (ibid.). Nishida wanted each of the East Asian nations to be free from imperial domination by the Western European powers (Nishida 1998d, 74). It is for this reason that he advocates that the Japanese must first develop their own national identity and that "the fundamental policy of the intellectual guidance, learning, and education of our nation's people must be grounded thoroughly and deeply in the underlying principles of our national policy" (Nishida 1998d, 75).

Ultimately, Nishida felt that every culture had a duty to become a "world-historical" culture—that is, to find within itself the elements that reflect the absolute as a world of creative, productive activity with a dialectical structure. Being familiar with Japanese culture, he was able to identify the elements of it that manifested this important quality. But he recognized that cultures interact with each other rather than developing in isolation and that cultures would never converge toward a monoculture dominated by an existing culture, but rather that they should strive to find the world-historical within themselves. The mission to act "world-historically" is universal, but its realization is necessarily plural and constantly evolving. No one culture will ever express the totality of absolute reality; but every culture expresses it within itself. Leading a moral life means to align our lives with the creative, productive activity of the absolute manifesting itself in and through the environment of our society and culture.

WHAT CAN WE LEARN FROM NISHIDA FOR OUR GLOBALIZED WORLD?

One could interpret Nishida's advocacy of a "world-historical" society as a desire that societies become explicitly religious. For instance, in "On the National Polity," Nishida criticizes Western societies for splitting church and state. Previous to the split, morality had been firmly grounded in religion. But Nishida believes that the split caused morality to be uprooted from its ground, resulting in an "abstract" morality that was not grounded in the historical world (Nishida 1998e, 86). He elaborates,

> At a certain juncture of the Middle Ages Europe presented the face of a Christian empire. But even here the dimensions of life concerned with transcendence and

immanence, the one and the many, stood apart and in opposition. There was a separation of Church and state. An abstract morality had to be introduced for the reason of the state's existence. The view of the divine nation such as we are able to see in Japan—where world-historical formation directly takes on a self-transcendent form within a racial formation itself, constituting a dialectical identity of transcendence and immanence—could accordingly not develop in the West. (Nishida 1998e, 86)

Nishida's lament over the separation of church and state was not meant as support for theocracy. Nor did he think that liberal states were incapable of becoming world-historical societies. In Nishida's view, it is not the case that every religion necessarily expresses the dialectic of immanent and transcendent that is the movement of absolute reality (Nishida 1998e, 92). He also did not believe that a state church is necessary for a society to be truly religious (Nishida 1998e, 92). Indeed, he supported many elements of liberal democracy, for instance, in his emphasis that a healthy political life and public forum are essential for the manifestation of a world-historical society (Nishida 1998e, 93). He gives as examples of world-historical societies the Greek *polis* and Rome (Nishida 1998e, 92–93), although he admittedly also mentions the "autocratic nations [of] Babylon and Assyria" (ibid.).

Moreover, Nishida emphasizes that the identity of state and religion does not justify religious-based militarism. Although he acknowledges that Japanese society is world-historical because it considers its founding to be a universal divine command (Nishida 1998e, 90), he rejected Japanese militarism. For instance, he felt that Japanese society diverged from its world-historical character in periods in which the country was dominated by the military, such as when military leaders seized power in the Kamakura period, thus enabling the reign of the *bakufu*, the government of the *samurai* (Nishida 1998e, 91).

That Nishida was not an advocate of theocracy is also clear when one considers that he was of the opinion that even the secular natural sciences and social sciences are able to reflect world-historical reality. For instance, he writes that all sciences and academic fields can manifest this reality: "All academic learning ... is established as the conceptual self-expression of the historical world. Logic is one form of this. At the ground of learning there must be a form that forms itself in the dialectical structure of the self's active intuition; and this must have the existential character of a particular historical-bodily existence" (Nishida 1998e, 89). Thus biology, physics, and chemistry are, to the degree that they have such a grounding form, also world-historical, that is, expressions of the unity of transcendence and immanence (Nishida 1998e, 89). For instance, in the case of biology, Nishida recognizes the presence of an "intuition of our biological bodily life" at the base of that science that reflects the world-historical nature of reality (Nishida 1998e, 89). Thus what is essential for a society to be "world-historical" and to provide the foundation of true morality is that it have the same form as the historical world—that is, it have a form that is dialectical in structure like the active intuition that is the creative wellspring of the individual and absolute reality (Nishida 1998e, 88).

In summary, Nishida's moral and ethical views are very relevant for our current globalized world. A society acts in a world-historical way when it promotes and protects a form of morality that reflects the interplay of individual and group that is the dialectical movement at the base of absolute reality. In concrete terms, this means adopting a morality that is grounded in the concrete cultural and social practices of a society, but which is at the same time creative and transformative. However, Nishida was also very clear that cultures are not monumental—they are created through interactions between their members and between cultures; it is only through this interaction that they can evolve and develop in ways that reflect the creative and productive nature of reality. All present forms of culture and society will come to an end just as all life will die; but we should strive to life in a way that is both rooted in our society and culture, and yet which accepts its inevitable change over time.

Our arts, our productive industries, our service industries—all aspects of a society—must be truly creative and connected to the source of human creativity. Above all, they should not cut off humans from the ability to discover their true selves and to realize this nature creatively in their everyday lives.

NOTES

1. Krummel points out that for Nishida, others are irreducibly individual, and yet, not being substances, they are "self-negating vis-à-vis one another" because they are in constant relationship with each other, creating groups and then dissolving them (Krummel 2015, 180).

2. Krummel writes that the historical world (*rekishiteki sekai,* 歴史的世界) is the world of "human interactivity" (Krummel 2015, 120).

3. In other writings, he is quite clear that he does not mean race as a biological category. For instance, in "On the National Polity," he writes that a historical society does not emerge by a purely biological process: "A historical society does not emerge from the mere environment." It follows from this that a "historical society" is not simply a race in the biological sense: "[a historical society] is reducible neither to environment nor race" (Nishida 1998e, 80). Of course, today, we know that race is not a valid biological concept at all.

4. In his early work, *An Inquiry into the Good* (1911), he gives the examples of "language, manners, customs, social systems, laws, religion, and literature" (Nishida 1990, 138).

5. This is the idea that is explored in Watsuji's classic, *Fūdo* [*Climate and Culture*] (Watsuji 1961).

6. In "On the National Polity," he speaks of a "people" rather than a society (Nishida 1998e, 78).

7. In *An Inquiry into the Good*, Nishida articulates for the first time what he means by social existence and its relationship to the individual. There, he writes not about the relationship between the individual and the species; rather, as befits the theoretical perspective Nishida adopts in that book, he writes about the relationship between individual consciousness and social consciousness. A social consciousness emerges when individuals live in community (Nishida 1990, 138). This social consciousness is expressed through the community's culture (ibid.), and Nishida thinks that it is essential to the creativity of every member. He writes, "Even the most original genius cannot step beyond the scope of this social consciousness; in fact, such a person is one who most displays the deepest significance of the social consciousness" (ibid.). In 1911, Nishida had not yet fully developed his dialectical analysis. However, he does think that both individual and social consciousness have a similar structure and are rooted in what he later calls the "historical world." He writes

If we analyze individual consciousness, we do not find a separate, unifying self. But because there is a unity upon which a unique character arises and various phenomena are established, we consider this unity a living reality. For the same reason, we can view social consciousness as a living reality. Like individual consciousness, social consciousness constitutes a system with a center and interconnections. (Nishida 1990, 139)

8. See also Feenberg (1999, 38–39).

9. Nishida specifically mentions the continuity in his work at various points. For instance, in "The Historical Body," he writes, "Because I have developed my system of thought over a very long period of time, my philosophical ideas might be said to have changed in various ways. But as a matter of fact, I think they have not changed all that much. I began my career as a philosopher when I wrote *Zen no kenkyū* (*Inquiry into the Good*) in 1911. Since then a considerable amount of time has indeed elapsed. I too have changed with the times in various ways, but I can say that the basic spirit of all my subsequent philosophical ideas had already emerged in that work" (Nishida 1998b, 37).

10. As an example of the prejudice common among philosophers even until today, take Descartes, who wrote that animals "have no intelligence at all, and that it is nature which acts in them according to the disposition of their organs. In the same way a clock, consisting only of wheels and springs, can count the hours and measure time more accurately than we can with all our wisdom" (*Discourse on the Method*, Descartes 1994, 141).

11. In *An Inquiry into the Good*, Nishida writes that "it is . . . by directly seeing God at the base of nature and at the base of the self that we can feel God's infinite warmth and attain to the essence of religion, which is to live in God" (Nishida 1990, 156).

12. In *An Inquiry into the Good,* Nishida writes that "our God must be the internal unifying power of the universe, which orders heaven and earth and nurtures the

myriad things in them; apart from this power there is no God" (Nishida 1990, 155; see also 156).

13. Nishida is referring to the last sentence in the passage on consciousness, where Fazhang writes, "Suddenly, [a deluded] thought arises; [this state] is called ignorance" (Hakeda 1893, 54).

14. Dilworth discusses the similarities that Nishida sees between Buddhism and Christianity (Dilworth 1987, 35–38).

15. For a discussion of how the Christian God is, according to Nishida, "a dialectical God who is both transcendent and immanent," see Krummel (2015, 177).

16. I believe that Nishida emphasizes the importance of departing from everyday views and discovering one's true self. However, Imono Mika has written an interesting article in which she emphasizes the importance of both activity and passivity in Nishida's philosophy (Imono 2016).

17. This use of an early work to explain some general themes in Nishida's philosophy is justified on many grounds. Krummel, for instance, sees the same continuity that I do between Nishida's final essay and themes from *An Inquiry into the Good* (Krummel 2015, 137). See also Nishida's comments in Nishida 1998b, 37; *supra* note 9).

18. Nishida rephrases this in *An Inquiry into the Good*, although he does not refer to the Prajnaparamita teachings. He writes that it is "because God is no-thing, there is no place where God is not, and no place where God does not function" (Nishida 1990, 82). For Dilworth's interpretation of the Prajnaparamita logic adopted by Nishida, see Dilworth 1987, 27–29). For a discussion of this passage and the relationship between nothingness and consciousness, see Krummel (2015, 171).

19. *Critique of Practical Reason.* Trans. Lewis White Beck. Indianapolis, 1956. P. 166. Quoted in Nishida 1990 at 131.

20. By "universal," Nishida seems to mean that a culture of "world-historical significance" must have "eternal value" (Nishida 1998e, 93). He gives the examples of Greek and Indian culture, whose ancient cultures died, but whose "legacies . . . live on today" because they are of universal significance (Nishida 19983, 94).

21. Nishida speaks of "nations" in "On the National Polity" (1998e, 84–85).

22. Nishida refers to Dōgen's (1200–1253) who said that "it is an illusion to try in practice to attain realization of the myriad things by pressing the self forward" (*Genjōkoan* 『現成公案』, quoted in Nishida 1998c, 70).

23. Nishida refers to Christ, who said that only those who are like innocent children may enter heaven (Nishida 1990, 133; reference to Matt. 18:3).

24. Nishida's intertwining discussion of the expressiveness of Japanese culture and the expressiveness of the world of active intuition strengthens the parallel I am identifying (1998a, 30–31). Nishida first describes Japanese culture as a culture of feeling (Nishida 1998a, 30), by which he means that it is not guided by law or ritual, but rather by "pure feeling" as expressed in Japanese aesthetic terms such as *mono no aware* (ibid.). He then follows this discussion of Japanese culture with a discussion of "active intuition." The world is "self-determining" in the sense that it is "active intuition," and this, Nishida explains, means that the world is "expressive" (ibid.). When individuals see things through doing and responding—through acting—their acting

is the manifestation of the self-expression of the world (ibid., 31). In *An Inquiry into the Good*, Nishida already writes about action as a mode of knowledge, which is the expression of the will of God. He writes that "in God, knowing is action and action is knowing. Reality is none other than the thought and will of God" (Nishida 1990, 162).

25. Dilworth writes that "what is primal, or primordial [in Nishida's philosophy is not reflexive principle of the self-completion of reason as in Kant's philosophy, but] rather the world's irrational, and pre-rational, concrete immediacy" (Dilworth 1987, 19). Perhaps Dilworth puts too much emphasis on the irrational nature of present experience. Nishida himself writes, in "The System of Self-Consciousness of the Universal" that everyday experience is just our true self intuiting (active intuition), and one of the things that the "true self" intuits is the everyday self that we perceive as the subject of our thoughts and feelings. He writes, "The self that truly sees must be a plane of intuition that includes this process-self-consciousness [the everyday self as the subject of experience]. Thus we can say that we feel our own life in the shining moon and in the insects crying in the fields" (Nishida 2005, 216; *NKZ* V:463). I don't think that this noetic activity of the true self (true self as active intuition) is irrational or prerational, unless by "rationality," Dilworth is referring to everyday thought. Nishida goes on, at the end of that work, to say that philosophy, as the "self-reflection of reason itself . . . must be the self-conscious development of reason itself" (ibid.; *NKZ* V:464). Krummel discusses how Nishida's philosophy conceptualizes the experience at the root of human consciousness as dialectical but not "a-rational" (Krummel 2015, 175).

26. Dilworth interprets Nishida's references to the everyday world as "linked to the Mahayana logic of the nonduality of samsara and nirvana" (Dilworth 1987, 36). Krummel instead emphasizes that the references to the "ordinary and everyday" in Nishida's philosophy are a reference to the fact that each individual "is the creative point of the absolute's self-determination" (Krummel 2015, 135; he continues his analysis of ordinariness on 136).

27. Nishida uses technical philosophical terms to explain this. He writes as follows, "Reality has the form of being and, at the same time, of non-being; it has the reciprocally mediating form of being qua non-being and non-being qua being. Thus, it is, at the same time, subjective and objective, noetic and noematic" (Nishida 1998a, 29). Using the more mystical terminology of his early writings, Nishida wrote that "God is none other than the world and the world is none other than God" (Nishida 1990, 169).

28. He writes in the last part of *An Inquiry into the Good* that when we "forget the self . . . an incomprehensible power beyond the self functions alone in all of its majesty; there is neither subject nor object, but only the true union of subject and object" (Nishida 1990, 174–175).

29. Dilworth sees in Nishida's discussion of death in "Nothingness and the Religious Worldview" a form of existentialism in which the individual must be aware of his mortality in order to be truly human (Dilworth 1987, 21). Krummel makes a similar point (2015, 165). I am not so convinced that Nishida advocates such a view—he seems to place more importance on the death of the "everyday self," not the

death of our mortal selves. Perhaps this is what Dilworth alludes to in his subsequent discussion (21–22). For the articulation of a view closer to mine, see Elwood (1994, 311–313). Stevens emphasizes that what is important about death for Nishida is not the future possibility of death but the eternal death of each moment—that is, each moment arises and passes away (2005, 98).

30. Feenberg describes this process of cultures awakening to their creative role as a "moment of subjectivity" that, in the case of Japan, is to be "recovered through a Zen-inspired Asian self-understanding" (Feenberg 1999, 28).

31. Even in his earliest works, Nishida advocated for worldwide self-actualization. He writes in *An Inquiry into the Good* that while "the nation is the greatest expression of unified communal consciousness," one should not be satisfied with simple nationalism, but instead work toward "a social union that includes all human-kind." He goes on to write that this should not mean the disappearance of nations, peoples, or cultures. Instead, he believed that "genuine universalism . . . does not require that each nation ceases to be" but rather "that each nation becomes increasingly stable, displays its distinctive characteristics, and contributes to the history of the world" (Nishida 1990, 141).

32. For a discussion of influences on Nishida in regard to his views about the relationship between culture and state, see Jacinto (1994, 147).

33. For a good survey of the various views taken in regard to the political orientation of Nishida's writings, see Arisaka (1996). See also Heisig and Maraldo (1994).

Conclusion

Japanese Cultural and Social Philosophy in the Twentieth Century

The primary purpose of this book has been to examine the cultural philosophy of Watsuji Tetsurō, Kuki Shūzō, and Nishida Kitarō to describe their views about the meaning of culture and the proper method for studying it. A secondary goal has been to assess these views with regard to their tendency toward cultural essentialism. As we have seen, essentialist and non-essentialist tendencies exist in the theories of each. On the one hand, each philosopher accepts the diversity of cultures, the possibility of cultural intermixing, and the existence of multicultural identity. On the other hand, each view incorporates essentialist aspects that can easily be coopted for political ends when "culture" overlaps with categories such as "nation," "ethnic group," and "race." While this book does not identify where to draw the line beyond which non-essentialism slips into essentialism, our study of culture should nonetheless help those wishing to theorize culture without crossing it.

As we have seen, the diversity of views about the nature of culture among the three philosophers is striking. Watsuji's phenomenological approach focused on the way in which culture and the creation of cultural meaning is experienced. In *Pilgrimages to the Ancient Temples in Nara*, he constructs the contemporary cultural meaning of Japan's Buddhist heritage through his encounters with objects (statuary, paintings, temples, and landscapes) and people (friends, family, temple staff, academics, and experts). The meaning of these encounters is generated by intellectual reflection and emotional response. In *Climate and Culture*, Watsuji applied this phenomenological approach intentionally and rigorously to the study of various climatic zones, and this led him to reflect on the social implications of cultural experience: that is, the nature of human existence that make such cultural experience possible. These reflections gave birth to his later theory of human existence as *betweenness* (*aidagara*), which describes the ontological structure of human existence which is necessary for the dialectic of individual and group to take place, and whose temporal and spatial structures he further elaborated in his three-volume work *Ethics*.[1]

Kuki' was inspired by Heidegger's hermeneutic method. He applied a modified form of it to extract the meaning of Japanese culture from a particular aesthetic sensibility or worldview, captured in the concept of *iki*. By means of this hermeneutic method, Kuki identified three sources of the meaning of *iki*: Buddhism, *Shintō*, and *Bushidō*. Methodologically, what is interesting about Kuki's approach is that it incorporates intuition into the process of human self-interpretation (hermeneutics). According to Kuki, humans exist in a context, i.e., in a world understood as a set of meanings in a constant state of change. But while human existence is a process of constant interpretation, we can also have intuitive experiences of the absolute, and these intuitions can provide an orientation in this world—the intuition of the absolute is a source of interpretative standpoints. Influenced by French philosophy, Kuki incorporated notions of intuition from Maine de Biran and Henri Bergson into Heideggerian hermeneutics.

While Kuki's modification of the hermeneutic method was revolutionary, so too was his view about the nature of the ethical ideals that Japanese culture embodies. While the stereotypical view of Japanese culture is that it downplays the importance of the individual and individual freedom (Sugimoto 2014, 3–4), Kuki argued that the normative foundation of Japanese culture is in fact the search for liberation and the maintenance of difference. He believed that the relationship between a *geisha* and her lover is the ideal precisely because it recognizes that each must maintain independence from the other and maintain the freedom of the other: it is a relationship that incorporates difference as an essential element. The view of Japanese society that underlies this ethics is not one oriented toward harmony and unity, but one that embodies the Buddhist ideal of the bodhisattva, who must use the encounter with each person as an opportunity to liberate him or her from the bonds of samsaric existence.

Nishida applied various analytical methods over the years, finally settling on a logical paradigm that David Dilworth translates as the "logic of the place of nothingness" (*bashoteki ronri*; 場所的論理; Dilworth 1987). One of his goals was to articulate the relationship between the "everyday self"—the self whom we believe ourselves to be most of the time—and our "true" self as the manifestation of the dynamic activity of reality (Dilworth 1987, 5–6). By applying this method, Nishida was able to describe the world as a world of constant productive activity and to explain human existence as part of this activity. For him, all human forms of expression, including cultural forms, are both the action of an individual and an expression of the whole of reality. Nishida's view of culture has metaphysical significance because the method he uses to grasp culture and the nature of the social relation underlying it was the very same method that he deployed to describe the structure of the world as a whole from a religious perspective. As a result, the goal that Nishida sets for each culture is necessarily a universal and religious one—just as individuals should live their lives in a way that reflects their true nature as an instance of the manifestation of the dynamic process of birth and death that characterizes reality as a whole, so too should cultures encourage their members to realize their true natures.

THE BACKGROUND TO A STUDY OF JAPANESE CULTURAL THOUGHT IN THE TWENTIETH CENTURY

A study of the cultural philosophy of these three philosophers cannot be complete without placing their views in the context of cultural studies in Japan more generally. Culture has historically played a very important role in Japan, and its study has provided the Japanese with a way to identify and reinforce what they perceive as shared cultural values. An example of this is the *Nihonjinron* literature, which literally means "the discourse of Japaneseness,"[2] a genre that has been in constant production since the end of the Second World War, although a version of it has always existed in Japan (Arisaka 2016, 762–763). As Yoshio Sugimoto explains, at the core of this literature is a view that "Japaneseness" comprises "a set of value orientations that the Japanese are supposed to share" (1999, 82). Of the three authors whose cultural philosophy we have studied in this book, the cultural philosophy of Watsuji and Kuki fit most closely with the *Nihonjinron* image, although their major works predated the period in which *Nihonjinron* emerged. As we have seen, Kuki in particular was interested in articulating a kind of taste as an "ethnic way of being" (*minzokuteki sonzai*; 民族的存在; 2004, 58), which picks up on many of the associations between culture, ethnicity, and race that can be found in *Nihonjinron*.[3]

Another important part of the background to this study is the political—the concepts of culture and society developed by Watsuji, Kuki, and Nishida can all have political consequences when deployed for such ends (Arisaka 2016, 761). Beyond discussions of cultural identity, the discourse of Japanese uniqueness has itself played an important political role in Japan, for instance, as a bulwark against colonialism at the end of the nineteenth and throughout the twentieth centuries (Parkes 1997, 306; Arisaka 2016, 757–59). As Maruyama Masao points out, Japanese politicians and thinkers of the nineteenth century considered it vital to centralize what had been until then a splintered feudal society in order to face the crisis brought about by American demands after the arrival of Commodore Matthew Perry in 1853. Maruyama writes:

> Faced with the external crisis [posed by the American demands], the most urgent necessity was the unification of the divided feudal political forces, and

the reinforcement of the national defenses by the establishment of a powerful central government capable of "manipulating the entire country of Japan as if it were its hands and feet" (Nobuhiro). Stabilization of national life and the development of industrial enterprises were proposed as the preconditions for this. (1974, 364)

On an ideological level, Fukuzawa Yukichi (1835–1901) states the common view of the intellectuals of the period that "the implantation of the concept 'nation' in the minds of the people of the entire country" had become urgent (quoted in Maruyama 1974, 367).[4] In subsequent years, the study of the uniqueness of the Japanese, including the special features of its culture, contributed to the building of a sense of common political cause in Japan and consequently a point of resistance against the perceived threat of European imperial domination (see generally Fukuzawa 2009, Chapter 10).

The interest in Japanese culture continued throughout the Meiji (1868–1912) and Taishō (1912–1926) periods as the process of industrialization and modernization of Japan, much of which was associated with Europeanization and Westernization, continued. The radical social transformation of Japan during this period inevitably led scholars such as Watsuji, Kuki, and Nishida to reflect on whether any aspects of the traditional Japanese way of life could or should be preserved in the face of the often alienating changes that surrounded them. We can turn once again to Fukuzawa for a statement of the confusion in which many intellectuals existed during this period. Having noted how the period after the Meiji Restoration had "caused dissatisfaction with [Japanese] civilization and aroused enthusiasm for Western civilization," he goes on to describe the resulting turmoil:

> The resultant complications and confusion in Japanese society almost defy imagination.... Contemporary Japanese culture is undergoing a transformation in essence, like the transformation of fire in water, like the transition from non-being to being. The suddenness of the change defies description in terms of either reformation or creation. Even to discuss it is extremely difficult. (2009, 2–3)

Natsume Sōseki, who spent a period of study in England from 1901 to 1903 in emotional anguish, describes the emotions that intellectuals like him felt during the Taishō period: "We are all aware that Japan today is not entirely secure. Japan is a poor country—and small. Anything could happen at any time. In that sense all of us must maintain our concern for the nation" (262). And yet, it was still important for the Japanese intellectuals of this era to deal with the perennial problems of human existence: Sōseki continues,

> Nations have always been most punctilious concerning the niceties of diplomatic language but not with respect to the morality of their actions. They swindle and cheat and trick each other every chaotic step of the way. That is why you will have to content yourself with a pretty cheap grade of morality when you make the nation your standard, when you conceive of the nation as an indivisible monolith. Approach life from a foundation of individualism, however, and you arrive at a far loftier morality. (262–263)

While Sōseki recommended a particular brand of individualism as a counterweight to the nationalism toward which the uncertainty of the era seemed to drive many of his contemporaries, others, including Watsuji, Kuki, and Nishida, engaged with Japanese tradition in order to uncover something in it that could serve as a basis for Japanese modernity. Their philosophies of culture and their views about the nature of society that animated them must be studied against the background of an uneasy tension that characterized the Japanese intellectual world in the first half of the twentieth century and that preoccupied many thinkers of that time.

However, another part of the political background was the colonial expansion of Japan after the Sino-Japanese war of 1894–1895 and Russo-Japanese war of 1905 until the end of the Second World War. During the period in which the three philosophers studied in this book were writing, Japan had expanded its empire to various parts of East and Southeast Asia, and as Yoko Arisaka points out, "Political philosophizing and historical context cannot be separated clearly" (2016, 763). Indeed, she is right to warn that there is a double edge to universalism: while the philosophy of Watsuji, Kuki, and Nishida helped the Japanese to coalesce around a sense of unity to resist European domination, the very same discourse could be used to justify Japanese domination in Asia (ibid.). It is for this reason that we have tried throughout our study of Japanese cultural philosophy to identify aspects of it that can be used in this way: to indicate essentialism elements that exist alongside non-essentialist ones.

INSPIRED BY WATSUJI: CULTURE AS AN ONGOING PROCESS OF RESPONDING TO THE PHYSICAL AND SOCIAL ENVIRONMENT

Watsuji's philosophy of culture has inspired many new ways of thinking about what it means to be human and how humans are related to the environment. They include Augustin Berque's *mésologie* (Berque 2011), a development of Watsuji's interpretation of the relationship between the natural and social environment (Berque 2012), Steve Bein's deployment of Watsuji to understand climate change (2017), and Erin McCarthy's development of Watsuji's relational and embodied notion of self (2010). Watsuji's insight was that culture is not limited to a set of particular practices or objects (art, architecture, etc.); culture is an ongoing process (temporal aspect) in which humans are engaged as they respond to the physical and social environment in which they live (spatial aspect). Culture is the expression of this activity that takes place as the interaction between people (and therefore manifest in our ethical relations) and between humans and the environment (and therefore manifest as "climatic" existence). Understood in this way, culture must necessarily differ across the globe: different kinds of adaptations and responses are required to live in different climatic and geographic zones, and this geographical difference therefore contributes to cultural difference.

While expressed in this way Watsuji's theory of culture is distinctly cosmopolitan, we have also seen that he had a tendency to lapse into geographic determinism (Berque 2012, 289)—to see differences in weather and landscape as the cause of cultural difference. In the process of shifting his role from cultural interpreter (indeed, even creator of culture) in *Pilgrimages* to the role of phenomenologist in *Climate and Culture*, certain essentialist and universalistic elements snuck into his thought. In *Pilgrimages*, Watsuji expresses the fact that culture is a kind of experience that we have as we interact with human artifacts (temples, art), the natural environment, and other people. His use of the phenomenological method to draw out the ontological structures of this interaction was accompanied by a tendency to essentialize culture by identifying it with particular forms that he believed this interaction took. Moreover, the role of cultural interpreter that Watsuji adopted in *Pilgrimages* became more authoritative in *Climate and Culture*. Because the early work took the form of a travel journal, the author's impressions and emotional responses were understood to be purely subjective; however the impressions of the author of *Climate and Culture* are presented as being objective.

However, when Watsuji is at his best, for instance at the beginning of *Climate and Culture*, he resists such a simplistic view: climate is not solely the sum of all environmental and physical phenomena—it is a way of experiencing the world. We experience our environment in our responses to it and in our interactions with others. For Watsuji, climate is a phenomenon—an aspect of our experience; it is not separate from human subjectivity, that is, our actual ongoing experiencing of the world.

Watsuji's engagement with European philosophy also provides some useful insights for those with an interest in comparative philosophy. In *Climate and Culture*, Watsuji attempted to situate his phenomenological approach in the context of the European philosophy that influenced him, and this comparison led him to essentialize culture by conceptualizing it—culture became simply an abstract category for understanding particular cultures. He also adopted from these European philosophers a speculative tendency—a desire to use the European concept of culture as a regulative concept for understanding culture throughout the world. Thus by trying to place his own phenomenological study of culture in the context of a European tradition, Watsuji ended up undermining his insight that culture is the way that particular groups experience the unique landscape of a local area. The culture of the temples of Nara is a local culture; but Watsuji sought to extend it to the whole of Japan. Similarly, Japanese culture is local to Japan, but Watsuji, adopting the universalizing gestures of Herder, Kant, Fichte, and Hegel, sought to extend features of Japanese culture to all cultures.

Watsuji's philosophy of culture as expressed in *Climate and Culture* thus manifests a tension between the tendency to consider culture as the expression of a specific social group (those sharing Watsuji's pilgrimage to Nara with him) and as the expression of a much larger group, a tension that belies the fact that the larger the group, the fewer experiences are shared.

Watsuji's phenomenological method could have saved him from slipping into essentialism, but his interpretation of Heideggerian phenomenology sometimes betrayed him. In particular, he had a tendency to psychologize phenomenology—to confuse *mitsein* (being with others) for a particular psychological attitude. This led him to consider culture and ethics to be about a particular mental state or spiritual attitude: a particular outlook on life. Thus in *Culture and Climate*, the culture of each climatic zone—the monsoon zone, the desert, and the meadows—is characterized by a particular way of looking at the world—changeable and unpredictable, pessimistic or cheerful. Indeed, in "The Japanese Spirit," Watsuji identifies Japanese culture with "ways of thinking" characteristic of the samurai. He criticizes Japanese Marxists for failing to recognize the particularly Japanese way in which they have adopted and adapted Marxist ideology. He writes,

> The special characteristic of young Marxists is . . . blindly to denounce Japanese tradition. Therefore, the fact that their very ways of thinking and of promoting their movement very clearly exhibit a special Japanese character is something which they themselves can certainly not feel. But their courage that does not calculate the cost, their spirit of self-sacrifice even in the face of death, their total submission, almost blind submission, to authority—where do these qualities differ from the ways of behavior which appeared in the samurai who fought the civil wars of the Sengoku era. Or again, are they not the same special Japanese qualities that were exhibited by the Christian martyrs of the early Tokugawa era? These qualities were astonishing to the Europeans of the time, but seen from the viewpoint of the way the Japanese warriors comported themselves, they were not especially strange. The same fearless attitude in the face of death

had just become linked to a new faith. In it there clearly appeared the character of the Japanese race that I have elsewhere called its *typhoon* [or monsoon] nature. (1998, 249–50)

We see here Watsuji's tendency to identify "culture" with a "way of thinking" that he labels "spirit." I believe this tendency is inconsistent with the phenomenological methodology, which is anchored in the particularity of experience of a particular person in a particular place interacting with a particular group of others.

Watsuji himself explains the reason for this slippage in the essay "The Japanese Spirit," where he identifies that his goal is to raise up Japanese spirit as an expression of "absolute spirit" (1998, 244–45). And here Yasuo Yuasa is no doubt right about Watsuji's motivation: to distinguish Asian and European cultures (1996, 311), to demonstrate the equal value of Asian cultures, and thereby to resist the racism and chauvinism of the West (1996, 314). Indeed, in "The Japanese Spirit," Watsuji writes about the necessity of finding something that, while anchored in Japanese tradition, is able to unify the Japanese in resisting colonization and the disintegration of Japanese culture as the influence of European culture, politics, and economics grew. He writes,

> In this framework, the problem of the Japanese spirit involves the problem of absolute spirit and at the same time the problem of its particular Japanese form. That particular form is nothing other than the Japanese form of human existence as it can be grasped through its objective manifestations. My position is that this problem can be treated only by taking the historical-climatic structures of human existence as foundational. If thinkers think they can grasp human existence in general apart from its particular racial formations, that will amount to overlooking the importance significance of the climatic character of active subjectivity in human existence, and accordingly will also only be able to grasp the historicity of human existence in merely abstract terms. The forms of racial particularity are not merely accidental, arbitrarily supplemental modalities of spirit. Rather, one finds the most essential determinations of human existence where the absolute spirit manifests itself through the forms of racial particularity. The significance of a world-historical mission that a particular race bears must be clarified only from here. (1998, 245)

The last few sentences make it clear that Watsuji wishes to maintain a place for Japan within the "world-historical mission," and that doing so requires grasping how Japanese culture is the expression of something universal— absolute spirit—that also expresses itself in the encroaching European culture. The danger inherent of Watsuji's strategy for resisting European colonialism is the assertion of a universal framework—which he labels the movement of absolute spirit—that every group must express in order to merit being called "world-historical."

Another tendency that emerges clearly in *Climate and Culture* is Watsuji's tendency to think of groups in terms of political entities such as nations. Research that he was undertaking at the time on the Japanese spirit may have inclined him toward this view. One way of putting this is to say that his phenomenological approach to ethics sometimes confuses phenomenological ethics as a study of human experience with phenomenological ethics as a study of the Japanese ethos. As we have seen, this confusion between culture, nation, ethnicity, and race continues in the views of those who write in the modern *Nihonjinron* genre (Arisaka 2016).

INSPIRED BY KUKI: CULTURAL IDEALS AS ETHICAL IDEALS—A JAPANESE ETHICS OF DIFFERENCE

Kuki's theory of culture will likely be of most interest to those interested in non-Eurocentric forms of an ethics of difference. While one might initially react to Kuki's notion of culture as being chauvinistic because of its exclusive focus on Japanese culture, it also has a critical potential. Indeed, the ideal relationship according to Kuki—the relationship that best expresses an idea of freedom unique to Japanese culture—is that between a *geisha* and her lover. It is strange to think of this relationship as a model for the ethical life, and Kuki's choice was no doubt meant to deny that the ideal could be found in the conventional attitudes of the conservative Japanese bourgeoisie. Kuki's message seems to be that even in samsara—in the fraught relationship between the *geisha* and her lover in which love is unrequited and emotional turmoil a constant—one can find the expression of the infinite. Indeed, perhaps only in this turmoil is one open to the revelation of the absolute.

The integration of a self-critical element in Kuki's notion of culture—that the absolute is expressed in a life that is apparently in turmoil—gives to Kuki's philosophy of culture a critical power that is not contained in Watsuji's. One can justly be critical of the heterosexism of Kuki's choice of ideal relationship and of the problematic portrayal of femininity that it implies. However, I believe that Kuki's iconoclastic choice opens the possibility of seeing nonnormative and transgressive cultures as embodying ethical ideals that can challenge the norm. What the norm considers dirty and amoral can express, as Kuki describes the life of the *geisha*, "the state of mind that is free of grime, unclinging, disinterested, and free from obstacles, and that has removed itself from any egotistical attachment to reality" (Nara 2004, 22).

In other work, I have tried to develop the critical nature of Kuki's ethics by demonstrating its similarities with that of Emmanuel Levinas (Mayeda 2012). For both Kuki and Levinas, the ethical relationship is one in which I recognize that I must always defend the freedom of the other by ensuring the other's independence from me. Indeed, the protection of this difference is essential to preserving the relationship. The relationship between the *geisha* and her lover, Kuki says, must be "a free-spirited flirtation, like a lotus leaf floating freely on the water" (Kuki 2004, 23). Of course, one might observe that the aestheticization of the relationship is itself a form of essentialism and that Kuki overlooks the complexity of Buddhist notions of the relationship between samsara and nirvana in his redeployment of the paradigm.

For Kuki, Japanese culture is expressed as a way of living together with others in accordance with certain eternally unattainable ideals. To seize its meaning, we cannot simply generalize based on specific instances of that culture as expressed in art or architecture. Rather, we must uncover the essential phenomena of consciousness—the experiences—that give it life. This experience is that of freedom, which we experience from time to time in exceptional moments of surprise and wonder. According to Kuki, the Japanese way of being in the world is based on an attitude and a way of life that is anchored in the experience of freedom that we can all access in these exceptional moments. It cannot be taken for granted that just because a person is Japanese that she will live up to the ethical ideal: she must choose well in each relationship to ensure that it embodies the ethics of freedom. Japanese culture, Kuki seems to say, is actually an orientation in life that inclines one toward choosing freedom despite the impossibility of realizing it in this life.

All individuals, whether Japanese or not, experience the absolute through metaphysical intuition which breaks the tedium of phenomenological experience (everyday experience of the sensual). But according to Kuki, for a culture to embody this intuition, it must take metaphysical freedom as its worldview and instill this worldview in its members as an attitude toward life, that is, as a culture.

INSPIRED BY NISHIDA: CULTURE AS WORLD RELIGIOUS CULTURE

We live in an era in which the secular and the religious seem to be at odds. Nishida's philosophy of culture provides a modern way of seeing the secular as sacred, to use the terminology of Herbert Fingarette. As was the case for Kuki, for Nishida, culture embodies ethical ideals. However, Nishida had a more universal approach than Kuki; each culture can be "world-historical": it can express something that he believed is captured in almost every world religion. What is this? It is an understanding that all beings are unique expressions of the absolute, be it conceived as God or absolute nothingness. To evoke the ethical view this embodied, Nishida often cited Kant, who wrote that what awoke in him the greatest wonder was the "starry heavens above me and the moral law within me," a passage which David Dilworth notes Nishida quoted in almost all of his works (1987, 14).

For Nishida, at every level, be it the individual, that of the group or of society as a whole, humans are dynamically active and therefore interactive. It follows that culture must also be the manifestation of the "historical body"—it is a manifestation of the activity of the world that emerges out of past activity (Maraldo 2017, 207). As Nishida explains, "The content of the historical world's self-transformation is culture" (Nishida 1987, 117). However, it is possible for the individual and for a culture to misunderstand themselves: to forget that they are expressions of the self-awareness of the world as dynamic activity. When this occurs, individuals become obsessed with their own thoughts, feelings, and desires—they collapse into the "standpoint of autobiography" (Nishida 1987, 113)—and cultures become mired in secular practices that do not reflect the true nature of what it is to be human (Nishida 1987, 119).

On the individual level, Nishida believed that each person's goal ought to be to return to his or her true self (Nishida 1987, 89), which means to "transcend the self" in the sense of recognizing that we and the world are expressions of "the dynamic equilibrium of the many and the one, a world constituted in the relation of simultaneous presence and absence" (Nishida 1987, 89). The social relation, and therefore also ethics, are essential for revealing this reality: when we interact with others, we recognize our own self-destruction (the limit that the other represents to me) and also our own self-constitution (the other's recognition and affirmation of me). The other's thoughts and feelings are inaccessible to me and therefore the possibility of true communication is always uncertain; and yet over time systems of cultural meaning have emerged that permit us to express ourselves and make ourselves understood. The I-Thou relationship is thus an excellent way of understanding the dynamic nature of the world as the play of self-contradiction, a play of the same and the different.

Nishida's concept of culture and the view of the social relation that it embodies are both vitalist and dialectical: we each live and experience the world as the dynamic movement of reality, which our relationships with others also express. In examining these relationships, we uncover the constant juxtaposition of self and other and thereby come to understand both our true nature and that of the world. As Ōhashi Ryōsuke explains, in Nishida's later philosophy, "the historical world is conceived of in terms of a mutual determination of self and world" (2016, 373).

CONCLUDING WORDS

While this book is a study of the cultural and social philosophy of three creative and original thinkers, at this point, the relationship between their views will no doubt also have become apparent. Thus it will not be surprising to see that the philosophy of Watsuji and Kuki can, in some ways, be understood as the development of different aspects of Nishida's view. Watsuji emphasized the dialectical relationship between individual and group, and therefore he characterized human existence as betweenness (*aidagara*)—the relationship between the two. Kuki was interested in maintaining the separation between self and other as the ground of ethical relationships, and so the absolute for him is something always other—something that one can only access from time to time in moments of wonder and surprise. Unfortunately, the consequence of Kuki's approach is that his concept of the absolute is hypostatized and frozen into a set of ideals—the ethics of the *geisha* and her lover embodied as a way of being with each other. One can tend toward the ideal, but for Kuki, one never reaches it.

Nishida's view, informed by his religious insight, may perhaps hold within it a possibility of liberation that is absent from the philosophy of Watsuji and Kuki. Watsuji had a gift for describing the dialectical relationship between self and other that is a part of Nishida's dialectical interpretation of the relationship between the self and reality; and yet his description of the nothingness that makes this dialectical movement possible does not have the depth or richness of Nishida's. And while Kuki's ethical ideal continues to ring true in the modern world in which we must go beyond simply accepting difference by acting to preserve and maintain it, at the heart of his ethical view is the impossibility of attaining this ideal and of realizing in this samsaric world the freedom and wonder that he experienced when he came in touch with the absolute. On the other hand, for Nishida, there is a true recognition that the failure to attain the ideal is nonetheless a manifestation of the dynamic movement of reality. He exhorted us, to use the language of Kant, to "will well" (2002, 4:393) even when our actions end up being out of alignment with the truth of reality. The cultural philosophy of Watsuji, Kuki, and Nishida all reflect their view that the nature of the social relation is ethical and that culture is a concrete manifestation of this ideal expressed in dynamic form through particular cultural practices.

NOTES

1. Augustin Berque has a very brief but helpful discussion of *aidagara* in Berque (2012, 288).

2. Arisaka calls *nihonjinron* the theory of "Japanese exceptionalism" (1996, 82).

3. As Sugimoto explains, "minzoku" can denote both "ethnicity" and "race." In his words, "Generally speaking . . . *Nihonjinron* defines the Japanese in racial terms with *Nihonjin* comprising most members of the Yamato race and excludes, for example, indigenous Ainus and Okinawans as groups who are administratively Japanese, but not 'genuinely' so. Furthermore, when *Nihonjinron* analysts refer to Japanese culture, they almost invariably mean Japanese *ethnic* culture and imply that the racially defined Japanese are its sole owners" (1999, 82).

4. For Fukuzawa's critique of British colonial practices in India, see (2009, 245–46).

Works Cited

ABBREVIATIONS

An Investigation of Climate: Watsuji 1961.
Koji Junrei: Watsuji 2014.
KSZ: *Kuki Shūzō Zenshū* (『九鬼周造全集』) Kuki, Shūzō. 1990. *The Complete Works of Kuki Shūzō*. Tokyo: Iwanami Shoten.
NKZ: *Nishida Kitarō Zenshū* (『西田幾多郎全集』). Nishida, Kitarō. 1965–6. *The Complete Works of Nishida Kitarō*. Tokyo: Iwanami Shoten.
Pilgrimages: Watsuji 2012.
TJZ: *Tosaka Jun Zenshū* (『戸坂 潤全集』). Tosaka, Jun. 1966. *The Complete Works of Tosaka Jun*. Tokyo: Keisō-Shobō.
WTZ: *Watsuji Tetsurō Zenshū* (『和辻哲郎全集』) Watsuji, Tetsurō. 1960–3. *The Complete Works of Watsuji Tetsurō*. Tokyo: Iwanami Shoten.

WORKS CITED

Note: In accordance with Asian convention, authors' names are in the order of family name followed by given name. In consequence, there is no comma separating the two.

Allison, Henry E. 2009. "Teleology and History in Kant: The Critical Foundations of Kant's Philosophy of History." In *Kant's Idea for a Universal History with a Cosmopolitan Aim: A Critical Guide*, 24–45. Edited by A. Oksenberg Rorty and J. Schmidt. Cambridge: Cambridge University Press.

Ameriks, Karl. 2009. "The Purposive Development of Human Capacities." In *Kant's Idea for a Universal History with a Cosmopolitan Aim: A Critical Guide*, 46–67. Edited by A. Oksenberg Rorty and J. Schmidt. Cambridge: Cambridge University Press.

Arisaka Yoko. 1996. "The Nishida Enigma: 'The Principle of the New World Order'." *Monumenta Nipponica* 51(1): 81–105.

———. 2016. "The Controversial Cultural Identity of Japanese Philosophy." In *The Oxford Handbook of Japanese Philosophy*, 755–775. Edited by B. W. Davis. Oxford: Oxford University Press.

Axtell, G. S. 1991. "Nishida Kitarō's Logic of Place and Western Dialectical Thought." *Philosophy East and West* 41(2): 163–184.

Ball, Stephen J. 2010. *Foucault and Education: Disciplines and Knowledge*. London: Routledge. First published in 1990.

Barnard, F. M. 1965. *Herder's Social and Political Thought: From Enlightenment to Nationalism*. Oxford: Oxford University Press.

Bein, Steve. 2011. "Introductions." In *Purifying Zen: Watsuji Tetsurō's Shamon Dōgen*. Edited by S. Bein. Honolulu: University of Hawai'i Press.

———. 2017. "Climate Change as Existentialist Threat: Watsuji, Greimas, and the Nature of Opposites." In *Japanese Environmental Philosophy*, 105–120. Edited by J. Baird Callicott and James McRae. New York: Oxford University Press.

Bellah, Robert N. 1910. *Time and Free Will: An Essay on the Immediate Data of Consciousness*. Translated by F. L. Pogson. London: George Allen & Unwin. Originally published as *Essai sur les données immédiates de la conscience*. Paris: Presses universitaires de France, 1889.

———. 1965. "Japan's Cultural Identity: Some Reflections on the Work of Watsuji Tetsurō." *The Journal of Asian Studies* 24(4): 573–594.

Bergson, Henri. 1932. "Les deux sources de la morale et de la religion." In *Henri Bergson: Œuvres complètes*. Paris: Arvensa Editions. https://www.arvensa.com.

———. 1969. *La pensée et le mouvant. Essais et conférences*. Paris: Les presses universitaires de France. Originally published in 1934 by Félix Arcan in Paris.

———. 2003. *La pensée et le mouvant. Essais et conférences*. Electronic version of Bergson 1969. http://classiques.uqac.ca/classiques/bergson_henri/pensee_mouvant/pensee_mouvant.html.

———. 2007. "Philosophical Intuition." In *The Creative Mind: An Introduction to Metaphysics*. Translated by Mabelle L. Andison. Mineola, NY: Dover. First presented as a lecture in Bologna on April 10th, 1911.

Bernasconi, Robert. 2000. "With What Must the Philosophy of World History Begin? On the Racial Basis of Hegel's Eurocentrism." *Nineteenth-Century Contexts* 22: 171–201.

Bernier, Bernard. 2006. "National Communion: Watsuji Tetsurō's Conception of Ethics, Power, and the Japanese Imperial State." *Philosophy East & West* 56(1): 84–105.

Berque, Augustin. 2011. *Fūdo: le milieu humain*. Paris: CNRS Éditions.

———. 2012. "Fûdo (le milieu humain): des intuitions watsujiennes à une mésologie". In *Repenser la nature: Dialogue philosophique, Europe, Asie,*

Amériques, 285–300. Edited by Jean-Philippe Pierron and Marie-Hélène Parizeau. Québec: Presses de l'Université Laval.

Bieda, Ken. 1970. *The Structure and Operation of the Japanese Economy.* Sydney, New York: Wiley.

Bourdieu, Pierre, and J.-C. Passeron. 1964. *Les héritiers, les étudiants et la culture.* Paris: Ed de Minuit. Translated as P. Bourdieu and J.-C. Passeron. 1979. *The Inheritors, French Students and Their Relation to Culture.* Chicago-London: University of Chicago Press.

Breazeale, Daniel, and Tom Rockmore, eds. 2016. *Fichte's Addresses to the German Nation Reconsidered.* Albany, NY: SUNY Press.

Bubner, Rüdiger. 1991. "Hegel and the End of History." *Bulletin of the Hegel Society of Great Britain* 12(1–2): 15–23.

———. 2003. *The Innovations of Idealism.* Translated by Nicholas Walker. Cambridge: Cambridge University Press. Originally published as *Innovationen des Idealismus. Neue Studien zur Philosophie.* Göttingen: Vandenhoek & Ruprecht, 1995.

Carter, Robert E. 2013. *The Kyoto School: An Introduction.* Albany, NY: State University of New York Press.

Cassirer, Ernst. 2011. *Zur Logik der Kulturwissenschaften.* Hamburg: Meiner.

———. 2015. "Herman Cohen and the Renewal of Kantian Philosophy." In *The Neo-Kantian Reader*, 221–235. Edited by Sebastian Luft. London: Routledge. Translation of "Hermann Cohen und die Erneuerung der Kantischen Philosophie." (1912) *Kantstudien* 17: 252–273.

Ching, Julia. 1993. *Chinese Religions.* Maryknoll, NY: Orbis.

Clark, John. 1997. *Reflections on Japanese Taste.* Sydney: Power Publications.

Cohen, H. Floris. 2005. "The Onset of the Scientific Revolution: Three Near-Simultaneous Transformations." In *The Science of Nature in the Seventeenth Century: Patterns of Change in Early Modern Natural Philosophy*, 9–33. Edited by Peter R. Anstey and John A. Schuster. Dordrecht: Springer. DOI: 10.1007/1-4020-3703-1.

Comte, Auguste. 1974. *The Essential Comte: Selected from Cours de philosophie positive (1830–42).* Edited by Stanislav Andreski. Translated by Margaret Clarke. London: Routledge.

Couzens Hoy, David. 1993. "Heidegger and the Hermeneutic Turn." In *The Cambridge Companion to Heidegger*, 170–194. Edited by Charles Guignon. Cambridge: Cambridge University Press.

Crawcour, Sydney. 1980. "Alternative Models of Japanese Society: An Overview." *Social Analysis* 5/6: 184–187.

Damasio, Antonio. 2018. *The Strange Order of Things: Life, Feeling, and the Making of Cultures.* Toronto: Penguin Random House.

Davis, Bret W. 2006. *Toward a World of Worlds. Nishida, the Kyoto School, and the Place of Cross-Cultural Dialogue*, 205–245. Edited by J. W. Heisig.

———. 2013. "Heidegger and Asian Philosophy." In *The Bloomsbury Companion to Heidegger*, 459–471. Edited by François Raffoul and Eric S. Nelson. New York: Bloomsbury Academic.

———, ed. 2016. *The Oxford Handbook of Japanese Philosophy*. Oxford: Oxford University Press. DOI: 10.1093/oxfordhb/9780199945726.013.26.

Dawkins, Richard. 1976. *The Selfish Gene*. Oxford: Oxford University Press.

Dear, Michael J., and Steven Flusty. 2002. *The Spaces of Postmodernity: Readings in Human Geography*. Oxford: Blackwell.

Dennett, Daniel. 1995. *Darwin's Dangerous Idea*. New York: Simon and Schuster.

———. 2017. *From Bacteria to Bach and Back: The Evolution of Minds*. New York: W.W. Norton.

Derrida, Jacques. 1978. "Violence and Metaphysics." In *Writing and Difference*. Translated by Alan Bass. Chicago, IL: University of Chicago Press. Originally published as "Violence et métaphysique. Essai sur la pensé d'Emmanuel Levinas." In *L'Écriture et la différence*. Edited by Jacques Derrida. Paris: Editions du Seuil, 1967.

Descartes, René. 1994. "Discourse on the Method." In *The Philosophical Writings of Descartes*, vol. 1, 101–151. Edited by John Cottingham, Robert Stoothoff, and Dugald Murdoch. Cambridge: Cambridge University Press. Originally published in 1637.

Dilworth, David A. 1987. "Introduction: Nishida's Critique of the Religious Consciousness." In *Last Writings: Nothingness and the Religious Worldview*, 1–45. Translated with an Introduction by David A. Dilworth.

Dilworth, David A., Valdo H. Viglielmo, and Agustin Jacinto Zavala, eds. 1998. *Sourcebook for Modern Japanese Philosophy: Selected Documents*. Westport, CT: Greenwood Press.

Dreyfus, Hubert L. 1993. "Heidegger on the Connection Between Nihilism, Art, Technology and Politics." In *The Cambridge Companion to Heidegger*, 289–316. Edited by Charles Guignon. Cambridge: Cambridge University Press.

———. 1995. *Being-in-the-World: A Commentary on Heidegger's Being and Time*. Cambridge, MA: MIT Press.

Dumas, Jean-Louis. 1972. "Taine, Lecteur de Hegel." *Les Études philosophiques* 2: 155–166.

Dupré, Louis. 1998. "Kant's Theory of History and Progress." *The Review of Metaphysics* 51(4): 813–828.

Durkheim, Emile. 1964. *The Rules of Sociological Method*. Edited by George E. Catlin. Translated by Sarah A. Solovay and John H. Mueller. New York: Free Press.

Elwood, Brian D. "The Problem of the Self in the Later Nishida and in Sartre." *Philosophy East and West* 44(2): 303–316.

Erismann, Christophe. 2008. "The Trinity, Universals, and Particular Substances: Philoponus and Roscelin." *Traditio* 63: 277–305.

Falser, Michael. 2015. "The Graeco-Buddhist Style of Gandhara: A "Storia Ideological," Or: How a Discourse Makes a Global History of Art." *Journal of Art Historiography* 13: 1–53.

Faure, Bernard. 1993. *Chan Insights and Oversights*. Princeton, NJ: Princeton University Press.

Feenberg, Andrew. 1999. "Experience and Culture: Nishida's Path 'to the Things Themselves'." *Philosophy East and West* 49(1): 28–44.
Fichte, J. G. 1978. *Reden an die deutsche Nation*. Meiner: Hamburg. Originally published in 1808.
———. 2008. *Fichte: Addresses to the German Nation*. Translated by Gregory Moore. Cambridge: Cambridge University Press.
Figal, Günter. 2000. *Heidegger zur Einführung*. Hamburg: Junius.
Förster, Eckart. 2009. "The Hidden Plan of Nature." In *Kant's Idea for a Universal History with a Cosmopolitan Aim: A Critical Guide*, 187–199. Edited by A. Oksenberg Rorty and J. Schmidt. Cambridge: Cambridge University Press.
Foucault, Michel. 1979. *Discipline and Punish: The Birth of the Prison*. New York: Vintage Books. First published in 1975 as *Surveiller et punir: Naissance de la prison*. Paris: Gallimard.
Fujita Masakatsu. 2002.「『「いき」の構造』再考」(*"Iki no kōzō" saikō*; "Reconsidering 'Iki no Kōzō'"). In *Kuki Shūzō no sekai*, 117–138. Edited by Sakabe Megumi, Fujita Masakatsu, and Washida Kyokazu. Kyoto: Minerva Shobo.
———. 2016. *The Development of Nishida's Philosophy: Pure Experience, Place, Action-Intuition*. Edited by Bret W. Davis. DOI: 10.1093/oxfordhb/9780199945726.013.21.
Fukuzawa Yukichi. 2009. *An Outline of a Theory of Civilization*, vol. III. Translated by David A. Dilworth and G. Cameron Hurst. New York: Columbia University Press. Translation of *Bunmeiron no gairyaku*『文明論之概略』(1875).
Funayama Shinichi. 1999. *Taishō tetsugakushi kenkyū* (『大正哲学史研究』, *Studies in the History of Philosophy in the Taisho Era*). Tokyo: Kobushi Shobō.
Furukawa Yūji. 2015. *Gūzen to unmei: Kuki Shūzō no rinrigaku* (『偶然と運命：九鬼周造の倫理学』, *Chance and Destiny: The Ethics of Kuki Shūzō*). Kyoto: Nakanishiya.
Gadamer, Hans-Georg. 2000. "Subjectivity and Intersubjectivity, Subject and Person." *Continental Philosophy Review* 33: 275–287. Translation of "Subjektivität und Intersubjektivität, Subjekt, und Person." In *Gesammelte Werke*, vol. 10, 87–99. Tübingen: JCB Mohr.
———. 2013. *Truth and Method*. London: Bloomsbury Academic.
Gerstle, C. Andrew. 2000. *18th Century Japan: Culture and Society*. London, New York: Routledge.
Graham, Julie. 1992. "Anti-Essentialism and Overdetermination: A Response to Dick Peet." *Antipode* 24(2): 141–156.
Grosz, Elizabeth. 2016. "The Other Within: The Relational Self in Nishida's Corpus." In *Critical Perspectives on Japanese Philosophy*, 219–251. Edited by T. Morisato.
Gunn, J. Alexander. 1922. *Modern French Philosophy: A Study of the Development Since Comte*. New York: Dodd, Mead and Co.
Haglund, Elaine. 1984. "Japan: Cultural Considerations." *International Journal of Intercultural Relations* 8(1): 61–76.
Hakeda, Yoshito. 1893. *The Awakening of Faith in the Mahayana*. New York: Columbia University Press. Reprinted 2006.

Hamlin, Cyrus, and John Michael Krois, eds. 2004. *Symbolic Forms and Cultural Studies: Ernst Cassirer's Theory of Culture.* New Haven, CT: Yale University Press.

Harris, H. S. 1991. "The End of History in Hegel." *Bulletin of the Hegel Society of Great Britain* 12(1–2): 1–14.

Hatab, Lawrence J. 2000. *Ethics and Finitude: Heideggerian Contributions to Moral Philosophy.* Lanham, MD: Rowman & Littlefield.

Hatano Seiichi. 1935. *Philosophy of Religion.* (*Shūkyō tetsugaku*; 『宗教哲学』). Tokyo: Iwanami Shoten.

Hegel, G. W. F. 1990. *Encyclopedia of the Philosophical Sciences in Outline and Critical Writings.* Edited by Ernst Behler. New York: Continuum.

Heidegger, Martin. 1977. "The Age of the World Picture." Translated by William Lovitt. In *The Question Concerning Technology and Other Essays*, 115–154. Edited by William Lovitt. New York: Harper & Row.

———. 1982. *The Basic Problems of Phenomenology.* Translated by Albert Hofstadter. Bloomington, IN: Indiana University Press. Translation of *Die Grundprobleme der Phänomenologie.* Published as vol. 24 of the *Gesamtausgabe.* Frankfurt a.M.: Vittorio Klostermann, 1975. Given as a series of lectures at the University of Marburg in the summer semester of 1927.

———. 1985. *History of the Concept of Time.* Translated by Theodore Kisiel. Bloomington, IN: Indiana University Press. Translation of *Prolegomena zur Geschichte des Zeitbegriffs.* Published as vol. 20 of the *Gesamtausgabe.* Frankfurt a.M.: Vittorio Klostermann, 1979. Given as a series of lectures at the University of Marburg in the summer semester of 1925.

———. 1996. *Being and Time.* Translated by Joan Stambaugh. Albany, NY: SUNY Press. Translation of Heidegger. 1953. *Sein und Zeit.* Tübingen: Max Niemeyer Verlag. Originally published in 1927.

———. 1999. *Ontology: The Hermeneutics of Facticity.* Translated by John Van Buren. Bloomington, IN: Indiana University Press. Translation of *Ontologie (Hermeneutik der Faktizität).* Originally given as a series of lectures at Freiburg University in the summer semester of 1923. Published as vol. 63 of the *Gesamtausgabe.* Frankfurt a.M.: Vittorio Klosterman, 1988.

Heisig, James W. 2006. *Frontiers of Japanese Philosophy*, vol. 1. Nagoya: Nanzan Institue for Religion and Culture.

———. 2012. "Nothing and Nowhere East and West: The Hint of a Common Ground." *Journal of the Theoretical Humanities* 17(3): 17–30.

Heisig, James W., and John C. Maraldo, eds. 1994. *Rude Awakenings: Zen, the Kyoto School, and the Question of Nationalism.* Honolulu: University of Hawai'i Press.

Herder, Johann Gottfried. 1969. "Ideas for a Philosophy of the History of Mankind." In *J.G. Herder on Social and Political Culture.* Edited by F. M. Barnard. London: Cambridge University Press.

———. 1985. *Gottfried Herder: Werke in zehn Bänden.* Edited by Günter Arnold, Martin Bollacher, et al. Frankfurt a.M.: Deutscher Klassiker Verlag.

———. 2004. *Another Philosophy of History and Selected Political Writings.* Edited by Iioannis D. Evrigesnis and Daniel Pellerin. Indianapolis: Hackett.

Hodge, Joanna. 1995. *Heidegger and Ethics.* London: Routledge.

Hodgson, Peter C. 2012. *Shapes of Freedom: Hegel's Philosophy of World History in Theological Perspective*. Oxford: Oxford University Press.

Husserl, Edmund. 1970. *The Crisis of the European Sciences and Transcendental Phenomenology*. Translated by David Carr. Evanston, IL: Northwestern University Press. Translation of Husserl. 1962. *Die Krisis der europäischen Wissenschaften und die transzendentale Phänomenologie: Eine Einleitung in die phänomenologische Philosophie*. The Hague: Martinus Nijhoff. Originally given as a series of lectures in Vienna in 1935 and published in 1936.

Inglis, Fred. 1993. *Cultural Studies*. Oxford: Blackwell.

Inoue, Mitsusada. 1979. "Postface." In *Fūdo: le milieu humain*, 321–330. Translated by A. Berque. Paris: CNRS Éditions, 2011.

Jacinto Z., Agustin. 1994. "The Return of the Past: Tradition and the Political Microcosm in the Later Nishida." In *Rude Awakenings: Zen, the Kyoto School, and the Question of Nationalism*, 132–148. Edited by J. W. Heisig and J. C. Maraldo. Honolulu: University of Hawai'i Press.

Janz, Bruce B. 2011. "Watsuji Tetsuro, Fudo, and Climate Change." *Journal of Global Ethics* 7(2): 173–184.

Jefferson, Thomas. 2011. "Notes on the State of Virginia." In *Call and Response: Key Debates in African American Studies*. Edited by Henry Louis Gates and Jennifer Burton. New York: W.W. Norton & Company.

Johnson, David. 2014. "Perception, Expression, and the Continuity of Being: Some Intersections Between Nishida and Gadamer." *Asian Philosophy* 24(1): 48–66.

Kant, Immanuel. 1956. *Critique of Practical Reason*. Translated by Lewis White Beck. Indianapolis: Bobbs-Merrill.

———. 2000. *Critique of the Power of Judgment*. Cambridge: Cambridge University Press. Translated by Paul Guyer and Eric Matthews. Translation of *Kritik der Urteilskraft* (1790).

———. 2002. *Groundwork for the Metaphysics of Morals*. Translated by Allen W. Wood. New Haven: Yale University Press. Translation based on the Akademie Ausgabe of *Kants Schriften*. Berlin: W. deGruyter, 1902.

———. 2007a. "An Answer to the Question: 'What is Enlightenment?'" In *Kant: Political Writings*, 54–60. Edited by H. S. Reiss. Cambridge: Cambridge University Press.

———. 2007b. "Idea for a Universal History with a Cosmopolitan Purpose." In *Kant: Political Writings*, 41–53. Edited by H. S. Reiss. Cambridge: Cambridge University Press.

———. 2014a. "Idea for a Universal History with a Cosmopolitan Aim." Translated by Allen W. Wood. In *Immanuel Kant: Anthropology, History, and Education*, 107–120. Edited by Günter Zöller and Robert B. Louden. Cambridge: Cambridge University Press. Originally published in 1784.

———. 2014b. "Review of J.G. Herder's Ideas for the Philosophy of the History of Humanity." Parts I and II translated by Allen W. Wood. In *Immanuel Kant: Anthropology, History, and Education*, 121–142. Edited by Günter Zöller and Robert B. Louden. Cambridge: Cambridge University Press. Originally published in 1785.

Käufer, Stephan, and Anthony Chemero. 2016. *Phenomenology: An Introduction.* Cambridge: Polity Press.

Kearney, Richard, and Mara Rainwater, eds. 1996. *The Continental Philosophy Reader.* London: Routledge.

Keller, Pierre. 1999. *Husserl and Heidegger on Human Experience.* Cambridge: Cambridge University Press.

Kleinschmidt, Peter. 1966. *Die Masken der Gigaku, der ältesten Theaterform Japans.* Wiesbaden: O. Harassowitz.

Kockelmans, Joseph J. 1994. *Edmund Husserl's Phenomenology.* West Lafayette, IN: Purdue University Press.

Krois, John Michael. 1987. *Cassirer: Symbolic Forms and History.* New Haven, CT: Yale University Press.

Krummel, John. 2015. *Nishida Kitarō's Chiasmatic Chorology.* Bloomington, IN: Indiana University Press.

Kuehn, Manfred. 2009. "Reason as a Species Characteristic." In *Kant's Idea for a Universal History with a Cosmopolitan Aim: A Critical Guide*, 68–93. Edited by A. Oksenberg Rorty and J. Schmidt. Cambridge: Cambridge University Press.

Kuki Shūzō. *Gendai Furansu tetsugaku kōgi* (『現代フランス哲学講義』 (*Lectures on Contemporary French Philosophy*)). KSZ 8.

———. 1939. *Ningen to jitsuzon tetsugaku* 『人間と実存』 (*Human Beings and Existence*). Tokyo: Iwanami Shoten.

———. 1998a. "The Expression of the Infinite in Japanese Art." Presented as a Lecture at Pontigny, France on August 17th, 1928. In *Sourcebook for Modern Japanese Philosophy: Selected Documents*, 207–2020. Edited by D. A. Dilworth, V. H. Viglielmo, and A. J. Zavala. Westport, CT: Greenwood Press.

———. 1998b. "The Idea of Time and the Repossession of Time in the Orient." Presented as a Lecture at Pontigny, France on August 11th, 1928. In *Sourcebook for Modern Japanese Philosophy: Selected Documents*, 207–220. Edited by D. A. Dilworth, V. H. Viglielmo, and A. J. Zavala. Westport, CT: Greenwood Press.

———. 2004. "The Structure of Iki." In *The Structure of Detachment: The Aesthetic Vision of Kuki Shūzō, with a Translation of Iki no kōzō.* Edited by Hiroshi Nara. Honolulu: University of Hawai'i Press.

LaFleur, William R. 1990. "A Turning in Taishō: Asia and Europe in the Early Writings of Watsuji Tetsurō." In *Culture and Identity: Japanese Intellectuals During the Interwar Years*, 234–256. Edited by Thomas J. Rimer. Princeton, NJ: Princeton University Press.

Lefebvre, Lucien. 1949. *La terre et l'évolution humaine: introduction géographique à l'histoire.* Paris: A. Michel.

Levinas, Emmanuel. 1987. *Time and the Other.* Translated by Richard A. Cohen. Pittsburgh: Duquesne University Press.

Liederbach, Hans Peter. 2012. "Watsuji Tetsurō on Spatiality: Existence Within the Context of Climate and History." *Shakaigakubu kiyō* (*Bulletin of the Sociology Department*) 114. https://www.kwansei.ac.jp/s_sociology/attached/0000021707.PDF.

Lucken, Michael. 2015. *Nakai Masakazu. Naissance de la théorie critique au Japon.* Dijon: Les presses du réel.
Luft, Sebastian. 2015. *The Space of Culture: Towards a Neo-Kantian Philosophy of Culture (Cohen, Natorp, and Cassirer).* Oxford: Oxford University Press.
Maine de Biran, François-Pierre Gontier. 1834. *Nouvelles considérations sur les rapports du physique et du moral de l'homme.* Paris: Ladrange.
———. 1841. "Influence de l'habitude sur la faculté de penser." In *Œuvres Philosophiques de Maine de Biran*, vol. 1. Paris: Ladrange. Originally published in 1802.
———. 1859. "Essai sur les fondements de la psychologie." In *Oeuvres Inédites de Maine de Biran.* Paris: Dezobry, E. Magdeleine et Cie.
Maraldo, John C. 2017. *Japanese Philosophy in the Making I: Crossing Paths with Nishida.* Nagoya: Chisokudo.
Marra, Michael F., ed. 2001. *A History of Modern Japanese Aesthetics.* Honolulu: University of Hawai'i Press.
———. 2004. *Kuki Shuzo: A Philosopher's Poetry and Poetics.* Honolulu: University of Hawai'i Press.
Maruyama Masao. 1974. *Studies in the Intellectual History of Tokugawa Japan.* Translated by Mikiso Hane. Princeton, NJ: Princeton University Press.
Marx, Werner. 1971. *Heidegger and the Tradition.* Translated by Theodore Kisiel and Murray Green. Northwestern University Press. Translation of Marx, *Heidegger und die Tradition: Eine problemgeschichtliche Einführung in die Grundbestimmungen des Seins.* Stuttgart: W. Kohlhammer, 1961.
———. 1992. *Towards a Phenomenological Ethics: Ethos and the Life-World.* Albany, NY: SUNY Press.
Mayeda, Graham. 2008. "Is there a Method to Chance? Contrasting Kuki Shūzō's Phenomenological Methodology in The Problem of Contingency with that of his Contemporaries Wilhelm Windelband and Heinrich Rickert." In *Frontiers of Japanese Philosophy 2: Neglected Themes and Hidden Variations*, 7–35. Edited by Victor S. Hori and Melissa Curley. Nagoya: Nanzan Institute for Religion and Cultures.
———. 2012. "Time for Ethics: Temporality and the Ethical Ideal in Emmanuel Levinas and Kuki Shūzō." *Comparative and Continental Philosophy* 4(1): 105–124.
———. 2016. "Kuki Shūzō: A Phenomenology of Fate and Chance and an Aesthetics of the Floating World." In *The Oxford Handbook of Japanese Philosophy*, 523–542. Edited by B. W. Davis. Oxford: Oxford University Press.
McCarthy, Erin. 2010. *Ethics Embodied: Rethinking Selfhood Through Continental, Japanese, and Feminist Philosophies.* Lanham, MD: Lexington.
———. 2016. *Watsuji Tetsurō: The Mutuality of Climate and Culture and an Ethics of Betweenness.* Edited by B. W. Davis.
McMullin, Irene. 2013. *Time and the Shared World: Heidegger on Social Relations.* Evanston, IL: Northwestern University Press.
Meacham, Darian, and Joseph Spadola, eds. 2016. *Maine de Biran: The Relationship Between the Physical and the Moral in Man.* London: Bloomsbury.

Mitchell, Don. 2000. *Cultural Geography: A Critical Introduction*. Oxford: Blackwell.

Moran, Dermot. 2000. *Introduction to Phenomenology*. London: Routledge.

———. 2011. "Gadamer and Husserl on Horizon, Intersubjectivity and the Life-World." In *Gadamer's Hermeneutics and the Art of Conversation*, 73–94. Edited by Andrzej Wierciński. Münster: Lit.

Morisato Takeshi, ed. 2016. *Critical Perspectives on Japanese Philosophy*. Nagoya: Nanzan Institute for Religion and Culture.

Najita Tetsuo, and H. D. Harootunian. 1993. "Japanese Revolt Against the West: Political and Cultural Criticism in the Twentieth Century." In *The Cambridge History of Japan*. Edited by Peter Duus. Cambridge: Cambridge University Press.

Nara Hiroshi. 2004. *The Structure of Detachment: The Aesthetic Vision of Kuki Shūzō with a translation of* Iki no kōzō. Honolulu: University of Hawai'i Press.

———. 2012. "Introduction to the Translation of Koji Junrei." In *Pilgrimages to the Ancient Temples in Nara*, ix–xxxiv. Translated by Hiroshi Nara. Portland: Merwin Asia.

Natsume Sōseki. 2009. *Theory of Literature and Other Critical Writings*. Edited by Michael K. Bourdaghs, Atsuko Ueda, and Joseph A. Murphy. New York: Columbia University Press.

Nicolas, Auguste. 1858. *Étude sur Maine de Biran d'après le journal intime de ses pensées*. Paris: Auguste Vaton.

Nishida Kitarō. 1973. *Art and Morality*. Translated by David A. Dilworth and Valdo H. Viglielmo. Honolulu: University of Hawai'i Press.

———. 1987. *Last Writings: Nothingness and the Religious World View*. Translated by David A. Dilworth. Honolulu: University of Hawai'i Press.

———. 1990. *An Inquiry into the Good*. Translated by Masao Abe and Christopher Ives. New Haven: Yale University Press. Translation of *Zen no kenkyū* 『善の研究』, NKZ 1.

———. 1998a. "The Forms of Culture of the Classical Periods of East and West Seen from a Metaphysical Perspective." In *Sourcebook for Modern Japanese Philosophy*, 21–36. Edited by D. A. Dilworth, V. H. Viglielmo, and A. J. Zavala. Westport, CT: Greenwood Press.

———. 1998b. "The Historical Body." In *Sourcebook for Modern Japanese Philosophy*, 37–53. Edited by D. A. Dilworth, V. H. Viglielmo, and A. J. Zavala. Westport, CT: Greenwood Press.

———. 1998c. "The World as Identity of Absolute Contradiction." In *Sourcebook for Modern Japanese Philosophy*, 54–72. Edited by D. A. Dilworth, V. H. Viglielmo, and A. J. Zavala. Westport, CT: Greenwood Press.

———. 1998d. "Fundamental Principles of a New World Order." In *Sourcebook for Modern Japanese Philosophy*, 73–77. Edited by D. A. Dilworth, V. H. Viglielmo, and A. J. Zavala. Westport, CT: Greenwood Press.

———. 1998e. "On the National Polity." In *Sourcebook for Modern Japanese Philosophy*, 78–95. Edited by D. A. Dilworth, V. H. Viglielmo, and A. J. Zavala. Westport, CT: Greenwood Press.

———. 2003a. *L'Éveil à soi*. Translated by Jacynthe Tremblay. Paris: CNRS Editions.

———. 2003b. "Je et tu." In *Nishida Kitarō 2003a*, 95–144. Translation of *Watashi to nanji*『私と汝』, NKZ 6: 341–427.

———. 2005. "General Summary." Translated by Robert Wargo. In *Wargo*, 186–216. From Nishida's longer work, *The System of Self-Consciousness of the Universal*『一般者の自覚的体系』. NKZ 5: 419–464.

———. 2011. "The Eternal in Art and Poetry." In *Japanese Philosophy: A Sourcebook*, 659–662. Edited by James W. Heisig, Thomas P. Kasulis, and John C. Maraldo. Honolulu: University of Hawai'i Press. This is an extract from Nishida's essay "Goethe's Background" (『ゲーテの背景』), published in NKZ 7: 321–330. First published in 1932.

———. 2015. *De ce qui agit à ce qui voit*. Translated by Jacynthe Tremblay. Montréal: Presses de l'Université de Montréal. Translation of *Hataraku mono kara miru mono e*『働くものから見るものへ』, NKZ 4.

Nishitani Keiji. 2016. *Nishida Kitarō: The Man and His Thought*. 2nd ed. Translated by Yamamoto Seisaku and James W. Heisig. Nagoya: Chisokudō. Translation of *Nishida Kitarō. Sono hito to shisō*『西田幾多郎——その人と思想』. Originally published in 1985.

Obama Yoshinobu. 2006. *Kuki Shūzō no tetsugaku: hyōhaku no tamashii*『九鬼周造の哲学：漂白の魂』(*The Philosophy of Kuki Shūzō: The Wandering Spirit*). Tokyo: Showado.

Ōhashi Ryōsuke. 2017. "The Kyoto School: Transformations Over Three Generations." In *The Oxford Handbook of Japanese Philosophy*, 367–387. Edited by B. W. Davis. Oxford: Oxford University Press.

Okakura, Kakuzō (Tenshin). 2007. *The Ideals of the East: With Special Reference to the Art of Japan*. Berkeley, CA: Stone Bridge Press. Originally published in 1904 by E. P. Dutton & Co.

Oksenberg Rorty, Amélie, and James Schmidt, eds. 2009. *Kant's Idea for a Universal History with a Cosmopolitan Aim: A Critical Guide*. Cambridge: Cambridge University Press.

Olafson, Frederick. 1998. *Heidegger and the Ground of Ethics: A Study of Mitsein*. Cambridge: Cambridge University Press.

Oswell, David. 2006. *Culture and Society: An Introduction to Cultural Studies*. London: Sage.

Paetzold, Heinz. 2008. "Anfänge Hegels in Japan. Aspekte der Philosophie Tetsuro Watsujis mit Blick auf Hegel." In *Anfänge bei Hegel*. Edited by Wolfdietrich Schmied-Kowarzik and Heinz Eidam. Kassel: Kassel University Press.

Parkes, Graham. 1997. "The Putative Fascism of the Kyoto School and the Political Correctness of the Modern Academy." *Philosophy East and West* 47(3): 305–336.

Peerenboom, R. P. 1991. "The Religious Foundations of Nishida's Philosophy." *Asian Philosophy* 1(2): 161–173.

Peet, Richard. 1985. "The Social Origins of Environmental Determinism." *Annals of the Association of American Geographers* 75(3): 309–333.

Pincus, Leslie. 1996. *Authenticating Culture in Imperial Japan: Kuki Shūzō and the Rise of National Aesthetics*. Berkeley: University of California Press.

Ray, Himanshu Prabha, ed. 2018. *Buddhism and Gandhara: An Archaeology of Museum Collections*. London: Routledge.

Ricoeur, Paul. 1967. *Husserl: An Analysis of His Phenomenology*. Translated by Edward G. Ballard. Evanston, IL: Northwestern University Press.

Robbins, Derek. 2005. "The Origins, Early Development and Status of Bourdieu's Concept of 'Cultural Capital'." *The British Journal of Sociology* 56(1): 13–30.

Sakabe Megumi. 1988. "Watsuji Testsuroo: A Case of Philosophical Thinking in Modern Japan." In *Traditional Thought and Ideological Change: Sweden and Japan in the Age of Industrialization*, 155–170. Edited by S. Cho and N. Runeby. Stockholm: University of Stockholm.

———. 1990. *Fuzai no Uta. Kuki Shūzō no sekai*『不在の歌──九鬼周造の世界』(*Songs of Absence: The World of Kuki Shūzō*). Tokyo: TBS Britannica.

Sakabe Megumi, Fujita Masakatsu, and Washida Kyokazu, eds. 2002. *Kuki Shūzō no sekai*『九鬼周造の世界』(*The World of Kuki Shūzō*). Kyoto: Minerva Shobo.

Sakai Naoki. 1997. *Translation & Subjectivity: On "Japan" and Cultural Nationalism*. Minneapolis, MN: University of Minnesota Press.

Scheler, Max. 1973. *Formalism in Ethics and Non-Formal Ethics of Values*. Translated by Manfred S. Frings and Roger L. Funk. Evanston, IL: Northwestern University Press.

Schopenhauer, C. F. Arthur. 1913. *Transcendente Spekulation über die anscheinende Üblichkeit im Schiksale des Einzelnen*. In *Arthur Schopenhauers sämtliche Werke*, vol. 4. *Parerga und Paralipomena: kleine philosophische Schriften*. Munich: R. Piper Verlag. Originally published in 1850.

Seamon, David. 1982. "The Phenomenological Contribution to Environmental Psychology." *Journal of Environmental Psychology* 2(2): 119–140.

Sevilla, Anton Luis. 2014. "Concretizing an Ethics of Emptiness: the Succeeding Volumes of Watsuji Tetsurô's Ethics." *Asian Philosophy* 24(1): 82–101.

Sikka, Sonia. 2006. "Kantian Ethics in Being and Time." *Journal of Philosophical Research* 31: 309–334.

———. 2011. *Herder on Humanity and Cultural Difference: Enlightened Relativism*. Cambridge: Cambridge University Press.

———. 2014. "Johann Gottfried Herder." In *Kant, Kantianism, and Idealism: The Origins of Continental Philosophy*, 83–106. Edited by Thomas Nenon. New York: Routledge.

———. 2017. *Heidegger, Morality and Politics: Questioning the Shepherd of Being*. Cambridge: Cambridge University Press.

Skidelsky, Edward. 2008. *Ernst Cassirer: The Last Philosopher of Culture*. Princeton, NJ: Princeton University Press.

Spengler, Oswald, and Charles Francis Atkinson. 1934. *The Decline of the West*. New York: A.A. Knopf. Originally published as *Der Untergang des Abendlandes* in 1918 (vol. 1) and 1922 (vol. 2).

Stefanovic, Ingrid Leman. 1994. "What is Phenomenology?" *Brock Review* 3(1): 58–77.
Stevens, Bernard. 2005. *Invitation à la philosophie japonaise. Autour de Nishida.* Paris: CNRS Editions.
Sugimoto Yoshio. 1999. "Making Sense of *Nihonjinron.*" *Thesis Eleven* 57: 81–96.
———. 2014. *An Introduction to Japanese Society.* 4th ed. Cambridge: Cambridge University Press.
Taine, Hippolyte. 1871. *History of English Literature*, vol. 1. Translated by H. Van Laun. London: Edmonston and Douglas.
Takada Tamaki. 2002. "Mukyū no chikasako: Kuki Shūzō to Haidega" 『無窮の近迫──九鬼周造とハイデガー』 (*Approaching Eternity: Kuki and Heidegger*). In *Fuzai no Uta. Kuki Shūzō no sekai*, 139–170. Edited by Sakabe et al. Tokyo: TBS Britannica.
Tanabe Hajime. 1924. "Genshōgaku niokeru tenkō: Heidegga no sei no genshōgaku" 『現象学に於ける転向ハイデッガーの生の現象学』 ("A New Shift in Phenomenology: Heidegger's Philosophy of Life"). *Shisō* 36(October 1924): 1–23. Reprinted in the *Complete Works of Tanabe Hajime*, vol. 4. Tokyo: Chikuma, 1963, 17–34.
———. 1934. "Shakaisonzai no ronri" 『社会存在の論理』 ("The Logic of Social Existence").
Tanaka Kyūbun. 1992. *Kuki Shuzo and the Phenomenology of Iki*. Edited by M. F. Marra 2001, 318–344.
Taylor, Charles. 1993. *Engaged Agency and Background in Heidegger*, 317–336. Edited by C. Guignon.
Teruoka Yasutaka. 2000. *The Pleasure Quarters of Tokugawa Culture*, 3–32. Edited by C. A. Gerstle.
Tipton, Elise K. 2008. *Modern Japan: A Social and Political History*. London: Routledge.
Toku Masami. 2015. *International Perspectives on Shojo and Shojo Manga: The Influence of Girl Culture*. London: Taylor and Francis.
Tosaka Jun. 1966. *Tosaka Jun zenshū (Complete Works of Tosaka Jun)*. Tokyo: Keisō-Shobō.
Tremblay, Jacynthe. 2007a. *Introduction à la philosophie de Nishida*. Paris: L'Harmattan.
———. 2007b. *L'être-soi et l'être-ensemble: L'auto-éveil comme méthode philosophique chez Nishida* [*Being-an-individual and Being-with-others: Self-Awakening as Philosophical Method in Nishida Philosophy*]. Paris: L'Harmattan.
Tu Wei-ming. 1985. *Confucian Thought: Selfhood as Creative Transformation*. Albany, NY: SUNY Press.
Vogel, Lawrence. 1994. *The Fragile "We": Ethical Implications of Heidegger's Being and Time*. Evanston, IL: Northwestern University Press.
Wargo, Robert J. J. 2005. *The Logic of Nothingness*. Honolulu: University of Hawai'i Press.
Watanabe, Masao. 1974. "The Conception of Nature in Japanese Culture." *Science* 183(4122): 279–282.

Watsuji Tetsurō. 1925. *Nihon seishinshi kenkyū*『日本精史研究』(*Research on the Japanese Spirit*). Tokyo: Iwanami Shoten. Republished in WTZ 4.

———. 1961. *Climate and Culture*. Translated by Geoffrey Bownas. Reprinted by Greenwood Press, Inc. in cooperation with Yushodo Co., Ltd., in 1988. Translation of *Fūdo*. Tokyo: Iwanami, 1935.

———. 1962. *Fūdo*『風土』. WTZ 8: 1–256.

———. 1963. *Natsume sensei no tsuioku*『夏目先生の追憶』(*Reminiscences of Natsume Sensei*). In *Watsuji Tetsurō* (『和辻哲郎』), 412–423. Edited by Karaki Junzō. Tokyo: Iwanami Shoten. First published in *Shinshōsetsu*『新小説』, 1917.

———. 1996. *Watsuji Tetsuro's Rinrigaku: Ethics in Japan*. Translated by Yamamoto Seisaku and Robert E. Carter. Albany, NY: SUNY.

———. 1998. *The Japanese Spirit* [『日本精神』(*Nihon seishin*)]. Translated by David Dilworth and A. Jacinto Zavala in Dilworth, Viglielmo, and Zavala, 231–261. Originally published in 1935 (Watsuji 1935). In WTZ 4: 281–321.

———. 2012. *Pilgrimages to the Ancient Temples in Nara*. Translated by Hiroshi Nara. Portland, ME: Merwin Asia.

———. 2014. *Koji junrei*『古寺巡礼』(*Pilgrimages to the Ancient Temples*). Tokyo: Iwanami.

Windelband, Wilhelm. 1910–1911. "Kulturphilosophie und transzendentaler Idealismus." *Logos: Zeitschrift für systematische Philosophie* 1: 186–196.

Woods, Allen. 2009. "Kant's Fourth Proposition: The Unsociable Sociability of Human Nature." In *Kant's Idea for a Universal History with a Cosmopolitan Aim: A Critical Guide*, 112–128. Edited by A. Oksenberg Rorty and J. Schmidt. Cambridge: Cambridge University Press.

Yoshino, Kosaku. 1992. *Cultural Nationalism in Contemporary Japan a Sociological Enquiry*. London, New York: Routledge.

Yuasa Yasuo. 1996. *Correspondence Between Yasuo Yuasa and Robert Carter*, 311–323. Edited by T. Watsuji.

Yusa Michiko. 1994. *Nishida and Totalitarianism: A Philosopher's Resistance*, 107–131. Edited by J. W. Heisig and J. C. Maraldo.

———. 2002. *Zen and Philosophy: An Intellectual Biography of Nishida Kitarō*. Honolulu: University of Hawai'i Press.

———. 2014. "Parsing the Topos and Dusting the Mirror: A Radical Internalization of 'Basho-Topos'." *Journal of Japanese Philosophy* 2: 7.

Index

Page references for figures are italicized.

ahimsa, 94
art: Ajanta wall paintings, 43–5, 49, 93; Buddhist, Chapter 2; Chinese, 44–46; Gandhara, 44–45, 58n20; Greek, 44–47

basho. See Nishida, Kitarō, *basho*
Bergson, Henri, 18–19, 139–42, 178, 181–82, 187–92; ethics, 189–91; example of the rose, 138; nature of the social, 187–92. See also Kuki, Shūzō, and philosophy of Henri Bergson
Berque, Augustin, 26, 55n2, 63, 93, 116, 261–62
Bubner, Rüdiger, 70, 82nn24–5
Buddhism: Prajnaparamita teachings, 236, 254n18; Pure Land, 47, 176–77, 248; *upaya*, 234. See also *dharmadhatu*; Nishida, Kitarō, and Buddhism; *samsara*; Zen Buddhism
Bushidō, 7, 27, 126–29, 134, 142, 154, 161, 166, 193n1, 258

chance, 166, 173, 178–80, 186–87, 192
Climate and Culture (Fūdo). See Kuki, Shūzō, *Climate and Culture*
colonialism, 259, 261, 264

Comte, Auguste, 14–16, 19
Condillac, Étienne Bonnot de, 14, 182
Confucianism, 7, 11, 37–38, 56–57n11, 192, 242; Five relationships, 37, 103, 242
culture, 1, 9–12, 25–26, 32–36, 44, 52, 62, 74, 76–77, 87-88, 91, 117–18, 130, 133–35, 142, 165–67, 268; and change, 27, 28n9, 47, 92; and climate, 5–6, 23, 26, 35, 49, Chapter 3, 87–8, 104, 262–63; and difference, 13, 25, 27, 48, 51, 61–62, 67, 78, 86, 89–90, 97–98, 107, 117, 249, 262; and essentialism, 22–24, 86, 92, 100–103, 114, 257, 261–62; and German Idealism, 6, 11–14, 63–71; and nationalism, 7, 21–25, 62, 86, 91, 103, 108, 114, 117, 230, 256n31, 261; and taste, 130–33, 135–36, 142, 145, 151–52, 156, 163. See also Kuki, Shūzō, Japanese culture; Nishida, Kitarō, and Japanese culture; Watsuji, Tetsurō, Japanese culture

dharmadhatu, 220n20
dialectic, 3–5, 8, 21, 26, 43, 49, 54, 58n19, 70, 104, 198–99, 202–15,

285

219n11, 229, 231, 240, 242, 245, 250–52, 254n15, 258, 267–68; of sameness and difference, 47–48, 174. *See also* Nishida, Kitarō, dialectic; Watsuji, Tetsurō, dialectic

Ethics: and difference, 258, 265–66, 268; of Emmanuel Levinas, 171, 266; of *geisha*, 170–74, 180, 258, 265

Febvre, Lucien, 93, 120n16, 122n33
Fichte, Johann Gottlieb, 63–68, 70, 80nn17–18, 85, 92, 108, 206, 263
Figure 5.1, *131*
Fukuzawa, Yukichi, 260

Gadamer, Hans-Georg, 48, 59n29, 99, 145, 149
Galileo, 239
geisha: ethics of, 170–74, 180, 258, 265; and freedom, 170–72, 180, 265
geographic determinism, 6–7, 23–24, 52, 64, 68–69, 86, 92–93, 100–108, 114–15, 117, 262. *See also* Watsuji, Tetsurō, geographic determinism
Goethe, Johann Wolfgang von, 34, 55n3, 134, 240

Hegel, Georg Wilhelm Friedrich, 2, 6, 11, 13–14, 61, 63–65, 68–70, 81nn20–25, 102, 108, 263
Heidegger, Martin: authentic historicity, 160–62, 165; authenticity, 110–12, 128, 157, 178–81; *Being and Time*, 5, 55, 71–73, 100, 112, 123n41, 128–29, 136, 139–40, 150, 157, 161, 163n3, 178, 193; and culture, 151–55, 161, 165; *Dasein* as being-toward-death, 178–79; ethics, 72–73, 82n27, 178–79; fate/destiny, 180; hermeneutics, 149–55, 258. *See also* Kuki, Shūzō, and Heidegger's hermeneutics; meaning and world, 75–76, 149–52, 178; phenomenology, 146–51, 153–54; possibility and impossibility, 177–80; spirit, critique of, 153. *See also* Watsuji, Tetsurō, interpretation of Martin Heidegger
Herder, Johann Gottfried, 2, 6, 11–13, 25, 28n13, 61, 63–67, 79n4, 108, 113, 119n12, 263
Husserl, Edmund: culture, 146, 148–49; intersubjectivity, 148–49; intuition, 147, 158–60; phenomenology, 146–49, 158

iki: and aesthetics, 133, 162; and Immanuel Kant, 134–35; as relational, 133, 155, 162; and resignation (*akirame*), 170–72, 180; as system of taste, *131*, 130–33, 151, 154, 156; as worldview, 134, 137, 140–41, 145, 155, 157–58, 161, 163, 258
imagination, 39–44
An Inquiry into the good (*Zen no kenkyū*). *See* Nishida, Kitarō, *An Inquiry into the Good*

Japanese nationalism, 7, 21–25, 54–55, 63, 86, 108, 114, 117, 230, 248, 261, 265

Kant, Immanuel, 13, 64, 66–67, 80n15, 204–205, 237, 242, 266, 268. *See also iki*, and Immanuel Kant; Nishida, Kitarō, and Immanuel Kant
Kuki, Shūzō: and Buddhist ethics, 166–67, 171–73, 177, 181, 258, 266; *Climate and Culture*, 2, 5–7, 13, 23, 26, 28n9, 34–35, 41, 44, 48–50, 52–54, Chapter 3, Chapter 4, 129, 162, 262, 265; contingency-necessity, 176, 179, 181; critique of (European) modernity, 126–28, 156–58, 160; cross-cultural understanding, 166–67; cultural chauvinism, 24–25, 265; culture, 7–8, 24–27, 130, 133–35, 142, 155, 157, 160–61, 163, 168–69, 178, 266; destiny/fate, 170–71,

180–81; *Ethics* (*Rinrigaku*), 5, 26, 50, 52, 109, 115; ethics and idealism, 162, 165–67, 172, 175–78, 193, 265–66, 268; ethics, 128–29, 134, 152, 156, 170–75, 182, 258, 265–66, 268; freedom, 26–27, 178, 258, 266, 268; and Heidegger's hermeneutics, 7, 127–29, 145–46, 151–52; hermeneutic method of, 130–31, 135–39, 151–52, 155–61, 258; intersubjectivity, 167–69; intuition, 2, 7–8, 145–46, 166, 168–70, 172, 178, 181–82, 258; Japanese culture, 128, 134, 154, 157, 161, 163, 169, 258, 265; metaphysical (mystical) dimension in philosophy of, 146, 155–56, 166–69, 180; nominalism, 139, 156, 161; and philosophy of Henri Bergson, 129, 135, 139–42, 157–58, 168, 170, 177–81, 187–93, 258; and philosophy of Maine de Biran, 4, 8, 167–69, 185–87, 192–93, 258; *Problem of Contingency*, 2, 8, 146, 158, 164n13, 169, 173–77, 190; role of surprise in ethics, 173–74, 176, 189, 266, 268; *sens intime*, 168–70, 177; social, 134, 155; space and time, 128, 155

landscape, 75–76, 87, 89–91
Levinas, Emmanuel. *See* Ethics- of Emmanuel Levinas

Maine de Biran, François-Pierre Gontier: destiny/fate, 185–86; ethics, 185–86; force, 184; God, 186–87; intuition, 186–87; philosophy of, 2, 178, 181–87, 195nn21–22; *sens intime*, 168–69, 177–78, 183–85; will, 184–85. *See also* Kuki, Shūzō, and philosophy of Maine de Biran
memes, 60n33

Natsume Sōseki, 34, 56n6, 79n1, 260–61

Neo-Kantianism, 12, 15, 17, 19–21, 28n14, 81n20, 100, 126, 143n5, 146, 181–82
Nihonjinron, 259–60, 265, 269n3
Nishida, Kitarō: active intuition (*kōiteki chokkan*), 199–200, 219–20nn11–12, 251–52, 254–55nn24–25; and art, 240–41, 243, 246–47; *basho*, 3, 8, 202–209, 220n20, 221nn21, 25–26, 30, 222nn34, 37, 223nn42, 45, 231, 233; and Buddhism, 201–202, 218, 231–33, 236, 245, 248–49; call and answer, 213–216, 218; choice, 232, 235; and Christianity, 201–202, 218, 231–32; communal consciousness, 198–99; compassion/love, 234–242, 246–47; creative activity, 216–18, 225–29, 238, 240–44, 250, 252, 258; culture and change, 226, 230, 252; culture and difference, 249–50; culture, 21–22, 215–18, 225, 229, 234, 238, 240, 247, 250, 258–59, 266–67; death (and life), 215, 255–56n29, 259, 267; dialectic, 8, 21, 198–99, 202–203, 209–11, 213–14, 227, 229, 233, 242, 250, 252, 267; environmental context, 227–28; eschatology, 246; ethics, 200–202, 218, 230–37, 241–47, 267; field of forces, 239–40; global culture, 248–49; God, 202, 211, 231, 233–34, 246, 255n27, 266; historical world, 3, 9, 22, 210–12, 215–18, 220n13, 225–30, 238, 240, 242–44, 247, 252n2, 258, 265–67; and Immanuel Kant, 204, 237, 242, 266; *An Inquiry into the Good*, 208, 210, 219nn9–10, 230, 231, 234–37, 242, 245–46, 253n7; interaction between cultures, 230, 249, 250, 252; intersubjectivity, 210–17, 252nn1–2; and Japanese culture, 244, 247–48, 254n24; and Judaism, 231, 233–34; logic of the predicate, 223n44; mirror, 201, 209, 223nn4–5, 232, 234; and modernity,

261, 263–65; and nationalism, 230, 248, 256n31; and Pascal's reed, 246; and race, 229, 252n3; relationship between 'I' and 'Thou', 213–15, 217; relationship to Kuki Shūzō, 4, 8, 268; relationship to Watsuji Tetsurō, 4, 8, 268; and science, 238–40, 251; self as expression of world, 198–99, 201; selfishness, 242, 245–46; sincerity, 242–43; social, 212–13, 215–18, 228–30, 238, 242, 247–52, 267; space and time, 206, 212, 222n36; spiritual life, 200–20, 231, 246–47, 251; true self and absolute negation, 232–33; true self, 226, 228, 231–38, 243, 246, 252, 258, 267; world-historical culture, 247–52, 265–66

Okakura Tenshin, 58n21, 165–66

Problem of Contingency. See Kuki, Shūzō, *Problem of Contingency*

race, 17, 28n6, 58n21, 64, 134, 229, 252n3, 257, 259, 264, 265
Rickert, Heinrich, 12, 15, 19–20
Roscelin of Compiègne, 139, 144nn19–20

samsara, 37, 141, 170–72, 177, 189, 234, 255n26, 265–66
Scheler, Max, 161, 198, 218n2
Schopenhauer, Arthur, 181
Showa Genroku Rakugo Shinjū (manga/anime), 125–26
spirit, 13–14, 18, 27–28n6, 46, 63–64, 68–70, 79n4, 81n20, 89, 101, 103–107, 153–54, 160; Japanese, 7, 46, 64, 79n7, 105, 248, 263–65. *See also* Watsuji, Tetsurō, spirit

Taine, Hippolyte, 14, 16–18
Taylor, Charles, 138
trace, 46–47

Watsuji, Tetsurō: betweenness (*aidagara*), 5, 32–34, 36, 43, 46, 53–55n2, 57n11, 72–73, 88n15, 109, 129, 257, 267, 268; climate and culture, 49–52, Chapter 3, 85–87, 89, 90, 96, 262; climate and politics, 101–102, 107–108, 117, 264; climate and space, 87–90; climate and time, 90–91; colonialism, 100, 107–108; cross-cultural exchange, 43–50, 52, 54–55, 91, 94, 96, 113, 117; culture and change, 52, 86, 89–92, 94, 96, 99, 103, 113, 117; culture and difference, 78, 89–90, 262; culture, 5–7, 15–16, 23–24, 26, 33, 44, 52–54, 118n5, 257, 261–63; desert, 88, 95–97; dialectic, 4–5, 8, 26, 43, 49, 54, 57n11, 70, 104, 268; *Ethics (Rinrigaku)*, 5, 26, 50, 54, 108–109, 113–17; geographic determinism, 103–108, 114–15, 117; interpretation of German Idealism, 13–14, 65–71; interpretation of Martin Heidegger, 5–6, 24, 55, 71–73, 78, 81–82n26, 100, 108–13, 115; Japanese culture, 102–104, 117; meadow, 88–89, 95; monsoon, 88, 93–94, 102; phenomenological method, 5–7, 33–34, 48–49, 53, 62, 67, 69–73, 76–78, 92, 100, 107–13, 262; *Pilgrimages to the Ancient Temples in Nara*, 5–6, 26, Chapter 2, 113–16, 257, 262; roads, 50, 55; social, 32, 54, 73, 89, 95–96, 109, 111–12, 115, 117; space, 33–35, 40–41, 46, 49, 52, 65, 70, 72–74, 80n15, 85, 87–90, 100, 109; spirit, 104–107, 109, 110, 112, 114, 263–65; three climatic zones, 86, 263; time, 33–35, 38–41, 46, 49, 54, 72, 74, 80n15, 90–91, 100, 109; transcendence (ecstasis), 76–77, 106
Windelband, Wilhelm, 12, 15, 19–20

Zen Buddhism, 245; Zen Master Dōgen, 254n22; Zen Master Linji Yixuan, 204; Zen Master Panshan Baoji, 236

About the Author

Graham Mayeda is Associate Professor of the Faculty of Law at the University of Ottawa, Canada. In addition to his research on legal philosophy, he also writes about twentieth-century Japanese philosophy with a particular emphasis on Nishida Kitarō, Watsuji Tetsurō, and Kuki Shūzō. He is also interested in European phenomenology and the philosophy of Martin Heidegger. He is the author of *Time, Space and Ethics in the Philosophy of Watsuji Tetsurō, Kuki Shūzō, and Martin Heidegger*.

www.ingramcontent.com/pod-product-compliance
Lightning Source LLC
Chambersburg PA
CBHW050858300426
44111CB00010B/1298